W9-CBW-871

The Remedy

Also by Richard D. Kahlenberg

Broken Contract: A Memoir of Harvard Law School

THE Remedy

Class, Race, and Affirmative Action

RICHARD D. KAHLENBERG

A New Republic Book
BasicBooks
A Division of HarperCollins*Publishers*

For Mom and Dad,
Rebecca, Cynthia, Jessica, and Caroline

Portions of this book first appeared in *The New Republic* "Class, Not Race" (April 3, 1995) and "Equal Opportunity Critics" (July 17, 1995).

Copyright © 1996 by Richard D. Kahlenberg
Published by BasicBooks, A Division of HarperCollins Publishers, Inc.

Designed by Laura Lindgren

ISBN 0-465-09823-1

96 97 98 99 ❖/HC 9 8 7 6 5 4 3 2 1

Contents

Acknowledgments

I BEGAN WRITING this book in the fall of 1993, but its intellectual roots—and my debts of gratitude—go much deeper. In college, I first became interested in issues of class and race when I wrote my senior honor's thesis on Robert Kennedy's 1968 campaign for president. Harvard Professor Richard Neustadt, my thesis adviser, heavily influenced my views on these issues as he guided my research on Kennedy's unique brand of urban populism, which united working-class whites and blacks. This book draws on interviews I conducted for my thesis with Robert Coles, Mario Cuomo, Jeff Greenfield, Richard Harwood, Arthur Schlesinger, Jr., and Adam Walinsky. All gave generously of their time.

As a law student, I wrote a paper, under the supervision of Harvard Law Professor Alan Dershowitz, proposing a shift to affirmative action based on class. His comments and criticisms were quite helpful to me. I described the paper in a two-and-a-half-page passage of a book I wrote about my law school experiences and received a flurry of letters on the subject, a show of interest that encouraged me to pursue the topic further.

When I worked as a legislative assistant for Senator Charles S. Robb, handling civil rights issues, among others, I had long discussions about affirmative action and class with the senator and with my colleagues, Susan Albert, Julius Hobson, Jr., Kerry Walsh Skelly, and Nicole Venable. Their thoughts and comments on the subject were very helpful to my thinking.

At George Washington University, where I was a visiting professor in the law school and a lecturer in the business school, I received helpful advice and support on the book from President Stephen Joel Trachtenberg. A number of my law school colleagues shared their thoughts and advice, including Jose Alvarez, Paul Butler, Burlette Carter, Jack Friedenthal, Larry Mitchell,

Bob Park, Josh Schwartz, and Lew Solomon. Charlie Craver and Chip Lupu were especially helpful. Scott Pagel and the library staff searched high and low for hard-to-find sources. My research assistant, Mike Hardin, provided invaluable assistance at the crucial early stages of this project. And Padmaja "Pat" Balakrishnan logged long hours providing clerical help. At GW's business school, I received good advice from Jill Kasle and Bill Davis. My students in a class on reforming affirmative action provided fresh insights. Thanks also to William Taylor and Mark Shields, who served as guest lecturers in the course and shared their views on class, race, and affirmative action.

At the Center for National Policy, a progressive think tank in Washington, I want to thank Maureen S. Steinbruner and Michael J. Petro for providing me the opportunity to finish up the manuscript—and to think further about the larger role of values in public policy.

In the course of writing the book, I had the opportunity to present my research at George Washington's National Law Center, the American University College of Law, the Georgetown University Law Center, the Brookings Institution, and the Economic Policy Institute. Thanks to those who provided helpful feedback to me as I developed my argument. In addition, I interviewed a number of people for this project whom I wish to thank: Jack Beatty, Charles T. Canady, Richard Cohen, Robert Coles (again), Jack Corrigan, Dinesh D'Souza, Thomas Edsall, Jeff Faux, Marshall Gans, David Garrow, Thomas Geoghegan, Nathan Glazer, David Halberstam, Tubby Harrison, Robert Laird, J. Anthony Lukas, Daniel Patrick Moynihan, Deval Patrick, Deborah Ramirez, Robert Reinstein, Charles S. Robb, Albert Shanker, Donald Slaiman, Jim Sleeper, William Taylor, Algera Tucker, and Carl Wagner. Thanks also to those who shared their thoughts but wished to remain anonymous.

At New Republic/Basic Books, thanks to Marty Peretz, who launched this project, and Peter Edidin, who signed me up. When Peter left Basic, the book went to Paul Golob, who has provided excellent advice. Paul radically restructured the book and provided thoughtful criticisms of its soft spots. He also urged me to push much of the academic material to the endnotes, a compromise that leaves the main text less cluttered but allows those readers who have a particular interest in the subject (or are troubled by a particular point) to see the argument unfold more fully. If the book succeeds, Paul deserves much of the credit. Attorney Richard Dannay and my mother-in-law, Dinah Moché, provided helpful advice on the book contract.

Several friends provided important comments, including Andrew Richards, Steven Bonorris, and especially Christopher Landau. John J. DiIulio, Jr., a tutor of mine in college, first got me thinking about affirmative action in 1982, and thirteen years later, he was still providing helpful critiques of my work. My parents, Richard and Jeannette Kahlenberg, and my sisters, Joy Kahlenberg Fallon and Trudi Kahlenberg Picciano, provided incisive comments, tempered by loving support. They hit me from the left, while Chris hit me from the right, and John from the center, and I think the book is better for it. My wonderful wife, Rebecca, offered her always sensible wisdom and has been remarkably patient and supportive. She and my fabulous daughters, Cindy, Jessica, and Caroline, put up with Daddy's writing another book, with good cheer and love. Thanks again, guys.

R.D.K.

Introduction
The Lost Thread

IN THE SUMMER of 1991, Judge Clarence Thomas began to visit various U.S. senators to round up support for his Supreme Court nomination. The fate of affirmative action was a central concern among Democrats, and as my boss, Senator Charles S. Robb of Virginia, and I prepared to meet Thomas, it was clear that the issue had to be raised. Robb, the son-in-law of President Lyndon Johnson, had a strong civil rights record, and he asked Thomas to explain his position on affirmative action. Thomas was not at all defensive about his opposition to racial preferences. Why, the judge responded, should his son receive a preference in college admissions over a poor white applicant from Appalachia?[1]

The question was disarming, not only because a black judge was telling a white senator that African Americans do not need special help, but more profoundly because a Republican was telling a Democrat that class matters. Implicit in the familiar criticism—that a child of a rich black doctor does not deserve a preference over the child of a poor white janitor—is the notion not only that race should not count, but that perhaps class should.[2]

The thesis of this book is that affirmative action, a well-intentioned but flawed instrument of public policy, should not be discarded but should be revamped so that preferences in education, in employment, and in government contracting are provided on the basis of class, not race or gender. The socio-economically disadvantaged of all races would benefit—the poor Appalachian student and the young Clarence Thomas of Pinpoint, Georgia—but not Clarence Thomas's son. Because of our nation's history of discrimination, minorities are disproportionately disadvantaged and would disproportionately benefit from such redirected efforts. The strong antidiscriminatory pro-visions of the Civil Rights Acts of 1964 and 1991 should remain, providing powerful tools against ongoing and future race and gender discrimination. And we should continue to promote race- and gender-based affirmative action to achieve the old noncontroversial goal of widening the net of applicants to ensure that women and minorities are not shut out of inter-views by the old boy network. But when the decision is to be made for hiring or admissions, any preferences should benefit disadvantaged people, across race and gender lines.[3]

Class-based affirmative action provides a principled third way out of the affirmative action thicket for those of us who see strong arguments on both sides of the question. Many Ameri-cans want to do *something* to remedy the lingering effects of our nation's discriminatory history and yet perceive the current system of racial preferences as unfair and damaging to our social fabric. Many reject the notion that because of past discrimina-tion, all women and people of color today deserve a bump up in competition against white males, but many are willing to say that those born poor face unequal chances, and that because of past discrimination, an extraordinary number of the poor are black. In a 1995 *Washington Post*/ABC News poll, 75 percent of those surveyed opposed racial preferences, but of those opposed, nearly two in three wanted to "change" the programs rather than "do away with them entirely."[4]

Until now, the compromise for many who are truly of two minds on the issue of affirmative action has been what some have called the "*Bakke* straddle": saying no to racial and gender quotas, but yes to affirmative action and more subtle forms of racial preference. The phrase refers to Justice Lewis F. Powell, Jr.'s, famous opinion in the landmark case of *Regents of Univer-sity of California v. Bakke* (1978). When the white applicant Allan Bakke sued the University of California Medical School at Davis, he argued that the admissions office practice of setting aside sixteen of one hundred seats for minorities was illegal. Powell, who held the swing vote on the Court, agreed that the quota was unconstitutional and illegal but said that the medical school could give a racial preference so long as race was treated as nothing more than a "plus factor." Harvard College, Powell noted, successfully used race as "one factor" without resorting to stated quotas.

This attempt to "find a middle ground," as Powell told his law clerk, pleased absolutely no one else on the Court—neither the four justices who said racial quotas were appropriate to overcome past discrimination nor the four who saw preferences as reverse discrimination and a clear violation of the Civil Rights Act of 1964.[5] Powell's "compromise" was widely denounced for sending a message that preferences are acceptable so long as they are subtle rather than explicit. Harvard's "plus system," it was noted, managed to come up with a remarkably consistent percentage of black students year after year.[6] As Powell's biographer John Jeffries notes, "Faced with two intellectually coherent, morally defensible, and diametrically opposed positions, Powell chose neither."[7]

Amazingly, this flimsy distinction, rejected by eight of the nine justices, has for almost twenty years provided the middle ground politicians have sought on the tricky issue of racial preferences. For many years, almost all politicians of both parties have told whites that they strongly oppose quotas, and they have told minorities that they favor affirmative action preferences. In 1995, for example, President Bill Clinton said he strongly supported race-conscious decision-making but opposed "quotas" and the use of preferences for "unqualified" candidates.[8]

But while the policy-making elite embraced the *Bakke* straddle, the American people never fully did. Most Americans realize that the world does not divide neatly between qualified and unqualified, and that the question is not whether unqualified minorities are receiving jobs but whether lesser qualified minorities and women are favored over more qualified white males. Clearly, we would not tolerate anti-black discrimination on the grounds that race was only "one factor" held against the applicant and that no "unqualified" white males were hired. Opponents of affirmative action seek to outlaw not only quotas for the unqualified but preferences for the less qualified as well.

The *Bakke* straddle, which endured for almost twenty years, is now under full attack from Republicans. In 1995, Senate

Majority Leader Robert Dole and California Governor Pete Wilson, both longtime supporters of affirmative action, called for its repeal. At the same time, activists in California are backing a 1996 ballot initiative to prohibit the state from employing race or gender preferences.[9] The state of racial preferences is always in flux—taking a step forward with the 1992 election of President Bill Clinton, taking a step back with the 1994 election of a Republican Congress—but opponents are clearly in the ascendance. Civil rights groups may be able to postpone the end of racial preferences, but that day will surely come.

Class-based affirmative action offers a more principled compromise, a middle ground that is politically and legally sustainable. Where opponents of affirmative action fail to provide actual equal opportunity for the poor, and proponents force an artificial equality of group result, class preferences provide a genuine form of equal opportunity for all individuals. Where opponents of affirmative action call for a color blindness that ignores history, and proponents offer the prospect of unending color consciousness, class preferences are at once color-blind and remedial, disproportionately benefiting those who have suffered most under our nation's history of discrimination. Where opponents of affirmative action place too little value on diversity and integration, and proponents raise diversity to a value above justice, class preferences provide a lively racial and economic integration, without sacrificing the greater goals of justice and equal opportunity. In short, class preferences are a way to remedy the historic racial wrongs of our country without resorting to "the disease as cure."[10] Class-based affirmative action is a remedy to the moral and political thicket of affirmative action, a way of meeting the goals racial preferences seek to achieve while avoiding the problems racial preferences create. And class-based affirmative action is the beginning of a remedy to something larger as well: the basic unfulfilled promise of equal opportunity for all individuals. The larger remedy may involve a whole host of other solutions, from labor reform to welfare reform, from health care reform to economic reform, but by getting people to refocus attention on issues of class, and to think about rebuilding class-based coalitions, need-based preferences will make those other remedies more likely to be enacted.

Any book critical of affirmative action is likely to hurt and provoke anger in civil rights groups, which have wedded themselves for thirty years to a strategy of racial preference. Many liberals have embraced a policy of "no retreat" on affirmative action and are likely to see any alteration as threatening, an effort to turn back the clock. Indeed, Nathan Glazer, a longtime critic of affirmative action, surprised readers in 1995 when he wrote that he is concerned "that African-Americans will see the abandonment of affirmative action as a terrible rejection by an indifferent and hostile society."[11] If no alternative is offered, Glazer is probably right. But replacing race with class preferences is not betrayal; it is restoration. A policy that unites people across racial lines and gives a leg up to the disadvantaged should not be seen as novel, much less threatening. In fact, the strategy and principle of class before race simply revives the thinking of two men—Martin Luther King, Jr., and Robert Kennedy—who could hardly be called hostile to the interests of black people. To endorse class preferences is simply to pick up a thread of thought lost after the twin assassinations of 1968. King and Kennedy were very different people and had their differences, but both, toward the end of their lives, were inexorably drawn to the conclusion that class inequality was the central obstacle to justice in the post–civil rights era.

In November 1967, King and the other leaders of the Southern Christian Leadership Conference began to plan a campaign that represented a new direction for the organization. "Gentlemen," he announced, "we are going to take this movement and we are going to reach out to the poor people in all directions in this country. We're going into the Southwest after the Indians, into the West after the Chicanos, into Appalachia after the poor whites, and into the ghettoes after Negroes and Puerto Ricans." He continued: "And we're going to bring them together and enlarge this campaign into something bigger than just a civil rights movement for Negroes."[12]

Not all of King's advisers were pleased with this change in direction. Some thought the focus should remain strictly on racial justice; others worried that to form coalitions with outside groups would mean relinquishing control of the movement.[13] But in the following months, King grew more and more committed to the idea, traveling across the nation to meet with Hispanics, Indians, and the white poor to plan what would become known as the Poor People's Campaign.[14] He told a rally in Selma that the focus needed to be on "class issues . . . with the problem of the gulf between the haves and have-nots."[15] King had stirred the nation with his dream of racial justice, but, in his last Sunday sermon, delivered at the National Cathedral in Washington, D.C., on March 31, 1968, King called his vision of economic justice nothing less than his "last, greatest dream."[16]

After the sermon, King traveled to Memphis to join a sanitation workers' strike, a miniature version of the multiracial economic-based coalition he was seeking to put together nationally. On this trip, on April 4, 1968, King was shot dead. Riots spread throughout the nation. Washington, Nashville, Detroit, Greensboro, Chicago, city after city—110 in all—went up in flames.

That night, Senator Robert F. Kennedy, then running for the Democratic nomination for president and in the midst of a heated campaign in the Indiana primary, was scheduled to speak to the worst section of the ghetto in Indianapolis. The city's mayor warned him not to go. But he went anyway and, speaking extemporaneously, informed the crowd of King's assassination:

> We can move in [the] direction [of] great polarization— black people amongst black, white people amongst white, filled with hatred toward one another. Or we can make an effort, as Martin Luther King did, to understand and comprehend. . . . What we need in the United States is not division; what we need in the United States is not hatred; what we need in the United States is not violence or lawlessness, but love and wisdom and compassion toward one another, and a feeling of justice toward those who still suffer within our country, whether they be white or whether they be black.[17]

The crowd wept, but left quietly. Indianapolis was one of the few large cities that did not burn.[18]

On April 7, Kennedy attended King's funeral in Atlanta. As he followed the mule cart carrying King's body, cheers broke out among the crowd. "Along the route Kennedy became the star," David Halberstam observed; a friend told the reporter, "It's as if they're anointing him." Hosea Williams, an aide to King, said, "After Dr. King was killed, there was just nobody else left but Bobby Kennedy."[19] Kennedy and King had been drawn together over time. Eight years earlier, Robert Kennedy had called a Georgia judge to ask that King be released from prison, and it was Kennedy who, through an intermediary, had suggested the Poor People's Campaign to King. For his part, King was prepared to endorse Kennedy in his bid for the presidency.[20]

As the riots tore through the nation, Kennedy became increasingly convinced, as King had been, that the racial lens through which liberals addressed social inequality was insufficient; he told Bill Haddad and David Halberstam that "it was pointless to talk about the real problem in America being black and white, it was really rich and poor, which was a much more complex subject."[21] Kennedy campaigned again and again on this basic theme, and by early May, his message appeared to be getting through to voters.

On Monday, May 6, 1968, the day before the Indiana primary, the Kennedy campaign began an extraordinary motorcade through the grimy streets of Indiana's grim steel towns: Gary, Hammond, Whiting. The year before, the city of Gary had divided sharply over the city mayoral election; white precincts voted white, black for black. Although the whites in Gary were registered Democratic by a five-to-one margin, 90 percent voted for the white Republican.[22]

But as RFK began the grueling, nine-hour motorcade through industrial northern Indiana, all the steel-mill families, black and white, came out to greet him. As the motorcade entered Gary, the city's black mayor, Richard Hatcher, climbed in to sit next to Kennedy on one side. On the other side of the candidate was Tony Zale, the former middleweight boxing champion who was a native-son hero of Gary's Slavic steelworkers. Kennedy rode through the industrial neighborhoods, black and white, with Hatcher and Zale remaining at his side, bridging the painful chasm between the races in Gary. "It was hard to escape the meaning of that kind of symbol," recalled the speechwriter Jeff Greenfield.[23] The city that had one year earlier divided, precinct by precinct, white versus black, came out in droves for Kennedy. For the moment at least, working-class whites and blacks put their differences behind them to cheer their candidate. The next day, not only did Kennedy sweep the black vote, winning 85 percent against his two primary opponents, but he also swept the white working-class wards, which four years earlier had given their votes to Alabama Governor George Wallace. The Harvard psychiatrist and Kennedy supporter Robert Coles told the candidate, "There is something going on here that has to do with real class politics."[24]

One month later, two months after King's assassination, Robert Kennedy was shot dead in Los Angeles, moments after declaring victory in the California presidential primary. The Poor People's Campaign, which had begun in May without its leader, racked by disorganization, violence, and unfocused demands, closed its tents on June 13, its goals unmet, its promise withered. By the fall, George Wallace was running for president as an independent, and in the general election, he gained back many of the white working-class voters to whom Kennedy had appealed. Richard Nixon was elected president.

The thesis of this book is that Robert Kennedy and Martin Luther King were right: after passage of the Civil Rights Act of 1964, class did become paramount over race in addressing problems of social inequality. The message has the potential to unite blacks and whites, and maybe even liberals and conservatives. While King and Kennedy were polarizing figures in their day, today King is honored by a national holiday and Kennedy is remembered as the last figure able to bring together blacks and conservative white workers. Since their deaths, diverse thinkers have spoken sympathetically about shifting away from race- to class-based affirmative action—from the late liberal Supreme Court Justice William O. Douglas to his conservative successors, Antonin Scalia and Clarence Thomas.[25] Among scholars, the list runs from Harvard's Cornel West on the left to the American Enterprise Institute's Dinesh D'Souza on the right.[26]

The argument for a new vision of affirmative action based on class proceeds in three parts. Part 1 (chapters 1–3) traces the evolution of affirmative action. Chapter 1 discusses the early aspirations of those leaders like King and President Lyndon Johnson who wanted to do something to remedy our history of discrimination. Chapter 2 discusses the ways in which affirmative action went astray from its original goals, as the object shifted from "compensation" to achieving "diversity"—a shift from short-term race consciousness to long-term race consciousness. The report card on affirmative action today provided in chapter 3 concludes that racial and gender preference programs are deeply flawed, though marginally better than doing nothing.

Part 2 (chapters 4–6) takes an in-depth look at the class-based affirmative action alternative. Chapter 4 builds the case for class-based preferences and argues that they do a better job of achieving the goals of race-based affirmative action while simultaneously meeting the best arguments against race and gender preferences. Chapter 5 outlines the mechanics of precisely how a class-based affirmative action program might work in education, entry-level employment, and contracting. This chapter fills in important details that other proponents of class-based affirmative action have failed to provide.[27] Chapter 6 addresses obvious concerns about class preference programs: Won't they promote class division? Aren't they much harder to administer than race- or gender-based preferences?

Finally, part 3 (chapter 7) speaks to the larger issues raised by the shift from a racial to a class emphasis. We examine the great possibilities open to those who pick up the lost thread with which Kennedy and King were beginning to weave a more equitable future.

Part 1

The Evolution of Affirmative Action

1 . The Early Aspirations of Affirmative Action

ON JUNE 4, 1965, President Lyndon Johnson rose to address the assembled graduates of Howard University on the great question facing the civil rights movement. With passage of the Civil Rights Act of 1964, a monumental achievement outlawing discrimination in employment and other fields, to what end should the nation, and the civil rights movement, now commit themselves?

Johnson was clear in saying the job of achieving racial equality was not complete. "Freedom is not enough," he declared. "You do not wipe away the scars of centuries saying: Now, you are free to go where you want, and do as you desire, and choose the leaders you please." He continued, using a powerful image that would be repeated over and over again in the coming years: "You do not take a person who, for years, has been hobbled by chains and liberate him, bring him up to the starting line of a race and then say, 'you are free to compete with all the others,' and still justly believe that you have been completely fair." Johnson defined "the next and the more profound stage of the battle for civil rights" as one in which Americans would seek "not just legal equity but human ability, not just equality as a right and a theory but equality as a fact and equality as a result."[1]

Written by the speechwriter Richard Goodwin and Assistant Secretary of Labor Daniel Patrick Moynihan, the address was warmly received by the civil rights community. It was meant to put Johnson ahead of the curve, to be proactive rather than reactive.[2] But in employing the sprint metaphor, Johnson was echoing an argument made earlier by Martin Luther King, Jr., in

3

his book *Why We Can't Wait*. The nation, King said, "must incorporate into its planning some compensatory consideration for the handicaps [the Negro] has inherited from the past." While some friends "recoil in horror" at the notion of compensatory treatment, King said, "it is obvious that if a man is entered at the starting line in a race three hundred years after another man, the first would have to perform some impossible feat in order to catch up with his fellow runner."[3] .

Johnson's speech drew its intellectual firepower from an internal government document, written by Moynihan, entitled *The Negro Family: A Case for National Action*. The Moynihan Report, printed in March 1965, said that the passage of antidiscriminatory laws, providing formal equal opportunity, would lead to the expectation of roughly equal group results. "This is not going to happen," Moynihan predicted. "Nor will it happen for generations to come unless a new and special effort is made." The problem, Moynihan believed, was that the legacy of slavery and segregation had left poor blacks, as a group, unable to compete fairly. "Individually, Negro Americans reach the highest peaks of achievement," he wrote. "But collectively, in the spectrum of American ethnic and religious and regional groups, where some get plenty and some get none, where some send eighty percent of their children to college and others pull them out of school at the eighth grade, Negroes are among the weakest." Going back to slavery, he said, "three centuries of sometimes unimaginable mistreatment have taken their toll on the Negro people."[4] Moynihan identified the primary impediment to black progress as the deterioration of the poor black family in America's ghettos. Because of past discrimination, a large proportion of blacks were being raised in disorder, dependent on welfare, and unable to compete with whites, even under a set of prospectively fair rules.[5]

Moynihan and Johnson saw the clear link between America's brutal treatment of blacks and their current depressed condition. A race of people were enslaved and told by the highest court in the land that the Declaration of Independence did not apply to them; the 1857 *Dred Scott* decision called blacks "beings of an inferior order, and altogether unfit to associate with the white race, either in social or political relations; and so far inferior that they had no rights which the white man was bound to respect."[6] In the early nineteenth century, black education was purposely suppressed and black literacy saw a devastating drop from 25 percent to 2 percent.[7] "The institution of slavery was dependent upon keeping the enslaved in a state of ignorance," the historian John E. Fleming explains, "for knowledge was the one factor which could have destroyed it. . . . Their lack of education, in turn, was used to justify and perpetuate slavery."[8]

Following the Civil War, the Freedman's Bureau expended $5 million in five years and called it a day.[9] After the 1896 Supreme Court decision in *Plessy v. Ferguson* legitimated "separate but equal" as a constitutional principle, the pattern continued. George Bernard Shaw, writing seven years after *Plessy*, exclaimed: "The haughty American Nation . . . makes the negro clean its boots and then proves the moral and physical inferiority of the negro by the fact that he is a bootblack."[10] In the twentieth century, blacks were segregated and told by one of the world's leading historians, Arnold Toynbee, that "when we classify mankind by color, the only one of the primary races . . . which has not made a single creative contribution to any of our 21 civilizations is the black race."[11] After World War II, white GIs could buy tract housing in New York and Pennsylvania with a $100 downpayment, while blacks were barred from doing so. "Those houses are now worth about $180,000," the civil rights activist and former Secretary of Transportation William T. Coleman, Jr., told the *Washington Post* in 1995. "That is family wealth blacks can't have."[12] This history continues to have direct consequences to this day. As Princeton's Michael Walzer points out, our nation's brutal history has left blacks in a state where they do not "qualify in anything like the way they would have had they developed under conditions of freedom and racial equality."[13]

Johnson, King, and Moynihan realized that unless something was done, beyond outlawing future discrimination, to address the continuing legacy of our nation's history, the evils of the past would be perpetuated into the future. Left unaddressed, this legacy of discrimination—the concentration of blacks in the lowest economic segments of society—was troublesome for three reasons. First, because blacks were disproportionately poor, they were disproportionately among those who lacked an equal starting place in life's race. This was the legacy of unequal opportunity. Second, because blacks were disproportionately poor, "black" was equated with "poor" in the white mind, and all blacks were stereotyped as either criminals and vagrants or as people to whom orders should be given, not taken from. This was the color-conscious legacy. Third, because blacks were disproportionately poor and not integrated into universities and professions, a whole group of white people had very little to do with blacks. Failing to integrate elite schools and professions would perpetuate white ignorance, prejudice, and hostility toward blacks. This was the segregation legacy. Johnson and King believed that by taking positive steps, the government could help ensure that blacks would not disproportionately continue to lack a fair start, laying the groundwork for a truly color-blind society in which skin color was no longer a fairly good proxy for social standing and hastening the racial integration that would bring about a decrease in prejudice and an increase in racial harmony.

• *Legacy of Unequal Opportunity.* Formal equal opportunity (embodied in the antidiscriminatory provisions of the Civil Rights Act of 1964) was "not enough," Johnson said, because poor blacks lacked an equal chance to develop their talents. "Ability is not just the product of birth," Johnson explained. "Ability is stretched or stunted by the family that you live with, and the neighborhood you live in—by the school you go to and the poverty or the richness of your surroundings."[14]

Moynihan's rough draft of the Howard speech explains the argument in greater detail. At birth, individuals differ in their natural capacity, but, Moynihan notes, "a person's capabilities are not just something he is born with. They are qualities which society can develop, or retard." Then he compares two groups, of equal natural ability, whose capacities are developed quite differently.

More and more we are finding it is possible to take one group of young persons, with a full range of talent and abilities, and feed them, house them, care for and teach them so well, that they all end up more capable persons than they started out. And we are finding it is possible to take an exactly similar group of young persons, and hardly feed them, and barely house them, and not care for them, and miseducate them. And they turn out much less capable persons than they were at the beginning. . . . If at the end of this process you give each group an equal opportunity to take the same set of examinations, or to compete in the same market place, you do not get equal results. You get unequal results.[15]

In years to come, proponents of affirmative action would stress this economic legacy of past discrimination. Justice Thurgood Marshall, for example, would point out that because of past discrimination, blacks had a four times greater chance of living in poverty, and a median family income only 60 percent that of whites.[16] He argued, in another case, that minority construction firms were hampered by "deficiencies in working capital, inability to meet bonding requirements, [and] disabilities caused by inadequate 'track record' "—barriers not faced by "experienced nonminority contractors."[17] Compensation was necessary to "achieve equal opportunity for all."[18]

• *Color-Conscious Legacy.* Likewise, some form of compensation was seen as necessary to reach a state of color blindness. Only by facing and addressing the legacy of past discrimination, Johnson said, would we "reach the time when the only difference between Negroes and whites is the color of their skin."[19] Johnson saw that simply proclaiming that we are a color-blind society does not make it true. To do nothing would freeze 400 years of oppression, solidifying the ill-gotten advantages held by many whites. Without some compensation, we would never get beyond the day when those picking up the garbage and cleaning the toilets and committing crimes were disproportionately black and those who are in the corporate suites were overwhelmingly white. Today, when one walks through the tree-lined streets of an affluent neighborhood and sees black and Hispanic people, one can still be fairly certain that they are not residents but employees of residents—there to mow lawns, take care of children, or clean houses. That is not a color-blind society.

- *Segregation Legacy*. So, too, to fail to remedy past discrimination was to ensure a perpetuation of past patterns of segregation—to ensure, in Justice Marshall's words, "that America will forever remain a divided society."[20] Integration was seen as essential, because the more contact whites had with minorities, the more tolerant each group was likely to become. With friendship and interaction, members of different races encounter one another as humans rather than as curiosities. Justice John Paul Stevens, arguing for an affirmative action plan for schoolteachers, said, "It is one thing for a white child to be taught by a white teacher that color, like beauty, is only 'skin deep'; it is far more convincing to experience that truth on a day-to-day basis during the routine, ongoing learning process."[21]

But it is crucial to remember, after thirty years of racial preferences, that in the early and mid–1960s, when Johnson, King, and Moynihan were grappling with how best to address the triple legacy of past discrimination, the initial idea of "affirmative action" was an extra effort to ensure that race was *not* a factor in hiring, combined with a vigorous effort to compensate the disadvantaged of *all races*.

While Johnson's Howard University address is today cited as supportive of racial preferences, Johnson never mentioned that possibility, an omission explicitly noted by news reports at the time.[22] The speech instead outlined a number of race-neutral need-based programs: "Jobs are part of the answer. . . . Decent homes in decent surroundings and a chance to learn—an equal chance to learn—are part of the answer. Welfare and social programs better designed to hold families together are part of the answer. Care for the sick is part of the answer."[23] Indeed, when the Bush administration said the Great Society programs helped cause the Los Angeles riots in 1992, the *Washington Post* ran excerpts of the Howard University speech on its editorial page "as a reminder of what the Great Society was about."[24]

Johnson's speech did open the door to other solutions— "there are other answers that are still to be found," he said— and he called for a White House conference to explore them. But at that subsequent meeting, Johnson did not back racial preferences. According to Rowland Evans and Robert Novak, Johnson administration officials kept "their fingers crossed" against the possibility that preferential treatment would be raised at the conference.[25] When a resolution on preferential treatment was introduced, the White House ensured that it was bottled up in committee.[26]

Johnson saw "affirmative action" as social mobility programs combined with an antidiscriminatory effort in which employers would broaden the pool of applicants to ensure that members of all races had a fair chance to compete, rather than as a system of preferences in which members of different races were held to different standards. Johnson's executive order 11246, which has been transformed over time to require racial preferences among corporations doing business with the government, actually called for federal contractors to take "affirmative action to ensure that applicants are employed, and that employees are treated during employment, *without* regard to their race, creed, color, or national origin."[27] A plan devised by Johnson's secretary of labor, Willard Wirtz, for racial quotas in the Philadelphia construction industry received "little backing" from Johnson himself[28] and was actually "rescinded" before Johnson left office.[29]

Moynihan believed there were race-blind, class-based ways to compensate for past discrimination. Although his report failed to provide specific policy proposals to address the legacy of past racial discrimination, Moynihan later recalled that "it always seemed to me that you would take care of this race problem in the context of a class problem."[30] In fact, on June 4, 1968—three years to the day after the Howard University speech—Moynihan gave his own commencement address, at the New School for Social Research, and came out firmly *against* the notion of seeking equal group result via racial quotas in university admissions. Moynihan said he feared that the failure to provide genuine equal opportunity, through race-neutral strategies such as "full employment, income supplementation, housing construction," and the like, was driving us to "government-dictated outcomes directed against those institutions most vulnerable to government pressure." He predicted that racial quotas at universities would quickly translate into quotas against disproportionately successful groups, such as Jews and Asian Americans.[31]

Likewise, Martin Luther King never endorsed racial preferences, arguing instead that there were nonracial ways to remedy past racial wrongs. King clearly believed that some sort of compensation for past discrimination was imperative, and in his book *Why We Can't Wait* he noted the precedents for giving preferential treatment—preferences in university admissions for the untouchables in India, and preferences in civil service employment for veterans following World War II. He wrote: "The ancient common law has always provided a remedy for the appropriation of the labor of one human being by another. This law should be made to apply for American Negroes." But having laid out the very best argument for racial preferences, King did not propose a bill of rights for the Negro but rather "a broad-based and gigantic Bill of Rights for the Disadvantaged, our veterans of the long siege of denial."[32]

As the decade wore on, King's commitment to class-based remedies grew stronger. In his work on the origins of the civil rights movement, the University of Pennsylvania sociologist John David Skrentny notes that while the Congress of Racial Equality (CORE) and the Student Nonviolent Coordinating Committee (SNCC) embraced race-conscious remedies, King's Southern Christian Leadership Conference (SCLC) did not.[33] And in King's 1967 testimony before the Kerner Commission, set up by Johnson to address the causes of urban rioting, he reaffirmed his class-based argument verbatim from *Why We Can't Wait*.[34] Even strong supporters of affirmative action like Derrick Bell, Joel Dreyfuss, Charles Lawrence III, Drew S. Days III, Frances Lee Ansley, and Jack Greenberg concede that in the last four years of his life, King's commitment to class-based solutions grew stronger and stronger.[35]

Other progressives took a tack similar to King's. In 1964 the Swedish economist Gunnar Myrdal came out in opposition to racial preferences, favoring instead race-neutral policies to "lift all the poor people" out of poverty.[36] In testimony before the Kerner Commission, Eli Ginzberg, chairman of the National Manpower Advisory Committee, advocated class-based, race-blind quota hiring by government contractors. He testified:

> I think your Commission should give consideration to taking a much more strenuous position of saying, "Look, the Negroes in the numbers that need to be fitted into the economy are not going to be fitted in easily, and let's stop fooling around and let's move to a quota system." You obviously include poor whites also. But to simply stipulate that larger employers—employers from fifty or a hundred workers up—will have to take one or two workers designated by the Employment Service as needing jobs.[37]

The Kerner Commission identified white racism as the central cause of unrest but proposed a wide variety of class-based initiatives. Its report recommended, for example, "efforts to improve dramatically schools serving disadvantaged children through substantial federal funding of year-round quality compensatory education programs" and "expanded opportunities for higher education through increased federal assistance to disadvantaged students."[38]

Robert F. Kennedy also spoke of a "special obligation" owed to blacks for years of slavery and segregation but proposed an aggressive expansion of government social mobility programs rather than a system of racial preferences.[39] In 1963, as attorney general, Kennedy testified before Sam Ervin's Senate Judiciary Committee on proposed civil rights legislation, and he strongly rejected what today might be considered a rather mild form of race consciousness. Ervin questioned Kennedy about a January 1963 equal opportunity directive issued by the New Orleans district of the U.S. Army Corps of Engineers. The directive required that if a Negro was among the top three candidates for a vacancy, failure to select him had to be justified in writing (whereas failure to select a white required no justification). Kennedy replied, "I would not issue those regulations. I don't think that they are wise regulations." Kennedy said he supported "a major effort to try to find Negroes who are eligible," rather than changing the standards of eligibility themselves.[40] In 1968 he told the journalist Jack Newfield, "You know, I've come to the conclusion that poverty is closer to the root of the problem than color. . . . We have to convince the Negroes and poor whites that they have common interests."[41]

After thirty years of race-based affirmative action, it may seem odd to rediscover that 1960s progressives proposed nonracial solutions to the problem of past racial discrimination.[42] But their notion was not that we should rewrite the history of the last three centuries by raising all blacks two rungs on life's ladder and knocking all whites down two rungs. That approach would be too speculative and crude, smacking of "payback" and inviting the response that the sons should not pay for the sins of the fathers. The notion was not compensation for compensation's sake, but rather, compensation to provide genuine equal opportunity, color blindness, and integration.

Johnson's fundamental aim was to address unequal starting places. When he said that "ability" is shaped by neighborhood, family, and school, he was describing, of course, class-based disadvantages. The logic of his argument about the insufficiency of formalistic equal opportunity applied to poor whites as well as to poor blacks, and not at all to advantaged blacks. Johnson knew that not all blacks lived in disadvantaged families and bad neighborhoods or attended deficient schools, and that some whites did.[43] Indeed, he noted in the Howard speech the incipient bifurcation in the black community: the "growing middle class minority" on the one side, and "the great majority of Negro Americans—the poor, the unemployed, the uprooted and the dispossessed, on the other." At the subsequent White House conference, Johnson detailed his concern about those blacks who were "jobless," "unskilled," and in "broken families," those "trapped in ghettoes and shanties."[44]

Moynihan was likewise concerned about unequal starting points. The problem was not a racial one per se, Moynihan wrote. "Given equal opportunities," he said, "the children of [black middle-class] families will perform as well or better than their white peers. They need no help from anyone, and ask none."[45] Moynihan's concern was the poor blacks growing up in broken homes for whom formal equal opportunity would not be enough. When he spoke of two groups with equal abilities, one unfed, ill housed, and miseducated, the other not, he spoke generally of blacks and whites, but the language was economic, not racial. To the extent that he was concerned about the breakup of the black family, the solution was jobs for unemployed blacks rather than preference programs that promoted an upper-middle-class black manager from junior to senior vice president.[46]

Martin Luther King, too, saw that compensatory treatment aimed at creating genuinely equal starting places needed to be class-based. King wrote: "While Negroes form the vast majority of America's disadvantaged, there are millions of white poor who would also benefit from [a Bill of Rights for the Disadvantaged]. ... It is a simple matter of justice that America, in dealing creatively with the task of raising the Negro from backwardness, should also be rescuing a large stratum of the forgotten white poor."[47]

The Kerner Commission had a similar logic in mind when it recommended broad class-based initiatives in response to urban rioting. While the focus of its report was Negroes living in the ghetto, the commission wrote, "This Nation is confronted with the issue of justice for all its people—white as well as black, rural as well as urban." The commission saw that a race-specific, class-blind approach was inappropriate since class divides within the black community were important to understanding urban rioting. Negro counter-rioters tended to be better educated and of higher income, the report noted, while the rioters tended to be lower-class blacks, whose hostility "is more apt to be a product of social and economic class than of race; he is almost equally hostile toward middle-class Negroes."[48]

Likewise, progressives in the 1960s knew that if color blindness was the ultimate goal, any race-based program would, at least in the short term, place the means in tension with the ends.

And if the purpose of integration was to decrease racial prejudice and increase social harmony, Johnson, King, and Moynihan
saw that race-based preferences were a problematic means of
achieving those ends.

First, many civil rights leaders were aware that any misplaced
focus on race, particularly a confusion of race and class, could fuel
white racism. When the Moynihan Report was publicly released
following the Watts riots in August 1965, Moynihan's talk of
family breakdown among blacks was denounced by civil rights
leaders for feeding racist stereotypes about the sexual promiscuity
of blacks—even though Moynihan clearly put the blame for black
illegitimacy on the legacy of white racism.[49] The problem of illegitimacy and associated pathologies, liberals said, was not one of
race, but of class. Moynihan, in comparing black and white illegitimacy rates, had failed to control for class and income; most of the
difference between racial groups disappears when you do so, they
argued. The civil rights leader Whitney Young, Jr., for instance,
said that while the pathologies of the Negro ghetto were undeniable, the report's title, *The Negro Family*, "stigmatized an entire
group of people when the majority of that group of people do not
fall into the category of the Negro family that Moynihan
describes. Moynihan did not point up that comparable data on
low income whites would show very much the same thing."[50]

If reaction to *The Negro Family* made Moynihan and
Johnson cognizant of the potentially stigmatizing effects of
focusing on race, they were also aware of the danger that special
treatment for blacks could arouse among whites. Three decades
later, Moynihan recalled:

> What I wrote was that we seek equality as a fact and as a
> result. That equal opportunity will not be enough. We have
> to seek equality. But I was still of the view that you could
> get it by a sufficient effort at—now shaken—but a suffi-
> cient effort at training and job creation and recognizing that
> they would have special needs. That you could bring people
> up to a condition that brought equality of results just by
> working with that. As against decreeing it, which I guess I
> always thought would be a source of awful ethnic conflict.[51]

Likewise, Martin Luther King saw that racial preferences were an unlikely means to achieve social harmony. King wrote to the freelance editor who was helping him to prepare *Why We Can't Wait*:

> Any "Negro Bill of Rights" based upon the concept of compensatory treatment as a result of the years of cultural and economic deprivation resulting from racial discrimination must give greater emphasis to the alleviation of economic and cultural backwardness on the part of the so-called "poor white." It is my opinion that many white workers whose economic condition is not too far removed from the economic condition of his black brother, will find it difficult to accept a "Negro Bill of Rights," which seeks to give special consideration to the Negro in the context of unemployment, joblessness, etc. and does not take into sufficient account their plight (that of the white worker).[52]

Years later, King's aide Bayard Rustin would echo King's sentiment: "Any preferential approach postulated on racial, ethnic, religious, or sexual lines will only disrupt a multicultural society and lead to a backlash," he wrote. "However, special treatment can be provided to those who have been exploited or denied opportunities if solutions are predicated on class lines, precisely because all religious, ethnic, and racial groups have a depressed class who would benefit."[53]

In the mid to late 1960s, then, the most thoughtful, progressive voices in America had come to two basic conclusions. First, the formal equality of opportunity embodied in the Civil Rights Act was not enough; affirmative steps were required to undo the present-day legacy of past discrimination. And second, for social, moral, and political reasons, compensation had to take the form of special help for the disadvantaged of all races.

2. Affirmative Action Gone Astray

I N THE LATE 1960s, after the assassinations of Martin Luther King and Robert Kennedy, the retirement of Lyndon Johnson, and the election of Richard Nixon, the direction of civil rights thinking changed dramatically. King and Johnson had spoken of compensating black America in the context of a broad, ambitious effort to create a Great Society, one with genuine equal opportunity, a genuine color blindness, and a naturally integrated future. The path chosen after their departures focused on a narrow zero-sum effort, pitting the very groups King had sought to unite against each other and following a theory of compensation that many Americans refused to accept. Then, in the late 1970s, came a second shift, just as important as the first but much more subtle, as the justification for affirmative action moved from compensation to diversity, from racial preferences as a temporary bridge to color blindness to racial preferences as a permanent way of life. In the first shift, affirmative action wandered from its noble roots; in the second, it broke with them completely and irretrievably.

FROM COLOR-BLIND TO COLOR-CONSCIOUS REMEDIES

The first great line of demarcation was King's assassination in 1968. In response to his death, and more profoundly to the riots that ensued, America—its universities, its new president, its businesses, and its civil rights leaders—decided not to answer the demands of Martin Luther King's Poor People's Campaign, which would have been very expensive, but rather to implement a system of explicitly racial preferences. Ignoring the fact that urban rioters were overwhelmingly poor, universities led the way by setting up racial preference programs that often ended up benefiting middle-class minority members who were quite distant from the rioting.[1] And the federal government began to push a system of racial preferences in employment that pitted the interests of white workers against those of blacks, so that each black gain under the program came at the expense of individual whites. The transition from King's class-based, race-blind remedy to the new race-based, class-blind preferences was swift and stunning.

In 1968 Marian Wright Edelman, an adviser to King, had helped facilitate the visionary Poor People's campaign,[2] but by 1974 she was supporting a University of Washington admissions program that favored the wealthiest minority member over the poorest white, reasoning that "all members of the minority groups were relevantly 'disadvantaged' for the purposes of the University policy."[3] The policy declared not only that all people of color are disadvantaged and that all whites are not disadvantaged, but that the richest minority member was more disadvantaged than the poorest white, and so was deserving of a preference.[4] It is remarkable that "affirmative action passed as a program on the Left," says the social critic Richard Rodriguez, given that "its supporters ignored the most fundamental assumptions of the classical Left by disregarding the importance of class."[5]

The shift from a race-blind class remedy to class-blind racial preferences was associated with a profound shift in the public policy goal. Where the first notion was that poor kids have unequal opportunities and, because of past discrimination, an extraordinary number of poor kids are black, the new notion was that *every* individual black needs a break against *every* individual white, no matter the class status of either. The goal was transformed from compensation in order to produce genuine equal opportunity to compensation to restore all people of color to the societal rung on the ladder where policy makers speculate they might have been but for historical wrongs.

When Allan Bakke, a working-class white applicant, was rejected from the University of California at Davis Medical School even though his scores were much higher than those of minority applicants who were accepted, some members of the Supreme Court reasoned that he had no complaint, because in the absence of past discrimination, those minority applicants would have beaten Bakke out on the merits. Wrote Justice William Brennan: "If it was reasonable to conclude—as we hold that it was—that the failure of minorities to qualify for admission at Davis under regular procedures was due principally to the effects of past discrimination, then there is a reasonable likelihood that, but for pervasive discrimination, respondent [Allan Bakke] would have failed to qualify for admission even in the absence of Davis's special admissions program."[6] This leap was never accepted by the American public.[7] The argument that even the most advantaged blacks deserve compensation, because if not for the accumulated sins of three hundred years they might have been even more advantaged, was very hard to swallow.

That is not to say that Americans reject the notion of compensation for historical wrongs entirely. Americans have supported compensation for past racial wrongs when (in Aristotle's formulation) the victims benefit, wrongdoers pay, and the reparations are proportionate to the crime. Consider, for example, the compensation provided for victims of the so-called Rosewood Massacre. In 1923 whites rampaged through the almost entirely black town of Rosewood, Florida, killing and looting and burning the town to the ground. The state of Florida failed to intercede in the weeklong massacre. Seventy-one years later, the state passed legislation to compensate identified survivors ($150,000 each) and provide college scholarships to all descendants of the victims.[8] The compensation was narrowly tailored so as to be paid, not to all blacks, but to actual victims or direct descendants—those directly linked with the wrong. Because the government was thoroughly implicated in each of the crimes, the wrongdoer paid.[9] And the dollar amount was deemed proportional to the documented crime. Like the U.S. government's reparations for interning Japanese Americans during World War II,[10] and Germany's reparations to Jews who were concentration camp inmates or survivors of inmates,[11] the Rosewood case presented a very strong case for compensation—and makes sense irrespective of each victim's economic status.

Likewise, documented acts of discrimination by a particular employer surely justify compensation for identifiable victims, restoring them to their proper place.[12] This, indeed, was the original meaning of "affirmative action" in labor law: to place victims where they would have been but for the illegal action.[13] Though more controversial, courts have also accepted the notion that when there is documented evidence of past discrimination by a particular employer—and all the victims may not be found, identified, and made whole—narrowly tailored and temporary remedies may give preferences to members of the same race who were not actual victims.[14] As President Reagan's solicitor general, Charles Fried, notes, while the victim-specificity requirement has considerable force in theory, "in practice it means that discrimination will often go unremedied, since by the time a lawsuit is done the specific victims will have scattered and there will be no one to compensate."[15]

But the Supreme Court never accepted the notion that racial preferences of the type employed in the *Bakke* case could be justified as compensation for general societal discrimination. Such preferences jettison not only the notion of victim-specificity and burdening wrongdoers but the rule of proportionality. For unless the nature of the wrong is carefully documented, the appropriateness of the remedy cannot be evaluated. Unless we carefully define the scope of the past discrimination, when it occurred, and which groups were affected, we cannot know the proper scope of the remedy, its appropriate duration, and its beneficiaries. In the *Bakke* case, for example, Justice Marshall eloquently outlined for page after page the brutal history of discrimination against blacks, concluding, "The experience of Negroes in America has been different in kind, not just degree, from that of other ethnic groups."[16] In fact, the Davis program benefited four ethnic groups, and two-thirds of its beneficiaries were not black.[17]

When past discrimination is not carefully documented, the Supreme Court has noted, the chances of stigma and resentment climb rapidly. As Justice Sandra Day O'Connor has written: "Proper findings . . . serve to assure all citizens that deviation from the norm of equal treatment of all racial and ethnic groups is a temporary matter, a measure taken in the service of the goal of equality itself."[18] And without careful findings, racial preferences may evolve into a politically driven spoils system, with each ethnic group trying to negotiate "a piece of the action."[19]

Some argue that the appropriate remedy for past discrimination is proportional racial representation. But most careful analysts flatly reject the notion that, but for societal discrimination, blacks, Hispanics, and women would all be found proportionately in each profession and school, and that each group would have an income 100 percent of the national average. While most Americans today reject the notion that racial groups are innately inferior, they also reject the notion that all group differences are the result of discrimination. A third category—the strong cultural differences between ethnic groups—surely help to explain different group results.[20] Racial and ethnic cultures differ widely not only in terms of cuisine and music but in ways that can have a dramatic impact on educational and financial achievement, such as median age of marriage and childbirth, family composition, family size, attitudes toward "success" in the majority culture, and language.[21]

To be sure, some of these cultural differences are themselves a product of discrimination.[22] But there does appear to be a core residual effect of culture, even after controlling for the effects of discrimination on economic status and on culture itself.[23] In the United States, the three top-performing groups between 1972 and 1989 had all themselves historically suffered discrimination. The annual incomes of Jewish American households stood at 155 percent of the national average, those of Asian Americans at 127 percent, and those of Irish Americans at 118 percent.[24] While these groups have not suffered discrimination on a par with that suffered by blacks, the fact that Jewish, Asian, and Irish Americans do better than whites generally suggests that cultural differences—apart from discrimination—play a powerful role in explaining group disparities.[25] How can discrimination explain that the out-of-wedlock birth rate among whites is higher (16 percent) than it is among Japanese Americans (6.5 percent) or among Chinese Americans (3.8 percent)?[26] Or that Asian Americans constitute 2.9 percent of the U.S. labor force but 11 percent of physicians, 7.2 percent of professors, and 7.1

percent of engineers?[27] And African Americans, who along with Native Americans have surely suffered more discrimination than other groups in our nation, are not at the very bottom rung of the economic ladder; blacks in America do better economically than Puerto Rican and Mexican Americans.[28] In 1993 Hispanics graduated from high school at a rate of 61 percent, compared with a black rate of 75 percent, and the median annual earnings of black men were greater than those of Hispanic men.[29] Blacks, Native Americans, and Hispanics all have mean on-the-job earnings above the level of Pennsylvania Germans.[30] Overall there is more income variation among white subgroups than there is between whites and blacks.[31]

Nevertheless, the notion of proportional representation received a strong public boost in 1969 from the unlikeliest of sources: President Richard M. Nixon. With the rioting of the late 1960s, the calls for some kind of racial compensation increased. In May 1969, James Forman burst into the Riverside Church in New York City, interrupted Sunday services, and declared that "white Christian Churches and Jewish Synagogues in the United States of America and All Other Racist Institutions" should pay some $500 million to black institutions to begin a larger program of reparations for slavery.

As Nixon took office, he had four major choices: he could ignore the need for compensation; he could adopt Martin Luther King's Bill of Rights for the Disadvantaged; he could answer Forman's call for cash compensation; or he could require employers and universities to use racial preferences. Nixon chose racial preferences, crossing the line that Lyndon Johnson had refused to transgress. Where Johnson had buried the Philadelphia Plan, Nixon resurrected it, imposing racial balancing requirements on the construction industry and unions in Philadelphia and, eventually, on all companies that had major contracts with the federal government.[32] On the merits, the Philadelphia Plan had a strong remedial basis, but the broader requirement did not.[33] Why would Richard Nixon, who was not known for a particularly strong civil rights record, choose to push this particular remedial option?

There is a good deal of evidence that Nixon was motivated in part by his desire to divide the Democratic political coalition of labor and civil rights groups.[34] The very dynamic that made King and Johnson uneasy about racial preferences was attractive to Nixon. If blacks and labor were both opposed to Nixon—and had allied themselves to defeat Nixon's agenda—racial quotas were an issue that would turn one group against the other.

According to one of Nixon's top aides, John Ehrlichman, Nixon "thought that Secretary of Labor George Shultz had shown great style constructing a political dilemma for the labor union leaders and civil rights groups. . . . Before long, the AFL-CIO and the NAACP were locked in combat over one of the passionate issues of the day."[35] When Senator Robert Byrd (D-W.Va.) tried to kill the Philadelphia Plan with a rider on an appropriations bill, Nixon rallied Republican support to reject the Byrd amendment. Shultz said defeat of the rider was "the most important civil rights issue in a long, long time,"[36] but according to the historian Hugh Davis Graham, the Philadelphia Plan involved anything but a straight civil rights question. In a meeting with Republican congressional leaders, Graham wrote, "Nixon emphasized the importance of exploiting the Philadelphia Plan to split the Democratic constituency and drive a wedge between the civil rights groups and organized labor. . . . The Philadelphia Plan would even the score against labor, Nixon said, for the administration's humiliating defeat over [Supreme Court nominee] Judge [Clement] Haynsworth."[37]

Initially, Democrats were skeptical of Nixon's use of racial quotas. Senator George McGovern expressed strong reservations about the Philadelphia Plan.[38] Bayard Rustin, in an address to the AFL-CIO in 1969, said the conflict between blacks and labor was "a source of tremendous satisfaction to the powerful enemies of the labor movement."[39] Nixon, Rustin said, was using the Philadelphia Plan "to divide black and white workers" by "deliberately throw[ing] black and white workers at each other's throats." Acerbically he asked:

Why, in fact, would a President who has developed a "Southern strategy," who has cut back on school-integration efforts, tried to undermine the black franchise by watering down the 1965 Voting Rights Act, nominated to the Supreme Court men like Haynsworth and Carswell, cut back on funds for vital social programs, and proposed a noxious crime bill for Washington, D.C.—which is nothing less than a blatant appeal to white fear—why indeed would such a President take up the cause of integration in the building trades?[40]

Some other civil rights leaders raised similar concerns. Clarence Mitchell, director of the Washington bureau of the NAACP, said the administration's handling of the Philadelphia Plan revealed "a calculated attempt coming right from the President's desk to break up the coalition between Negroes and labor unions."[41] The Nixon administration was put in the position of having to lobby civil rights groups to strongly support the plan.[42] When the plan was voted on in Congress, Republicans in the House supported racial preferences 124–41, while a majority of Democrats (115–84) opposed them.[43]

Nixon had successfully driven a wedge between his domestic political opponents, labor and blacks, just as he would later drive a wedge between his international enemies, the Chinese and the Soviets.[44] The problem, of course, was that over time it became clear that in Nixon's effort to divide enemies, he had chosen the "wrong" side politically.[45] In 1969 he had wanted to break up the coalition and to punish labor. By 1970, however, there were signs that labor and the white working class, long the base of the Democratic Party, might actually become a strong Republican ally, particularly on Nixon's Vietnam policy. The pivotal event, says the University of Pennsylvania's Skrentny, was the Hard Hat March in the spring of 1970, when thousands of construction workers and others marched in support of Nixon's Vietnam policies.[46] According to the White House speechwriter William Safire, "Most of the zip went out of [the Philadelphia Plan] after the hardhats marched in support of Nixon and the war."[47]

By the fall of 1970, the Republican strategist Kevin Phillips would write an op-ed piece in the *Washington Post* arguing that the Philadelphia Plan, along with the president's expansion of welfare and push for suburban integration, "have all detracted from the Nixon administration's ability to use the 'social issue,'" to attract northern, blue-collar, and Catholic voters.[48] Ehrlichman responded to the Phillips editorial in a memo to the president:

> *Philadelphia Plan:*
> While anti-labor and pro-black, the legislative battle drove a wedge between the Democrats and labor which has stretched the membrane. The Plan itself is not widely understood in non-labor circles, in my view. Labor understands it and hates it. In due time, if we administer it without undue zeal it can become a "slow and reasonable" approach to civil rights.[49]

Over time Nixon did more than slow his support for the Philadelphia Plan; he disowned it. Meanwhile, the Democrats resolved their qualms and became more forthright in their support of racial preference schemes. In fact, McGovern, who had been hesitant about the Philadelphia Plan, chaired the Democratic reform commission that established racial and gender quotas for the 1972 convention. The issue created a major flap when the delegation from Cook County, Illinois, was unseated for failure to have proportionate numbers of black delegates.

By August 1972 Nixon had told all federal agencies to avoid the use of quotas. The next month, Secretary of Labor James D. Hodgson issued a directive backing away from hiring goals for federal contractors.[50] And in his 1972 reelection campaign, Nixon ran against quotas. Thomas and Mary Edsall describe the stunning reversal:

> Nixon, in 1972, seeking to secure the shifting loyalties of the white working class, turned presidential rhetoric against the major civil rights initiative of his own first administration—the Philadelphia Plan. Although Nixon had fought for the plan in 1969, by 1972 he sought to reap political reward from stockpiled blue-collar resentments: "When young people apply for jobs . . . and find the door closed because they don't fit into some numerical quota, despite their ability, and they object, I do not think it is

right to condemn those young people as insensitive or even racist."[51]

Nixon attacked McGovern as "the quota candidate" and said that a fixed quota system is "as artificial and unfair a yardstick as has ever been used to deny opportunity."[52] At the Republican Convention in 1972, Nixon derided the Democratic convention rules as "quota democracy," arguing, "the way to end discrimination against some is not to begin discrimination against others."[53]

On the Supreme Court, a similar pattern could be seen among progressives: initial skepticism by some liberals about the idea of racial preferences, but eventual support for the policy. Following in the tradition of King and Johnson, Justice William O. Douglas balked at the constitutionality of racial preferences and advocated race-blind preferences for the disadvantaged. In the 1974 case of *DeFunis v. Odegaard*, involving racial preferences in law school admissions, Douglas wrote:

> A black applicant who pulled himself out of the ghetto into a junior college may thereby demonstrate a level of motivation, perseverance, and ability that would lead a fair minded admissions committee to conclude that he shows more promise for law study than the son of a rich alumnus who achieved better grades at Harvard. That applicant would be offered admission not because he is black but because as an individual he has shown he has the potential, while the Harvard man may have taken less advantage of the vastly superior opportunities offered him.[54]

Likewise, the liberal California Supreme Court Justice Stanley Mosk, in addressing the *Bakke* case at the state level, backed special consideration for the disadvantaged but said that outright racial preferences were illegal.[55]

By the time the U.S. Supreme Court considered *Bakke* in 1978, however, Douglas had retired and the Court's liberal wing would stand foursquare behind racial preferences and quotas. Four justices—William Brennan, Byron White, Thurgood Marshall, and Harry Blackmun—supported as lawful and constitutional the University of California at Davis's system of racial quotas and preferences as a way of "remedying the effects of past societal discrimination."[56] Four conservative justices—John Paul Stevens, Warren Burger, Potter Stewart, and William Rehnquist— declared Davis's preference program a violation of Title VI of the Civil Rights Act of 1964. Justice Lewis F. Powell provided the Court's liberals with a decisive fifth vote in favor of racial preferences in university admissions, arguing that preferences (though not quotas) in medical school admissions were constitutional and lawful if used as a way of "obtaining the educational benefits that flow from an ethnically diverse student body."[57] Though Powell alone espoused this theory of diversity, he provided the swing vote and authored the controlling opinion in *Bakke*.[58]

Still, the Court's liberals clung to the notion of eventual color blindness, saying racial preferences were only a temporary means by which our society would advance to its ultimate color-blind stage. In Justice Blackmun's familiar words, "In order to get beyond racism we must first take account of race."[59] Short-term race consciousness, he said, was necessary before the country could "achieve its professed goal of a society that is not race conscious." He added: "I yield to no one in my earnest hope that the time will come when an 'affirmative action' program is unnecessary and is, in truth, only a relic of the past."[60] And Justice Marshall argued: "If we are ever to become a fully integrated society, one in which the color of a person's skin will not determine the opportunities available to him or her, we must be willing to take steps to open those doors."[61]

While some opponents of preferences were always skeptical of their temporary nature,[62] the public record is replete with examples of proponents of affirmative action pledging their impermanence. Congressman Robert Drinan (D-Mass.) called race and gender preferences "an interim strategy,"[63] and Eleanor Holmes Norton, chairman of the Equal Employment Opportunity Commission under President Carter, acknowledged that "there is a general consensus in our society" that affirmative action "ought to be temporary."[64] Most proponents did not specify a time limit, though a few did. Whitney Young, Jr., of the National Urban League called for "a decade of discrimination in favor of Negro youth,"[65] and Justice Blackmun said he hoped that affirmative action programs would be unnecessary "within a decade at most."[66]

Proponents believed that prospective antidiscriminatory measures, primarily the Civil Rights Act of 1964, would address ongoing and future instances of discrimination; once we had remedied the remaining vestiges of past discrimination, we could move on to a color-blind society. The Supreme Court was very careful and rigorous in its insistence that affirmative action was justified not to combat contemporary discrimination but to address "the legacy of unequal treatment."[67] Indeed, in *City of Richmond v. Croson* (1989), Marshall specifically noted that the issue "is not present discrimination but rather whether past discrimination has resulted in the continuing exclusion of minorities."[68] One could cite literally hundreds of invocations of the notion that affirmative action is meant to remedy the lingering effects of *past* discrimination[69]—from the opinions of Justices Marshall, Brennan, and O'Connor,[70] the Congress,[71] and the executive branch.[72] In his famous argument about the fairness of life's race, Johnson was not saying that the racetrack itself had potholes (the Civil Rights Act was meant to address prospective barriers), but that the past has a legacy still felt today—the "scars of centuries" and the impact of being "hobbled by chains" in past years.[73] Most supporters of affirmative action realized that racial preferences were an extraordinary tool (discrimination in itself) that made sense only as a remedy for the legacy of *past* discrimination, precisely because prospective antidiscrimination statutes cannot themselves reach back and eradicate that history.

By the early 1970s, then, many leaders had jettisoned the notion of addressing the legacy of past discrimination in the context of a Bill of Rights for the Disadvantaged or a War on Poverty. Racial preferences were seen as a necessary, but temporary, tool to lead the nation to a color-blind future.

FROM COMPENSATION TO DIVERSITY

Over time, however, a new theory emerged that largely replaced the temporary compensatory notion of affirmative action with a vision of a much more permanent race consciousness. Where affirmative action was initially justified as compensation for past discrimination—short-term racial consciousness to achieve color blindness—the new justification, "diversity," discarded the aspiration of color blindness in the long run.[74] The distinction between compensatory preferences and diversity preferences, though often ignored, is at least as profound as the divide between color blindness and color consciousness.

Advocates of compensatory affirmative action argue that they still believe in the goal of color blindness, but that in order to get from here to there we need a transition period in which race is taken into account. By contrast, the new advocates of diversity argue that the color-blind ideal was wrong all along. Race does matter, and it always will, because race is not just skin color but a substantive cultural characteristic of such great importance that it ought to be a significant factor in the distribution of benefits and burdens. In the new way of thinking, to deny the central and fundamental importance of race is itself a form of racism, and race consciousness is a good thing, in both the short run and the long run.[75] This is a striking departure from the mainstream civil rights movement, which, as William Julius Wilson points out, had always seen "a society without racial preferences" as "the long-term goal."[76]

On the Supreme Court, progressives were initially wary of citing diversity as a justification for racial preferences. In *UC v. Bakke*, Justice Brennan and others distanced themselves from Powell's diversity rationale, arguing that "the central meaning" of the opinion was that governmental institutions could use racial preferences "to remedy disadvantages cast on minorities by past racial prejudice, at least when appropriate findings have been made."[77] But by 1990 support for diversity as a justification for preferences had found a liberal majority.[78] In *Metro Broadcasting v. FCC*, the Court upheld a pair of minority broadcast license preferences on the grounds that minority ownership would lead to increased diversity in programming.[79] In his valedictory opinion, Brennan explicitly embraced race-conscious diversity goals, "even if those measures are not 'remedial' in the sense of being designed to compensate victims of past governmental or societal discrimination."[80] Brennan cited, favorably, Justice Powell's diversity rationale from *UC v. Bakke*—the very opinion from which Brennan had distanced himself years earlier.[81]

Off the Court, the rhetoric of Democratic politicians mirrored this shift. In the early 1970s, the McGovern Commission had urged quotas at the Democratic National Convention in order to "overcome the effects of past discrimination,"[82] but in 1992, Bill Clinton shed the rhetoric of compensation, stating simply that his administration would "look like America."[83] Clinton may have been merely continuing in the long-standing presidential tradition of rewarding groups who helped elect him,[84] but it is noteworthy, nevertheless, that Clinton chose to employ the language of "diversity." Diversity may be seen as more politically palatable than compensation because it is justified not as atonement for white sins but as a way to further common interests. So strong is the Clinton administration's commitment to diversity that when the school board in Piscataway, New Jersey, laid off an equally qualified white teacher, the Clinton Justice Department defended the action not on the grounds that Piscataway needed to remedy past discrimination, but on the grounds of increasing diversity within a particular teaching department.[85]

Today most educators highlight their commitment to "diversity" rather than "compensation," calling diversity "the hallmark" and "the core" of the university experience.[86] As president of Harvard, Derek Bok openly denigrated the compensatory rationale for affirmative action, stating in 1985:

> I am not very keen on viewing preferential admissions as some way to atone for the injustices of the past. . . . I am not sure the [minority] students we admit are the ones who most need atonement. I had a great friend last year who was a captain of the women's track team. Once I met her in the Yard and she says, "I'm so tired out that I don't know whether I can run this weekend." I say, "Why?" "Well, I was over in Italy, celebrating my birthday." I don't think of any reparations being due to her, but I do think she was a very talented person who I think would add something to the student body and be heard from later in life, and so I am glad she's here.[87]

In higher education, the diversity rationale is so predominant today that Professor Stephen Carter talks about the compensatory model in the past tense: "Back in the 1970s," he says, special admissions programs were justified "as compensation for [past discrimination], the contemporary concept of 'diversity' not yet having been unearthed."[88]

In the business world, too, diversity is offered as an end in itself. Companies employ preferences not to redress past discrimination, they say, but to reach new markets. "To hell with the law," Nutrasweet Chief Executive Officer Robert E. Flynn told the *New York Times*. "You can't send someone from the north side of Chicago to sell Nutrasweet in Singapore. You need a team to reflect the markets you are going to serve."[89] Even conservative newspapers like the *Washington Times* and the *Wall Street Journal*, which have little sympathy for compensatory arguments, consider race a qualification on diversity grounds. "In some cases, the ethnic background of a candidate can be a qualification," says David Threshie, the publisher of the *Orange County Register*.[90]

The new diversity argument, while commonplace, is quite radical. It jettisons the old argument for racial preferences—"we're not ready" to be color-blind—and questions the aspiration toward color blindness itself. Race, it is argued, is an important social construct and always will be, and it may appropriately be used to distribute benefits and burdens, now and forever more. The diversity argument appeals not to morality or the need to right wrongs but to a hard-nosed notion of "racial realism." Advocates of diversity point out that few of us are color-blind purists; diversity, in their view, involves a simple recognition of social reality. They note, correctly, that our constitutional and statutory law provide three general exceptions to qualify the basic presumption in favor of color blindness.

First, the law carves out an exception for liberty interests and associational rights. While the Congress has chosen to extend prohibitions against racial discrimination into many parts of the private sector—employment, housing, hotels, and restaurants—it has left a limited sphere of autonomy for private individuals to discriminate, which falls under the right of association. An employer or landlord could be forbidden to discriminate by race, but the prohibition does not extend to the employer or landlord's choice of friends, or spouse.[91] Where we would rightly be appalled if a landlord advertised for a white tenant, the personal advertisement of a single white male "in search of" a single white female is read without batting an eye.[92] (Indeed, one survey found that the majority of personal ads designate race.)[93] Just as the government may not forbid racial intermarriages, neither can the government tell you that you must be race-blind when choosing a marriage partner.[94] In addition to the libertarian justification, there is also a cultural pluralism argument that says, in the private sphere, it is healthy to permit different subcultures to grow and develop within the larger society. The *pluribus* should flourish in the private sphere, whereas in the public realm—publicly financed education, employment, commerce—we come together, as an *unum*. Still, this liberty right has been narrowly construed. When private clubs take on a more public character—membership, for example, comes to entail substantial business opportunities—they may properly be regulated by the government for such things as race and gender discrimination.[95]

Second, the law allows, indeed requires, the government to be race-conscious (ironically enough) in enforcing antidiscrimination principles.[96] For one thing, to ensure that employers are engaging in noncontroversial "old-style" affirmative action (widening the net of applicants so that minorities know of opportunities when they come available), job applicants must disclose their race on employment forms. Even conservatives like Jesse Helms say they support this type of affirmative action, so long as the standards are not bent, because it is consistent with the antidiscriminatory principle.[97] Likewise, the courts and the Congress have backed so-called disparate impact suits, a highly race-conscious tool that is necessary for effective enforcement of the antidiscriminatory merit-based principle. In the famous 1971 case of *Griggs v. Duke Power*, the Supreme Court found that hiring practices that have a disproportionately negative impact on minorities must be specially justified, even when intentional discrimination is not alleged. In *Griggs*, the employer had required that applicants for low-skilled jobs have a high school diploma—a requirement that effectively screened out a disproportionate number of blacks but was not particularly relevant to performing the jobs. The Supreme Court interpreted Title VII to mean that when such disparate impact occurred, employers had to justify the practice by a "business necessity" standard—a standard that Duke Power could not meet. The Congress reaffirmed *Griggs* with passage of the Civil Rights Act of 1991.[98] If the government could no longer label people by race, both old-style affirmative action and the 1991 act would be unenforceable.

Third, the law acknowledges that in very narrowly defined cases, realism and common sense allow private employers and government to take race or gender into account. The Civil Rights Act of 1964 recognizes the principle that in certain circumstances some criteria normally thought to be impermissible—religion, sex, or national origin—may actually be bona fide occupational qualifications.[99] Thus, a Roman Catholic school of theology may properly require that a religion professor be Catholic, even though requiring that a job applicant be Catholic in most other contexts would be illegal. A fashion designer may properly insist on hiring women to model the women's clothing, an owner of a strip joint that caters to heterosexual men would be justified in saying that only women need apply for the job of stripper, and a hotel manager may insist that a restroom attendant match the gender of the room he or she is assigned to attend.[100] Wet nurse and sperm bank donor are other jobs for which gender is obviously a bona fide qualification.[101] Although the 1964 act does not include a specific exemption for race, one can imagine circumstances where race should obviously count. For example, if a police officer is needed to go undercover into an all-black gang, the police chief of an all-white police force would clearly be justified in hiring a black officer for the job, even if that officer had a somewhat lower score than a competing white applicant.[102] Others argue that race is relevant to certain acting roles. Clearly, a white actor could not have played the role of the black suitor in *Guess Who's Coming to Dinner*.

On a constitutional level, the Court has likewise held that racial classifications, while subject to "strict scrutiny," are not inherently invalid. Even the Court's most vociferous proponent of color blindness, Antonin Scalia, concedes that in cases of "social emergency rising to the level of imminent danger to life and limb"—such as a racial prison riot, where there is a need to temporarily separate the races—the principle of color blindness may be bent.[103] But the exception is a narrow one. The Court has found that a long-term separation of the races in a prison— even for the benign purpose of keeping the peace—is unconstitutional.[104] And the Court's decision to make an exception to the color-blind rule in allowing the imprisonment of Japanese Americans during World War II in the *Korematsu* case has given the Supreme Court reason for pause before allowing "emergencies" to justify additional exceptions to the rule against racial classifications.[105]

The diversity rationale for racial preferences takes color consciousness much further than the previous three exceptions. Where the liberty exception is limited to purely private decisions, the enforcement exception serves the pursuit of color blindness, and the realism exception is quite narrowly tailored, diversity is public in nature, questions the very worthiness of the color-blindness goal, and is hardly narrow in scope. The diversity exception says that race is a bona fide consideration in many circumstances and in the long term. So far the argument has been accepted by the courts in only the narrowest of circumstances, but it has gained strong currency outside the judiciary, particularly in elite circles.

Whereas the old liberal vision saw race as superficial, as "skin color," and supported affirmative action only as a method of compensating and moving on to long-run color blindness, the new vision sees race as ethnicity, race as culture.[106] If the old liberal vision said race is something to get beyond, the new vision says race involves profound differences that are not to be ignored. The new vision emphasizes these differences between people, calling attention to aggregate differences and asserting that group differences are so important that they justify differential treatment. Under the new thinking, people don't "happen" to be black or white; their race is essential to their identity and to their claim on benefits. In discussions of gender, proponents argue not only that women speak with a "different voice,"[107] but that where that voice is underrepresented it becomes an element of merit.

Some reject the new vision's emphasis on difference as separatist at best, and racist and sexist at worst. But the real issue is not whether aggregate differences exist. Most people today do recognize that race is more than skin color and celebrate the cultural diversity and differences of America's ethnic groups. The real controversy comes when we ask whether those *aggregate* differences should be considered a bona fide qualification for *individuals* seeking positions. Beyond the extreme cases—the cop going undercover in a black gang—the waters get muddy very quickly. The diversity argument started in the university setting and then spread to the occupational arena; we will trace these developments in turn.

Educational Diversity

The diversity argument was first advocated in the university context, and it is in education where the theory continues to have its greatest resonance.[108] An educational institution is meant to teach, not only through its professors but through its student body. The greater the diversity of student backgrounds, the greater the exposure of each one to different ways of thinking. Just as universities give geographic preferences to ensure rural representation, they also naturally give racial preferences, the argument runs. The claim is in part that minorities will bring to the discussion the perspective of those who have experienced discrimination.[109] But if racism were to end tomorrow, diversity preferences would still be justified because race is a proxy for a distinctive culture, whether it be African American, Asian, Latino, or Native American. Residents of Montana have never suffered discrimination, but they are wanted for their differing perspective.

College admission decisions, it is argued, rest on social utility, not moral desert. Race is just like athletic ability, geography, or legacy status, proponents say, and preferences are not particularly fair but nevertheless are justified because they contribute to the institution. Indeed, the New York University law professor Ronald Dworkin argues that a university's decision to accept the smartest person—a decision usually cloaked with the term "merit"—with its implication of moral desert, is itself merely a utilitarian decision to accept or hire the person who is most likely to contribute the most.[110] It is not that some are more "worthy," but that they are more "valuable." Universities "use" students rather than "judge" them.[111] The smart individual has no "right" to attend a university, it is argued; the university reserves the right to admit the individuals it deems most useful, which may, in late–twentieth century America, involve considerations of race.[112]

Some critics question the whole notion of "minority viewpoints." When pressed, it is often awkward and difficult to define what is meant by the term. Are black views more liberal? Not on the Middle East, abortion, or the environment, says the Yale Law School professor Stephen Carter.[113] The columnist Richard Cohen asks, "What exactly is the female position on North African refugees? What is the African American position on Guatemalans slipping into Mexico and hoping to come to the United States? And what is the Hispanic position on the need for population control programs in the Asian subcontinent?"[114]

But while the notion that there is a "black" position on discrete issues is ludicrous, it is less easy to dismiss the notion that in general, black or female life experiences help shape a worldview that may have tangible import in a wide variety of issues. At least when achieved without preferences, the benefits of diversity in the university setting should be clear to all who today acknowledge that there are strong and important cultural differences between racial groups. Even opponents of racial preferences, in the words of the Reagan administration solicitor general Charles Fried, concede: "It would be silly to deny that there are many communities with distinct cultural attributes, and it would be Philistine to deny the richness their diversity lends to national life."[115] All other things being equal, having a rich diversity of students should enhance the learning experience for all.

Occupational Diversity

So, too, in the occupational setting, proponents of diversity argue that race can be an element of merit in being a better teacher, lawyer, professor, social worker, judge, newspaper reporter, police officer, TV station owner, or salesperson. Indeed, some argue that job candidates, by virtue of race or gender, may make better role models—a principle important to all the professions listed above and to virtually all other noncriminal professions as well. Increasingly, proponents of affirmative action do not argue that racial minorities should be properly represented in various professions because they are the same as whites and would have been there in proportionate numbers absent past discrimination. Instead, it is argued, minorities are different, and precisely because they are different, they are valuable to the employer. In particular, the new school of thinking says race can be relevant to a number of occupations because people of color will better serve minority constituencies and provide role models to less advantaged minority workers.[116]

The notion of serving minority constituencies is at the heart of preference schemes in a wide variety of professions. To begin with the most commonly cited example, some argue that a city plagued by tense relations between police and a minority community has a compelling reason to count race as a positive factor in new police hiring.[117] Says Clinton's former deputy attorney general, Philip B. Heymann: "I think it's very important that law enforcement does not look like a foreign occupying force, and to do that, you have to have diversity."[118] Likewise, others believe that social workers, like drug counselors, are more effective if they racially match the drug addicts with whom they are working. Thus, the Drug Abuse Education Act of 1970 provides "for the use of adequate personnel from similar social, cultural, age, ethnic and racial backgrounds as those of the individuals served under any such program."[119] Others argue that black doctors can better relate to black patients, and so black skin is an element of merit in selecting who will become doctors.[120] Black newspaper reporters are in a better position, it is said, to cover black regions of a city because it is more likely that sources will trust them, relate to them, go out for drinks with them, and give them the real story.[121] Some argue it is equally appropriate to count race as an element of merit in picking judges so as to instill greater confidence in the legal system among minority communities.[122]

The argument that race is a bona fide occupational qualification has been extended by some to other professions. Harvard Law School's Elizabeth Bartholet argues, for example, that employers "should be willing to consider blackness in a positive sense," not as compensation for past discrimination, but because "there is a need for more black lawyers who are interested in working with minority communities, for more black teachers who are capable of efficiently communicating with black students and their parents, and for more black academics who are interested in focusing their teaching and scholarship on problems particularly significant to minority groups."[123] Harvard Law Professor Duncan Kennedy concurs, at least with respect to legal academics: "We are treating race as a credential (as a proxy for culture and community) because we anticipate terrific work from some of these applicants," he writes, "work that we don't think we can get from the whites they replace."[124]

In the area of sales, it is argued that companies may want to give a preference to help open new markets. One company told the Citizens' Commission on Civil Rights that "minority insurance agents brought in minority customers who were not previously insured by that company."[125] Defending the right of private employers to grant preferences, Senator John Danforth (R-Mo.) argued that if an "employer wants to sell to customers in the inner city, and the employer does not have enough blacks on the work force, and they say: Hey, we really want to hire some blacks, because that is good business," an employer should be able to consider race as an element of merit.[126]

In addition, it is commonly argued that race should be considered a plus factor in providing "role models." The argument applies with particular force to high-profile positions. In 1980 Ronald Reagan, a staunch opponent of racial and gender preferences, noted that "appointments can carry enormous symbolic significance" when announcing that he would appoint a woman to the Supreme Court.[127] President Bush, though he denied it, clearly thought Clarence Thomas's race was a qualification for the Supreme Court,[128] and before the appointment Senator Orrin Hatch said he personally hoped Bush would appoint a person of color to replace Justice Thurgood Marshall.[129]

The role model argument, which draws on the findings of the sociologist John Ogbu, says that unless women and people of color see themselves reflected in leadership and professional roles, they are unlikely to put in the hard work and effort required to attain those positions. Ogbu's influential book *Minority Education and Caste* argues that certain "caste minorities" throughout the world underperform academically not primarily because of inadequate "home environment, school environment, or heredity," but because educational performance "is directly related to typical adult roles in the contemporary postschool world." We need, he says, to reverse the presumed causal connection. Instead of saying that blacks are concentrated in the lower portions of the occupational hierarchy because they do not work hard in school, it may be that African Americans "often reject academic competition with members of the dominant group" and "fail to work hard in school" because "such efforts have not traditionally benefited members of the groups." To support his argument that it is the societal *role* a group plays that is key to academic performance—rather than the group's culture per se—Ogbu notes that certain caste minorities, like West Indians in Britain and the Barakumin in Japan, do *better* in the United States than they do in their native lands precisely because their traditional societal role is unknown here. Indeed, the Barakumin, who do much worse in Japan, do better economically than other Japanese in the United States.[130]

WHY THE SHIFT?

Why has the diversity rationale, once disdained, now become so prominent? The answer lies, in part, in four strategic advantages that diversity offers over the compensatory rationale.[131]

First, diversity circumvents the heavy burdens placed by the Supreme Court on racial compensation schemes, particularly the requirement that evidence of past discrimination be produced to justify racial preferences as a remedy. Liberals lost the argument that general past societal discrimination justifies preferences, and that someone like Allan Bakke is not hurt by affirmative action because, but for past discrimination, he would have been rejected on the merits anyway.[132] A majority of the Court now holds that all governmental racial preference programs that are remedial in nature must be supported by clear findings of past discrimination.

The requirements can be quite burdensome. In the 1989 case of *City of Richmond v. Croson*, the Supreme Court struck down Richmond's 30 percent construction set-aside for minorities even though prior to adoption of the program, less than 1 percent of the city's prime contracts had gone to blacks—in a city 50 percent black.[133] The Court held that a congressional finding of discrimination in the construction industry *nationwide* was insufficient to justify the set-aside; specific findings for the city of Richmond were necessary. On the other hand, Richmond's well-documented history of discrimination, particularly in its educational system, was insufficient since it did not relate to the construction industry.[134] The findings had to be both localized and industry-specific.[135]

The diversity rationale neatly circumvents the need for proving past discrimination.[136] In *Bakke*, preferences were upheld, despite the lack of a factual predicate of discrimination, because diversity was good for education. And in *Metro Broadcasting*, the racial preferences of the Federal Communication Commission (FCC) were upheld, without findings of past discrimination, as a way of promoting diversity on the airwaves. Justice Kennedy, in his dissent, noted that the list of minority groups benefiting from the diversity preferences happened to coincide precisely with the beneficiaries of an earlier remedial statute.[137]

Second, the diversity rationale neatly disposes of pesky questions about when affirmative action will end. Compensatory affirmative action was always advertised as temporary, and the passage of time has created both legal and political problems. The legal problem is that those affirmative action programs that the Court approved as having an adequate factual predicate must also, in order to gain approval, have a self-destruct mechanism. And as the most egregious forms of discrimination are reined in, the likelihood of new court-ordered affirmative action remedies drops precipitously. The political problem is that even where the courts may be willing to tolerate a continuation of a particular remedial program, the public may not be. When Senator Robert Dole attacked affirmative action, he said: "Slavery was wrong. But should future generations have to pay for that?"[138]

Since diversity is unrelated to historical wrongs, its rationale—making sure viewpoints are represented—applies in perpetuity, so long as the slightest imbalance exists.[139] To Bob Dole's complaint about the continuing relevance of slavery, Bill Clinton can properly respond that slavery has nothing at all to do with promoting diversity. The time bomb is thereby defused.

Third, by shifting to a utilitarian rationale, diversity theory makes moral claims about hurting innocent parties or benefiting undeserving minorities look naive. The compensatory rationale was a rights-based theory, open to the moral complaint that white males should not pay for the sins of their fathers, and that employees should not have to pay for the discrimination of employers. By contrast, the diversity rationale jettisons complicated moral arguments about compensatory justice for a utilitarian notion that preferences are good for the institutions that offer them.

Diversity, then, blunts the major philosophical argument made by opponents of racial compensation: that affirmative action sometimes hurts innocent whites and helps undeserving minorities.[140] No innocent white is hurt, and no undeserving minority benefits, because admitting or hiring minorities with lower scores is no sacrifice to "merit." The minority preference is deserved because the minority students add something that the white students do not; in the words of a *Columbia Law Review* editor, "diversity is part of quality."[141] At its worst, as the civil rights attorney Jack Greenberg notes, Justice Powell's logic in *Bakke* "approved admitting blacks because in part it helped whites."[142] Black representation is useful to white students because a black presence will help whites learn what black people are like. Blacks, then, are not treated as ends in themselves, but as tools to educate whites. Indeed, as we shall see in chapter 3, blacks can actually be directly hurt by diversity policies.

Because there is no moral claim, only a utilitarian one, a countervailing white moral claim looks unsophisticated. Diversity proponents portray themselves as hard-nosed realists, noting that institutions are merely looking out for what's best for them. In an unusual argument for progressives—given their traditional concern for fairness over efficiency—they say: you have no claim to be treated fairly. Grow up. They address the unfairness argument posed by Clarence Thomas—how can my privileged son deserve a preference on equality opportunity grounds?—by saying the program has nothing to do with fairness.[143]

Fourth, diversity brings in new allies for the political and legal fights, particularly women and gays. The compensatory rationale for affirmative action always faced the political difficulty that programs were vulnerable to repeal by the majority of the population that was disadvantaged by them. But the diversity argument has at least the potential to address this political difficulty by adding new allies who do not come in under the old compensatory rationale.

The compensatory argument did not work well for women and gays. While our nation surely has a history of discriminating against both groups, the legacy of past discrimination is not nearly as strong as it is with respect to African Americans and other racial and ethnic groups. Because ethnic and racial groups tend to marry among themselves, past discrimination against blacks and Latinos and Native Americans leaves a more distinct economic legacy than it does for women, who tend to form economic units with the perpetrators of discrimination—men.[144] As a result, white women are much less economically disadvantaged than blacks and can readily compete in a number of educational and employment arenas without preference.[145] But by expanding the argument for preferences to diversity, women may theoretically be included in the coalition supporting affirmative action.[146]

But do diversity preferences really circumvent the legal and political problems faced by compensatory affirmative action? Or does the new theory simply raise more problems than it solves?

3. A Report Card on Affirmative Action Today

A FTER THIRTY YEARS, how well do affirmative action programs, as employed in practice, measure up against the stated goals of the scheme's early proponents? How well do they provide genuine equal opportunity? Do they advance us toward a color-blind future (assuming that is a goal still worth pursuing)? Do they provide the benefits of integration—reducing prejudice and fostering social harmony? How well do they compensate for past discrimination?

GOAL NO. 1: GENUINE EQUALITY OF OPPORTUNITY

The first and central goal of affirmative action, according to Justice Brennan's opening line in the *Bakke* decision, was to "achieve equal opportunity for all."[1] Indeed, the early programs, such as the UC Davis Medical School program challenged by Allan Bakke, were framed in terms of helping "economically and/or educationally disadvantaged" applicants.[2] The program was theoretically open to poor white students and was means-tested for minorities. "Ethnic minorities are not categorically considered under the Task Force Program unless they are from disadvantaged backgrounds," the UC guidelines declared.[3]

But over time, as affirmative action programs evolved from the race-blind class-based structure to class-blind racial preferences, the goal shifted from equality of individual opportunity to equality of racial group results.[4] While the new goal is normally criticized for going too far, it is in some senses quite modest.[5] To the extent that affirmative action, at its ultimate moment of success, merely creates a self-perpetuating black elite along with a white one, its goal is timid, certainly more conservative than a genuine equality of opportunity, which gives blacks, whites, and other Americans of all economic strata a fair chance at success. Even if all the racial numbers work out, so that there are a perfectly proportionate number of blacks and whites as doctors and lawyers, we have made only a small step toward substantive equal opportunity if those doctors and lawyers still all come from the highest income groups within their race, assuming the natural talent for being a doctor is more democratically spread.[6]

‣ If the goal is genuine equality of opportunity—allowing individuals to use their natural talents to the fullest—then in a society that outlaws racial discrimination (making caste illegal), affirmative action makes sense to the extent, and only to the extent, that race serves as a proxy for the remaining injuries of class. Affirmative action has in fact survived in part because there is a strong overlap between race and class in the United States. And in practice, some evidence suggests that the average recipient of affirmative action preferences may be somewhat less well off economically than the average displaced white male. While it is impossible to know the actual economic status of the dis-preferred—because they are not normally identified—we do know that in university admissions the affirmative action beneficiaries are often, as a group, less well off than the white students admitted. (And we can presume that those admitted are not wildly better off than those who were on the cusp of getting in but were displaced by affirmative action applicants.)

Thus, at Berkeley the median family income for freshmen entering in the fall of 1992 was $31,000 for Chicanos, $44,000 for African Americans, $50,000 for Asian Americans, and $77,000 for whites.[7] Berkeley's chancellor also notes that the parents of white students were much more highly educated: nearly 70 percent had postgraduate degrees. By contrast, almost half (49 percent) of Chicano students had parents with high school educations or less, and 41 percent of African American students had parents who did not have four-year college degrees.[8] And nationally—to use one measure of the college applicant pool—black students taking the SAT are clearly worse off than their white counterparts. Thirty-eight percent of blacks taking the SAT came from families with incomes below $20,000 in 1990, compared with 10 percent of whites. And while 40 percent of black SAT takers had parents who attended college, 61 percent of whites were in that category.[9]

But race is an imperfect proxy for class. The obvious problem, as Clarence Thomas argued in his confirmation hearings, is "that all disadvantaged people aren't black and all black people are not disadvantaged."[10] Thus, affirmative action is, in the words of Harvard Professor Alan Dershowitz and his student Laura Hanft, "classically overinclusive (including advantaged blacks) and underinclusive (not including disadvantaged whites)."[11]

The great failing of affirmative action is in not acknowledging that the legacy of past racial discrimination—real as it is—is not today's only impediment to opportunity. To argue that the most advantaged black applicant is more disadvantaged than the poorest white blinks at reality and is patronizing at best. The very term "disadvantaged" connotes "poor" before it connotes "minority"; indeed, when we say that African Americans and women are "disadvantaged," we cite evidence of *economic* status—income, unemployment, and poverty rates—to prove their disadvantage.

Under the current system, there is nothing to stop wealthy blacks from receiving preferences over poor nonblacks. Dinesh D'Souza, for example, tells the story of two applicants to Berkeley: Thuy Nguyen, a Vietnamese boat person who had lived in a refugee camp in Thailand, and Melanie Lewis, an African American daughter of an engineer. Both scored 1000 on the SAT, and Nguyen's GPA was actually slightly higher than Lewis's (3.8 vs. 3.6). Nguyen was rejected and Lewis accepted.[12] At the University of Michigan, says Joseph Adelson, the wealthy daughter of a black ambassador, attending a prestigious Ivy League college, was preferred in graduate admissions over a comparably qualified white welfare daughter who was schooled at a public university.[13] The columnist Richard Cohen tells about losing a promotion at the *Washington Post* because, as he was told, "we needed a woman." The fact that this particular woman was "from a very old and still-affluent American family" did not matter to the *Post*.[14] Cohen was incredulous. "I said, 'Look, I'm the first person in my family who went to college. I went to school at night, worked during the day time.' I said, 'I have to make way for Theodore Roosevelt's granddaughter? She's a victim?' "[15]

But how often does this happen? We know that blacks as a group are more disadvantaged than whites; the liberal essayist Michael Kinsley argues that "black" is not a bad shorthand for "disadvantaged."[16] Assuming that the typical black and the typical white are involved, more advantaged blacks receive preferences over less advantaged whites probably something like 29 percent of the time. While in 1940 race was a pretty good proxy for class—only 8 percent of black men made more than the average white man—by 1980 some 29 percent of working black men made more than the median white.[17] In 1993 the figure was roughly the same.[18]

In 1965, when Lyndon Johnson raised the notion of compensation, one-tenth of blacks were middle-class. By 1990 the figure was one-third.[19] From the 1960s to the 1980s, the chances of a black man becoming part of the economic elite have increased tenfold.[20] The chance of making more than $50,000 (in 1991 dollars) more than doubled for blacks between 1967 and 1991, according to Census Bureau statistics.[21] The percentage of blacks earning over $100,000 also more than doubled.[22] *The Economist* notes that in the past two decades the percentage of blacks earning more than $50,000 in 1990 dollars increased faster (46 percent) than the percentage of white families (35 percent) did.[23] In some 130 cities and counties nationwide, blacks have a higher household median income than whites do, everywhere from small towns to the New York City borough of Queens.[24] All told, between 1967 and 1994, writes Henry Louis Gates, Jr., the black middle class has quadrupled.[25]

Measured occupationally, black progress is equally obvious. The National Research Council notes that the occupational distribution among races has improved and that, in fact, "the proportion of employed workers in better jobs increased more rapidly for blacks than for whites and that this upgrading continued throughout the 1970s and 1980s."[26] In *The Truly Disadvantaged*, William Julius Wilson wrote that black occupational progress was faster than for whites in many areas.[27] Between 1970 and 1990, the percentage of black managers increased 138 percent, the percentage of black college professors rose 45 percent, the percentage of black physicians increased 64 percent, and the percentage of black lawyers increased 162 percent.[28] There is a sad side of the story for the black community as well: the perpetuation of the black underclass is a continuing tragedy. But one cannot deny the tremendous progress that has been made in the last three decades.

Moreover, there is some empirical evidence to suggest that in practice affirmative action is an even worse proxy for disadvantage than it is in theory. While 29 percent of black men earn more than the average white man, marketplace forces push institutions to provide limited preferences to the most advantaged minorities—the offspring of the 29 percent—at the expense of the most disadvantaged whites—thus canceling out some of the net gain in equal opportunity. The phenomenon is widely noted and generally accepted by both proponents and opponents of affirmative action.[29] On the one hand, says William Julius Wilson, "the race-specific policies emanating from the civil rights revolution, although beneficial to more advantaged blacks (i.e., those with higher income, greater education and training, and more prestigious occupations), do little for those who are truly disadvantaged."[30] On the other hand, says Queens College Professor Andrew Hacker, the burden of affirmative action falls largely on working-class whites. "In actual fact, talented advertising executives and successful surgeons have little to fear from minority preference. The whites who lose out are generally blue-collar workers or persons at lower administrative levels, whose skills are not greatly in demand."[31] How true are these two claims, and are they inconsistent?

As to the first claim, it would seem intuitively true that a program that gives preference to any person of color (without any form of means testing) will benefit those who are in the best position to take advantage of it: the most advantaged members of minority groups.[32] In addition, because affirmative action is concentrated in areas where blacks are underrepresented—competitive positions—often only the most educated minorities will be competing.[33] The empirical data generally confirm the logic, though the context remains important.

First, and most obviously, in the area of government set-asides—for construction contracts, broadcast stations, and the like—the minority beneficiaries tend to be quite well off. Section 8(a) set-asides are designed for "economically disadvantaged" minorities, but those beneficiaries who own companies that provide services, from computer processing to construction, are likely to be at least middle-class. In 1989 the average personal net worth of beneficiaries was $160,000, twice the national average, and eight times the net worth of the average black family.[34] Moreover, there is some evidence that the funds do not even trickle down to black neighborhoods. According to one survey of the 8(a) program, between 1988 and 1993, only 22 percent of the Small Business Administration (SBA) funds went to minority companies located in minority areas, and the "lion's share" went to firms "whose headquarters were located in primarily white, well-to-do neighborhoods."[35]

Other federal racial preference programs are not even means-tested. For example, the Federal Communication Commission preferences for broadcast licenses, notes Michael Kinsley, "amount to the anointing of black millionaires."[36] In 1995 the FCC's minority tax certificate program, which provided enormous tax breaks to large white-owned cable companies if they sold to minority-controlled firms, came under scrutiny when the media giant Viacom Inc. sought to use the tax certificate program to defer between $440 million and $640 million in capital gains taxes, perhaps indefinitely.[37] What made matters worse was that the minority purchaser was one of the architects of the program during the Carter administration. In moving to repeal the legislation, Speaker of the House Newt Gingrich said, "This is not about helping the disadvantaged. This is about simply rigging the game on behalf of one set of millionaires over another."[38] The minority purchaser, Frank Washington, was reduced to pleading, incongruously, "I have played by the rules."[39]

In the employment context, studies by both the Labor Department and Jonathan Leonard of Berkeley have found that affirmative action programs involving federal contractors had the greatest impact on "higher paying managerial, professional, and craft occupations."[40] The Yale economist James J. Heckman confirms the "pro-skill bias" of affirmative action, noting the existence of several studies that found particularly large wage gains for educated minority workers in high managerial and professional jobs.[41] The economist Glenn Loury concurs: "It is clear from extensive empirical research on the effect of affirmative action standards for federal contractors that it is mainly those blacks in the higher occupations who have gained from this program."[42] In their study of black progress since the 1940s, the economists James Smith and Finis Welch conclude: "Young college-educated blacks were the main beneficiaries of affirmative action."[43]

When women are the beneficiaries of affirmative action, primarily in the employment and contracting contexts, the chances of wealthy beneficiaries is even greater, since women as a group are spread more evenly throughout socioeconomic strata than are minorities.[44] When women were added to the highway construction set-aside program, minorities protested that wealthy white women would win the lion's share of the benefits, and there is some evidence that that is precisely what has happened.[45]

Even if one is not disposed to feel particularly upset about those instances in which disadvantaged whites lose out to affluent minorities receiving preference, one still might be concerned that in benefiting the most advantaged minorities, affirmative action is doing very little for poor minorities. For if affirmative action is obviously overinclusive of advantaged minorities—a fair number, it turns out—and underinclusive of disadvantaged whites, it is also, in practice, underinclusive of disadvantaged minorities. For "millions of struggling black Americans," says Stephen Carter, affirmative action is "stunningly irrelevant."[46] Some, like Professor Donald Judges, go further, asserting that affirmative action not only neglects members of the black underclass, it hurts them by diverting political energies.[47] Shelby Steele argues, "I think the unkindest cut is to bestow on [upper-middle-class] children like my own an undeserved advantage while neglecting the development of those disadvantaged children on the East Side of my city who will likely never be in a position to benefit from a preference."[48]

The conventional wisdom also says that those whites who bear the brunt of affirmative action are the least advantaged. The early and high-profile cases involving Marco DeFunis, a relatively poor Sephardic Jew who worked his way through college and law school,[49] and Allan Bakke, a Vietnam veteran and son of a milkman and schoolteacher,[50] certainly provided anecdotal evidence for the charge. Cheryl Hopwood, a rejected white applicant to the University of Texas Law School, fills out the 1990s profile: raised "under difficult circumstances" by a widowed mother, Hopwood worked her way though high school, community college, and California State University at Sacramento.[51]

Proponents and opponents of affirmative action alike acknowledge that victims are often disadvantaged whites. In 1979 Antonin Scalia, then a law professor at the University of Chicago, argued that it was the more recent white immigrants, Italians, Jews, Irish, and Poles, "who, to a disproportionate degree, are the competitors with the urban blacks and Hispanics for jobs, housing, education—all those things that enable one to scramble to the top of the social heap where one can speak eloquently (and quite safely) of restorative justice."[52] He repeated the populist objection in his dissent in *Johnson v. Santa Clara County* eight years later, arguing that those who lose out are the "unknown, unaffluent, unorganized."[53] Among left supporters of affirmative action, Derrick Bell says that too often affirmative action and other civil rights remedies fail to "place as much of the burden as possible on upper- rather than lower-class whites."[54] Liberals Alan Freeman, Owen Fiss, Michael Walzer, and Frances Ansley all echo this concern.[55]

Affirmative action programs often pit whites and blacks of the same class against each other,[56] but in some contexts—such as delegate selection for national political party conventions and in university admissions—wealthy minorities can benefit at the expense of poor whites. After the 1968 Democratic National Convention, the Democrats reformed their party rules to ensure that a certain percentage of the delegates were minorities and women; it did not take on the more difficult task of ensuring that all classes were represented. As it happened, the move for racial, gender, and age diversity actually exacerbated the economic homogeneity of the delegates. As one study of the Democratic Party found, after the race and gender quotas were adopted, the percentage of college-educated delegates shot up "from 58 percent in 1972 to 70 percent in 1974, a level exceeding that of 1968 (61 percent)."[57] The change, writes the political scientist Byron Shafer, resulted in a major class shift.

> Before reform, there was an American party system in which one party, the Republicans, was primarily responsive to white-collar constituencies and in which another, the Democrats, was primarily responsive to blue-collar constituencies. After reform, there were two parties responsive to quite different white-collar coalitions, while the old blue-collar majority within the Democratic Party was forced to try to squeeze back into the party once identified predominately with its needs.[58]

Universities have a double incentive to take wealthy people of color over poor whites. Privileged minorities bring both the ability to pay full tuition and the ethnic diversity that enhances status. Poor whites, by contrast, bring no cash and add no racial diversity. In 1991 David Karen reported that the expansion of access to elite colleges for blacks and women has not been extended to those with lower socioeconomic status.[59]

As the black middle class continues to expand, the black poor will increasingly be crowded out. At Berkeley during the 1980s, for example, when the university was making an intensive drive to diversify ethnically, an internal study found that "remarkably little progress" was made in achieving socioeconomic diversity. Two-thirds of the blacks in Berkeley's 1987 entering freshman class had families with incomes above the national mean (which is, in turn, much higher than the black family mean). In fact, between 1977 and 1987, in a time of great affirmative action pressure, the study found that the proportion of freshman whose mothers and fathers had graduated from college actually increased.[60] At Harvard, one study found that most African American students "will come from middle-class homes and have attended predominantly white schools."[61] Fully 70 percent of Harvard's black undergraduates have parents who are managers or professionals.[62]

And the vast majority of colleges face a pressure much more intense than Harvard's: a financial imperative to admit students who can pay the bills. As noted earlier, affirmative action does probably provide a net benefit in genuine equal opportunity and economic diversity, but if one wants to reach the economically disadvantaged, one must do so directly. To achieve economic diversity, seeking racial diversity will not do, Berkeley found; a separate economic category was proposed and adopted. At the University of Texas Law School, Judge Sam Sparks noted in the *Hopwood* case that the affirmative action program, combined with a system of rating students by the prestige of their undergraduate institution, had the effect of burdening disadvantaged whites disproportionately. Disadvantaged whites may have been offered positions at elite colleges but turned them down for economic reasons, Sparks noted, so the racial preference system "had the somewhat ironic effect of affecting the rights of the less advantaged" nonminorities the most.[63] When the existence of alumni preferences for advantaged whites is factored in, the unfairness to poor whites is exacerbated further.

The truth, then, is that affirmative action is pervasive—it affects people at almost all stations, whether for good or ill. But even spreading the burden of affirmative action evenly is by definition regressive. (The gasoline tax is regressive, for example, because everyone pays the same amount, even though some are less able to pay than others.) If an upper-middle-class white kid cannot get into Princeton, she can go to Rutgers. But if a working-class kid with low skills applies for a job and does not get it because of racial preferences, going one notch down finds her not at Rutgers but on the unemployment rolls. And clearly, those whites who lose out from preferences are generally younger and more vulnerable, and have little in common with the powerful whites who make personnel decisions.

In the end, though, the important point is that race-based affirmative action, while it should help disadvantaged applicants, often does not. And when it does not, when it prefers Clarence Thomas's son over the son of a white Appalachian miner, it is not an "abuse" of the system but a logical fulfillment of its aims as currently structured. Overall, then, race-based affirmative action may provide some net increase in equal opportunity, given the overlap between race and class, but because its goal has shifted over time toward equality of racial group result, it does a highly imperfect job of providing genuine equal opportunity.

Grade: B-

GOAL NO. 2: LONG-RUN COLOR BLINDNESS

How well do today's affirmative action programs promote long-run color blindness? Those programs that remain remedial in nature and seek to provide a temporary bridge to a color-blind future may help get us there.[64] But as "temporary" programs grow increasingly permanent and the justification for preferences shifts from compensation to diversity, the question is not whether these programs promote color blindness—they do not—but whether color blindness is worth holding on to in the first place.

Today proponents of diversity argue that color blindness is naive: just as universities need athletes and trumpet players, they need blacks to strengthen the institution; just as an employer hires someone with a particular flair for sales for work in that area, so she might count race as a plus in hiring individuals to reach new markets. These utilitarian considerations, proponents say, are very different from the old type of race-conscious decision-making, which was based on a prejudice against blacks and other minorities.

But it is important to note that under the Civil Rights Act there is no requirement that illegal racial discrimination be based on theories of white supremacy or notions of racial superiority. A white employer who refuses to hire blacks because he thinks it would be "bad for business" is just as guilty as one who does not hire blacks because he thinks they are innately inferior.

Indeed, the act is not even limited to protecting minorities or women and speaks generically of "race" and "sex" discrimination. In practice, the act has been interpreted to allow race and gender preference programs if they are part of a bona fide affirmative action plan. But outright discrimination—say, an African American employer who does not want to hire "honkies"—is just as illegal as discrimination by whites against blacks.[65]

The factor that sets race and gender apart from athletic prowess, trumpet playing, or a flair for sales is their immutability: race and gender are beyond an individual's ability to control. The notion that people should generally be judged by factors within their control is one of the common threads behind those criteria or classifications that are covered by the Civil Rights Act of 1964 (as amended) or that have been held to be "suspect" or "semisuspect" under the equal protection clause of the Fourteenth Amendment. The two overlapping lists now include race, color, religion, sex, national origin, disability, and illegitimacy.[66] While religion is technically mutable, Barry Gross points out that "if we consider one's religion not a matter of mere profession but rather of belief, then it cannot be helped, for no one can rationally be ordered to believe or not to believe in something."[67] And while illegitimacy is technically mutable (when a father acknowledges paternity), the condition is beyond the personal control of the child.[68] Even Justice Brennan, who supported racial quotas in *Bakke*, acknowledged that racial classifications "are contrary to our deep belief that 'legal burdens should bear some relationship to individual responsibility or wrongdoing,' and that advancement sanctioned, sponsored, or approved by the State should ideally be based on individual merit or achievement, or at the least on factors within the control of an individual."[69]

The rule is not an absolute one. The fact of immutability does not end the inquiry, either under the Civil Rights Act or under equal protection doctrine. Under the Civil Rights Act, we have noted, a fashion designer may insist that a model for women's clothing be female; an airline may insist that its pilots not be blind—even though gender and blindness are immutable.[70] And the equal protection clause allows classifications to withstand strict scrutiny where there is a compelling state interest and narrowly tailored means. But in both sets of cases, there must be a very good reason to rebut the strong moral presumption against judging people on bases that are immutable or beyond their control. Only when the social utility of judging a person based on immutable factor is overwhelming is the presumption overcome. The courts have ruled that compensating for past discrimination is one such compelling interest, when clear findings of discrimination are made and the remedy is narrowly tailored. But are the benefits of racial diversity a compelling interest? We look first at education, then employment.

Education

Race is said to be just like other college admissions factors, but in fact it is quite different. One's academic record—grades and test scores—is at least marginally within one's control, depending on the amount of effort exerted; moreover, the social utility of this admissions factor is clear: society has an interest in training the best possible physicists, doctors, and lawyers.[71] Likewise, a demonstrated commitment to service—or the binding pledge of a medical school applicant to serve a neglected indigent population after graduation—is both socially useful and in large part a matter of personal choice.[72] Athletic ability also provides marginal utility in the form of entertainment (for society) and enhanced reputation (for the university) and is moderately within the individual's control, since natural (and therefore arbitrary) factors do not completely determine athletic ability the way they do race.[73] Veterans' preferences likewise differ from race preferences in that serving in the armed forces is today normally a matter of choice, and society may properly reward veterans for their sacrifice and contribution.[74] By contrast, racial preferences *are* similar to two commonly used educational preferences— legacy and geographic preferences—that have nothing to do with applicants' personal efforts. But far from justifying the case, the similarity places race preferences in bad company. Legacy and geographic preferences are very hard to justify because their social utility is marginal and does not rebut the strong presumption that we should be judged by factors within our control.[75]

The argument that racial preferences are "no worse than" legacy and geographic preferences hardly rings with the moral authority traditionally invoked by civil rights advocates.[76]

Does the social benefit of having a racially diverse class—the enhancement of robust discussion through the inclusion of "minority views"—overcome the presumption against judging individuals by immutable factors? On the positive side of the ledger, it seems highly plausible to think that, all other things being equal, discussion of important issues is enhanced in a racially diverse environment. The educational benefits of diversity may, however, be smaller than proponents think, for two reasons. First, to the extent that racial and ethnic groups on university campuses commonly find themselves (voluntarily or involuntarily) in segregated enclaves, the viewpoint diversity rationale may be limited to the classroom. At Berkeley, for example, a *New York Times* reporter observed "blacks and whites rooting for the same team but sitting in different sections. Floors in the undergraduate library are, in practice, segregated by race. Rarely does a single white or two comfortably join a dining room table occupied mostly by blacks."[77] Nowhere can the T-shirt be found: "It's a black thing, let me explain it to you so you can learn." That is the import of the decline in the term "integration" and the rise of "diversity."[78]

Second, race is, as all proponents of diversity will admit, an imperfect proxy for viewpoint. It would be appalling to take the race viewpoint notion literally: Mr. Jones, could you give us the black perspective on *Roe v. Wade*, please?[79] So proponents of diversity are caught in a bind: to avoid the charge of racism, they must avow that not all blacks think alike, but in so doing they concede that race is not a precise proxy for viewpoint.[80] The social benefit, then, is that some minority students may bring differing viewpoints to bear in the classroom, if not beyond.

But when *preferences* are used to achieve racial diversity, social costs are also imposed that must be weighed against the educational benefits. One of the major costs is legitimization of a phenomenon we were supposed to be getting away from: racial stereotyping. The message that diversity policies send is that racial stereotyping is now permissible; that race can be used as a proxy for viewpoint; that I can look at your skin color and have a pretty good idea of how you think or feel or act; and most important of all, that I can legitimately act on that stereotype. "In race-obsessed America, racial stereotypes are back in fashion," Stephen Carter notes, "only now the stereotypes are the friends, not just the enemies, of people of color." He observes that, "in an earlier era," to say there is a particularly black way of thinking "might have been marked down as frankly racist. Now, however, [such comments] are almost a gospel for people who want to show their commitment to equality."[81] Though thinking of members of racial groups "in the aggregate" is the very definition of a word we used to use to denote racism—*prejudice*—prejudging individuals by the color of their skin or surname is now deemed permissible, even progressive.

Proponents of diversity try to differentiate the new stereotypes from the old bad ones in two ways. First, they argue that the new stereotypes are not the inaccurate misconceptions of bigots but rather are based on the reasoned findings of empirical studies. As Justice Brennan said in *Metro Broadcasting*, the FCC had conducted studies that found racial ownership translates into diversity in broadcasting; the group treatment is the "product of 'analysis' rather than a 'stereotyped reaction.' "[82] But a basis in fact cannot truly distinguish good from bad stereotypes. As Randall Kennedy points out, even though it is empirically true that white people have access to more education than black people do, that is not an excuse to use race as a proxy for educational attainment.[83] The white jewelry store owner or cab driver can also cite "studies" to justify barring young black men from their stores or cabs. (The FBI says blacks commit robbery at five times the national average).[84] Empirically speaking, the sexist admissions officer is correct to think that, statistically, it is more likely that a male law school or medical school graduate will get more person-hours out of his degree than a female graduate, since it is still more likely that female doctors or lawyers will take time off with a child than that their male counterparts will.[85]

The second way to try to distinguish the old prejudice from the new is to say that the first involved a negative stereotype, and the second promotes a positive, inclusive stereotype. But that cannot be true, for in any decision based on stereotype the rejected individual feels excluded and the accepted individual feels included. The cab driver who, in passing up the black passenger, picks up a white rider is also employing a positive (perhaps erroneous) stereotype about white people. The admissions officer who turns down a white applicant in favor of a black is also employing a negative stereotype of the white applicant (she will not add much to the class discussion). For the rejected applicant, the stereotype is hardly inclusive.

It is likely that cab drivers will use racial stereotypes whether or not universities employ diversity preferences, but there is something very troubling about the government placing its imprimatur on racial generalizations.[86] For there can be no doubt that government, university, and employer policies on racial preferences leave their mark on the way people think. Over the years opponents of civil rights repeatedly invoked the notion that it was fruitless to pass laws concerning racial issues because one cannot legislate morality. In 1958 President Eisenhower would invoke the assertion of the Yale sociologist William Graham Sumner that "stateways cannot change folkways"[87] as an excuse for inaction, saying, "Laws themselves will never solve problems that have their roots in the human heart and in human emotions."[88] But liberals argued the opposite at the time. Harvard Professor Gordon Allport wrote, "Let the line of public morality be set by authoritative pronouncements, and all the latent good in individuals and communities will be strengthened."[89]

The subsequent history of this nation supports Allport over Sumner. The passage of legislation, along with the announcement of certain court decisions, not only changed the behavior of the American public but also helped to bring about a sea change in public attitudes. In 1963 nearly half of whites said they would move if a black family moved in next door. By 1990 the figure was 5 percent.[90] The proportion of whites favoring integrated schools jumped from 32 percent in 1942 to 92 percent in 1985, while the proportion saying blacks deserve equal employment opportunity rose from 44 percent in 1944 to 97 percent by 1972. The support for integrated restaurants and hotels is so high that pollsters no longer ask the question.[91] And, as the civil rights lawyer William Taylor notes, even opponents of the civil rights movement now pitch their argument in terms of a "color-blind" society.[92] This development would not have come as a surprise to Allport, who noted in the 1950s that a law that changes outward action, "psychology knows, has an eventual effect upon inner habits of thought and feeling."[93]

For the moment, the new pro-black diversity stereotypes appear to cut in the favor of African Americans. But Stephen Carter notes that the "sharp rhetorical arrows" about the distinct viewpoints of minorities one day may be turned against blacks. He asks, "Is it a good thing, is it a safe thing, to encourage white America to continue to think in racial terms?" Carter is also rightly concerned that the new stereotype associating skin color with viewpoint places pressure on minorities to conform, to provide the requisite "minority" views.[94]

What, then, is the net social utility of racial preferences in university admissions? On the one hand, the educational benefits of bringing together diverse people are important. People who are likely to have diverse life experiences will learn from one another and reduce social misunderstanding. On the other hand, the costs of using preferences to create diversity—the legitimation of stereotyping and, as we shall see, the risk of increased prejudice and increased racial tension—are also great. On pure grounds of social utility, the argument is fairly close. But whether one argues that the social utility is marginally good or bad, neither argument is sufficient to overcome the strong presumption against judging people on immutable characteristics. For that, the social interest must be compelling and unambiguously positive.[95]

Employment

In the employment sector, similarly, race is plausibly considered a bona fide occupational qualification because preferring minorities can better serve minority constituencies and provide positive role models. But there is also a social downside to providing preferences to achieve each such purpose. When the positive social utility of the new racial preferences is weighed against the negative, we are not even close to approaching the compelling social purpose required to rebut the presumption against being judged by immutable factors.

Downside of the Argument That Minority Constituencies Are Better Served Assume for the moment that it is empirically true that black teachers can more effectively reach black students, and that black police officers will, by virtue of race, do a better job of policing black ghettoes. What is the social downside to accepting this argument? The problem is that once we allow the racial views of constituencies to dictate the choice of personnel, we open a can of worms that is ultimately much more dangerous to blacks than whites. The notion that race or gender may frequently be relevant, in a permanent sense—because it is good for, say, "customer relations"—should in fact set off alarm bells.[96]

For when racial preferences are justified by reason of social utility rather than as compensation for past wrongs, there is nothing to stop white people from plausibly making the same arguments. Whites can also argue about "the facts of life" in giving preference to whites when the constituency to be served is white. Sure, black teenagers relate better to black police officers, but what if a statistical survey found that white corporate clients are more likely to "relate better" to white lawyers?[97] Black customers might be more trusting of black salespeople, but what about the employer who has a Japanese company as a major client and feels that the Japanese businessmen would prefer working with a white male over a black female? If black teachers "communicate more efficiently" with black students, why should we not also think that white teachers communicate better with white students? When the constituency is not black inner-city residents but potential Democratic voters, why is it not accurate to say that a Democratic Party, desperately trying to reestablish its connection with Reagan Democrats, should choose as its chairman a white ethnic rather than an African American?[98] A political campaign would be justified in hiring only white workers to campaign door to door in areas where residents are known to be intolerant of minorities. Many employers may justify racial preferences for people of color not because they remedy past discrimination but because they are good for business. But what of an employer who believes diversity is bad for business and uses a racial preference for whites to keep the workforce homogenous? What if employers have nothing against African Americans but believe that mixing black and white workers leads to increased racial tension and decreased productivity? In the past, American employers separated Italian and Irish immigrants for that very reason.[99] A baseball owner could say he needs to hire white ballplayers rather than black players, "when they're equally qualified," not because he himself is bigoted but because statistical studies show that more of his predominantly white constituency will come to games if there are more white players.[100] When an airline's customers are mostly businessmen who overwhelmingly want female flight attendants, why does it not, to use Senator Danforth's phrase, make "good business" sense to hire only women?

We have heard this reasoning before—that it is good business to discriminate. In an earlier era, these arguments lost. The alleged desire of white baseball fans to watch white players crumbled under the moral force of Jackie Robinson. The claims of airline customers were rejected in a famous case, *Diaz v. Pan American World Airways*, in which the Fifth Circuit Court dismissed the notion that being female was a bona fide occupational qualification for being a flight attendant. Despite polls showing an overwhelming majority of customers preferred female flight attendants, the court said that bigotry or sexism should not be allowed to shape the law.[101]

One can try to differentiate the old cases from the new by saying that the black teenagers have a reason to suspect white police officers—a history of police brutality—but that is, of course, a stereotype as well. Not all white police officers are racist—not even many of them are—and, of course, black officers are capable of brutality as well. It may be true that sending a black cop to speak to a predominantly black high school class is more likely to get the message across in the short run, but giving in to such racialism only widens the gap between the races.[102] Consider whether this distinction from the *ABA Journal* between white lawyers playing to white juries and black lawyers playing to black juries holds water: "Even though few lawyers want to acknowledge or discuss it, lawyer-matching is a time-honored tradition. The twist is that while it once might have been done for the wrong reason of bowing to bias or stereotype, it is now practiced as a way of putting clients or circumstances in the best light in a multicultural society."[103]

The related problem with using race as a bona fide occupational qualification is that it can pigeonhole people of color in certain slots. If a black reporter is given extra points because he is especially qualified to cover blacks, it is unlikely he will be assigned to cover the largely white financial industry. If a newspaper argues that it has to have a black as editor of the metropolitan desk, then, as Ellis Cose notes, "logic dictates that if certain managerial tasks are best handled by blacks, others are best left to whites. What that logic has meant in terms of the larger corporate world is that black executives have landed, out of all proportion to their numbers, in community relations and public affairs, or in slots where their only relevant expertise concerns blacks and other minorities."[104] If it is true that a white actor should not play an Asian role, then, Arthur Schlesinger notes, the black actors Morgan Freeman and Denzel Washington will no longer be able to play certain Shakespearean roles, as they have, and will be confined to black roles.[105] If one says a firm needs to hire more black lawyers because black attorneys play better to inner-city juries, what happens when the attorney is told that he cannot try an exciting case in the suburbs because a white lawyer will do better with a white jury?[106] When a female lawyer is removed from a case because the client fears the judge is sexist?[107] And if blacks are given a plus, as Bartholet suggests, to focus "their teaching and scholarship on problems particularly significant to minority groups," are not all academics who happen to be black more likely to be viewed as black academics?[108]

Downside of the Role Model Theory Likewise, providing role models—while plausible and broadly accepted by elites as a rationale for racial preferences—does not rise to the level of social utility required to overcome the presumption against distributing benefits and burdens by skin color. Whatever the empirical evidence on the importance of role models, using racial preferences for this purpose bears a high social cost: the message is conveyed that there are such unbridgeable differences between blacks and whites that whites cannot possibly serve as role models for blacks, or blacks for whites. The courts have rejected the role model theory as racist, arguing that we do not want to legitimate racialism through public policy. In the 1986 case of *Wygant v. Jackson Board of Education*, in which the school board's affirmative action plan linked the number of black schoolteachers with the number of black students, the Supreme Court said the notion of black teachers for black students and white teachers for white students was precisely what we were supposed to be overcoming.[109]

There are other social costs as well. If large preferences are given, minority or female "role models" are likely to perform less well in their jobs. The message sent to young minorities, whites, women, and men is not the one we usually associate with role models. And for liberals, the role model theory sends the strange message that the best way to help the disadvantaged is to help an elite—a veritable "trickle-down" civil rights policy.[110]

Ultimately, using race as a qualification—either to promote role models or to improve service to minority constituencies—works much better in theory than in practice. Consider, for example, the application of the theory at Harvard Law School in the fall of 1982. Black students mounted a boycott of a course on civil rights taught by Jack Greenberg, head of the NAACP Legal Defense and Education Fund (LDF). Greenberg, according to one analyst, was "perhaps the most knowledgeable and successful civil rights lawyer in America" and had dedicated his life's work to the cause.[111] But as Stephen Carter notes, "Greenberg, to his apparent disadvantage, is white," prompting the Harvard Black Law Students Association (BLSA) and Harvard's Third World Coalition to call for his ouster and the appointment of a minority professor "who can identify and empathize with the social, cultural, economic and political experience of Third World communities."[112] Derrick Bell likewise called for "a teacher whose credentials include experiences in and with American racism similar to those the students have already suffered." The president of BLSA also suggested that Greenberg "relinquish directorship of the NAACP Legal Defense and Education Fund to a Black attorney."[113] The negative stereotype, Carter says, is that "a white person . . . cannot possibly understand what it is like to be nonwhite."[114]

All of this is, of course, very far from the thinking of many mainstream civil rights leaders. While Greenberg's color had raised concerns in certain circles from the very beginning, Thurgood Marshall, in nominating Greenberg to succeed him as director general of the NAACP Legal Defense and Education Fund, signaled his rejection of that concern. Indeed, according to Greenberg, Marshall said the fact that Greenberg was white "shouldn't be an issue—after all, that was what our fight was about, a country with no racial distinctions." Greenberg's appointment was approved by the LDF board unanimously and won nearly unanimous support among the black press. At the time of the Harvard boycott, a number of black leaders rallied to Greenberg's side. Carl Rowan called the boycott "racist, anti-intellectual," and "anti-civil rights." Bayard Rustin called it "nothing more than blatant racism." And Randall Kennedy defended Greenberg, comparing him to the abolitionist Thaddeus Stevens.[115]

But Greenberg's supporters were largely (with the exception of Randall Kennedy) from an older generation. While some black students came to tell Greenberg that they personally disagreed with the boycott, not a single black law student took the course. "My reaction to all this," Greenberg wrote in 1994, "was that I scorned those boycott leaders and their followers who, caught in their racist enterprise, scrambled for other justifications, and I pitied those who disagreed with the boycott, but wouldn't break ranks and risk retaliation. From which group, I wonder, will we enlist the civil rights leaders of the future?"[116]

While permanent race consciousness is all the rage among critical race theorists, a man who spent his life fighting the tyranny of racism in South Africa holds another perspective. On October 6, 1994, South African President Nelson Mandela told a joint session of Congress: "We are human together or nothing at all. The phrase you use, the concert of your being which is fundamental to the understanding of your society, the notion of a melting pot has in time begun to address a reality that encompasses the globe . . . whatever our different complexions, whatever our different racial characteristics, whatever our different gender features, we are nonetheless—all of us—part of one indivisible and common humanity."[117] Critical race theorists would see these words as quaint and outdated, but they bespeak the experience of a man who knows well the dangers of racialism.

Arguments of diversity, resting solely on social utility, in the end pale in comparison to the mighty authority invoked by the early civil rights movement. As the columnist Charles Krauthammer notes, the placards of thirty years ago, "Solidarity in Support of Justice," tower over today's puny posters, "Solidary in Support of Diversity." He writes: "Diversity is indeed a value for a multiracial society. But one can hardly say of it, as King said of justice, that it 'rolls down like waters,' or, like righteousness, 'like a mighty stream.' "[118] The color-blindness ideal, at least in the long run, is still worth holding on to. The demons of racialism in the public sphere are far more of a threat to equality than today's proponents of diversity realize.

Grade: F

GOAL NO. 3: THE BENEFITS OF INTEGRATION: REDUCED PREJUDICE AND GREATER SOCIAL HARMONY

A third goal of Lyndon Johnson and Martin Luther King was to take affirmative steps to eliminate segregation's ongoing legacy. Integration in school and workplace, it was argued, would reduce racial prejudice and bring greater social harmony. In the university setting, for example, once individuals from various ethnic groups were brought together, they would realize that they were bound by a common humanity and recognize that differences, as Justice Stevens wrote, were only skin deep.[119] Given our nation's history, we must dispel the myths that arise from separation and ignorance.

Normally, integration would increase social harmony. But integration achieved through racial preferences has not worked as planned; if anything, racial preferences seem to have increased negative stereotyping and racial hostility. Because the integration rationale for racial preferences is justified on utilitarian grounds (as opposed to the moral grounds of public school desegregation), we must weigh the practical costs and benefits.

Cost: Increased Racial Prejudice

When racial preferences are used to achieve integration, the preferences, by their very nature, may send a negative message to both blacks and whites that blacks cannot make it on their own.[120] Worse than the existence of a preference per se is the subpar performance that inevitably follows any sizable preference scheme. As we shall see, SAT scores and grades do have some predictive value, so it is not surprising that any type of preference that involves a sharp deviation from academic criteria—athletic, legacy, racial, or disadvantaged—is likely to result in having the preferred disproportionately concentrated in the lower part of the class.[121] The more weight given to the preference, the more concentrated the effect. If racial preferences are mere tiebreakers, as is often argued, then they are unlikely to have a major impact on performance.[122] If they are sizable, the pattern of performance (in class, in exams, in dropout rates, in bar exam passage, etc.) may be large.

So how substantial a factor are racial preferences in university admissions? There should be an easy, straightforward, and readily accessible answer to this empirical question, but, unfortunately, the issue is shrouded in secrecy.[123] Because defenders of affirmative action are completely silent on the weight of racial preferences, to find a comprehensive compilation of data on the question, one must turn to such an extreme source as Charles Murray and Richard Herrnstein's book *The Bell Curve*. They found that for classes entering the nation's most elite colleges in 1991 and 1992, the median difference in SAT scores between the white and black mean was 180 points. In other words, the average African American student had an SAT at the 10th percentile of white students. Latinos were 129 points below the white mean, putting the average Latino student at the 20th percentile among white students. The gap between black and white

SAT scores ranged from a low of 95 points at Harvard to a high of 288 points at Berkeley.[124]

For those who are hesitant to rely on *The Bell Curve*, other public data are available, primarily from litigation over affirmative action programs at the University of Washington Law School (1974), the UC Davis Medical School (1978), and the University of Texas Law School (1994). In addition, data are available from Berkeley, the University of Virginia, Harvard, and a few other colleges and law schools. All of the data unmistakably confirm the substantial weight of racial preferences in university admissions.[125] At the University of Texas Law School, for example, the court found that "the presumptive denial score for nonminorities was higher than the presumptive admission score for minorities."[126]

Defenders of affirmative action point out correctly that scores are not all that matter, that universities look at a number of race-blind factors, including essays. Reference to these other factors was cited by Georgetown's Dean Areen as the reason (rather than racial preference) for the lower LSAT scores of black law students. But this reasoning was patently false. As the University of Texas law professor Lino Graglia wryly points out, "We were to understand, apparently, that there is an inverse correlation between high LSAT scores and GPAs and the ability to write an essay on why one wants to be a law student at Georgetown."[127]

It is not at all surprising, then, that as a group minorities in affirmative action programs perform less well than the student body as a whole, a track record that is often more visible to white students than the confidential nature of grading would suggest. At the undergraduate level, the main public manifestation of poor performance is dropout rates. A 1989 Department of Education study found that, of high school graduates entering four-year colleges in 1980, 52 percent of whites had graduated, while only 26 percent of blacks and Hispanics had graduated.[128] A 1992 National Center for Educational Statistics report confirms the two-to-one dropout rate.[129] Looking only at largely white campuses, the black dropout rate nationwide is five times that of whites.[130] The pattern can be seen at such varied institutions as Cornell, MIT, the University of Wisconsin, Oberlin, Ohio State, San Jose State, and Berkeley.[131]

Some of the lower retention rate stems from the economic fact that students of color generally come from less advantaged backgrounds and have a hard time paying for college.[132] But actual performance is central to the dropout rate. In 1986 only 62 percent of Latinos admitted to Berkeley through an affirmative action program maintained a 2.0 grade point average, compared with 90 percent of regularly admitted students.[133] One study found that in the Berkeley freshman calculus class, the failure rate was 5 percent among Asians and 50 percent among blacks.[134] At ten top law schools in the late 1970s, black students had a first-year mean GPA in the 8th percentile.[135] When racial quotas were imposed at tuition-free Boston Latin, a selective public school, the failure rate for black and Hispanic students went from being comparable to that of whites to double that of whites.[136]

Beyond attrition rates, there is another way students sense the academic performance of their peers. Even when students do not know their classmates' grades, professors often do, and they frequently "express amazement" when African Americans perform well academically.[137] The attitude filters down to the students. One black law student, writing in the Atlantic Monthly, told of the anguish in class: "The silence, the heavy sense of expectation, fell on all of the blacks in a classroom whenever one of us was called upon for an answer."[138]

Racial patterns of academic performance become highly public in law schools, where only those who do best academically make the law review. In 1981 the elite Harvard Law Review had eighty-nine members, none of whom were African American, Hispanic, or Native American. (There was one Asian American.)[139] Harvard's solution: preferences for law review selection, which only exacerbated awareness of minority underperformance. At the low end, poor law school performance is manifested in low bar passage rates. In 1986 nearly 90 percent of UCLA law students admitted under the regular program passed the California bar exam, but only 30 percent of those admitted under the diversity program passed.[140] In Florida the bar passage rate among blacks was 43 percent in 1991, compared with 75 percent for whites.[141] In medical school, poor performance is manifested in failure rates on the National Board of Medical Examiners test.[142]

Likewise, among teachers, aggressive affirmative action programs by universities (and hiring school districts) has led to a large disparity in passage rates on minimum competency exams. Andrew Hacker contrasts passage rates in a number of states:[143]

TEACHER COMPETENCY EXAMS: PASS RATES

	White	Black
Alabama	86%	43%
Arizona	80	44
Arkansas	88	33
California	76	30
Connecticut	54	18
Georgia	94	54
Louisiana	78	15
Mississippi	70	40
New York	85	50
North Carolina	94	54
Virginia	98	69

Table 3.1

Some proponents of affirmative action argue that this phenomenon is overplayed. What does it teach white students if blacks are absent from elite universities entirely?[144] But while a dearth of minority students at elite colleges might indeed stigmatize, the phenomenon is at least contained. Under the current system of racial preferences, Robert Klitgaard explains, when top schools seek diversity, there is a ripple effect at lesser schools: minority students underperform compared to white students at each and every institution down the line. He writes:

Suppose the top school wanted 7 percent of its students to be black. It would have to stretch academically, perhaps 120 to 150 points at the margin on each SAT aptitude test, to get that many blacks. This stretching, however, takes away precisely those blacks who would have been admissible without preferential treatment at schools two and three. These schools therefore must stretch to get the same percentage of blacks as before, and then this stretching process might ripple back through the rest of the schools.[145]

While all preferences result in concentration of the preferred (blacks or athletes, or the poor) in the bottom, the problem, as Christopher Jencks points out, is that stereotypes about minorities are much more damaging than those about athletes. "Encouraging the nation's future professional and managerial elite to think that athletes are dimwits does no serious social harm," Jencks writes, "because very few undergraduates remain athletes after they graduate, and those who make a career out of sports reap such spectacular rewards that they can survive jokes about their academic skills. A policy that encourages the nation's future leaders to believe that blacks are slow learners will, in contrast, do incalculable harm over the long run because blacks cannot shed their skin after graduation."[146] The poor performance—as opposed to preferences per se—also makes self-doubts real.[147]

On one level, it is blatantly unfair to say that because of white racism we must be careful not to give too many breaks to blacks, lest we feed more white racism. It is unfair, as Shelby Steele points out, that "white incompetence is always in individual matter, while for blacks it is often confirmation of ugly stereotypes."[148] This is surely true when racial preferences are advanced as a matter of compensatory justice. White racism should not veto what justice requires. But when the argument is social utility—that integration through preferences will reduce prejudice—the empirical accuracy of the contention is highly relevant.

Now, one should be skeptical when whites who are hurt by affirmative action argue that it is truly in the self-interest of blacks to eliminate preferences—just as one needs to be suspicious when oil companies argue that off-shore drilling is good for the environment.[149] One must suppose that for people of color living in a world where many whites are racist with or without affirmative action, the net increase in prejudice may be tolerable if that is the cost of getting the opportunity to attend a more selective university. That is why it is crucial to the argument that blacks and women—whose surface self-interest should yield overwhelming support for preferences—are indeed highly ambivalent. The interpretation of polling data is always tricky, and it is especially so with "affirmative action."[150] But when the issue is defined not vaguely as "affirmative action" but as "preferences," we can have more confidence about minority opinion.[151] Dozens of polls consistently indicate that at least half of the African American population opposes racial preferences in hiring and college admissions.[152] Among women, support for affirmative action is thin throughout the world, including the United States, where only 25 percent of women support preferential treatment. According to the social scientists Paul M. Sniderman and Thomas Piazza: "Affirmative action is opposed nearly as often by women, who would stand to benefit by it in this case, as by men, and it is overwhelmingly rejected by both."[153]

While conservative blacks have been called hypocritical for opposing preferences even as they have benefited, it may be, as J. Anthony Lukas has pointed out, that people like Clarence Thomas are in a unique position to know the downside of preferences; they know how excruciating it is "to feel your talent ripening within you and yet know others see you as the undeserving beneficiary of misguided social programs."[154] And black ambivalence about the impact of preferences extends to liberal black student groups, which have rejected special remedial courses for blacks. When the Detroit Symphony Orchestra applied affirmative action to its hiring procedure in 1989, a number of black musicians opposed the move. "Now even when a black player is hired on the merits of his playing, he will always have the stigma that it was to appease some state legislator," Michael Morgan, the black assistant conductor of the Chicago Symphony Orchestra, told the *New York Times*.[155] When the *Harvard Law Review* contemplated expanding its affirmative action program to women, some of the strongest opponents were female members of the review. Even the black novelist Toni Morrison was concerned when forty-eight black writers weighed in prior to her receipt of the Pulitzer Prize for distinguished fiction in 1988. She said: "It was too upsetting to have my work considered as an affirmative action award."[156]

Cost: Increased Racial Tension

The second argument behind using racial preferences to achieve integration is that bringing people together from different backgrounds to a university will promote racial harmony. The theory holds up quite well when integration flows from antidiscriminatory principles, but when racial preferences are used to achieve integration—a practice accepted by the elite but never by the vast majority of whites—the means work at cross purposes with the ends, and the result is likely to be greater racial hostility, not less.

Some conservatives have concluded that affirmative action is partly responsible for the recent increase in racial violence on campuses.[157] One need not go that far to see that, when white teenagers see themselves as more likely to be victims of race discrimination than blacks—as a 1992 poll found—affirmative action is not contributing to racial harmony.[158] Particularly disturbing is a recent finding that the "mere mention" of affirmative action policies raises white hostility toward blacks. When affirmative action is not mentioned in the poll question, 26 percent of whites believe that African Americans tend to be irresponsible, but when affirmative action is discussed in passing, the number climbs to 43 percent.[159]

Some supporters of affirmative action say white resentment is minimal, pointing out that only 3 percent of race, gender, and ethnicity discrimination cases filed between 1990 and 1994 were pursued by white males.[160] The statistic is highly misleading, however, since lawyers are less likely to take "reverse discrimination" suits given the much more difficult legal standard they face.[161] And in practice, white resentment is likely to be multiplied. As Professor Kent Greenawalt explains, if a minority applicant receives a job owing in part to a racial preference, the employer may be tempted to tell all fifteen white applicants that they might have gotten the job but for the preference.[162] A law school that admits fifty black students may have to pass over a thousand white applicants with higher paper qualifications.[163] Rejected whites who rightly conclude that they would have been admitted with their test scores had they been black, incorrectly conclude (in 950 of 1,000 cases) that they would have gotten in but for affirmative action.[164]

In a 1986 survey conducted by Michigan's Institute for Social Research, fully 75 percent of whites said it was "very likely" or "somewhat likely" that they would be denied a position because of affirmative action.[165] In a recent Gallup poll, 21 percent of whites said they already had been a victim of reverse discrimination, compared with 36 percent of blacks saying they had been a victim of discrimination.[166] The Democratic pollster Stanley Greenberg conducted focus group discussions with working-class voters in Michigan in 1985 and found that "discrimination against whites has become a well-assimilated and ready explanation for their status, vulnerability and failures."[167]

This phenomenon is compounded by intense media interest in affirmative action programs. The Detroit Symphony story is a case in point. Even though affirmative action is not a raging issue among musical organizations, its treatment as front-page news in the *New York Times* may have left whites with the impression that affirmative action is more widespread than it in fact is. Thus, African Americans suffer the stigma that they "can't make it on their own" without, in many cases, actually receiving the preferential treatment about which whites complain. The same could be said of the *Metro Broadcasting* case. Justice Brennan emphasized that the FCC's diversity preference program was quite small.[168] Given that fact, and given the enormous publicity associated with the Supreme Court case, one has to wonder whether the program is in the long-run interests of minorities.[169] Likewise, for all the ink spilled about President Clinton's diversity hiring, the journalist Bob Woodward found that in the area about which the president cared most—the economy—the key players included seventeen white males and four white women, no blacks, no Hispanics, no Asians, and no Native Americans.[170]

It is somewhat unfair to key the success of affirmative action to white resentment, just as it is unfair to tie it to the level of white racism. Certain segments of the white population have always resisted the advancement of African Americans, and increased racial hostility did not—and should not have— blocked efforts to desegregate schools or integrate neighborhoods.[171] So, too, where there is a conflict between strong cases of compensatory justice and social harmony, justice surely should prevail. But when judged on social utility—the grounds on which the diversity argument rests—the increase in racial tensions is highly relevant.

Moreover, white resentment about affirmative action is different in nature from white opposition to other black gains. While affirmative action did not, as some claim, create David Duke, it does seem to rile whites who would otherwise take a more positive view of racial progress.[172] In the 1950s and 1960s, it was clearly true that white attitudes on various civil rights issues came down, essentially, to the question, "Are you sympathetic to Negroes as a group, are you indifferent to them, or do you dislike them?"[173] But when Delegate Eleanor Holmes Norton puts opposition to affirmative action in California on a par with white resistance to *Brown v. Board of Education*, she misreads the broad shift in white attitudes over forty years.[174] And when President Clinton dismisses white anger over racial preferences, saying that white males are having a hard time psychologically, he minimizes the legitimate beef that arises when skin color is used against a group.

White opposition to affirmative action is different in kind from white opposition to civil rights. Opponents include, predictably, the hard-core racists, but opponents also include those deeply and genuinely committed to the larger principle of nondiscrimination—people who support civil rights, voting, and fair housing legislation, who see affirmative action as a contradiction to, rather than a fulfillment of, what Gunnar Myrdal called the American Creed. After reviewing the data, Sniderman and Piazza concluded: "The common suggestion that affirmative action has become a litmus test revealing whites' 'true' feelings toward blacks is plainly wrong." Where once you could ask one civil rights question and have a good idea of what the answers on other civil rights issues would be, "today, social welfare policies and race-conscious policies are evaluated in distinguishably different terms."[175] Says William Julius Wilson, "Many white Americans have turned, not against blacks, but against a strategy that emphasized programs perceived to benefit only racial minorities."[176]

On the other side of the equation, has affirmative action contributed to social harmony by reducing minority hostility toward whites? Logically, this would seem likely to happen, but there is some evidence that the benefit is small. A 1992 UCLA study found that the group that has benefited most from affirmative action—middle-class blacks—are actually *more* alienated than poor blacks.[177] Despite a generation of racial preferences, parts of the black community are so thoroughly alienated that they will cheer O. J. Simpson's acquittal and march behind Louis Farrakhan—on the very ground where whites and blacks once united behind Martin Luther King.[178]

In sum, the separatist means of affirmative action appear to negate the integrative benefits. Preferences do not increase respect for minorities, they impose a stigma; they lead not to racial harmony but to racial resentment. Say Sniderman and Piazza, "Wishing to close the racial divide in America" with affirmative action, "we have widened it."[179]

Grade: F

GOAL NO. 4: COMPENSATION FOR HISTORICAL WRONGS

Finally, how well do affirmative action policies compensate for the historical wrongs suffered by African Americans and, to a lesser degree, other American victims of past discrimination? To answer this question, we must distinguish between two types of programs. Narrowly tailored programs responding to documented discrimination form the first set. The second set consists of programs that seek a rough equality of group result, on the supposition either that proportional representation approximates distributions we would have seen but for past discrimination or that proportional representation brings diversity benefits. Affirmative action programs in the first group come about as close to compensating for past discrimination as possible and deserve a grade of A. But the vast majority of racial and gender preference programs today fall into the second category and do a fairly poor job of compensating for past discrimination.

The broad compensatory programs that seek a rough racial balance to counteract past *societal* discrimination do a poor job of compensating, as we saw in chapter 2. Because there is not a neat link between discrimination and underrepresentation, proportional representation ends up overcompensating certain groups.[180] Worse yet, racial balancing may in practice disproportionately burden those groups that themselves have been victims of discrimination historically.

Diversity programs have all the flaws of broad compensatory racial balancing programs and, moreover, do not even pretend to be in the business of compensation. At universities, for example, diversity can mean actively recruiting *foreign* students, to whom the United States owes no compensation, and who in most cases are hardly disadvantaged.[181] Because diversity is keyed to underrepresentation rather than past discrimination, it forfeits the moral claim of being compensatory and cares not whether the policy actually hurts groups historically subject to discrimination. The central premise of the diversity model is that racial groups are, in the aggregate, culturally distinct; that difference is the ticket to special preferences. Its goal, therefore, *cannot* be compensation, since those very cultural differences that diversity recognizes translate into varying levels of performance in various fields. Incredibly, President Clinton has actually highlighted the amoral and noncompensatory nature of the diversity rationale as a positive aspect. In responding to a press inquiry about his Justice Department's decision to back the firing of a white teacher to maintain diversity, Clinton said: "As long as it runs both ways, or all ways, I support that decision. That is, there are other conditions in which if there were only one white teacher on the faculty in a certain area, and there were two teachers, they were equally qualified, and the school board or the school administrator decided to keep the white teacher also to preserve racial diversity."[182]

Indeed, even though the diversity rationale may often in practice help members of groups that have been victims of injustice, the theory has nothing to do with their interests at all. It is the institution that benefits from diversity, and at worst, that institutional interest can translate into having black and Asian and Chicano people around to help enrich the educational experience of whites.[183]

A policy tethered not to past discrimination but to underrepresentation will be inappropriate as a remedy for past discrimination, not least because all underrepresented "groups" are not racial.[184] The logic of diversity argues for preferences for any underrepresented group that might have something different to offer. At Harvard Law School, for example, conservative students were severely underrepresented in the late 1980s.[185] As a matter of diversity, conservatives could persuasively argue that they would make debate robust; as a matter of justice, of compensatory fairness, granting conservatives a preference is absurd. At many law schools, students are generally in favor of abortion rights. Under the viewpoint rationale, it would be entirely proper for a law school to provide a preference for an ardent pro-life advocate and vocal conservative who agrees to speak up in class. But it would be very difficult to argue that pro-life applicants have been discriminated against. Indeed, in the early 1990s, Georgetown Law School specifically sought to hire a "conservative" for its faculty. One can agree or disagree with this use of diversity, but it clearly has nothing to do with compensatory justice.

In the racial context, diversity not only ignores the compensatory goal, it can sometimes serve to defeat compensatory aims, punishing groups historically victimized by discrimination, including Asian Americans and even African Americans.[186] (Jews and homosexuals, both the victims of centuries of discrimination, have also seen diversity used against them.)[187] The goal of proportional representation has clearly hurt Asians at elite California schools like Berkeley, and at other universities as well. In 1988 Asians were more than twice as likely (32.8 percent) as whites (15.8 percent) to be UC-eligible—which cut against the goal, identified by UC President David Gardner, of creating a "desirable ethnic mix."[188] A Berkeley admissions official told the *Chronicle of Higher Education*: "Asians are overrepresented by three times their high school population. How will the university justify overrepresenting Asians at the expense of others?"[189] Berkeley, wrote Dinesh D'Souza, was not "prejudiced against" Asians—"there were just too many of them." The solution: Asian Americans needed a higher score than whites to be admitted to the undergraduate university. The California state auditor general concluded that between 1981 and 1987 Asian American applicants had on average higher scores than whites but were admitted at lower rates than whites.[190] In 1994 Asian Americans who enrolled at Berkeley continued to need higher SAT scores and GPAs than whites.[191] "It's something everyone's going to face sooner or later," Berkeley's Vice Chancellor Roderic Park says. "We're just there first."[192]

At UCLA, a Department of Education investigation found that the graduate mathematics department gave illegal preferences to whites over Asians.[193] At the elite public magnet school Lowell High School in San Francisco, Chinese Americans have to score much higher than whites to be admitted into the program. Indeed, at one point, the gap between what Chinese Americans needed to get in compared with requirements for whites was *larger* than the gap between what whites needed compared to blacks and Spanish-surnamed students.[194] Brown, Stanford, and Yale have also been accused of holding Asians to a higher standard than whites.[195] Researchers have found that stereotypes about Asian narrowness—"They're all pre-meds," or, "They don't participate in extracurriculars"—do not explain the lower rates of admission.[196] Asian Americans understand what is going on. A 1988 Field Institute poll in California found that 80 percent of Asian Americans oppose preferences, an even higher rate of opposition than the poll found among whites.[197]

In practice, then, diversity policies often benefit groups that have never been discriminated against (WASPs) and hurt groups that have (Asians, Jews, and homosexuals), a point actually emphasized by a few supporters of preferences. For example, one University of California administrator tapped into anti-Asian sentiment by arguing that if racial preferences were repealed, Berkeley would become "90 percent Chinese and 10 percent white."[198] But worst of all, diversity can be used to hurt the group most victimized by discrimination in this country: African Americans.

Today the majority of minorities are nonblack; many are recent immigrants. Not only have nonblack minorities diluted the benefits of affirmative action for African Americans, they have in some instances used affirmative action to exclude blacks. While it was always theoretically true that diversity could hurt blacks, in recent years Hispanic groups have actually used the sword of affirmative action to argue for cutting the "overrepresentation" of blacks in a number of areas.[199] In 1994, for example, blacks constituted 10.3 percent of the nonmilitary workforce nationwide, but 20.8 percent of the U.S. Postal Service workforce. In some big cities, like Los Angeles and Chicago, the overrepresentation is much greater. The vice chairman of the Postal Service's board, a Hispanic, complained, and the postmaster general replied, "We are committed to making progress in affirmative action and being a leader in workforce diversity."[200]

In Compton, California, too, the role model and diversity theories are being used by Hispanics against blacks. The city is 51 percent Latino, and the school population 59 percent Hispanic, and yet the teachers and administrators are only 5 percent Hispanic and 72 percent black. Hispanic activists do not cite discrimination but argue instead that "we need Latino teachers who understand not only the language of the children but their background." They also argue for more city hall jobs, since only 11 percent of full-time city employees are Hispanic. The local head of the NAACP is put in the position of complaining that Latinos "want all the businesses. They want all of City Hall, all the schools. Now they're talking about the post office."[201]

In Los Angeles, blacks constitute 10.5 percent of the population, but 28 percent of county workers, while Hispanics make up 40 percent of the population but hold just 21 percent of the government jobs. The 1976 county-enacted affirmative action policy calls for a workforce that reflects the population, and now blacks at places like the Martin Luther King, Jr./Drew Medical Center in Watts are complaining: "They are lowering standards for them [Hispanics.]"[202] Mamir Grant, head of an organization representing Los Angeles black city workers asks, "Whatever happened to merit?" adding: "I'm not in favor of affirmative action. It shuts blacks out."[203]

In Washington, D.C., the U.S. Commission on Civil Rights recommended in early 1993 that the predominantly black D.C. government provide affirmative action for Latinos for city jobs until they were proportionately represented. Moreover, as the conservative critic Linda Chavez points out, the commission's target for government employment "is based on a population figure that includes both legal and illegal immigrants."[204] The claim for proportional representation appears to have less to do with compensation than with diversity—or, more probably, with politics.[205]

The problem is likely to occur in city after city. In New York City, blacks hold nearly 40 percent of government jobs, though they constitute only 25 percent of the employed labor force. In Chicago, blacks outnumber Latinos citywide by two to one, but in the city workforce the ratio is nearly four to one.[206] "It's the ultimate nightmare of affirmative action," Ricky Gaull Silberman, vice chairman of the federal Equal Employment Opportunity Commission, told the reporter Jonathan Tilove in 1993. "It is its Achilles' heel."[207]

The problem is not only that Latinos have suffered less discrimination than blacks, but that many Hispanics are recent immigrants to whom no compensation is owed.[208] In 1965, when affirmative action programs began, less than half of U.S. immigrants were from the Third World, and their number (115,000) was fairly small. By 1991, 90 percent of immigrants were coming from the Third World, and their total had mushroomed to 1.68 million. In twenty years, some thirteen million Third World immigrants have arrived, all of them eligible for affirmative action.[209] This angers whites, but it also angers black Americans. Some argue that resentment of preferential treatment for Cubans was a contributing factor to the 1980 riots in Liberty City, Florida.[210]

In all areas where blacks are today overrepresented, whether it be in certain public housing projects, in certain universities, or in professional sports, the theory of diversity can be used against them.[211] Some blacks have already suffered. Strong proponents of diversity might stand by the use of anti-black preferences, but on a compensatory score, these programs fail miserably.

Grade: C

Measured by its own standards, today's affirmative action programs fail to do a very good job of providing genuine equal opportunity, long-run color blindness, the benefits of integration, or compensation for past discrimination. This does not mean that declaring an end to affirmative action would do a better job; in fact, I think that would be marginally worse. But there is a third way, which addresses both the noble aspirations of proponents of affirmative action along with the legitimate criticism of opponents. We can "do better," to use Robert Kennedy's words. It is to that alternative that we now turn.

Part 2

Class-Based Affirmative Action

4. The Case for Class-Based Affirmative Action

C LASS-BASED affirmative action, a system of preferences for the economically disadvantaged in education, entry-level employment, and contracting, will achieve the legitimate goals of affirmative action while avoiding the major pitfalls associated with racial and gender preferences. This chapter presents a three-part case for class-based preferences. First, they will help fulfill the promise of genuine equal opportunity. Second, they will indirectly compensate for past discrimination, bring about a natural integration, and provide a bridge to a color-blind future. Third, they should survive the legal and political attack that will, in the end, sharply curtail or even kill race- and gender-based preference programs.

EQUAL OPPORTUNITY

The central and overriding argument for class-based affirmative action is that it will help move us from today's inadequate system of formal equal opportunity toward a more genuine system of equal opportunity under which individuals born into very different circumstances can flourish to their full natural potential. In a society with substantial inequalities of wealth, the notion of equal opportunity is, as University of Texas Professor James Fishkin has written, "the central doctrine in modern liberalism for legitimating the distribution of goods in society."[1] Equal opportunity exists when individuals have equal life chances to develop their natural talents to the fullest, should they choose to take the time and effort to do so. Says Fishkin, "According to this notion, I should not be able to enter a hospital ward of healthy newborn babies and, on the basis of class, race, sex, or other arbitrary native characteristics, predict the eventual positions in society of those children."[2] It stresses equality to the extent that social factors should not be allowed to inhibit the chance to develop one's natural talents. It stresses liberty to the extent that it does not guarantee equal results: the naturally talented are allowed to do better than the untalented to the extent, and only to the extent, that individuals work hard to achieve what they are capable of achieving. In academic circles, the notion of equal opportunity and meritocracy has been criticized from both the left and right, but the ideal holds up fairly well and is widely accepted in mainstream thought.[3] Endorsed by political figures as varied as Ronald Reagan, Richard Nixon, Hubert Humphrey, and Franklin Roosevelt, equal opportunity is, as Gary Wills notes, "the great agreed-on undebated premise of our politics. Left and Right, liberal and conservative, Democrat and Republican, all work from this basis."[4]

Equality of opportunity is so ingrained in the American psyche that both sides of the affirmative action question pay homage to it. Writing in support of affirmative action in *Bakke*, Justice Brennan declared, in the very first line of his opinion, the need to "achieve equal opportunity for all."[5] Writing in opposition to affirmative action in the *Harvard Law Review*, the attorney Morris Abram called for "equality of opportunity and a fair shake for individuals."[6] But neither Brennan nor Abram gets us there. We have seen that racial preference schemes, which aim at equality of racial group result, fail, but the opponents of affirmative action, who call for a strict "meritocratic" system for advancing, fail, too.

The meritocratic scheme provides formal equal opportunity, in that individuals are judged on "merit," not on "irrelevant" characteristics like race, gender, religion, national origin, sexual orientation, or class origin. However, this system, sometimes referred to as a "career open to talents," fails to correct for "background unfairness," which is inherent in class differences.[7] As the British critic R. H. Tawney said, what is required depends "not only upon an open road, but upon an equal start."[8]

The difference is crucial. As long as antidiscrimination laws work, race and gender are not impediments per se, but class differences (whether a product of past discrimination or not) remain, and civil rights legislation does nothing to address that inequality.[9] Some are born poor and underprivileged, others wealthy and advantaged. In this sense, antidiscrimination laws may be seen as necessary but not sufficient for achieving substantive equal opportunity.[10]

Failing to provide genuine equal opportunity and settling for a sterile formalistic equal opportunity undercuts the practical and moral rationales that buttress equal opportunity in the first place. Functionally, providing equal opportunity, but not equal result, is an efficient way in a complex society of sorting people and motivating them. In a seminal essay, the Princeton University sociologists Kingsley Davis and Wilbert E. Moore suggested that stratification is endemic to all societies as a way of ensuring that "the most important positions are conscientiously filled by the most qualified persons."[11] The moral, and secondary, justification for equal opportunity is that people who work hard and contribute the most should be rewarded for their effort.[12] Inequalities, says Tawney, were thus thought to be "twice blessed. They deserved moral approval, for they corresponded to merit. They were economically beneficial, for they offered a system of prizes and penalties."[13]

On the functional side, if we are trying to place the most talented in the most important positions, formal equal opportunity is not enough. Failing to correct for the social positions into which people are born runs the great risk of missing most of the latent talent of the poor. Thomas Jefferson, who envisioned a "natural aristocracy" in America to replace the "artificial" aristocracy of wealth and heredity that had ruled Europe, fought for free public education, including university-level education, and an end to inheritance laws that perpetuated aristocracy.[14] "Worth and genius would thus have been sought out from every condition of life, and completely prepared by education for defeating the competition of wealth and birth for public trusts," Jefferson wrote.[15] He expected to find talent in all segments of society—the "aristocracy of virtue and talent," he said, is "scattered with equal hand through all [nature's] conditions."[16] Jefferson was disturbed that elite private schools were open only to the wealthy aristocracy.[17]

Likewise, if equal opportunity is meant to motivate people to work hard, and if the poor and the working class believe, based on experience, that they cannot compete no matter how naturally talented they are, then we undercut the goal. Writes Tawney: "The most seductive of optical illusions does not last for ever. The day when a thousand donkeys could be induced to sweat by the prospect of a carrot that could be eaten by one" is long over.[18] If the most talented are stifled or unmotivated, society does not reach its potential for technological or spiritual advancement. In this sense, the drive for egalitarian measures such as equal school funding, far from undermining free enterprise, makes it work. According to the education critic John Coons, there is "no graver threat to the capitalist system than the present cyclical replacement of the 'fittest' of one generation by their artificially advantaged offspring."[19]

On moral grounds, if we want to reward hard work—and in practice we often measure hard work by what is produced—failing to provide an equal start is morally indefensible.[20] To reward individuals born with advantages arising from their parents' effort makes no moral sense. Indeed, Theodore Roosevelt, in pushing for a heavily progressive inheritance tax in 1906, argued that a commitment to rugged individualism required each generation to run its own race.[21]

How Much Social Mobility Exists in the United States?

The key empirical question is this: how close do we come to providing genuine equal opportunity today, to providing an equal start as well as an open road? If, as Lyndon Johnson said, ability is not just the product of birth but the product of family and community and schooling, do our various social programs give children born into different economic circumstances substantive equal opportunity?

Some Americans are satisfied that we have achieved genuine equal opportunity. Unlike race, they say, class is mutable. They point to people like Ross Perot and to Bill Clinton—the quintessential meritocratic president, "son of a salesman and a nurse," whose "ticket out of Hot Springs was high scores on college entrance exams"—as evidence that in this country class is a matter of choice, not fate.[22] While various economic classes obviously exist in America, the very real possibility of social mobility—the temporary nature of class—makes the term "classless society" highly appropriate. In this way, the United States is different from Europe, the argument runs. Invoked is Tocqueville's observation that "among democratic peoples new families continually rise from nothing while others fall, and nobody's position is quite stable. The woof of time is ever being broken and the track of past generations lost."[23] And since Tocqueville's time, social mobility has increased, it is argued, with the growth of free public education, inexpensive state colleges, and the rise of standardized tests, which remove the prejudice of class.[24] The government already spends billions of dollars every year on programs like Head Start to provide equal starts. (Some, of course, argue that these programs are too generous and advocate cutting them back.) We have, they say, done the best we can to provide equal opportunity for each younger generation without mandating equal result for the older generation. (A few conservatives even argue that the extent to which children of the poor largely end up poor themselves, and rich parents tend to have kids who grow up rich, is not itself evidence of unequal opportunity but rather a manifestation of genetic differences between the rich and poor.)

Accordingly, some argue that class-based preferences, as a correction for unequal starting places, are unnecessary. Abigail Thernstrom, for example, argues that class-based preferences will "simply exacerbate the already serious problem of victim status creep." Instead, she suggests, "those who truly care about the less fortunate will embrace quite a different policy—one that delivers the message that, black or white, rich or poor, with effort and discipline the chances are good you can make it. America is a land of opportunity. It's a message of hope, and it's even true."[25]

Thernstrom appears to have chosen her words carefully. For the claim that America is the "land of opportunity" is quite different from the more ambitious American goal of "equal opportunity." Thernstrom cannot argue that a child growing up in a ghetto, a barrio, or a trailer park, consigned to grinding poverty and lousy schools, has anything approaching equality of opportunity, and so the goal is adjusted downward: we now seek mere opportunity, which presumably is satisfied when once in a while poor children go on to achieve dramatic success.

But statistically speaking, the evidence is quite strong that social mobility is limited, that privilege tends to perpetuate itself. And while we have made great strides in providing greater opportunity through social programs, there are numerous real-life barriers that remain unaddressed by current public policy. Finally, the genetic argument, that the poor are poor because they are of lesser genetic stock, is simply not supported by the scientific evidence.[26]

First, how much intergenerational mobility is there? How many sons and daughters of the poor or working class become wealthy, compared with the sons and daughters of the rich? How typical is Bill Clinton's or Ross Perot's story? The question has been the subject of a wealth of studies. Though most focus on boys, similar questions can be asked of girls.[27] Here are some relevant findings:

• In 1979 Northwestern University's Christopher Jencks found: "If we define 'equal opportunity' as a situation in which sons born into different families have the same chances of success, our data show that America comes nowhere near achieving it. . . . The sons of the most advantaged fifth could expect to earn 150 to 186 percent of the national average, while the sons of the least advantaged fifth could expect to earn 56 to 67 percent of the national average." Occupationally, the same pattern emerges. Writes Jencks: "Sons from the most favored fifth of all families had predicted Duncan scores [measuring occupational status on a scale of 0 to 96] of about 64, while sons from the least favored fifth of all families have predicted scores of about 16." Jencks also found that "those who do well economically typically owe almost half of their occupational advantage and 55 to 85 percent of their earnings advantage to family background."[28]

• John Brittain of the Brookings Institution found that a son in the bottom 10 percent is predicted to have an income less than half the income of a son born into the top 10 percent. Sons born in the top 5 percent could expect to earn more than three times that earned by the bottom 5 percent. Put another way:

> The son ranking 10 percent from the top in background had a 51 percent chance of having a 1976 family income of $25,000 or more, compared to a 2 percent chance for his disadvantaged opposite number. The son from the middle of the top 5 percent in background rank had nearly a 40 percent chance of achieving an upper-middle-class income of $35,000 or more. The chance for the son with the poor background is negligible. Even a more fortunate son who starts life in the middle of the pack had only a 2 or 3 percent chance of reaching the $35,000 income level in 1976.[29]

• The sociologists Peter Blau and Otis Dudley Duncan, who pioneered mobility studies, found that in 1962 males studied between 25 and 64 had a 10.2 percent chance of being salaried professionals, but if their fathers had been salaried professionals, the chance was 31.9 percent; if their fathers had been farm laborers, the chance was 1.9 percent.[30]

• Samuel Bowles and Herbert Gintis found that even when controlling for ability (which itself is influenced by class advantages), children from the top 10 percent of income are twenty-seven times as likely as children from the bottom 10 percent to themselves end up in the top 10 percent of the income bracket. Of one thousand children born into the bottom tenth, only four will make it to the top tenth.[31]

• In 1991 the economist David Zimmerman, now at Williams College, found that only 12 percent of boys born into the bottom quartile rose as adults to the top quartile. Sixty-nine percent were in the lower half. Zimmerman found that sons received a 4 percent advantage for every 10 percent that their father's income exceeded the average.[32]

• In 1992 the University of Michigan's Gary Solon found that if a boy is born into the bottom 5 percent of the economic distribution, his chance of staying in the bottom fifth is one in two, his chance of rising above the median is only one in four, and his chance of making the top fifth is one in twenty.[33]

Historians have also found that the amount of social mobility in the United States has been greatly exaggerated.[34] And while America is supposed to be the quintessential nation of equal opportunity, a number of studies have found that our level of social mobility is not much different than that of the class-conscious countries of Europe. The sociologists Seymour Martin Lipset and Reinhard Bendix, for example, found that opportunities to rise were not greater for Americans than for Europeans.[35] Zimmerman's 1991 study confirmed this phenomenon, finding the correlation between father's and son's incomes almost identical for the United States and Britain.[36] And while one might expect the degree of social mobility and opportunity to have increased over time, as social programs have grown, the National Research Council found that in recent years opportunities for upward mobility have actually declined for low-income people.[37]

These figures are likely to strike many readers as wrong. We are always hearing about people who started with nothing and built up a fortune, the immigrant who came to America with no education or money and has children and grandchildren who went on to great success. But we tend to hear more about exceptional success stories than about routine failures.[38] In addition, equal opportunity seems more prevalent than it is because *absolute* and *relative* mobility are often confused: absolute mobility involves general progress in education and material success across generations; relative mobility measures whether people born into different classes in the same generation have equal shots at success. When there is educational progress across society, the son of a high school graduate is more likely to go to college (absolute mobility), but he does not necessarily keep up with the son of the college graduate who does postgraduate work (relative mobility). To test whether equal opportunity exists, we need to know the degree of relative mobility—the degree to which the sons of street sweepers do as well, not as their fathers, but as the sons of lawyers. Until recently, our nation has had a great deal of absolute mobility, which has masked the lack of relative mobility.[39]

Real Life Barriers Remain Unaddressed

In analyzing the vast class-based environmental differences that bombard American children and adolescents, we begin by pointing to the enormous differences in family wealth. Despite the New Deal, the Fair Deal, the New Frontier, the Great Society, and on and on, enormous inequalities persist. At each stage of childhood—from birth to elementary school to high school to college—the chances are decidedly unequal for individuals who are born with the same talents and work at the same level of effort. We first turn to the enormous differences in income and wealth among American families and then look at how well the various government initiatives to provide greater equal opportunity have worked.

Family Differences Since its founding, our nation has been considered more egalitarian than Europe, not only because of our supposedly high rates of social mobility but also because—as Tocqueville noted—we have a broad, solid middle class.[40] But today, as Labor Secretary Robert Reich notes, "we have the most unequal distribution of income of any industrial nation in the world."[41]

In 1993 the top one-fifth of the American public took home almost as much income as the bottom 80 percent. The differential between the top and bottom fifth was more than 13:1.[42] The gap has been growing over the past fifteen years. Between 1979 and 1993, according to the Labor Department, real family income for the top 20 percent increased by 18 percent, while the bottom 20 percent saw a 17 percent decline.[43] Income inequality is at its highest rate since the Census Bureau began keeping records in 1947.[44]

In the workplace, pay gaps skyrocketed. In 1979 American chief executive officers made on average 29 times as much as the average manufacturing worker. In 1985 the multiple was 40, and by 1988 the figure was 93 times as much—prompting even *Business Week* to question the disparity.[45] But the gap continued to grow, and by 1990 CEOs earned 113 times the wage of the average worker; by 1995 the multiple was 150. By comparison, Japanese and German CEOs continue to have a pay differential similar to those of U.S. executives in 1979—between twenty and thirty-five times the wage of the average worker.[46]

Wealth differences are even more pronounced than income differences. According to the congressional Joint Economic Committee (JEC), the top 10 percent of the American population owns two-thirds of net wealth, while the bottom 90 percent owns one-third.[47] A 1983 Federal Reserve study, which focused specifically on financial assets, found that the top 2 percent held 54 percent of assets, that the top 10 percent held 86 percent of assets, and that a majority of Americans (the bottom 55 percent) had no net fungible assets.[48] The MIT economist Lester Thurow found in 1987 that the Forbes 400 list of the richest Americans had "effective control" over "40 percent of all fixed, nonresidential private capital in the United States."[49]

Conservatives have justified these inequalities as merely reflecting inequality of *result*, arguing that what matters is not the ultimate degree of inequality but whether the gains were obtained fairly, in a system of equal opportunity.[50] The problem, of course, is that vast inequality of parental result translates, necessarily, into unequal opportunities for the next generation.

Alex Kotlowitz provides chilling documentation of how unequal results translate into unequal opportunities for innocent children. Consider, for example, what it is to be like Lafeyette and Pharoah Rivers, growing up without a father, among drug dealers and killers in a Chicago housing project. Imagine being let out of your fifth-grade class early one day, as Lafeyette was, and sitting inside your apartment, looking out the window for your little brother, when a drug shooting begins. Kotlowitz tells the story:

> Lafeyette ... watched hopefully for Pharoah as the children poured out of the Henry Suder Elementary School, just

a block away. Panicking, many of the youngsters ran directly toward the gunfire. Lafeyette and his mother screamed at the children to turn back. But they kept coming, clamoring for the shelter of their homes. Lafeyette finally spotted his brother, first running, then walking, taking cover behind trees and fences. But then he lost sight of him. "Mama, lemme go get him. Lemme go," Lafeyette begged. He was afraid that Pharoah would run straight through the gunfire. Pharoah would later say he had learned to look both ways and that's why he'd started walking. "My mama told me when you hear the shooting, first to walk because you don't know where the bullets are coming," he explained.

When, on another occasion, Kotlowitz asked ten-year-old Lafeyette what he wanted to be when he grows up, Lafeyette responded, "If I grow up, I'd like to be a bus driver." "If," Kotlowitz writes, "not when."[51]

Or imagine, as Jonathan Kozol reports, being a child in the Anacostia section of Washington, D.C., where a principal complains that, "on Fridays, in the cafeteria I see small children putting chicken nuggets in their pockets. They're afraid of being hungry on the weekend." Or being a child in the South Bronx, witnessing murders and rapes, but also having to deal with issues that middle-class kids would never dream of, like untreated dental problems. Kozol writes:

> Although dental problems don't command the instant fears associated with low birth weight, fetal death or cholera, they do have the consequence of wearing down the stamina of children and defeating their ambitions. Bleeding gums, impacted teeth and rotting teeth are routine matters for the children I have interviewed in the South Bronx. Children get used to feeling constant pain. They go to sleep with it. They go to school with it. Sometimes their teachers are alarmed and try to get them to a clinic. But it is all so slow and heavily encumbered with red tape and waiting lists and missing, lost or canceled welfare cards,

that dental care is often long delayed. Children live for months with pain that grown-ups would find unendurable. The gradual attrition of accepted pain erodes their energy and aspiration.[52]

Then there are the working-class kids who grow up much better off than the poor kids but with their own disadvantages. The National Institute of Health's Melvin Kohn and others have argued that working-class fathers, after being pushed around all day on the job, are, as a group, more likely to be authoritarian.[53] The social critic Lillian Rubin, in her interviews with white working-class families, noticed that none of the homes had living room lamps for reading. The working-class mothers and fathers she interviewed were themselves universally products of the working class—40 percent with alcoholic parents, close to 40 percent the children of divorce or desertion. Rubin was struck when she asked the working-class mothers what they valued most in their husbands. " 'He's a Steady Worker; he doesn't drink; he doesn't hit me'—these are the three attributes working-class women tick off most readily." When Rubin interviewed professional middle-class family women, not one mentioned those qualities; these were taken for granted, and middle-class wives focused on "intimacy, sharing, and communication."[54]

Next consider the child of the upper-middle-class and upper-class professional. Not only is this child not likely to experience the impediments of the poor—the violence and want—he is more likely to enjoy the distinct positive advantages that come from having parents who know the value of education firsthand and provide a stimulating intellectual environment in the home. He is, says Rubin, raised in an environment where "the sky's the limit."[55] This will not always be true—upper-status parents will sometimes be so busy with work as to neglect a child—but even so, the University of Maryland economist Mancur Olson is surely correct when he says, "On average, the more successful families pass on the larger legacies of human and physical capital to their children."[56]

Equalizers Don't Equalize Some conservatives, while conceding that children grow up in very different families, would argue that there is not much we can do about that, and that our country evens out the different family environments by the time a teenager leaves his family in three significant ways. We provide (a) a progressive tax system and welfare state, which eliminate gross inequalities; (b) free public education through age eighteen; and (c) a system of standardized tests, which allow the naturally smart to advance, irrespective of class prejudice. Do these equalizers equalize opportunity?

One would think, with all our social reforms—a stiff inheritance tax, progressive marginal tax rates, and welfare payments to the poor—that America has done a fairly good job of addressing inequality of wealth and income. But the evidence suggests the opposite. According to the Brookings Institution's John A. Brittain, "The relative gap between rich and poor in America has remained substantially impervious to egalitarian public policy." Even when marginal tax rates reach 91 percent, Britain says, the *after-tax* income of the top 10 percent "consistently averages around twenty times that of the lowest tenth." Great wealth has survived nominally high estate taxes as well, he says: the top 1 percent continues to hold 25 percent of all personal wealth "decade after decade."[57] MIT's Lester Thurow has come to similar conclusions about the minimal effect of transfer payments and gift and inheritance taxes on inequality of wealth and income in the United States.[58] The Center on Budget and Policy Priorities, using Congressional Budget Office (CBO) data, found that "the richest 1 percent of all Americans now receive nearly as much income *after taxes* as the bottom 40% of Americans combined. Stated another way, the richest 2.5 million people now have nearly as much income as the 100 million Americans with the lowest income."[59] Between 1980 and 1990, after-tax income inequality rose faster than inequality measured before taxes.[60] Of the twenty-four leading industrial countries, only Australia and Turkey have lower tax rates than the United States.[61] The argument here is not that all incomes should be equal, but that children continue to be born into strikingly different economic circumstances under existing efforts at redistribution.

Public education is supposed to be the great democratizer. As John Dewey envisioned it, rich and poor would come together and share the common schooling available to all. But are the schools today a model for promoting equality of opportunity? Dozens of studies have looked at this question, and most conclude that schools tend to reproduce the existing social hierarchy.[62] The problem, notes the *New Republic*'s Mickey Kaus, is that "common access to schooling isn't the same thing as access to common schooling."[63] At the most basic level, we lack equal educational funding: there are often large gaps in per-pupil expenditure between poor and wealthy school districts.[64] The federal government's effort to provide greater funding to poor school districts through Chapter 1 of the Elementary and Secondary Education Act of 1965 has had a limited impact. While the federal government provides more than $6 billion a year through the program, federal spending amounts to only $6 of every $100 spent on public education.[65] The money is spread thinly: some 93 percent of the nation's school districts receive Chapter 1 funds.[66] And attempts by the Clinton administration to focus the money more clearly on poor districts in 1994 were largely blocked by representatives of wealthier districts.[67]

Some conservatives point out that James Coleman's landmark 1966 study, *Equality of Educational Opportunity*, found that school funding is a small determinant of educational achievement. But the weight of evidence confirms the commonsense notion that school funding does make a difference.[68] Indeed, the Coleman report argued for *greater* funding for schools with high concentrations of poverty than for schools with wealthier populations, to compensate for the disadvantage that students from poor backgrounds bring to school and for the additional disadvantage of attending school with other poor students.[69] Coleman found that poor black sixth graders in middle-class schools were twenty months ahead of poor black sixth graders in poor schools. The same was true of poor white sixth graders.[70] Overall, Coleman reported, "attributes of other students account for far more variation in the achievement of minority group children than do attributes of staff."[71]

So in America, poor students are at a triple disadvantage:

they come from disadvantaged family environments; they go to schools with high concentrations of poverty; and instead of receiving much more funding per pupil to make up for those two disadvantages, they often receive less. On top of these disadvantages, add a fourth: even in schools with some socioeconomic mix, poor students are likely to be segregated from the more affluent students through tracking. Without getting into the merits of the debate over the value of tracking, we do know that tracking is widespread—83 percent of school districts use it— and that it undercuts some of the equal opportunity potential of public schools.[72]

In sum, the current public educational system, far from tending to compensate for unequal starting places, tends to legitimatize and freeze socioeconomic status. Even the conservative economist Milton Friedman acknowledges:

> At the elementary and secondary level, the quality of schooling varies tremendously: outstanding in some wealthy suburbs of major metropolises, excellent or reasonably satisfactory in many small towns and rural areas, incredibly bad in the inner cities of major metropolises. The education, or rather the uneducation, of black children from low income families is undoubtedly the greatest disaster area in public education and its most devastating failure. This is doubly tragic for it has always been the official ethic of public schooling that it was the poor and the oppressed who were its greatest beneficiaries.[73]

This was the central insight of the Coleman report: far from removing the handicaps that come from varying family backgrounds, public schools actually accentuate them. As children progress through their school years, the initial gap between children from high-status and low-status families does not close but actually widens.[74]

Thus far, we have limited our discussion to public schools, but it is, of course, the right of wealthy parents to opt out of the public schools entirely, to buy what they see as superior opportunities for their children. Although the elite preparatory schools like to say they have opened up their doors and are more democratic, make no mistake as to whose children predominate. According to one study, two-thirds of the students at the twenty top prep schools had parents whose income was three times the national median, while almost half the student families had incomes four times the national median.[75] At one prep school, 40 percent of the students' parents were listed in the Social Register, a status claimed by .00265 percent of American families.[76]

Besides public education, the college board exams are meant to be the great democratizers. When you take an SAT, what counts is brains and effort, not race or social class. But many who have looked at the issue more closely conclude, as the journalist James Fallows has, that "in most instances, the tests simply ratify earlier advantage—that as engines of mobility, they have sputtered and died."[77]

It is not surprising that the accumulation of profound advantages and disadvantages we have outlined leave their mark on academic achievement, including the College Board exam. We know that these tests do not simply measure innate intelligence but significantly reflect class and family background. Indeed, the designers of the SAT themselves concede: "The SAT measures developed verbal and mathematical reasoning abilities that are involved in successful academic work in college; it is not a test of some inborn and unchanging ability."[78] Indeed, in 1993 the College Board changed the name of the SAT from the Scholastic Aptitude Test to the Scholastic Assessment Test, to dispel the impression "that the SAT measures something that is innate and impervious to change regardless of effort or instruction."[79]

To add insult to injury, affluent students in recent years have compounded their advantage with SAT preparation courses. While the Educational Testing Service (ETS) once held that coaching had no impact on scores, the debate has now shifted to the question not of whether but of how much coaching can help.[80] And there is little question that the courses benefit the affluent disproportionately.[81]

While much ink has been spilled on the disparate racial impact of the SAT, researchers have found that the class impact is profound—and that, indeed, the racial impact is in part a reflection of the class impact. This has been consistently true over time. Thus, in the mid–1970s the mean income at each level of SAT performance painted a striking picture, as it did in 1985.[82] In 1994, according to the College Board, SAT scores broke down as follows[83]

SAT SCORES BY FAMILY INCOME

Family Income	Combined SAT Score
Less than $10,000	766
$10,000–20,000	812
$20,000–30,000	856
$30,000–40,000	885
$40,000–50,000	911
$50,000–60,000	929
$60,000–70,000	948
$70,000 or more	1000

Table 4.1

Not once does the correlation make a false step.[84] Overall, as the National Academy of Sciences (NAS) points out, children from the top socioeconomic 20 percent on average score at the 65th percentile, while the bottom socioeconomic 20 percent scores on average at the 35th percentile.[85]

None of this is to say the test is itself biased, since it makes no claim to measure "innate" natural intelligence plus effort. The test is meant to predict freshman year grades, and since rich kids (through no doing of their own) have access to much better training than do poor kids, one would expect the "learned ability," and ability to do well in college, to be higher for the rich. The bias, then, appears not to be in the tests per se but rather reflects our entire social structure. The SATs have, in turn, an enormous impact on who gets into selective colleges, and who gets into selective colleges has a large impact on who gets ahead in America.[86]

Equality of opportunity is a brilliant synthesis of liberty and equality *only* if individuals actually have an equal chance to develop their natural talents. But because the shrinking of government programs means that America is unlikely to commit the social resources necessary to create more equal starting places, and because we do not want to interfere with the integrity of the family (from which much inequality stems), class-based affirmative action for disadvantaged young adults of all races is a highly appropriate tool for promoting genuine equal opportunity. Providing limited, class-based preferences to young people starting off on their own—in college or in entry-level jobs—provides a better approximation of genuine equal opportunity than either racial preferences or a policy of inaction.

Class preferences make sense for the same reasons of efficiency and moral desert that provided the original justification for equal opportunity. It is true that on grounds of efficiency, we normally care only about who can do the best job, not who has faced the most obstacles. As the Harvard philosopher Robert Nozick notes, those who judge who are the winners of life's various races "usually do not care about desert or about the handicaps labored under; they care simply about what they actually get."[87] If a corporate board is deciding between two fifty-year-olds for the position of chief executive officer, efficiency surely dictates that the board choose the individual who has a track record of producing the most; past record, in this case, is a fairly accurate predictor of future achievement. However, when we are dealing with adolescents who are beginning their adulthood, there is a strong efficiency argument for looking at obstacles faced, to get a better assessment of long-term potential. A poor applicant from the inner city who scores 1000 on the SAT surely has more potential than a wealthy student with private tutors who scores 1050. Indeed, one study found that the most successful Harvard graduates were those with lower SATs from blue-collar backgrounds.[88] In deciding between two eighteen-year-olds who have applied for an entry-level position or for admission to a competitive university, the future potential is less well known; looking beyond the track record to consider the obstacles faced is surely relevant to determining long-run potential. A seventeen- or eighteen-year-old taking the SAT has three-quarters of her life ahead of her. If there is a time to factor in obstacles, this is it.[89]

Second, it is highly appropriate, for reasons of moral desert to correct for a teenager's class position. While sociologists and policy makers will debate the extent to which an adult's economic class is mutable—Republicans stressing the role of individual initiative and Democrats the role of environmental forces—all agree that for children and adolescents, their class position is essentially not theirs but that of their parents.[90] Adolescents are, of course, responsible for their own actions, but they are not responsible for their class or socioeconomic status, or for the disadvantages that stem from that status. A teenager from a lower-class background should get the benefit of a preference; only those who as individuals work hard and apply themselves should advance from within the group to whom such preferences are awarded. Because the class-based obstacles and disadvantages that face adolescents are not in any sense of their own making, a preference correcting for that unfair and immutable condition makes perfect moral sense. Those who work hard and do fairly well despite obstacles do deserve a hand up, and failure to offer that hand is to underestimate the long-run potential of such adolescents.

In sum, class-based affirmative action provides what other systems do not. Unlike formalistic equal opportunity, it corrects for background injustice. Unlike racial preferences, it does not hit poor whites with a regressive tax; does not benefit advantaged minorities; does benefit poor whites; and does benefit poor people of color. Where the laissez-faire system provides only formal equal opportunity, and where affirmative action provides only equality of group result, class-based affirmative action provides genuine individual equal opportunity.

COMPENSATION, INTEGRATION, AND A COLOR-BLIND FUTURE

While the main thrust behind class-based preferences is the goal of providing genuine equal opportunity, the program should also provide a more satisfying means of achieving the related goals of racial preferences—compensation for past discrimination, the benefits of racial integration, and a color-blind future.

A system of class-based preferences implicitly compensates those groups that have been historic victims of discrimination by addressing the ongoing economic legacy of discrimination. Because minorities have been discriminated against, they are disproportionately poor and would benefit disproportionately from a class-based approach. Unlike a system of racial preferences, class-based preferences do not assume a direct linear link between an individual's race and his rightful position in life's competition—a link that claims Allan Bakke would not have been admitted to UC Davis Medical School on the merits but for past discrimination. But unlike the laissez-faire approach, class preferences are rooted in social history. For example, the fact that blacks were excluded from housing opportunities and therefore do not today have the net worth enjoyed by whites is accounted for in a class-based preference. Class preferences will benefit the victims of past discrimination to the extent that the legacy of discrimination is reflected in their current economic status.

Despite all the progress made by minorities in the past three decades, they remain as a group disproportionately poor. Accordding to recent Census Bureau and Labor Department statistics, the 1990 median household income of black families was 58 percent that of whites. In 1990 black children were almost three times as likely to live in poverty (44.8 percent) as white children (15.9 percent).[91] The poverty rate among Hispanic children is nearly as high as among black children.[92] If one considers, instead of the "snapshot," the chances of being poor at some point while growing up, the chances for white children are 45 percent, and for blacks 85 percent.[93] If a class preference had gone to families in the lowest income quartile in 1990, 41.3 percent of black families would have benefited, compared with 17.2 percent of white families.[94]

We know from experience that existing class-based programs benefit blacks disproportionately. The widely popular GI Bill, which helped educate returning World War II veterans, led to an 85 percent increase in black college enrollment.[95] The old Comprehensive Employment and Training Act (CETA) program had a minority enrollment of 50 percent.[96] Some school systems have found that race-blind need-based mechanisms can be highly effective in boosting minority scores. In Montgomery County, Maryland, the school board puts extra funding not in schools with large concentrations of minorities but in those with the highest percentage of low-income or poorly per-forming students, irrespective of race. As a result, a large gap between whites and blacks has been nearly eliminated.[97] In the public works arena, New York City's class-based preference program involving public contracting gave preferences not to women and people of color but to small businesses located in depressed areas. It ended up channeling 45 percent of set-asides to blacks, Hispanics, and women.[98]

Conversely, when student loan and grant programs were cut back in the 1980s, black enrollment in higher education dropped off sharply.[99] Between 1976 and 1986, financial aid shifted sharply away from grants to loans.[100] Because black families are less financially secure than white families—even within the same income categories—minority students are much less likely to take on loans. According to one study, "Fewer than one-third of low-income minority aid recipients secure a government secured loan, compared with more than two-fifths of low-income white aid recipients." The result was predictable. Whereas 48 percent of black high school graduates in 1977 attended college—a rate nearly equal to the white rate—by 1986 the rate was 36.5 per-cent.[101] Writes Princeton Professor Paul Starr, "Minority access to higher education depends as much, if not more, on strong national support for college financing, than on affirmative action admissions."[102] Without assuming scientific causal links between past discrimination and the current economic position of indi-vidual members of racial minority groups—or assuming that all racial groups would be proportionately represented but for dis-crimination—class-based preferences indirectly recognize the current effects of past discrimination.

It is true that class preferences will benefit large numbers of whites as well as minorities. Obviously, poor and working-class whites are included in the program not for reasons of historical compensation but because the goal is broader than merely com-pensating for past discrimination; it includes the grander aim of providing genuine equal opportunity for all Americans. If the legacy of discrimination were the only impediment to equal opportunity, then an exclusively race-based preference would be appropriate. But it is not. Even on purely compensatory grounds, however, class preferences—combined with narrow and temporary racial preferences in rare instances—will do the best job.

The reason is this: if one believes that there is a strong link between discrimination and current economic position—as proponents of affirmative action do—then those blacks who suffered the worst kinds of discrimination are concentrated at the lower rungs of society, while the most advantaged blacks are those who suffered least.[103] Roger Wilkins, for example, points out that "racism has always hurt some blacks more than others"—slaves in the South obviously more than free blacks in the North—and that today's "inner city poor are poor because they have been scarred more deeply by the legacy of slavery than the rest of us."[104] But as we have seen, affirmative action benefits often go to the most advantaged blacks—those least likely to have been discriminated against. Thus, the relationship between the degree of compensation and the degree of desert is inverted.[105] In this sense, by helping the most disadvantaged blacks, class-based affirmative action arguably does a *better* job of compensation for past discrimination than race-based affirmative action does. No longer aiding middle-class minorities—as affirmative action has done for a generation—class-based affirmative action takes up the slack of compensating poor and working-class minorities, the most victimized in the first place. "Ironically," William Julius Wilson argues, "the shift from preferential treatment for those with certain racial or ethnic characteristics to those who are truly disadvantaged in terms of their life chances would not only help the white poor, but would also address *more effectively* the problems of the minority poor."[106]

It is absolutely crucial to remember that those who initially believed that we need to compensate for past discrimination did not also believe that compensation had to take the form of a race-specific measure. Martin Luther King, we should recall, felt strongly that some form of compensation was necessary, and in fact, he was criticized for raising the notion of debt.[107] But he concluded that there were nonracial ways to remedy racial wrongs, and that the injuries of class needed addressing along with the injuries of race; he proposed the Bill of Rights for the Disadvantaged.[108]

Because class-based preferences indirectly compensate for past discrimination, and because they disproportionately benefit minorities, they will also provide more racially integrated universities and workplaces than a system without preferences. If one's goal is racial balancing per se, then class preferences are less efficient than racial preferences. But as we saw in chapter 3, when race is used to provide a false integration, it undermines the very goals of integration—decreasing racial prejudice and increasing social harmony. Class preferences will disproportionately benefit minorities, hastening racial integration, but without the increased racial prejudice and hostility associated with racial preferences. At the same time, because class preferences maintain the commitment to addressing past discrimination, people of color will feel less hostile toward the majority than they would if affirmative action were eliminated altogether. Likewise, class preferences will increase the number of minority role models without conveying the message that skin color itself is a qualification. Building on the growing supply of role models created by a generation of race-based affirmative action, class-based preferences will make even more minority role models available, but without using race as the means.[109]

By the same token, class-based preferences are likely to do an excellent job of moving our society toward a genuinely color-blind future. Proponents of affirmative action say we need to do something about our racial history to get beyond race. Opponents say using color-conscious means contradicts the very message of color blindness we are trying to send. Class-based affirmative action addresses both concerns. It will have a racially integrative impact, without using race-conscious means. Means and ends will not work at cross-purposes; both will pull in the same direction. Class-based affirmative action is at once color-blind and cognizant of our nation's history. Ours is a history of racial discrimination resulting in a concentration of blacks in the lower segments of society, and class-based affirmative action implicitly addresses that history, in a color-blind manner.

LEGAL AND POLITICAL NECESSITY

Finally, even for those who would stand by racial and gender preferences on the merits, there are urgent legal and political reasons to look for other means of achieving the goals of affirmative action. While affirmative action has managed to survive for thirty years, the scope of this particular remedy has and will continue to be circumscribed by both the judicial and political branches. As a matter of necessity, and survival, proponents of affirmative action will want to look at the class alternative. For at the end of the day, a program with as little public support as racial preferences faces a highly unstable and uncertain future.

Legal Impediments

While the Supreme Court was initially open to the notion of compensatory racial preferences, over time the Court has grown increasingly wary. Strong public opposition to preferences helped elect conservative presidents who, in turn, have appointed conservative justices to the Court. After a series of close decisions, some supporting affirmative action, others opposing, the 1989 *Croson* decision saw for the first time a solid 6–3 majority willing to subject state affirmative action programs to the same "strict scrutiny" standard used to strike down Jim Crow laws. As we saw in chapter 2, that standard is tough to meet. And in June 1995, the Court, by a 5–4 vote, applied the strict scrutiny standard to federal programs in the case of *Adarand Constructors Inc. v. Pena*, explicitly overruling the pro–affirmative action ruling in *Metro Broadcasting*.[110]

Beyond its application to federal construction set-asides, *Adarand* severely threatens the very heart of affirmative action—implementation of Lyndon Johnson's executive order 11246, which requires affirmative action of all companies doing business with the federal government in excess of $50,000. When Richard Nixon used Johnson's executive order to require racial quotas in the Philadelphia construction industry, his remedy might well have passed the *Adarand* test: the Philadelphia Plan involved a temporary remedy for discrimination by six trades in a five-county area with a well-documented history of discrimina-

tion. But Nixon subsequently applied affirmative action requirements to all federal contractors nationwide, whether a history of
discrimination existed or not, and this will surely fall under the
strict scrutiny prescribed in *Adarand*. More ominously, *Adarand
v. Pena* showed that five members of the Court are willing to
explicitly overrule precedents on affirmative action, threatening
pro–affirmative action decisions like *Bakke* and *United Steel
Workers v. Weber*.[111] The Clinton administration has tried to put
a favorable "spin" on the *Adarand* decision, emphasizing that
seven of nine justices said affirmative action is not always forbidden.[112] But as the *New Republic*'s Jeffrey Rosen points out,
the last time five members of the Supreme Court upheld a racial
classification against strict scrutiny was 1944.[113] Yale Law's Paul
Gewirtz concludes that the new standard will be so tough to
meet that supporters of preferences must realistically look at
alternatives.[114]

While the Supreme Court was once the haven to which civil
rights activists would turn, today it is likely to have a hostile
reaction to race-based preferences. Indeed, on statutory questions it is the Congress that has had to go back seven times since
1975 to respond to unfavorable Supreme Court decisions—the
most recent congressional enactment being the Civil Rights Act
of 1991, reversing a series of unfavorable Supreme Court inter-
pretations of civil rights laws.[115] And when the Court renders
antipreference decisions on constitutional grounds, quick legislative fixes are, of course, unavailable.

As a simple legal matter, then, there is a strong argument that
even those who support affirmative action need to look, rather
urgently, for different remedies. Rather than turning to new theories to support racial preferences, in the vain hope of convincing a
majority of justices on the Supreme Court, supporters of affirmative action need to seriously consider programs based on class.
For while almost any race-based preference is today vulnerable to
attack by the Supreme Court, the Court is almost sure to uphold
the constitutionality of class-based affirmative action programs.
In contrast to race-based affirmative action, class preferences are,
as the legal columnist Stuart Taylor notes, "legally unassailable."[116]
And therein lies a great legal irony.

The Fourteenth Amendment to the Constitution, ratified following the Civil War, provides, in part, that "no State shall . . . deny to any person within its jurisdiction the equal protection of the laws." In hundreds of cases, the Supreme Court has tried to define what those vague words mean, and over the years the members of the Court have developed a body of case law that says the Court will require a powerful justification for legislation that classifies individuals on "suspect" grounds. Race is the paradigmatic suspect classification, and the Court has also found classifications involving gender, illegitimacy, and alienage to be "semisuspect," requiring a somewhat higher level of justification than other types of legislation.

For many years, lawyers on the left tried to add "class" to the list of suspect classifications and seemed to come close at times.[117] But as Professor John Ely notes, "The once glittering crusade to extend special constitutional protection to the poor has turned into a rout."[118] It is now well established, as a matter of constitutional law, that while race is clearly a suspect classification, class is clearly not.[119] It is for this very reason that lawyers on the left have traditionally tried to pitch arguments seeking to overturn state action in terms of race rather than class. Where a unanimous court would strike down the racial unfairness of school segregation in *Brown v. Board of Education*, the Court refused to strike down the class-based unfairness of inequitable public school funding in *San Antonio v. Rodriguez*.[120]

Today, ironically, we are faced with precisely the opposite dynamic. In the remedial phase, most of the racial laws being subjected to constitutional challenge are not those that hurt people of color but affirmative action remedies meant to help them. But because the Court has held race to be a suspect classification, and because it applies the same strict scrutiny to "benign" racial classifications as it does to the old anti-black classifications, those seeking to help people of color have a strong legal incentive to avoid racial remedies. Conversely, the very failure of the left to have class included in the list of suspect classifications means that benign class-based remedies for the poor face no double-edged sword. To a lesser degree, we have already seen this phenomenon play out with respect to gender-based affirmative action: because gender is not fully suspect, gender preferences are easier to sustain.[121]

Finally, as has been noted, Justices Scalia, O'Connor, and Thomas have gone out of their way to explicitly advocate forms of class-based affirmative action as a constitutional alternative to race-based programs. Indeed, following the Supreme Court's decision in *Croson*, the ACLU pointed to a class-based construction set-aside program in New York City as a way cities could remedy past discrimination in a clearly legal manner.[122]

In sum, then, even if proponents of racial preferences have no moral qualms about the current regime, there are strong legal reasons to consider the class-based affirmative action alternative. The diversity justification for affirmative action, which has temporarily circumvented the legal requirements that racial preferences be justified by documented discrimination and temporary in nature, is highly unstable. Whereas once there were reasons to pitch arguments in terms of race in order to persuade the Court to intervene to help, now there is every reason to pitch remedies in terms of class so that the Court will not intervene to hurt.

Political Impediments

Those racial and gender programs that do manage to survive judicial scrutiny may well be rescinded by political bodies or by voter referenda. Racial preferences have always been highly unpopular. While some polls show opposition to the nebulous "affirmative action" is soft, researchers have found that "the idea of quotas and preferential treatment is the reef on which affirmative action founders."[123] In most national polls, racial preferences in employment or education—even those not involving quotas—are opposed by more than 80 percent of whites and 50 percent of blacks.[124] White opposition is strong even under the best scenarios for preferences: when two otherwise equally qualified candidates are involved,[125] and when an employer has proven to have discriminated in the past.[126] In theory, women should throw their hefty electoral support behind gender preferences, but polls show white women oppose preferences almost as often as white men do.[127]

"Rarely is public opinion, particularly on such a controversial issue, as united as it is over this question," George Gallup concluded in the late 1970s.[128] More recently, President Clinton's pollster Stanley Greenberg (who personally favors racial preferences)[129] conceded:

> There is no debate on affirmative action. Everybody's against it. There is a very small share of the [white] electorate—zero—that believes they have personal responsibility for this. That they ought to be paying for the injustice. . . . They can't even begin to understand the logic on it. It does not even reach the level of common sense for the majority of Americans. . . . It's odd that the Democratic party takes it as an accepted principle, whereas the base which we need to reach in order to win elections takes it as a conventional wisdom that it's an injustice to the middle class. It is a political problem of historic proportions.[130]

Moreover, in contrast to many other areas of public policy, positions on racial preferences are held deeply. Twice as many individuals change their mind when given a "gentle nudge in the form of counter-argument," on issues of social welfare as on issues of racial preferences.[131] Affirmative action is not an abstract question to Americans; it's one that touches them personally.

Until recently, however, affirmative action programs have managed to survive repeated assaults.[132] Attacks on the programs during the Nixon, Ford, and Reagan administrations all failed.[133] Attempts by members of the Bush administration to outlaw race-based scholarships and to eliminate federal preferences were seen as political blunders and sent officials reeling in retreat.[134] From the 1960s through the mid-1990s, programs have proliferated, despite their unpopularity, in large part thanks to an unlikely alliance between civil rights groups, business interests, and educators.[135]

But the Republican sweep of Congress for the first time in forty years and the rise of the vaunted "angry white male" in 1994 had a dramatic impact. Following the midterm elections, political commentators began speaking openly about the prospect of seeing "the end" of affirmative action programs. Joe Klein, writing in *Newsweek*, said race and gender preferences were likely to end on President Clinton's watch.[136] The *New Republic* asked, "Is Affirmative Action Doomed?"[137] Where for many years programs for racial set-asides flew through Congress without opposition, in 1995 it was the *repeal* of the FCC's minority tax certificate program that sailed through the House and Senate.[138] Where President Bush's education secretary, Lamar Alexander, saved minority scholarships in 1991 (with a wink, telling college administrators "with a warm heart" they could count race as "one factor"), four years later he endorsed a California initiative to repeal race as a factor in UC admissions and took credit for saying, "Scholarships based on race alone are wrong."[139] Where President Bush quickly backed away from a directive abolishing federal affirmative action guidelines in 1991, Senator Robert Dole introduced even more sweeping legislation to roll back programs in 1995.[140] In July 1995, the University of California, once on the cutting edge of the diversity movement, saw its racial preference program repealed by the Board of Regents. And Democratic Senator Joe Lieberman, chairman of the Democratic Leadership Council, announced that he supported the outright repeal of preferences called for in the California Civil Rights Initiative.[141] Similar ballot initiatives have sprung up in six other states.[142]

Sharp cutbacks are likely, but even if proponents of racial preferences manage to dodge the bullet again in the short run, five undeniable trends make repeal of affirmative action increasingly likely: (1) the passage of time; (2) the growth in our nation's ethnic diversity; (3) the flattening of our nation's standard of living; (4) the increasing legal challenge to racial preferences; and (5) the growing sophistication of affirmative action opponents.

The Time Bomb The passage of time may be affirmative action's worst enemy. As originally envisioned, racial preferences were supposed to be "temporary." Just how temporary remains a contentious issue and can be answered either by looking at minority progress or by measuring the passage of time. Either way, many Americans—and certainly many Republicans—say the time to end preferences has come. Indeed, the passage of time is precisely the way in which politicians like Bob Dole explain their evolving views on affirmative action.

The question of minority progress presents a mixed picture: some portions of the black community have made very good progress, while many African Americans on the bottom are doing worse than ever.[143] This may suggest to many Americans that affirmative action, which in practice primarily benefits middle- and upper-middle-class minorities, has in fact succeeded. When American voters see the growing black middle class—the number of African Americans earning professional degrees in medicine and law rose by 35 percent from 1977 to 1987, and the proportion of black households with incomes above $50,000 in real terms increased by 46 percent between 1970 and 1990—they begin to wonder whether affirmative action is still necessary.[144] Whereas in 1967, when affirmative action got its start, one in seventeen blacks made more than $50,000 in constant dollars, by 1989 the proportion was one in seven.[145] The irony, of course, is that affirmative action is designed to be the victim of its own success. More and more we are faced with a new set of circumstances: do the sons and daughters of "affirmative action babies" deserve the preferential treatment that would make them "affirmative action grandchildren"?

When we refer to time in evaluating whether affirmative action should end, support for affirmative action erodes even more steadily. Proponents of affirmative action are caught in a bind. If they argue that thirty years of affirmative action is not enough time to remedy three hundred years of slavery and segregation, they seem to imply that three hundred years of affirmative action is more appropriate—an idea that is likely to reduce the slim white American support for racial preferences even further. On the other hand, if they emphasize that preferences are truly temporary and limit their duration, they run into the embarrassment of deadlines passed: to wit, Whitney Young, Jr., and Harry Blackmun's calls for a decade of affirmative action.

Given the bind, most supporters of affirmative action fail to provide a definite date when preferences should end, leading many to suspect that preferences will in fact be perpetual. Already some erstwhile supporters of affirmative action have begun to argue that it has run its course. In the Carter administration, it was harder to find a more ardent champion of affirmative action than Secretary of Health, Education, and Welfare Joseph Califano.[146] But Califano says affirmative action was meant to last "for at least a decade and possibly a generation."[147] By 1989 he would write: "Affirmative action has pried open some important doors for blacks, but it was never conceived as a permanent program and its time is running out."[148] Similar statements have been made by liberals like Carter's counsel Stuart Eizenstat and Dukakis's campaign manager Susan Estrich.[149] George Shultz, who championed the Philadelphia Plan as Nixon's secretary of labor, also says it is now time to end affirmative action.[150]

Likewise, as the legacy of segregation and images of Bull Connor fade, the next generation of Americans is beginning to grow weary of "transitional inequality." A 1992 poll of 15–24-year-olds found that white teenagers think they are more likely to be the victims of reverse discrimination than blacks are to be the victims of old-style discrimination.[151] It is not surprising that Third Millennium, a group of post-baby boomers, calls for "a new approach to affirmative action that focuses on economic status," or that the young editors of Berkeley's newspaper support the university's shift from race to class preferences.[152] While it is true that the Reaganites' boast in 1980 that they would dismantle affirmative action turned out to be an empty one, affirmative action was then little more than a decade old. As we begin to close in on the thirtieth birthday of affirmative action programs, the case becomes more and more difficult to sustain.

Demographic Trends The second inexorable trend that threatens the political viability of affirmative action is our nation's increasing diversity. For many years, our nation thought in terms of two categories, black and white.[153] In 1970 blacks outnumbered all other minorities combined by almost two to one, but by 1990 the other minorities outnumbered blacks.[154] Sometime in the next few decades, the number of Hispanics alone is projected to surpass the number of blacks.[155]

In addition to the dramatic shift within the minority community, there has been a related growth in the size of the total minority population. Between 1960 and 1990, the percentage of Americans who are people of color grew from 10 percent to 25 percent.[156] By 2050 the non-Hispanic white population is projected to drop to 53 percent—by which time, the *Washington Post* observed, "our terminology of 'majority' and 'minority' will become meaningless."[157]

This increasing diversity poses two problems for race-based affirmative action that are not faced by class preferences. First, growing diversity places stress on the compensatory rationale for affirmative action, which, at root, was about the sins of slavery and segregation. As blacks decline in their share of the minority population, more and more preferences will go to other minority group members, who, blacks rightly argue, do not suffer from the same legacy of discrimination. As we saw in chapter 3, preferences can and have been used *against* blacks if they are overrepresented compared with other minorities, as they are in the U.S. Postal Service. The question, as Professor Deborah Ramirez puts it, is this: "Should affirmative action programs treat Latinos and Asians as whites, or as blacks, or as something in between?"[158] The compensatory concern is especially acute to the extent that preferences benefit immigrants who have suffered no harm, and whose ancestors have suffered no harm, in this country. (Today the vast majority of immigrants are people of color.)[159] Politically, providing these immigrants with preferences is likely to be highly troubling to both blacks and whites.

Second, the increase in diversity undercuts the notion that affirmative action is safe, since it involves the political majority helping a small powerless minority. As a constitutional matter (and as a matter of fairness as well), one of the reasons to be less concerned about "reverse" discrimination is that, in theory, the majority is discriminating against itself, so that, if things get out of hand, it can always eliminate the policy.[160] In California, non-Hispanic whites now constitute 57 percent of the population and are projected to become a minority by the year 2000.[161] A number of the nation's largest cities are already majority-minority.[162] Politically, whites are likely to pull back while they feel that they are still in electoral control. It is no accident that

California is the first state to see a repeal of affirmative action placed on the ballot.

Flattening Social Mobility The third trend troubling to affirmative action involves America's failure to produce a rising living standard to match the post–World War II boom. As this realization settles in, affirmative action will become more unpopular, and class-based affirmative action is likely to prove more attractive. When affirmative action was first broadly proposed in 1965, the nation's economy was growing fast and the standard of living was rising.[163] Between 1947 and 1973, the standard of living doubled as median family income rose (in 1987 dollars) from $15,422 to $30,820.[164] Such prosperity argued in favor of affirmative action—it is easier to accommodate racial preferences when the cost appears lower—and against class preferences, because the widespread absolute social mobility helped obscure the class barriers to relative social mobility.[165]

Since 1973, however, all this has changed. The American standard of living has been flat.[166] As Daniel Patrick Moynihan notes, the record of stagnant family income between 1970 and 1985 represents "the longest stretch of 'flat' income in the history of the European settlement of North America."[167] In December 1990 the *New York Times* would note that "most Americans are entering the 1990s worse off than they were in the early 1970s. Only those Americans in the top 20 percent have escaped stagnation; their incomes have grown significantly."[168] Meanwhile, Americans are working harder to keep up.[169] As a result, some Americans are more open to looking for scapegoats, like affirmative action, but are also more open to programs that level the playing field for those lacking genuine equal opportunity.

Legal Trends and the Loss of Business Fourth, as legal trends continue to tighten up on the instances when affirmative action is justified, big business, which has strongly supported affirmative action, may find it to be in its self-interest to jettison racial preference programs. In the past, business has not supported racial preferences out of the goodness of its heart; some employers have embraced racial preferences as an easy way to avoid so-called disparate impact lawsuits, which arise when the workforce is racially imbalanced.[170] Under the Civil Rights Act of 1991, employers have the burden of justifying those practices that statistically result in too few minorities being hired or promoted. Rather than going to the trouble of defending these employment practices, some employers simply resort to hiring by the numbers. If the courts declare racial hiring illegal (as many argue they will),[171] businesses will need to look for an alternative method of hiring, one that not only avoids using racial preferences but yields a racially balanced workforce.

Business may see class-based preferences as a new way out of the disparate impact bind, since preferences based on disadvantage will have a "positive" disparate impact, that is, they will increase the number of minority hires.[172] Rather than fighting a losing battle to reinstate the right to use race preferences, businesses may very well focus their efforts on trying to negotiate for federal help in the requirement that they hire poor and working-class entry-level workers, a disproportionate number of whom will be minority.[173] In short, the political support from business for affirmative action may well be contingent on legal support from the courts. Once the legal support wanes, business's political support —so crucial to the program's survival to date—is likely to deteriorate.

Credible Alternatives The fifth and final change that is likely to toll the death knell for affirmative action is the increasing sophistication of opponents. Where conservative opponents of affirmative action used to call for a cold turkey repeal of preferences, today they often speak of replacing affirmative action with an alternative. In April 1995, for example, House Speaker Newt Gingrich declared that while he was opposed to racial preferences, "I'd rather talk about how do we replace group affirmative action with effective help for individuals, rather than just talk about wiping out affirmative action by itself."[174] Similarly, the successful effort to roll back preferences at the University of California explicitly endorsed replacing race and gender preferences with class-based preferences.[175] By contrast, that very same week Senator Phil Gramm's attempt to repeal racial set-asides (without offering a substitute) fell flat.[176] Any alternative is likely to make opponents appear more reasonable, "inoculating" them from appearing mean.[177] Moreover, alternatives should draw some political support from members of the Democratic Party as well, particularly those who are anxious not to be caught on the wrong side of the preference argument but, absent an alternative, would feel morally obligated to support some version of the status quo.

Affirmative action has survived in part because until recently critics lacked a credible substitute. Indeed, many opponents of preferences have been defiant in their failure to talk about alternatives. The Hoover Institution economist Thomas Sowell, for example, argued: "No one who extinguishes a forest fire or removes a cancer has to 'replace' it with anything. We are well rid of evils."[178] And when liberal Senator John Kerry criticized affirmative action in 1992, his failure to offer an alternative vision was attacked by proponents of affirmative action as a major weakness.[179]

If opponents of affirmative action could get bipartisan support for an alternative, they would solve a central problem plaguing earlier attempts to curtail affirmative action. When Ronald Reagan and George Bush talked about cutting back on affirmative action, they did so in the context of otherwise miserable civil rights records.[180] Even if they had offered alternatives, civil rights groups could easily discredit the idea by reference to the source. A good-faith bipartisan effort to come up with a constructive alternative to affirmative action could not so easily be written off.

The Political Appeal of Class-Based Affirmative Action

If several trends are running strongly against race-based preferences, the time has rarely been better for the political fortunes of the class-based alternative.

In the past, there were some signs that class-based affirmative action might have strong political appeal. When the issue of class preferences arose during Clarence Thomas's nomination hearings in 1991, the Democratic silence was deafening. When Thomas explained to the Senate Judiciary Committee that, while he opposed racial preferences, he supported preferences for the disadvantaged of all races, Democrats did not attempt to refute him. A nominee who was widely and vigorously denounced by Democrats on issues of gender (abortion and sexual harassment) was left virtually untouched on this issue. It fell to the Republicans to probe the nominee on his views about class-based affirmative action, and the Republicans even chose to highlight his theory in the Judiciary Committee report.[181]

The idea percolated for a number of years among academics and journalists, with supporters running the ideological gamut from Alan Dershowitz, Cornel West, and Mark Shields to Clint Bolick, Charles Murray, and Richard Herrnstein—and dozens of others.[182] But it was not until affirmative action began to come under serious attack following the 1994 elections that politicians across the political spectrum began to seriously flirt with the idea. Among conservatives, Newt Gingrich and Jack Kemp have supported need-based affirmative action.[183] And New York Governor George E. Pataki and New Jersey Governor Christine Todd Whitman have explored the idea.[184] Among Democrats, President Bill Clinton jumped on board for a time, declaring, "I want us to emphasize need-based programs where we can because they work better and have a bigger impact and generate broader [public] support."[185] Senator Joe Lieberman (D-Conn.) has said that he is looking at alternatives to race- and gender-based preferences, and Senator Charles S. Robb (D-Va.) has called class-based affirmative action "intriguing and thoughtful."[186] Nowhere was the coming together more evident than in California, where the conservative architects of the California Civil Rights Initiative say they prefer class-based affirmative action, and the Democrats considered backing the class-based alternative.[187] While there is no agreement on the particulars of a class-based affirmative action program, the broad idea appears to be garnering surprisingly diverse support.[188] In fact, a 1995 *Newsweek* poll found much greater popular support for income-based preferences than for race-based preferences.[189] In a March 1995 *Los Angeles Times* poll, 58 percent of respondents supported affirmative action for economically disadvantaged individuals.[190] And a September 1995 *Washington Post* poll found that 60 percent of whites and 44 percent of blacks agreed that "affirmative action should be for low-income people, not for persons of a specific race or sex."[191]

When Clinton and Gingrich suggested support for class-based affirmative action, Clinton was attacked by his left, and Gingrich by his right.[192] In the presidential review of affirmative action programs, civil rights and feminist groups lobbied hard against any class-based alternatives, calling for "no retreat" from the status quo. In an earlier era, labor would have championed broad-based help for the disadvantaged, since racial polarization always gives labor's opponents the upper hand. But with the notable exception of Albert Shanker, president of the American Federation of Teachers, labor did nothing to support a class-based alternative to racial preferences.[193]

Nevertheless, both Clinton and Gingrich continued to explore the idea, apparently attracted by its potential to restore the winning combination that passed the great civil rights legislation of the 1960s—the Civil Rights Act of 1964 and the Voting Rights Act of 1965. The formula for success was a policy with unquestionable moral underpinnings and a relatively inexpensive price tag.[194] "The power of the civil rights movement under Martin Luther King was its universalism," says Cornel West. It was then seen as "a moral crusade for freedom," rather than "an expression of a particular interest group."[195] And unlike demands for welfare, the civil rights movement sought not handouts but a chance for those who worked hard to compete fairly.[196] Moreover, the early agenda of the civil rights movement was relatively cheap. Unlike the major social programs launched by Roosevelt and Johnson—AFDC, Medicaid, Medicare, and Social Security—the cost of administering the civil rights apparatus was small. Bayard Rustin exaggerates only slightly when he says, "The civil rights King struggled for did not cost the American public one penny."[197] Likewise, affirmative action programs, though lacking in broad moral support, have survived in part because they are relatively cheap.

Class-based affirmative action, more morally sound than race-based affirmative action and less costly than the Great Society, has the potential to replicate the great success of the early civil rights movement. It is color-blind and yet responds to the moral desire to do something about the legacy of our nation's history.[198] Like education, it provides disadvantaged people with not a handout but a chance to prove themselves if they work hard; it also goes to poor youth, who are morally blameless for their economic position. But unlike education programs, class preferences are fairly cheap and will not bust the budget.[199]

There is a school of thought that is highly critical of the notion that the civil rights movement succeeded because of its strong moral message. NYU's Derrick Bell, for example, argues that almost every initiative that helped blacks was undertaken because the initiative was seen as furthering the interests of whites.[200] But if that is true, then vigorous use of racial preferences was doomed from the beginning. And a shift from racial preferences to class preferences is inevitable, since the change is surely in the self-interest of whites who will themselves benefit— or will benefit if they fall on hard times. Whether one subscribes to the benign view (whites will support class preferences because they are fairer) or the more malign view (whites will support only programs that help at least some whites), both point to the political efficacy of nonracial, class-based programs.[201]

If class-based affirmative action is morally sound and politically and legally unassailable, will it work? We turn next to that question.

5. The Mechanics of Class-Based Affirmative Action

H OW MIGHT class-based affirmative action work in practice? How is "class" to be defined? Should only the poor benefit, or lower-middle-income Americans as well? Should there be a sliding scale of benefits? In what contexts should class preferences apply? University admissions only? Employment as well? Public contracting? Should class preferences apply to people of all ages? To promotions as well as hiring? How would the idea be implemented? Would preferences be voluntary or mandatory? How substantial should the preferences be? Would class preferences entirely displace racial and gender preferences?

Some blanch at the weight of these questions. "The difficulties of measuring disadvantage seem insurmountable," says the Citizens' Commission on Civil Rights.[1] "There isn't one simple or generally accepted way to identify or determine 'need,' " says the National Women's Law Center (NWLC).[2] The columnist Michael Kinsley asks, "Does Clarence Thomas, the sharecropper's kid, get more or fewer preference points than the unemployed miner's son from Appalachia?"[3] *The American Lawyer*'s Stuart Taylor, Jr., likewise wonders, "How many points for attending an all-black inner city school vs. a second-rate white suburban school? How many for family income under $10,000? Under $20,000? For a mediocre small-town school? A deserting father? An alcoholic mother?"[4]

Most proponents of class-based affirmative action have failed to explain their idea with any degree of specificity.[5] The questions of implementation are indeed serious and difficult, but they are not impossible to answer. At the university level, admissions committees deal every day with precisely the types of apples-and-oranges question that Kinsley and Taylor pose. Should a law school admit an applicant with a 3.2 GPA from Yale or a 3.3 from Georgetown? How do you compare the two if one applicant worked for the Peace Corps but the other has slightly higher LSATs? In fact, as we shall see, a number of universities already give preferences for disadvantaged students in addition to racial minorities, and class preferences have been employed in certain employment and public contracting contexts as well.

In setting up a framework for class preferences, we should be guided by three principles. First, we must keep firmly in mind our primary goal: providing a system of genuine equality of opportunity, where natural talents may flourish to their full potential. To do this, we want to create an obstacles test: if a given individual has done quite well, despite various impediments, then she is very talented and/or very hardworking and therefore deserves an edge because she has great long-run potential. The goal is not to absolve people from responsibility for their own actions (*pace* the Menendez brothers). Rather than excusing pathological behavior, an obstacles test reveals those individuals in whom there is something special worth developing, since they have faced serious obstacles and been relatively successful anyway.

Second, we want a system that can in fact be administered. When the Manhattan Institute's Abigail Thernstrom ridicules the notion of providing preferences to someone with "a handicapped mother, an alcoholic father, a depressed sister and a drug-dealing brother," she is absolutely right.[6] We want the system to ask for information that is verifiable. We may be interested in knowing whether an applicant did quite well even though he grew up in a household with no books and did not have enough "quality time" with his parents, but it is much easier to verify the parents' income, education, and occupation. An unenforceable system will be fraught with abuse, which is possible both on the part of the applicants and (to the extent preferences are compulsory) on the part of employers and universities. Verifiable and objective measures of disadvantage guard against both types of abuse. Moreover, stiff penalties for fraud will stick only when the measures of disadvantage are objective.

Third, we want a program that will actually be adopted in our nation's republican form of government. A theoretically sound program, even one that is administrable, is merely idle chatter if it has no chance of passage politically. Unlike racial remedies, which are sometimes imposed by the judiciary, there is virtually no chance that class-based affirmative action will be imposed by the Supreme Court as constitutionally required.

One possible approach, which seeks to adhere to the three principles, is outlined in this chapter. People may differ on the particulars, but the point is not that the plan is a perfect one, but that there are objective and quantifiable ways to measure disadvantage and make a system work.

WHAT CONTEXTS?

In what contexts would class-based affirmative action apply? If we are trying to provide genuine equal opportunity, rather than equal result, class-based affirmative action would apply with most force at "meritocratic crisis points" relatively *early* in life.[7] As noted in chapter 4, for people in their late teens who are applying to college or for an entry-level job, being economically disadvantaged is not at all their "fault" and yet may hide their true potential. With this basic guideline in mind, we consider the applicability of class-based affirmative action to education, employment, and public contracting.

In education, class-based affirmative action makes sense in the university admissions process, both because applicants are still young and because universities already have access to a wealth of information about applicant backgrounds. Colleges and graduate schools are in many ways the modern gatekeepers, deciding who gets ahead and who does not, so it is natural that many of the discussions of class-based affirmative action have focused on university admissions.

Since 1991 Berkeley has given special consideration to applicants "from socioeconomically disadvantaged backgrounds ... regardless of race or ethnicity."[8] In recent years, between 16 percent and 18 percent of the freshman class has received a leg up in admissions, based on a disadvantage index that measures parental income, education, and occupation.[9] Temple University Law School has, since the 1970s, given preference to "applicants who have overcome exceptional and continuous economic deprivation."[10] Nearly 50 percent of the class is admitted under the Special Admissions and Curriculum Experiments (SPACE) program, which gives special consideration primarily to minority and disadvantaged applicants.[11] At Hastings College of Law in California, 20 percent of the class is set aside for disadvantaged students through the Legal Equal Opportunity Program (LEOP).[12] And in New York, the Higher Educational Opportunity Program (HEOP) provides financial incentives for colleges to admit low-scoring disadvantaged students of all races.[13] Even the UC Davis Medical School program challenged by Allan Bakke was limited to "disadvantaged" minorities, a system that Davis apparently did not find impossible to administer.[14]

If required of universities, such preference systems would need to be accompanied by guarantees of financial aid and some form of remedial education—perhaps a mandatory summer program prior to the beginning of the first year. Just as important, class-based affirmative action would mean modifying or eliminating existing preferences that tend to *hurt* those from lower social economic classes—such as alumni preferences and preferences for applicants from preparatory schools.[15] If a university insisted on providing alumni preferences, it would forgo federal funding. Application of the class preference principle to elementary and secondary schooling should also be explored.[16]

In the employment arena, class-based preferences could be implemented by public employers and federal contractors. In 1994, for example, the Clinton administration issued regulations for section 3 of the 1968 Housing and Urban Development Act (as amended in 1992), requiring a hiring preference for low-income workers in the federal construction of new public housing.[17] Hiring preferences have for years been provided to veterans for civil service jobs. The case for public employment preferences is particularly strong for applicants just graduating from high school and not pursuing college, on the theory that at that age their class-based handicaps hide their true potential and are not at all of their own making.[18]

Since preferences are somewhat harder to apply to entry-level employment than to university admissions (employers do not necessarily have access to the same information on an applicant's class background), the definition of class might be simplified. But it is crucial that class preferences not be limited to university admissions alone, for to do so would bypass all those students who go straight from high school to the job market. In 1991 just 34.1 percent of all whites between eighteen and twenty-four were enrolled in college; the figure for African Americans was 23.6 percent, and for Hispanics 18 percent.[19] Among young adults from the bottom quartile of family income, just 30 percent go to college.[20] Giving preferences in college admissions is crucial, because college is more than ever the key to upward mobility, but preferences must apply to entry-level employment as well if we are to impact the lives of the majority of poor and working-class students in this country.[21]

Preferences make less sense in promotions and in lateral hiring of older employees, particularly for skilled positions. Ross Perot, for example, does not today deserve a preference simply because he was born poor.[22] Entry-level job holders often require training and are in that sense analogous to university students; more senior positions, by contrast, may require instantaneous, high-skilled performance. But the fact that class preferences would not apply to promotions later in life is no reason for alarm. Giving preferences for promotions in *either* the race- or class-based affirmative action context makes less sense than it does in initial hiring. The argument for preferences is strongest when we are giving individuals a fair chance to prove themselves. Just as universities that provide admissions preferences do not provide racial preferences in grading, so in employment the case for preferences is much stronger in hiring than in promotion.[23] And giving an individual a chance at a first job is important. The sociologists Otis and Beverly Duncan and David Featherman report that "the occupational level at which a man begins his career is substantially predictive of the level at which he will be found at any age between 25 and 64."[24] The guiding principle, then, must be a fair shot at performing, not a guaranteed equal result. To combat ongoing racial and gender discrimination in promotion—the so-called glass ceiling—the Civil Rights Act of 1991 requires that employers continue to justify race or gender imbalances in promotion by the legal standard of "business necessity."

Preferences could also be appropriately tailored to public contracting. At first glance, the general notion of benefiting low- and lower-middle-income people seems difficult to apply, since most owners of companies in a position to bid are not low- or lower-middle-income.[25] But race-neutral class-based preferences can nevertheless be framed to give a leg up in contracting to those companies headed by individuals who are disadvantaged *relative* to the competition, and/or to companies that employ workers who are disadvantaged and/or are located in disadvantaged census tracts.

In the Richmond set-aside case, Justice Scalia noted that states could "adopt a preference for small businesses, or even for new businesses—which would make it easier for those previously excluded by discrimination to enter the field. Such programs may well have a racially disproportionate impact, but they are not based on race." Justice O'Connor spoke even more broadly about taking race-neutral steps to address the barriers to many small and minority-owned businesses. "Simplification of bidding procedures, relaxation of bonding requirements, and training and financial aid for disadvantaged entrepreneurs of all races," she wrote, "would open the public contracting market to all those who have suffered the effects of past societal discrimination or neglect."[26]

Many federal programs already give a preference to small businesses, and even those programs that are in practice race-based (such as the section 8[a] set-aside program) use disadvantaged status as a criterion. To the extent that the racial component of preferences for companies owned by "socially and economically disadvantaged" individuals should drop away after *Adarand*, programs to help small struggling businesses will remain. For example, before the *Adarand* decision, the FCC had proposed providing a 25 percent discount for wireless communication licenses to women and minority-headed companies with $40 million or less in revenue. After *Adarand*, the FCC proposed that all small businesses with revenues below $40 million receive a 25 percent bidding credit.[27] Likewise, shortly after the District of Columbia's racial set-aside program was struck down as unconstitutional, the District government established a 50 percent set-aside for local small businesses owned by disadvantaged people of all races.[28]

Alternatively, programs can look at a business's location or employees. In 1980 Mayor Edward Koch instituted an affirmative action program in New York City based on economic deprivation rather than race or ethnicity. The program established a 10 percent subcontracting set-aside to small firms (those with annual gross receipts of less than $500,000 or $1.5 million for heavy construction) located in New York City that did at least 25 percent of their business in depressed areas or employed—as at least 25 percent of their workforce—economically disadvantaged workers. Depressed areas were defined as economically deprived by census tracts, and economically disadvantaged workers were legally defined as the hard-core unemployed (out of work for forty weeks or more). Bonding requirements were waived for certified subcontractors, and the city offered technical assistance and working capital loan guarantees as well. The program disproportionately helped women and people of color. Although Koch's successor, David Dinkins, abolished the program in favor of a more traditional set-aside scheme, the Koch plan has served as a model for cities that have seen their own racial set-aside programs struck down in the courts under *Croson*.[29]

In a similar vein, Philadelphia Mayor Edward G. Rendell has proposed that 15 percent of federal contracts be set aside in a race-neutral manner to distressed urban areas.[30] In 1995 President Clinton proposed supplementing race and gender construction set-asides with a set-aside for employers who locate in "distressed areas" or employ a large percentage of workers from such areas.[31] And Republican Senator Christopher Bond has called for set-asides for historically underutilized business zones (HUBZones) to funnel contracts to business in communities with low incomes and high unemployment.[32]

DEFINING CLASS

How should class be defined? The classic Marxist definition of class divides those who own the means of production from those who do not,[33] but that definition is obviously unhelpful, since, according to Lawrence Mishel of the Economic Policy Institute, only 1 percent of American households receive more than half their income from capital.[34] In an early study of social mobility, Harvard's Seymour Martin Lipset defined class in terms of manual versus nonmanual occupations, and others have looked at blue-collar versus white-collar occupations; those definitions, however, are becoming obsolete. The child of a middle-income steelworker may be more advantaged than the child of a single-parent bank teller. If our concern is with what Max Weber called one's "life chances,"[35] we want to define those obstacles that will help us find the diamonds in the rough, those people who have extraordinary natural talent and a strong drive but whose full potential is obscured by traditional meritocratic criteria.

There are three basic ways to proceed: with a simple, moderately sophisticated, or sophisticated definition. The simple method is to ask college or entry-level employment applicants their family's income and to measure disadvantage by that factor alone, on the theory that income is a good proxy for a host of economic disadvantages (such as bad schools or a difficult learning environment). The second way to proceed, using the moderately sophisticated calculus of class, would look at what sociologists believe to be the big three determinants of life chances: parental income, education, and occupation. The third alternative, using the sophisticated calculus of disadvantage, would count these three factors plus such factors as net worth, the quality of secondary education, neighborhood influences, and family structure. Later in this chapter, we will consider which type of definition makes the most sense in which contexts, but for now we will explore how one could objectively measure each factor in a verifiable manner.

Simple Definition of Class
The simple definition of class—looking only at family income—can be implemented simply by looking at tax returns. Bard Col-

lege, for example, makes eligibility for its class-based Higher Education Opportunity Program contingent upon a notarized copy of IRS form 1040 or letters from a social service agency detailing an applicant's family income. Income figures can be adjusted to factor in family size using a formula readily available from existing antipoverty programs.[36] In addition, where a national pool of applicants is considered, income adjustments could be made to reflect large regional differences in cost of living.[37] Again, we already have a federal formula worked out on this issue as a result of the Federal Employees Pay Comparability Act.[38] Those who for privacy reasons object to disclosing family income would not be forced to do so but would forgo the chance of receiving a class preference.[39]

The Moderately Sophisticated Definition of Class

A second definition of class would consider what sociologists consider the three main determinants of socioeconomic status (and what educators consider the key factors in a child's academic achievement): the income, education, and occupation of the parents.[40] This moderately complex definition of class is currently employed by Berkeley.[41]

Parents' Education Parents' education is highly correlated with academic achievement and life chances. In fact, some studies suggest that a parent's educational level is a better predictor of a child's educational attainment than parental income.[42] (A private school teacher with a master's degree may make less than a unionized sanitation worker but provide her child with greater educational advantages.) At Berkeley, for example, 68 percent of fathers of the 1987 freshmen class had completed college, compared with 27 percent of fathers of similar age statewide. While 56 percent of Berkeley freshman had mothers who attended college, the statewide figure was 14 percent.[43] The most straightforward way to measure parents' education is by number of years of schooling, though there are also ways to grossly evaluate the relative quality of university educations at various institutions.[44] Berkeley divides students between those whose parents received a four-year college degree and those whose parents did not.[45]

Parents' Occupation Parental occupation is another important determinant of a child's success. For example, a father's occupational status is a better predictor of his son's occupational status than the father's wealth.[46] Occupation is a good predictor partly because it is closely tied to both education and income.[47] Some say that occupation has an independent impact on a child's life chances above and beyond education and income.[48] Whether or not this is true, there is an argument for counting occupation as a good check against fraud in the reporting of income and education.

For many years, occupation was designated by the father, but today it would be assigned to the "higher ranking" of the parents (or the average of the two). By considering occupation, we account for the fact that, even within the same family income group, a child growing up in a family where the father is an attorney earning $60,000 a year and the mother is home with the children is more advantaged than the child in a family where the father earns $40,000 a year as a steelworker and the mother $20,000 a year as a secretary.

On the surface, this category would seem to open up a hornet's nest administratively. Skeptics would say it is impossible to determine which parental jobs give children an advantage and which do not. But it is clear that certain distinctions are widely agreed upon in the job market: salaried employee versus wage earner, mental versus physical labor, autonomous and self-directing managers and professionals versus those who receive commands and punch a time clock.[49] It is clear that different jobs have more or less power, more or less compensation, and more or less autonomy. They have greater or lesser societal importance (function) and require greater or lesser talent or training (scarcity).[50]

In fact, various attempts to objectively rank occupations have been remarkably consistent over time. Because adult children rarely remember their parents' income, the mobility studies of sociologists normally focus on the parents' occupation. Over the years sociologists have come up with rather elaborate rankings of occupational status; by necessity, they are actually quite good.[51]

In the early 1920s, F. E. Barr compiled the Barr Scale of 120 occupations, ranked 0 to 100 by a team of judges, based on the degree of intelligence required to perform the job. Several decades later, Otis Duncan provided the Index of Occupations, based on the 1960 census, providing scores of 0 to 96 based on income and educational levels for each occupation.[52] In addition, the National Opinion Research Center (NORC) polled typical Americans in 1947 and 1963 on the relative occupational prestige of a number of professions. From these various sets of data, the correlation is almost perfect, and the pecking order unambiguous.[53]

The NORC found that opinions about the relative standing of occupations were the same in 1963 as they were in 1947 and 1925. "Whereas they had expected to see significant shifts in the relative prestige given various jobs," wrote the sociologists Richard Sennett and Jonathan Cobb, "they found instead that over the course of two generations, despite a major depression and substantial changes in the occupational structure, Americans retained a relatively stable picture of what constitutes more prestigious and less prestigious work." In fact, Sennett and Cobb argue, the hierarchy of occupational roles today is roughly consistent with the analogous hierarchy in an ancient myth of Purusha from India, upon which that society's caste system is built.[54] The sociologist Donald Trieman's cross-cultural study of sixty societies found a "remarkably high" correlation (0.8) in relative occupational prestige across all pairs of countries.[55]

Likewise, the federal government has no problems classifying civil service jobs clearly in grades 1–18,[56] nor the Census Bureau in establishing various occupational groupings.[57] The bureau's rankings, devised in the 1940s by Dr. Alba M. Edwards, factor in "the nature of the work, the skill and training involved in it, the income it brought, and common opinion about its prestige." Edwards's basic scheme is still used today.[58] The Department of Labor, too, has an elaborate occupational code, which reflects relative status.[59]

There are then, a range of options on how to rank occupations. Broader categories are easier to administer; finer categories strive for greater fairness. Something in the middle, such as that employed by Berkeley, probably makes sense.[60]

The Sophisticated Definition of Class

The sophisticated definition of class would include not only income, education, and occupation but also factors such as wealth, schooling opportunities, neighborhood influences, and family structure.

Wealth While wealth normally correlates with income, inquiring about net worth helps fill out the "snapshot" picture provided by income in a given year. On the high end, one can imagine the wealthy entrepreneur who happens to take a year off to travel as his son applies to college, placing his assets into capital growth funds with very little income. On the low end, looking at assets can be a rough proxy for whether a child once suffered living in poverty—and for how long. Whereas some 20 percent of children may be poor in a given year, nearly 50 percent experience some poverty in their first eighteen years.[61] A child might have lived in poverty for seventeen years, although her mother's job now places her in the middle class. Net worth, which by definition accumulates over many years, helps capture this phenomenon. In addition, as William Coleman has noted (see chapter 1), African Americans have lower net worths than whites of the same income group, in part because of residential discrimination; including wealth in our calculus helps reflect that legacy as well. And for financial aid in college admissions, net worth is already disclosed.[62]

Schooling Opportunities There is broad empirical evidence that the quality of a child's primary and secondary schooling, including the quality of his fellow students, has a major impact on his life chances. While family background is extremely important to academic success, high concentration of poverty in a school is a serious obstacle above and beyond hailing from a poor family. We know that poor children start off behind in first grade. Students in high poverty schools (76–100 percent poor) score in the 33rd percentile on reading tests, while students in low poverty schools (0–19 percent poor) score in the 60th percentile, according to the Department of Education's National Assessment of Educational Progress. By the eighth grade, however, the gap has widened to 22nd percentile for poor, and 65th percentile for rich. The same pattern holds for math.[63] The data also show that poor children in schools with high concentrations of poverty are three times *more likely* to score in the *bottom* 10 percent nationally as poor children in schools with low poverty concentrations. Meanwhile, poor children in the high-poverty concentration schools are two times *less likely* to score in the *top* half as poor children in low-poverty schools.[64] What is truly striking, however, is that nonpoor students attending schools with high concentrations of poverty perform, on average, less well than poor children attending nonpoor schools.[65]

While it may seem impossible to rank schools by "quality," admissions officers at selective colleges have detailed knowledge about various high schools; today, however, it is precisely that knowledge of disadvantaged high schools that makes their graduates less, not more, likely to be admitted.[66] As Dinesh D'Souza points out, putting school atmosphere into the mix "might seem an extraordinarily complex calculus," but "colleges already have access to, and in many cases use, this data."[67] To objectively quantify school quality, a calculus could consider readily available figures such as the percentage of students at each school who receive free or reduced-price lunches, median test scores on standardized tests, and per pupil expenditure. Berkeley is considering giving special consideration to students from high schools with low graduation rates.[68]

Neighborhood Influence A number of studies have found that living in certain low-income communities can have a negative impact on an individual's life chances—increasing the likelihood, for instance, of dropping out of school or having an out-of-wedlock child—even when controlling for class.[69] This is an additional burden that the underclass—those 6 percent of the poor living in highly concentrated poverty—face over those who are merely poor.[70] One study in Chicago suggests that poor black students whose families reside in middle-class black or white suburban neighborhoods have a higher high school graduation rate than those left behind (95 percent versus 80 percent) and are more likely to go on to college (54 percent versus 21 percent.)[71] As with other criteria, there is some scholarly debate over the degree to which concentration of poverty and neighborhood influences affect life chances.[72] But the bulk of the evidence seems to support William Julius Wilson's thesis that neighborhood matters, and in any event, the debate impacts how to weigh this factor in a definition of "class" more than about whether to count it in the first place.[73]

There are many ways to objectively measure neighborhood influence. The percentage of households living in poverty is the most common, but other possible indicators include median family income, male unemployment rate, and percentage of female-headed households, by zip code or census tract.[74] Others have suggested looking at the crime rate in an area as a factor indicating disadvantage.[75] One federal proposal to provide regulatory relief for distressed communities extends benefits to census tracts in which more than 33 percent of the population lives in poverty, 45 percent or more of out-of-school males work less than twenty-six weeks in a year, 36 percent or more of families with children are headed by a single parent, or 17 percent or more of residents receive public assistance.[76]

Family Structure The final factor to consider, family structure, primarily refers to the absence or presence of two parents but might also refer to a parent's age. Growing up in a single-parent family obviously has a generally negative impact on family income, since families headed by single mothers are six times as likely to be in poverty than all other American families.[77] But as Moynihan noted in 1965, the tested IQ of children is lower when the father is absent, even after you control for class.[78] More recently, Sara McLanahan and Gary Sandefur, in their book *Growing up with a Single Parent*, conclude that "children who grow up in a household with one biological parent are worse off, on average, than children who grow up in a household with both of their biological parents," not only because they have less income but because, even controlling for income, "adolescents who have lived apart from one of their parents during some period of childhood are twice as likely to have a child before age twenty, and one and a half times as likely to be 'idle'—out of school and out of work—in their late teens and early twenties."[79]

For a long time, discussion of the subject was taboo, but today everyone from former Vice President Dan Quayle to Secretary of HHS Donna Shalala agrees that children who live with two parents have a better chance of making it in our society.[80] As the columnist E. J. Dionne, Jr., explains, "This ought not be a complicated proposition. The fact is that raising children is an immensely time-consuming endeavor. Single parents have a tougher time of it than married parents do, in large part because one person has exactly half the potential time available that two people do." But there is a second effect when a parent leaves rather than dies. "Psychologically, a kid is obviously better off knowing that he or she is important enough that both a father and a mother are willing to be there. What happens to your sense of self-worth if your father simply disappears?"[81]

One problem with employing this criterion is that individual family structures are constantly changing. A child born out of wedlock may later be legitimated, while intact marriages undergo separations and divorces; spouses may remarry or be widowed. Today half of all American children will spend some time in a single-parent home before the age of eighteen, though at any one time the figure is 30 percent.[82] (Some 85 percent of the students at Washington's elite prep school Maret are children of divorce.)[83] Ideally, we want to know how long a child lived with one parent. Short of that, the line could be drawn between those children living with one parent whose parent never married (50 percent) and those who are children of divorce (50 percent); the former are more disadvantaged.[84] In addition, there is an argument for factoring in the age of a child's parents, since there is a disadvantage to being born to a mother who is still a minor.

Some will find the notion of rewarding out-of-wedlock birth, divorce, or teenage childbirth abhorrent.[85] But recall that the preference goes not to the parent but to the illegitimate child, who has faced an impediment not faced by the legitimate child and whose status as illegitimate is not of her own making. (If the child herself has an out-of-wedlock birth, she receives no additional preference and is less likely to be in a position to win a coveted job or university slot, competing as she is with other illegitimate children who have not given birth out of wedlock.) And it is absurd to say that preferences for the child will somehow provide an incentive for mothers to have out-of-wedlock births. A pregnant teenager bringing a child into the world without a husband is unlikely to be thinking hard about maximizing her child's life chances, much less about the possibility that, eighteen years down the line, her offspring could have a small edge at getting into Harvard.

Of the three definitions, the sophisticated one is the fairest and should be employed whenever practical—certainly by university admissions officers, who already have access to a wealth of information. The more factors that are included, the less likely it is that an applicant will successfully manipulate the system or commit outright fraud, since the factors interrelate: fudging in one area will stick out in another. In entry-level employment, by contrast, a simpler definition of class may suffice, since employers do not have access to the same data as universities and parental income (or occupation) is a fairly good proxy for many of the factors in the sophisticated definition. (If a job applicant's parents are poor, it is more likely that they also will have little education and low-status occupations and will live in neighborhoods with bad influences and bad schools.)[86]

A seven-part test of disadvantage will inevitably be ridiculed by those who favor inaction. You cannot assign a number to disadvantage, it will be said. At some philosophical level, this is surely true, but neither can you put a number on intelligence or intellectual promise, and yet universities do that every year when they come up with index scores based, for example, on GPA and LSATs. Some critics always greet new proposals for social progress as "Orwellian." Consider social security: "You mean you're going to give every man, woman, and child in the United States a social security number? And keep track of how much they put into the system as they switch employers over an entire lifetime? Even though computers haven't been invented yet? Are you crazy?" Or consider college financial aid: "You mean you are going to ask every applicant filing for aid to state their parents' income and assets?" Or, indeed, affirmative action: "You are going to ask every employer to report the ethnicity of each and every worker? What about when their ethnicity is unclear? What if a company has forty thousand employees?" Indeed, what is truly Orwellian is to do what we do today—have a teenager take a three-hour standardized test and then have that number stick with them, without controlling for disadvantage. Adding a number for disadvantage to the calculus just makes deciding who gets ahead and who does not a little fairer.

Proponents of affirmative action need to be especially chary of arguing the inadministrability of class preferences since similar "good in theory but not in practice" arguments apply with full force to race-based affirmative action.[87] And while it is often assumed that class-based affirmative action is more difficult to administer than a program based on race, there is nothing inherently harder about the first than the second.[88] Race seems simpler only because we have avoided a number of ambiguities.

While class preferences involve the tricky question of establishing who should qualify for preferences, race-based programs face the question of which groups should be protected. Most programs benefit blacks, Hispanics, Asians, and Native Americans, but claims have been made by Arab, Italian, Polish, and Cajun Americans as well.[89] Even if an institution can agree on the broad list of minorities who should benefit, there is the thorny question of subgroups. The broad administrative categories employed in the past do not work very well anymore. For instance, "Hispanics"—a construct that exists nowhere in the world but the United States[90]—includes not only Mexican Americans and Puerto Ricans, whose peoples were conquered, but also groups like Nicaraguans, who, notes Nathan Glazer, "were neither conquered by the United States nor subjected to special legislation."[91] Worse, the category includes immigrants from Spain, whose ancestors, Richard Cohen notes, "colonized most of the New World, oppressing, enslaving, exploiting and often eradicating the people they encountered."[92] Among Asian Americans, should East Indians count? Should Filipinos be treated differently from other Asians?[93] Even among blacks, there is contention over whether West Indians and Caribbeans should count.[94] Many of these subcategories make a great deal of sense and their recognition makes programs more fair, but each subdivision makes administration of race-based programs more difficult.[95]

And while most affirmative action programs to date have ignored the question of immigration, as more slots meant to remedy past discrimination go to those never subjected to discrimination in this country, the pressure will intensify to require beneficiaries to document place of birth—or their ancestors' place of birth—further complicating administration of race-based preferences.[96] Likewise, to be fair, some argue that we should calibrate preferences so that blacks would receive a greater preference than Hispanics and Asians.[97] Finally, there is the unpleasant task of deciding which individuals can properly claim to be a member of the preferred minorities.[98] According to a study by the National Center for Health Statistics, nearly one-third of people who called themselves Asians were identified by independent observers as black or white; 70 percent of American Indians were so identified; and 5.8 percent of those who self-identified as black were categorized as white by a census observer. Another study, by the Centers for Disease Control and Prevention, found that an "astounding number" of infants who died had different races designated on their birth and death certificates.[99]

Determining who is Hispanic, critics argue, is even more difficult and has given the Census Bureau fits for years. Defining Hispanics as those who speak Spanish pulls in people who may not be of Latin origin, whereas defining them as those with Spanish surnames, the preferred method, mistakenly pulls in (a) non-Hispanic white women married to Hispanics and (b) recent immigrants from Spain, and excludes (a) Hispanic women who marry Anglos and take their husband's last names, (b) Hispanics who have Anglicized their names, and (c) children of Hispanic mothers and non-Hispanic fathers.[100]

Cases of outright ethnic fraud are not unknown and require extensive evidence to adjudicate.[101] But beyond these fairly rare cases, there is a very real and growing question of how we should treat a new category of people who consider themselves "multiracial."[102] For purposes of compensatory justice, when whites marry people of color, the legacy of discrimination is only half as strong.[103]

In the end, proponents of affirmative action should be wary of using the argument of complexity against class preferences. Racial preferences are just as easy to ridicule. To paraphrase Kinsley, does a new Indian immigrant get fewer or more points than a third-generation Latino whose mother is Anglo?

At bottom, questions of administration can be aimed at any number of existing programs, including student loans, food stamps, social security—and race-based affirmative action. Not only is it possible to come up with an objective list of verifiable criteria that can measure disadvantage, but we shall see in chapter 6, it is actually in the interests of African Americans to push for the most complex definition.

Finally, even if sorting by race were much easier than looking at individual disadvantage, that fact should not be dispositive. As Justice Douglas noted in the *DeFunis* case: "We have never held administrative convenience to justify racial discrimination."[104] It may appear somewhat easier for an admissions committee to sort by race rather than class, but as Temple University President Peter Liacouras asks: "What part of a faculty or administrative member's work is as socially important as to decide fairly who will share in the American Dream?"[105]

WHAT CUTOFF?

What should be the cutoff for beneficiaries? Should only the underclass benefit, all the poor, or working-class teenagers, too? Indeed, should the upper-middle class benefit vis-à-vis the rich? Should the cutoff point depend on the context?

Taking the last question first, it clearly makes sense to provide a relative cutoff depending on the context. The poverty line is an *absolute* standard (the cost of feeding a family multiplied by three).[106] But since our concern here is with providing genuine equal opportunity in life's race, the goal is to correct for *relative* inequality of opportunity. A relative standard is also more easily applied across different contexts than an absolute standard. Applicants to elite colleges may be predominantly wealthy and upper-middle-class, in which context a working-class applicant is relatively disadvantaged. As a practical matter, in the context of higher education it may be impossible to find enough students in abject poverty who, even with a remedial program, will be capable of doing the work. At Berkeley, for example, students who met the strict requirements of the Educational Opportunity Program—neither parent attended a four-year college, and parents could not afford to pay more than $1,000 in educational expenses—often did not have grades and board scores indicating any likelihood of success. Accordingly, Berkeley determined that its socioeconomic measure of disadvantage had to be broader: it needed to define "socioeconomic disadvantage in the Berkeley context" differently.[107] A two-tier system was established, with a sizable preference for students from families of four with income below approximately $23,000 and a smaller preference for students with family income between $23,000 and $33,000 (the state median).[108] By contrast, a metropolitan police force may recruit primarily from working-class communities, in which case the preference should go only to those from poor families, who lack comparative equality of opportunity.

What should be the relative cutoff for beneficiaries? At one extreme would be a finely tuned, elaborate, sliding scale system in which one receives preferences based on one's percentile ranking in socioeconomic status, so that even an individual in the 98th percentile would receive a preference, albeit a slight one, over someone in the 99th percentile. At the other extreme would be a system in which only those so disadvantaged as to come from the bottom 5 percent of applicants could benefit. What are the arguments for pushing in either direction? As a matter of fairness, a system providing preferences at the 98th percentile overstates the impact of social position on opportunity, since gross social inequality—between the wealthy and the poor—is most reliably a cause of unequal opportunity. Strictly speaking, upper-middle-class children may as a group lack the advantages of the rich, but the degree may be too small to comfortably generalize about it. To calibrate down to the percentile—in effect, "class norming" the SAT in college admissions—suggests an exactness to the science of sociology that is insupportable.

On the other hand, there are two powerful reasons to include others besides those at the very bottom of society in a preference program. First, the injuries of class extend beyond the very poorest. The offspring of the working poor and the working class lack advantages, too, and indeed, SAT scores correlate lockstep with income at every increment. Allan Nairn, author of a study on the Educational Testing Service, notes:

> It is not simply a matter of penthouse versus tenement. The ETS score discriminates not only between the rich and a *minority* of Americans (the very poor) but also between the rich and a *majority* of Americans (the members of the working and middle classes). The SAT discriminates among virtually all levels of the country's class structure—across both income and occupation. The more money a person's family makes, the higher that person tends to score; people from homes with $21,000 incomes tend to score higher than people from homes with $18,000 incomes; people from white collar homes tend to score higher than people from blue collar homes.[109]

Likewise, social mobility studies find that the rich have enormous advantages over the middle class, and that children born to the top 5 percent are some twenty times more likely to be wealthy than children born at the median income.[110] These statistics suggest that unfairness is not confined to the underclass.

Second, as a political matter, it is axiomatic that a program aimed only at the very poor, while perhaps more politically viable than a race-specific program, is less viable than programs with a broader base of beneficiaries. After analyzing the history of social programs in the United States, Harvard Professor Theda Skocpol came to three conclusions:

> First, when U.S. antipoverty efforts have featured policies targeted on the poor alone, they have not been politically sustainable, and they have stigmatized and demeaned the poor. Second, some kinds of relatively universal social policies have been politically very successful. Third, room has

been made within certain universal policy frameworks for extra benefits and services that disproportionately help less privileged people without stigmatizing them. What I shall call "targeting within universalism" has delivered extra benefits and special services to certain poor people throughout the history of modern American social provision, and new versions of it could be devised today to revitalize and redirect U.S. public social provision.[111]

While Skocpol's thesis has been criticized by those who point out that universal programs are more expensive than targeted ones, that criticism applies with less force to preferences; broadening the group of beneficiaries makes good political sense.[112]

A middle ground would be to provide a substantial preference to those at one-half the median socioeconomic status in the applicant pool and below, and a smaller preference to those between one-half the median and the median itself. The one-half the median guideline, a well-established measure of disadvantage, has been embraced by, among others, the philosopher John Rawls. In defining "the least fortunate group," Rawls says the one-half-median mark (of wealth and income), though arbitrary, "has the merit of focusing attention on the social distance between those who have least and the average citizen."[113] Measuring deprivation in terms of half the average or mean income is also generally accepted by economists and laypeople alike, Arthur Okun notes.[114] Polls have shown that for decades Americans have defined poverty as half the average income—irrespective of what the average income is.[115]

In addition, a smaller preference should go to those from lower-middle-income families. One federal program now provides a two-tiered preference, with one preference for very low-income (below 50 percent of the median) and another preference for low-income (between 50 percent and 80 percent of the median).[116] Providing a moderate preference for those whose incomes are up to, say, 100 percent, or even 80 percent, of the median will strike many readers as too generous. But in 1994 median family income was just $32,264.[117] Consider the reaction of the labor lawyer Thomas Geoghegan to a similar figure in 1986:

In fact, I have no idea how anyone else lives, how the bottom four-fifths of the country gets along. When I hear that the median family income in America is $29,000 a year (in 1986), I take out my passport and wonder what country I have wandered into. Did you know that? $29,000 a year? That means the income of roughly half the families in America is below that. Why isn't this fact on the front page of *The New York Times* every day? Imagine what it would be like on $29,000 a year, or less, just you and your family of four—with both you and your spouse working?[118]

Families living below the median share in only 20 percent of the nation's income.[119] And before becoming too concerned about giving a break to a student at the 49th class percentile, consider that, in 1991, 60 percent of American households did not buy a single book all year, and only 2 percent bought "serious" books.[120] Consider that 75 percent of American workers have not completed college, and that 93 percent have no more than two years of schooling beyond a bachelor's degree.[121]

There is nothing sacred about providing special benefits only to those below the poverty line. The Earned Income Tax Credit (EITC), which has broad public support, provides working families with tax relief up to $26,673 and is slated to cover 45.1 percent of families in Mississippi and 42.3 percent of families in Washington, D.C., in 1996.[122] Likewise, when health care was debated in 1994, a group of Senate moderates, dubbed the "mainstream" coalition, supported health care subsidies for families earning up to 240 percent of the poverty line.[123] In 1994 that figure translated into benefits for a family of four earning $36,338—a figure higher than the national median.[124]

Note that failure to provide some degree of preference up to the median will mean that those between one-half the median and the median itself are likely to be the ones who will lose out when the poor are preferred. The poor will receive a break; the middle and upper classes will continue to enjoy advantages; and the lower-middle class will be squeezed. Note also that a sliding scale may be implemented in the class context with much greater ease than in a race system. While it is difficult to calibrate the difference between discrimination against African Americans and against Asians, socioeconomic status, which falls neatly on a continuum, does not present this same challenge.

IMPLEMENTATION

How would a class-based affirmative action program be implemented? Would it be voluntary or mandatory? Would it apply to the public sector only, the private sector as well, or some hybrid? The basic legal framework in which race-based affirmative action is today grounded provides a good starting place for the implementation of class-based preferences. The underlying philosophy is that those in the private sector (universities and employers) should not be required to provide preferences, but that those who choose to receive federal funding and to make contracts with the federal government are rightly held to a higher standard. In addition, indirect incentives will encourage private employers to consider class preferences as a way of complying with the racial balancing requirements of the Civil Rights Act of 1991.

Federal Government
The federal government should take the lead by providing preferences in its own entry-level employment to disadvantaged applicants who are qualified. Federal managers would be required to set goals for entry-level hiring and to have a strong justification for failing to meet those goals. Preferences would not be employed for promotions, since the idea is to provide disadvantaged young people with a chance to prove themselves, not to promote preferences as a way of life.

Recipients of Federal Aid
Those institutions receiving federal aid could, as a condition of receipt of that aid, be required to provide reasonable class-based preferences in entry-level employment and education. This mechanism would bring under the program almost all universities and state and local governments. The program would require not only entry-level employment preferences but also the kind of educational preferences discussed earlier: preferences in tracking

in primary and secondary education, and preferences in university admissions. Those institutions not wishing to employ preferences would not be forced to but would forfeit federal aid.[125]

Some argue that at the university level we should rely on voluntary preferences, since dictating university admissions might pose a threat to academic freedom. But we have already crossed that bridge. Title VI of the Civil Rights Act already prohibits universities that receive federal funds from discriminating against racial minorities.[126] Likewise, the Civil Rights Act's employment discrimination requirements, which initially exempted universities, now apply to them, arguments of "academic freedom" notwithstanding.[127] Universities that feel strongly about not giving a break to poor and working-class students, or that wish to discriminate based on race, would be free to do so, but the federal government need not subsidize those decisions.

Requiring class preferences also appears necessary because most universities are unlikely to provide them on their own. While some universities purport to count disadvantage informally as a plus in admissions (Harvard, in the *Bakke* case, said it preferred "disadvantaged economic, racial and ethnic groups,"[128] and New York University Law School includes in its "diversity considerations" a category for "socioeconomic conditions"[129]), it is clear that the class preference most universities employ today is for the wealthy.

Researchers have found that advantaged private school students have "a significant edge in admissions" at Ivy League and other prestigious colleges over public school students with the same SAT scores. Indeed, one study comparing a leading selective public high school with sixteen elite boarding schools found that students at the boarding schools were twice as likely to get into Harvard, Yale, and Princeton even though their SAT scores averaged 150 points *below* those of students at the public high school.[130] We have already discussed the enormous affirmative action programs for alumni children, but it is significant to note that those legacies who do not apply for financial aid have a higher rate of acceptance at Harvard than those legacies who do.[131]

In the Harvard class of 1975, for which data are public, no preference was given for disadvantaged students, but being an alumni child boosted an applicant's chances of acceptance by 33 percent, and being from a private school boosted chances by 10 percent—holding grades and test scores constant.[132] Other schools varied in their approach to disadvantage: at Williams and Colgate, disadvantage slightly improved an applicant's chances of being admitted, while at Bucknell it hurt slightly, but in all cases racial and alumni preferences were far more important.[133]

If universities were employing aggressive class preferences today, on the theory that poor and working-class students add diversity or show greater potential than advantaged students with the same scores, disadvantaged students would have a higher rate of acceptance when test scores are controlled. In fact, the opposite occurs.[134] James C. Hearn found that 35 percent of the exceptionally able high-income students ($38,000 or more) attended highly selective colleges, while only 10 percent of exceptionally able lower-income students ($16,000 or less) attended a highly selective college.[135] Overall, in 1986, when the national median family income was $28,000, only one in twelve students at highly selective private colleges came from families with incomes below $20,000. By contrast, while only 20 percent of American families made above $50,000, more than 60 percent of the families of the elite freshmen did.[136]

Part of the problem may be latent class prejudice.[137] But the main reason universities fail to give preferences to the poor and, indeed, give hefty preferences to the rich has to do with financial considerations. Government grants and loans rarely make up the entire shortfall at expensive private schools (or even at some public schools); the schools must therefore make up the difference.[138] And the problem is likely to get worse as more and more colleges, like Brown University in the early 1990s, abandon "need-blind" admissions. By 1994 there were reportedly fewer than twenty schools that still admitted students without regard to ability to pay.[139]

Even racial preference programs fail to add much economic diversity. All the incentives point in one direction: a college scores as many diversity points for admitting advantaged people of color as for admitting less advantaged minorities, and in doing so they also avoid the financial costs of providing aid. Universities gain no similar cachet for admitting poor and working-class white students, and since any preference means lower SAT medians (and lower prestige), schools understandably shy away from highly expensive preferences for poor students.[140]

If universities are required to provide class-based preferences, they will obviously want to negotiate to have the federal government pick up part of the tab for remedial education and financial aid for the increased number of poor and working-class students. In this way, the cost of eliminating racial preferences would be increased funding of higher education, to the benefit of poor and working-class people of all races.

Federal Contractors

Private companies doing business with the federal government (or at least those with $50,000 in contracts or more than fifty employees) could be required to use class preferences in filling entry-level positions, just as such companies are currently required to use racial preferences.[141] The existing affirmative action provisions, outlined in executive order 11246 and revised order 4, cover some 42 percent of the private workforce in this way.[142] As with the current program, companies that do not reach their hiring goals would risk losing federal contracts.[143] Again, to help share the cost of providing preferences, federal contractors may wish to negotiate from the government more generous grants for any extra remedial training necessary for disadvantaged entry-level hires.[144] In addition, to shift some of the burden of administration to the government, employers may wish to push for a program under which a student graduating from high school who wishes to benefit from a class preference would fill out a standard form providing readily accessible data: her high school, her place of residence, family structure, and parents' income. A family tax return, providing much of this information, could be attached. Net worth would not be requested. Those who are concerned about privacy would not be required to complete the form but would lose the opportunity to qualify for a preference.

Private Institutions That Do Not Receive Federal Aid or Make Federal Contracts

In the purely private sector—companies that do not do business with the federal government—current racial affirmative action requirements generally do not apply, and indeed, Title VII specifically says preferences are not required under the act (except when preferences are ordered as a remedy for proven past discrimination by an employer). However, all employers with over fifteen employees (a definition that covers 86 percent of the non-farm private-sector workforce)[145] are required to justify racial imbalances under the *Griggs* disparate impact analysis. Under current law, many employers choose not to defend hiring practices that result in a racially imbalanced workforce and instead use preferences to make sure their numbers work out. The Supreme Court provided some support for this general practice in the 1979 case of *United Steelworkers of America v. Weber*. But if *Weber* is overturned by the Court—or if voluntary racial preferences are outlawed—some employers might find an incentive to use nonracial class preferences, which disproportionately benefit minorities, as a way of avoiding disparate impact litigation. Under this plan, *Griggs* itself would not be repealed,[146] so the pressure for class preferences would be indirect, since a business necessity defense would still work to explain disparities. But those employers who today use racial preferences to avoid lawsuits but find they are no longer able to do so legally might very well turn to class preferences.[147]

HOW SUBSTANTIAL SHOULD PREFERENCES BE?

How much of a preference should disadvantaged applicants receive? Under a voluntary "class plus" system, how large should the plus be? Under a government system of goals, what is a reasonable target? If a college or government employer misses its target, what gap in traditional criteria is a reasonable excuse?

At the one extreme, we can imagine a quite aggressive preference system under which all economic groups in the general population—or at least the applicant pool—must be proportionately represented at a university or in an employer's entry-level workforce so long as all those admitted or hired are minimally qualified to do the work. There would be debate over what "minimally qualified" means, but most universities now have a fairly good idea of how far down they can reach before the chances of failure grow too high.

At the other extreme, we can imagine a very minor preference that would correct merely for the degree (if at all) to which grades and board scores underpredict students' actual first-year grades. If after a year the preferred group has a median first-year GPA below the median of the nonpreferred, we would say that the preference was too large and should be adjusted.

Again, a middle ground between the extremes seems most appropriate. If the goal is to give a chance to those who have the greatest long-run potential, in practice the preferences need to be larger than a mere correction for underprediction of first-year grades. Eighteen years of poor preparation will not be made up overnight. As Justice Douglas argued in regard to a law student admitted on a class preference, the applicant "may not realize his full potential in the first year of law school or in the full three years, but in the long pull of a legal career, his achievements may far outstrip those of his classmates whose earlier records appeared superior by conventional criteria."[148]

Indeed, there is debate over whether scores actually underpredict the performance of the poor (as measured by first-year grades) at all. The National Academy of Sciences says the scores are a pretty good predictor across class lines, while others say it is obvious that those who can afford coaching will perform less well in college than their artificially high scores suggest.[149] In his 1978 annual report, Harvard Dean Henry Rosovsky said that "the correlation between test scores and social status is generally higher than the correlation between college performance and social status."[150]

On the other hand, class preferences will not be able to make up for the entire social deficit, and so proportional representation is too ambitious a goal. First, some naturally bright poor children may internalize certain values associated with the so-called culture of poverty (present-day orientation, weak work ethic, etc.). They may naturally be smart and may even work fairly hard compared with their peers, but to the extent that they apply themselves less than do their more advantaged peers their long-run potential is stunted. Second, there are limits to the usefulness of a preference for a naturally bright and personally driven child who has nevertheless had an abysmal education and is completely unprepared for rigorous study, since it is cruel to admit a child to an elite university who has no chance of succeeding. Admitting students who would be unlikely to perform adequately does no one any good.

Using this information, as well as input from universities and employers, reasonable goals should be set: short of proportional representation, but with greater representation than we see today. Universities that do not meet their goals would have to justify their failure to find qualified applicants. Putting some pressure on universities to increase their numbers should result in aggressive recruitment of qualified but disadvantaged students who now either do not attend college or attend institutions below their potential.[151] In addition, regulations could effectively require remedial programs by saying that failure to meet a goal is justified only if a remedial program was tried.

In education, carefully crafted remedial programs can be highly effective. At Georgia Tech, for example, the Challenge Program, a nonracial five-week program given prior to freshman year, has been extremely successful in boosting minority achievement. In 1992, 10 percent of African American and Hispanic students received a perfect 4.0 grade point average—double the proportion of whites.[152] The absolute number of blacks and Hispanics with 4.0 GPAs in 1992 exceeded the total number for the period 1980–90, before the remedial program was revamped to encourage higher expectations and to reach members of all races.

According to Professor Leslie Espinoza, intensive in-residence summer programs for law schools run by the Council on Legal Educational Opportunity (CLEO) produce graduation rates of almost 80 percent, a "remarkable" accomplishment "considering that most CLEO students would not have been admitted to law school without the program."[153] Some summer programs provide an opportunity for students to prove themselves, and strong performance is a condition of admissions.[154] Other summer programs, like those at Texas Tech University School of Law and Wayne State University Law School, allow minority students to take one or two first-year classes so that they will have a more manageable, reduced first-year course load when the other students arrive.[155]

In the employment arena, some job training programs have proven effective.[156] And while critics rightly point to the failure of many remedial education and training programs, some of those programs have not succeeded in large measure because the same critics have effectively starved them of funding.[157]

WHAT SHOULD HAPPEN TO RACE-BASED AFFIRMATIVE ACTION?

For the most part, class-based preferences are designed to supplant rather than supplement race-based preferences. Current antidiscriminatory protections, including the Civil Rights Act of 1991, would remain, and in fact, in forfeiting racial preferences, supporters of affirmative action should bargain for increased funding of antidiscriminatory enforcement. The trade would not have to happen all at once, and civil rights groups might negotiate a phaseout of race-based affirmative action over a certain number of years, combined with an assurance that class-based programs would be aggressively pursued.[158]

The end goal would be a world without racial preference, except in those limited instances when such preferences are justified as a narrow remedy to documented discrimination of the kind envisioned in *Croson* and *Adarand*. The new regime would effectively overturn *Bakke* (which legitimated racial preferences to achieve educational diversity);[159] *Weber* and *Johnson* (which legitimated voluntary racial preferences when past discrimination is presumed and has not been documented);[160] and executive order 11246 (which effectively requires mild preferences, even when no past discrimination has been documented.)[161] Though even those remedies meeting *Croson* and *Adarand* remain politically unpopular, they present the very strongest case for compensatory justice and, in practice, will occur only infrequently.[162]

But even in cases where the *Croson* test is met and racial preferences are justified, there are two ways in which such short-term preferences can be made more equitable. First, even corporations and universities that have discriminated and employ racial preferences will not be exempt from class-based affirmative action requirements, as they are today.[163] This policy would allow for compensation where there has been documented injury but would maximize the chances that compensatory race preferences will go to disadvantaged minorities, and that the cost will be borne by advantaged rather than poor whites.

Second, the burden of compensation should fall to the maximum extent possible on the wrongdoing employer rather than on innocent white employees, a goal that has generally been embraced by observers across the political spectrum but often ignored in practice.[164] By requiring findings of past discrimination, we have already eliminated the worst burden shifting—the *Weber* dodge, in which employers elude back-pay requirements by agreeing to give preferences prior to the finding of discrimination—and the "they told me to" defense of federal contractors who justify racial preferences as compliance with executive order 11246. In addition, when a court finds discrimination and orders promotions of minorities, the court can shift the burden of such programs from the passed-over white employee to the employer by requiring the employer to promote the minority candidate but pay the white employee the higher wage he would have received with the promotion.[165]

But it is important to keep the issue in perspective. The general rule will be class, not race. Except in those very rare instances where racial remedies meet the stringent requirements of *Croson*—in which case, the remedy is class plus race—class preferences alone will be the rule.

6. Six Myths About Class-Based Preferences

O
PPONENTS OF class-based preferences raise a number of objections to the program. Some of the criticisms are legitimate and thoughtful, but all are answerable. Some can be answered by referring to competing principles or values. Others can be addressed by structuring the class preference program in a certain way. In this chapter, we address six myths about class-based affirmative action: that shifting from race to class preferences will (1) eliminate a powerful antidiscriminatory tool; (2) lead to all-white universities; (3) spark Marxist class warfare; (4) undercut capitalist and pro-family incentives; (5) unfairly treat people as members of groups; and (6) fail because they address symptoms rather than root causes.

MYTH NO. 1: SHIFTING FROM RACE TO CLASS PREFERENCES REMOVES AN IMPORTANT TOOL TO COMBAT ONGOING RACIAL DISCRIMINATION

An increasing number of people argue that affirmative action is necessary, not to address the legacy of past discrimination, but as a prophylactic against more subtle forms of ongoing and future discrimination. Commerce Secretary Ron Brown, for example, argues that affirmative action "continues to be needed not to redress grievances of the past, but the current discrimination that continues to exist."[1] Northwestern's Christopher Jencks concurs that "the most plausible argument for reverse discrimination today is . . . that we need formal discrimination in favor of blacks to offset the effects of persistent informal discrimination against them."[2] President Clinton himself defended affirmative action on the grounds that "the evidence suggests, indeed screams, that . . . the job of ending discrimination in this country is not over."[3] They argue that because discrimination continues to exist, racial preference must continue to exist, and that anyone who favors ending preferences must believe that racism "is a thing of the past."

The logic is as faulty as it is common.[4] The notion of fighting discrimination with discrimination made sense only to the extent that the first discrimination occurred in the past and could not be corrected through prospective antidiscriminatory laws. It was the more complicated problem of remedying the present-day legacy of past discrimination that justified racial preference. It is only because discrimination in the past cannot be undone by prospective antidiscriminatory statutes that racial preferences are a reasonable option. Future discrimination—the potholes in Lyndon Johnson's racetrack—were under the jurisdiction of antidiscriminatory laws. Racial preferences were almost never meant to be a "backstop" to antidiscrimination laws to counteract current discrimination.[5] Even some of those who have made the new prophylactic argument concede that they have changed their tune.[6]

For one thing, if it is true that racial preferences are necessary to combat current discrimination because antidiscrimination laws are inherently ineffective, then racial preferences and race consciousness cease to be transitional. If, after the progress we have made, American society is so racist to the core that antidiscriminatory statutes cannot possibly do the job, then we shall have racial preferences for a very, very long time to come. Some proponents of race preferences want it this way; they can thus dismiss questions about when preferences will end. But the shift loses the support of all those who are willing to back transitional preferences only as long as they are truly temporary.

Even if one is willing to live with a system of permanent race consciousness, racial preferences as a remedy for future discrimination are, depending on the context, either (a) unnecessary and counterproductive (education and employment) or (b) inappropriate (social discrimination). Racial preferences are unnecessary in the education field because the primary problem facing blacks there is not ongoing racism on the part of teachers or university admissions officers but the inheritance of class—inadequate education for poor and working-class people, a disproportionate number of whom are minority. Moreover, a system of racial preferences, premised in part on the notion that minorities are different, is an odd way to counteract the subtle or unconscious racism of teachers who expect less of black students. And though racism still exists in the area of employment, as I shall argue, our antidiscriminatory laws do a fairly good job of counteracting discrimination because disparate impact suits and old-style affirmative action (recruitment, advertising, etc.) serve as adequate backstops against subtle forms of racism. In a third residual category, which I label "social discrimination" (housing, services, clubs, criminal justice, etc.), I shall argue that antidiscriminatory laws have been much less effective—precisely because in this realm there is no concept of disparate impact—and need to be strengthened, but that racial preferences as a backstop are entirely inappropriate.[7]

My argument, then, is not that racism has been scrubbed from the American soul. Far from it.[8] The new calls for repeal of the Civil Rights Act of 1964 are dangerous and wrong.[9] Our residential housing is highly segregated. Affluent blacks endure the infuriating insult of being unable to hail cabs. Professional "testers"—equally qualified blacks and whites who apply for the same job—still unearth discrimination in employment.[10] My argument is that we have fairly good tools to combat present-day discrimination without having to resort to the disease as cure. As William Julius Wilson has argued, where racism was once sanctified by law and life chances were more a function of race than class, today the very existence of stratification among blacks suggests that life chances now have more to do with class than race.[11]

Educational Discrimination

The argument for using racial preferences to combat current discrimination in education assumes that (a) the elementary and secondary educational system, which prepares students for the contest of selection in higher education, is consciously and unconsciously biased against minorities; and (b) selective educational institutions are themselves consciously or unconsciously biased against minorities.

There is no doubt that our nation has a long history of racial discrimination in elementary and secondary education, of which the de jure segregation of schools is only the most obvious manifestation. But today there are powerful tools to combat such discrimination, tools that require the complete and total dismantlement of de jure segregation, root and branch. Although the remedies are often imperfect, they are clearly more powerful than the remedies to address class-based educational inequality.[12] Where de jure racial segregation was declared unconstitutional in *Brown v. Board of Education*, unequal funding of public schools was upheld in *San Antonio v. Rodriguez*.[13] So, too, if tracking procedures unfairly discriminate against racial minorities, they can be struck down where there is no such protection for the poor.[14]

Many subtle forms of unconscious racial bias by school teachers or administrators may be harder to ferret out, but as we have seen, systems of racial preference tend to exacerbate, rather than remedy, unconscious bias. On the right, Shelby Steele says, "I don't think racial preferences are a protection against this subtle discrimination; I think they contribute to it."[15] And on the left, Paul Starr notes that "affirmative action policies have helped to perpetuate [white] racism." By lowering expectations of blacks as a group, "affirmative action provides a basis for expectations and attitudes that used to be based wholly on prejudice."[16]

What of the selective educational institutions themselves? It would be hard to argue that admissions officers reject minority candidates based on race, since we know that universities do precisely the opposite—assigning enormous preferences to minorities and actively wooing them with generous scholarships.[17] Instead, the argument is made that admission exams—the SAT, LSAT, and the like—are "culturally biased" against minorities.

What does it mean to be "culturally biased"? It obviously cannot mean *merely* that certain racial or ethnic groups do better or worse on a particular measure. Asian Americans do better as a group than whites on most standardized tests, yet few would argue that the test is culturally biased against whites.[18] Instead, what is normally meant by bias is that the tests do not predict what they purport to predict as well for one group as for another. That is, if a 1000 SAT score predicts a grade point average of 3.0 for the general population, but blacks with that SAT scores actually have a mean GPA of 3.5, then the test under-predicts for blacks and is biased against them.

Does this happen? According to the definitive study, conducted by the National Academy of Sciences National Research Council, the answer is no. Everyone from Charles Murray to Stephen Jay Gould agrees that there is no statistical bias in the tests in the sense that they underpredict black performance.[19] Indeed, the National Research Council found that, if anything, the opposite occurs—that standardized tests overpredict the grades of blacks at colleges and law schools.[20] This finding does nothing to confirm theories of genetic inferiority. The correlation of a culture-bound test with a culture-bound college curriculum and grading system says nothing about the innate intelligence of the test taker.[21] The SAT does test culture, as do college grades, but that measure is not insignificant.[22] Indeed, as Alexander Bickel argues, "culture in a larger sense is what universities aim to transmit and what students must work and achieve in."[23] The melting pot remains important on the public level—there is no escaping that the public culture must be mastered. Cultural pluralism suggests that speaking "Black English" at home or in certain communities should not only be tolerated but perhaps even encouraged; but in the public sphere, in education and employment, telling young African Americans that Black English will get them just as far as standard English is nothing short of a cruel hoax. As Thomas Sowell argues, "Since there are no culture-free societies, all performances will be in some given culture, so that attempts to predict performance are therefore attempts to predict what will happen within a particular cultural context."[24] Of course, standardized tests do not come close to measuring everything that is important—creativity, character, leadership. And they certainly do not predict who will be a good lawyer, doctor, or businessperson. But until someone devises such tests, we are stuck with muddling along and doing the best we can with what we have.

Finally, if the tests are indeed statistically biased and do not predict as well for blacks, Hispanics, and Asians as for whites, Title VI makes use of such tests illegal.[25] Derrick Bell notes that the current system—which continues to employ the SAT, LSAT, and other traditional screening devices while lowering standards for minority applicants—"has served to validate and reinforce traditional policies while enveloping minority applicants in a cloud of suspected incompetency."[26]

Employment Discrimination

In the field of employment, there are fairly good tools to deal with ongoing discrimination. Today, if a black student graduated first in his class at Harvard Law School, served as an editor of the *Harvard Law Review*, clerked for the Supreme Court, and was then turned down by Philadelphia's law firms—as William T. Coleman, Jr., was in the 1940s—everyone would agree that he would have an unbeatable case of intentional discrimination.[27] But, of course, discrimination is more insidious today and therefore more difficult to prove; laws aimed at intentional discrimination put the burden on the minority victim to prove his or her case. So current law goes much further, requiring employers to justify hiring practices when they have a disproportionately negative impact on minorities, and requiring federal contractors to employ (among other things) old-style affirmative action. And since 1972 the Equal Employment Opportunity Commission has been empowered to aid plaintiffs in bringing lawsuits against private employers. Between 1972 and 1989, according to former EEOC official Alfred Blumrosen, the agency filed nearly 90,000 cases in federal court and settled more than 250,000 cases in favor of minority plaintiffs.[28]

Disparate Impact Suits Title VII disparate impact suits require employers to give a good reason (business necessity) for a particular employment practice that has a negative impact on minorities. In the landmark case of *Griggs v. Duke Power*, the Court ruled that Title VII is violated not only when an employer intentionally discriminates against individuals for their race but also when an employment practice has an unintended and unjustified adverse impact on certain racial groups. In *Griggs*, the employer, Duke Power, required low-level workers to have a high school diploma. The Court declared that hiring practice illegal because it disproportionately hurt blacks and was unrelated to job performance. The Court wrote: "The Act proscribes not only overt discrimination but also practices that are fair in form but discriminatory in practice."[29]

According to the EEOC's interpretation of this requirement, an employer that hires individuals of a particular race at a rate less than 80 percent of the rate for the group most often hired is engaging in an employment practice of adverse impact.[30] Thus, if 50 percent of whites males who apply are hired, and other groups are hired at less than a 40 percent rate, an adverse impact has occurred. This rule applies not only to an employer's entire workforce but to subgroups as well; a firm with the right number of minority workers overall, but with white workers concentrated at the top and blacks at the bottom, can also be subject to a successful disparate impact suit. Employers that lose disparate impact cases—that is, they cannot justify the imbalance—are liable for back pay, even though the discrimination was unintended.[31]

Some proponents of racial preferences say that *Griggs* is not tough enough and that hiring goals or quotas are necessary to keep employers from discriminating; others say that the requirement that employers bear the burden of justifying imbalances in their workforce will lead employers to informally adopt quotas to fend off litigation.[32] But the *Griggs* decision, which was reaffirmed in the Civil Rights Act of 1991, is a highly sensible middle ground. On the one hand, it acknowledges that statistics are relevant to ferreting out discrimination because intentional discrimination is very hard to prove; in addition, *Griggs* places the burden on employers to justify practices that result in racial imbalances. On the other hand, if an employer has a good justification for a racial imbalance, it should not be required to employ preferences. Indeed, section 703(j) of the Civil Rights Act says that employers may not be required "to grant preferential treatment" to address imbalance, and many employers have successfully used the "business necessity" defense.[33] While some conservatives complained about the Civil Rights Act of 1991, the final bill struck a middle ground that most senators, from Ted Kennedy to Orrin Hatch, felt was acceptably balanced. The bill passed overwhelmingly in the Senate, 93–5, nearly matching the unanimous nature of the Supreme Court's initial decision in *Griggs*.[34]

Old-Style Affirmative Action Another important nonpreferential tool in the antidiscriminatory arsenal is old-style affirmative action. This noncontroversial form of affirmative action requires employers to broaden the pool of applicants and to make sure that informal barriers do not keep minorities and women from having the chance to fairly compete for positions. Since many jobs have traditionally been filled through word of mouth, it is crucial that employers be required to look beyond the (white) old-boy network. When individuals fill out employment applications, it is entirely appropriate that potential employees indicate their race and gender, not to enable the decision to hire to rest on that fact but to ensure that the applicant pool draws on all segments of society. When it does not, employers should be required to advertise in newspapers aimed at minority groups underrepresented in the pool. The Citizens' Commission on Civil Rights is clearly right in its belief that tools are needed to combat "the persistent use of practices such as word-of-mouth recruiting, 'old boy' networks, aptitude and other tests not related to job performance." Disparate impact suits and old-style affirmative action meet those objectives.

Effectiveness of Antidiscriminatory Tools But what if antidiscriminatory tools do not work? In 1992 median black family income was 54 percent of white family income.[35] Women make 71 percent of what men make.[36] The Glass Ceiling Commission found in 1995 that, at the upper levels, 97 percent of senior managers at Fortune 1000 industrial companies are white males.[37] Is that not clear evidence that the Civil Rights Acts of 1964 and 1991 are fairly impotent, and that we should turn to preferences as more powerful medicine?

While these statistics are troubling, and grounds for suspicion, they do not point to a need to resort to preferences to combat current discrimination, for four reasons. First, group cultural differences will to some extent explain disparities in income: there is no reason to believe that, absent discrimination, all groups would be at 100 percent of the national median income. West Indian blacks, for example, who are physically similar to African Americans and victims of their own long history of discrimination, earn 94 percent of the American average. Thomas Sowell found that second-generation West Indian immigrants earn *more* than the American average family income.[38] As we saw in chapter 2, ethnic groups differ, in the aggregate, in family structure, average age of marriage, language, and the value placed on education; men and women differ, in the aggregate, in responsibility for child raising.[39] Second, differences in outcome surely reflect in some part the legacy of *past* discrimination (which affirmative action, race- or class-based, properly attempts to address) rather than a deficiency in the antidiscriminatory laws intended to combat *current* discrimination. Indeed, if some of the current disparities among ethnic group performance were not a result of past discrimination, the major argument for affirmative action would be severely undercut.[40] Third, the widely noted economic bifurcation of the black community provides strong evidence that antidiscrimination laws are having a positive impact on curbing discrimination.[41] Under a system of widespread ongoing discrimination, we would not see bifurcation, says William Julius Wilson; we would see, as we did in the pre-1964 days, the vast majority of blacks concentrated in the lower echelons with no room for escape.[42] Fourth, even if there are deficiencies in the antidiscriminatory regime we employ—and there surely are—laws can be strengthened, and agency funding boosted, before we cross the line to using prophylactic preferences. Tougher sanctions against those guilty of discrimination and expanded use of tests and audits should be part of any trade of race- for class-based preferences.[43]

Social Discrimination

Finally, in the social realm, racism remains strong, and we generally do not have the powerful disparate impact tool that has been fairly effective in the fields of education and employment.[44] One of the most flagrant examples is the inability of blacks, particularly accomplished upper-status blacks, to receive certain common services from whites, or even from other blacks. The paradigmatic example is the professional black male trying to flag a taxi.[45] Testers have found discrimination in retail sales as well; for instance, blacks pay on average $400 more than what whites pay for the same automobile.[46] Likewise, there is fairly widespread agreement that the rate of desegregation in the workplace has not been matched by residential desegregation. Americans are more likely to work with people of differing races, but are still likely to return home to a highly segregated neighborhood, numerous studies show.[47] The pattern represents discrimination more than self-segregation.[48] And there is also a wealth of information suggesting that racial bias continues to infect parts of our criminal justice system. The Los Angeles tapes—of Rodney King's beating and of Mark Fuhrman's rantings—are chilling reminders of this bias.[49]

But while racial discrimination in services, housing, and criminal justice continues to exist, and while it is horrifying and must be dealt with firmly, one must ask, in what sense is providing racial preferences in education and employment and contracting a proper remedy for social discrimination? The whole point about discriminatory taxi cab drivers is that even black professionals—who may have been lifted into the middle class by affirmative action—are passed by. (And make no mistake: what angers most people is not cab drivers refusing to pick up disheveled black [or white] thugs, but refusing to pick up Cornel West dressed in a three-piece suit). To address the problem of racial and gender discrimination in retail sales, commentators do not recommend that we mandate that car dealers give a $400 discount to all black buyers to offset discrimination; they urge tougher penalties for those who discriminate.[50] And how would a racial preference system work to combat housing discrimination?[51]

To combat discrimination in applications of the death penalty, would we really want a racial preference that made a defendant more likely to receive the death penalty for killing someone black?[52] The logical answer to police brutality is not racial hiring preferences—black officers are no more immune than white officers to the impulse to beat victims—but better training and tough sanctions for violators. And yet one nevertheless hears the argument that affirmative action—racial preferences in employment and education—are somehow fair as a counterweight to ongoing forms of anti-black discrimination by the justice system's application of the death penalty, by cab drivers, or by those responsible for racial hate crimes like the one in Howard Beach. President Clinton, for example, cited the fact that certain law enforcement officers attended a racist gathering in Tennessee as evidence of the continued need for federal racial preference programs.[53] The logic seems to be that the unfairness of racial preferences to whites is answered by the fact that in many ways blacks still have it worse in our society. Even if there might be some inequity in preferring a wealthy black over a poor white in college admissions, when you ask JFK's old question—would whites want to exchange places with blacks—whites still say no.[54] The logic is flawed. Hate crimes should be punished fully, but they hardly justify a minority preference in broadcast ownership or admissions to Berkeley. The logic can also be poisonous. In most cases, the impulse to do something positive for blacks is generous and genuine, but sometimes the logic of evening the score can turn sinister—and a Reginald Denny is beaten, or a double murderer is set free.[55]

While laws barring racial and gender discrimination are not perfect, they do offer a basic legal protection against current bias, protection that does not exist against the injuries of class. The barriers of class go much deeper than prejudice per se.[56] Being born poor keeps people down, not so much because of bias but because of lack of opportunity to get a good education, to progress, to develop one's natural potential. This is the difference between discrimination and deprivation. Whereas racial prejudice is an obvious failing, a departure from the system, the barriers of class are endemic, built into the very system itself.[57] An African American who is subject to discrimination can sue, and many thousands do each year. A poor person—whether white or black—faces additional obstacles and generally has no recourse. We live in a nation, Marian Wright Edelman reminds us, "where small babies die of cold quite legally."[58] That is why race preferences are unnecessary to combat current discrimination, but in a society where inadequate investments are made in equal education and equal opportunity, class preferences make perfect sense.

Mini-Myth: Class-Based Programs Should Supplement, Not Supplant, Race-Based Programs

A related argument says that the injuries of race are not reducible to class, and that strategies aimed at lifting up the poor and working class must supplement, rather than replace, race-based programs.[59] President Clinton, for example, backed a "class plus race" approach when he called for federal set-asides for racial minorities and for businesses located in poor communities.[60] Why not do both?

In the broadest sense, we should. Race and class both need to be addressed. To the extent that "doing both" means implementing class preferences supplemented by vigorous enforcement of antidiscrimination laws (both disparate impact and disparate treatment) and old-style affirmative action, we should do both. Moreover, narrowly tailored racial preferences in the public or private sphere are appropriate in extreme cases that genuinely satisfy the *Croson* and *Adarand* test: where discrimination is documented, and a narrowly tailored, truly temporary race-based remedy is justified. Beyond that, a program of class- and race-based preferences is certainly a step in the right direction, since it eliminates the blatant unfairness of providing Clarence Thomas's son a preference over a poor white coal miner's kid. (And the fact that civil rights groups are now willing to discuss race plus class preferences is a healthy development.) But outside those very rare cases in which racial preferences will survive strict scrutiny, class preferences should fully replace race preferences, for both substantive and political reasons.

On the merits, to say that class should supplement rather than replace race preferences really means that preferences should go not only to poor and working-class blacks (who will qualify under a class program) but to upper-middle-class and wealthy people of color as well. The fight to save preferences for advantaged people of color highlights all the very weakest points about affirmative action generally. It cuts against the goal of equal opportunity by making the bizarre claim that wealthy African Americans are just as disadvantaged as poor whites and poor blacks. It cuts against our goal of long-run color blindness. It feeds the same resentment and prejudice that existing programs do—only more so, since all the focus is on helping advantaged blacks whom most people believe deserve the preference least. And given that upper-middle-class blacks are the least likely to have suffered the legacy of discrimination and the most likely to have received a generation of compensation already, it highlights the weakest case for compensatory action.[61]

Politically, there is strong reason to believe that if we insist on retaining race preferences, class preferences are unlikely to be adopted. The attraction to conservatives of class preferences is the tradeoff: the elimination of race-based affirmative action. Adding class on top of race is to the conservative mind even worse than what we have today.[62] And among the broader population, there is some polling evidence that adding class on top of race would not solve the political dilemma of affirmative action.[63]

MYTH NO. 2: SHIFTING TO CLASS PREFERENCES WILL LEAD TO ALL-WHITE UNIVERSITIES, HURTING ALL STUDENTS EDUCATIONALLY

Some argue that any race-neutral program, even one that is class-based, will not produce a "desirable ethnic mix" at elite universities.[64] This was certainly the fear of educators when they adopted race-specific programs in the late 1960s and early 1970s.[65] The problem is that while blacks and Hispanics are disproportionately poor and should disproportionately benefit from class preferences, they tend to do worse on the SAT than whites and Asians of the *same* income group.[66]

But if the program is carefully and thoughtfully designed, racial diversity will decline less than critics fear.[67] And educationally, the new enrichment of class diversity will more than offset any decline in racial diversity. Finally, I will argue, our goal must be genuine equal opportunity for individuals, not equality of group results.

To begin with, of course, many high-achieving minority students will be admitted to universities without any preference, class- or race-based. When white liberals say that an institution will become "all-white" without affirmative action, they underestimate the number of highly talented people of color who will be admitted to institutions on race-blind criteria. This is particularly true after a generation of desegregation and affirmative action, which have resulted in a sixty-point closing of the gap between black and white SAT scores.[68]

Structuring the Class-Based Program

Moreover, there are three steps to take in constructing a class-based program that will ensure that the programs are both essentially fair and effectively boost minority enrollment: (1) eliminate unfair geographic and legacy preferences; (2) set up a generous class-based program with the goal of filling a large number of seats with poor and lower-middle-class students; and (3) define class in a more sophisticated manner than as just parental income. As Berkeley Chancellor Chang Lin Tien noted on the eve of the repeal of race-based affirmative action at the University of California, "We can come up with some tricks."[69] Having said that, the idea is not to use class as a Trojan Horse for race. The change is very real: many poor whites will benefit under the new system, and the people of color who benefit will be quite different from the more privileged group that tends to benefit today. The idea is to provide a genuine equal opportunity that will yield a healthy economic and racial diversity.

First, legacy preferences, which perpetuate past discrimination (and benefit the most affluent alumni most), have a negative disparate impact on people of color, as do geographic preferences, which tend to benefit white Protestants.[70] Eliminating both is consistent with fairness (see chapter 3) and would help people of color. By contrast, athletic preferences, which reward in part the individual effort of athletes, disproportionately benefit blacks and should be retained.[71]

Second, universities are more likely to achieve racial diversity if they set up generous programs for poor and working-class students, either by providing a fairly large "plus" for disadvantage or by setting large goals. Assume, for example, that a university now informally sets aside ten seats for blacks in a class of one hundred. Under a new class-based affirmative action program, assume the university sets a goal of forty seats for students who come from the bottom 50 percent economically. Even if 75 percent of the class preference seats go to nonblacks, there is no net loss of black seats. The absolute number of African Americans is still ten.[72]

Third, universities may be able to boost the number of minorities admitted by using a sophisticated definition of class that is both fairer than using straight income and more beneficial to people of color. While it is often noted that blacks do worse on the SAT than whites of the same income, it is important to go further and grapple with the question of *why* this is so.[73] One major reason is that income comparisons alone are unfair to African Americans because blacks are generally more economically disadvantaged than whites of the same income group; black poverty is on average worse than white poverty. While this does not justify using race as a proxy for "worse poverty," it does argue for devising a definition of class that reflects the fact that even within the same income category, blacks are, in the aggregate, more disadvantaged than whites.

In 1965 Lyndon Johnson's Howard University speech noted two major differences in black and white poverty: black poverty was more concentrated and isolated than white poverty, and it was associated with a higher level of family breakdown. Today Roger Wilkins points not only to the higher incidence of single-parent families among the black poor but to the associated problem of children having children.[74] Thus, just as race-based affirmative action helped the most advantaged minorities the most, a simplistic definition of class (income only) may primarily help the most advantaged members of the poor and working class, who tend to be white.[75] Within the same income categories, blacks tend to be more disadvantaged than whites in three ways: (1) wealth, (2) family structure, and (3) concentration of poverty. Some will argue that these criteria—particularly family structure—reflect cultural differences and should not be included in a definition of disadvantage, but unlike the transmission of cultural values, which inhere in the child, these are disadvantages imposed on the child whether the child agrees or not.

Wealth Disparities While median black income hovers around 60 percent of white income, median black household wealth is much, much lower—around 9 percent of the white median.[76] Paul Starr, citing a study by Melvin Oliver and Thomas M. Shapiro, notes that, "astonishingly, white households with annual incomes between $7,500 and $15,000 have higher mean net worth and net financial assets than black households making $45,000–$60,000."[77] These differences appear to reflect the impact of several factors. Past housing and lending discrimination provide one explanation.[78] As Raymond Franklin notes, "Denial of access to the housing market on equal terms has meant that blacks are constrained in the type of housing they can obtain, and therefore, the homes they do obtain tend to appreciate at a significantly lower rate than those purchased by whites."[79] Second, the wealth gap reflects the fact that many middle-class black families are new to the middle class and are unable to build on a base of wealth inherited from previous generations. In a 1995 study, Rand economist James P. Smith found that while one in three white households receive a financial inheritance, just one in ten black households do.[80] In a study conducted by Zena Smith Blau in Chicago, 82 percent of middle-class black mothers had working-class backgrounds, compared with 32 percent of white middle-class mothers. To Blau, this fact—the class origins of the parents—helped explain why the children of middle-class blacks did about as well on IQ tests as the children of working-class whites.[81]

Third, the wealth gap, particularly at the low end, reflects the fact that black poverty tends to be more persistent than white poverty (and the impact on a child is correspondingly greater).[82] David Ellwood compared the number of years that a child born between 1967 and 1973 was likely to have lived in poverty from birth to age ten. While 8 percent of whites lived in poverty for more than four of their first ten years, the figure for blacks was 56 percent. When considering even more persistent poverty—seven of a child's first ten years—the black/white ratio grows to 11:1, with 34 percent of black children living in such persistent poverty, compared with just 3 percent of whites. "Think about the implications of these simple statistics," Ellwood writes. "Only 8 percent of white children will know as much economic deprivation as the typical black child."[83]

It is not surprising, therefore, that the black/white wealth ratio is most highly skewed within the lowest income groups. The median net worth of blacks with less than $900 in monthly income was 1 percent that of whites of similar income, while the net worth of blacks with $4,000 or more income per month was 46 percent that of whites with comparable income.[84]

Family Structure Within income categories, minority and white family structures differ in three ways, all to the relative disadvantage of African American and Latino children: in the incidence of single-parent families; the incidence of very young mothers; and the incidence of large families.

The overall statistical difference between black and white families is well known. In 1991, 78.5 percent of white children under eighteen lived with two parents, compared with just 35.9 percent of African American children.[85] In 1991, 58 percent of black households were headed by women, compared with 17.9 percent of white households, a ratio of 3:1. Nationally, the black out-of-wedlock birth rate is 3.59 times higher than for whites. Among children whose mothers have never been married, the black multiple is 13:1 (2.69 percent of white children versus 35.3 percent of black children).[86] Some of this difference disappears when controlling for class—that is, poor whites have high rates of illegitimacy and female-headed households, too. But a residue remains.

Second, black children are more likely to be born to very young mothers. Says Wilkins: "The parents are themselves no more than children."[87] In 1992, among teenage girls between the ages of fifteen and seventeen, blacks had 81.3 live births per 1,000 girls, compared to 51.8 live births for whites.[88] Taking these two factors together, unmarried black teenagers have a birth rate four times that of unmarried white teens.[89] Finally, blacks and Latinos who tell the SAT statisticians they have a certain family income are also somewhat more likely to live in larger families than whites (see chapter 2), and the income is likely to be stretched more thinly. Family size must therefore be counted in as well.

Concentration of Poverty Third, black poverty is generally more concentrated than white poverty, and since that factor is crucial to life chances, it should be counted in a class preference proposal. Poor blacks are six times as likely to live in areas of high poverty concentration as poor whites.[90] The impact is important. "As a consequence," writes the National Research Council, "poor blacks, to a much greater degree than poor whites, interact mainly with other disadvantaged people. Black poor children attend schools with other poor children, go to churches with impoverished congregations, and deal with merchants geared to do business with a poor clientele."[91] The University of Chicago's Mark Testa says: "Poor whites reside in areas which are ecologically and economically very different from poor [black areas]. Any observed relationships involving race would reflect, to some unknown degree, the relatively superior ecological niche many poor whites occupy with respect to jobs, marriage opportunities, and exposure to conventional role models."[92]

Researchers have found that once non-income differences are accounted for, racial gaps in achievement dissipate or even disappear entirely.[93] But if all this is true—if black poverty is generally worse than white poverty—why not just count race along with class? The answer, of course, is that the differences are true only in the aggregate. While pointing to group differences, both Johnson and Wilkins conceded that such differences "are not racial differences,"[94] and that the black poor are not "different in the eyes of God."[95] Obviously, not all poor blacks live in single-parent families, just as not all poor whites live in two-parent families. And a growing number of whites do live in concentrated poverty. In 1994, *U.S. News and World Report* identified fifteen white slums with all the social pathologies associated with the underclass.[96] The number of Americans living in underclass white neighborhoods is 1.6 million, according to the Urban Institute, up 85 percent since 1980.[97] The answer, then, is not to use race as a (not entirely accurate) proxy for particularly devastating forms of poverty, but to use those indices that happen in practice to disproportionately benefit blacks.[98]

Education: Class Diversity

Thus far, we have been measuring diversity in purely racial terms. But from an educational standpoint, class preferences are likely to create not only more racial diversity than a policy of inaction but much more class diversity than race-based affirmative action ever has. And there is a strong argument that class is at least as important as racial diversity from a pedagogical standpoint. Bringing together people of genuinely different social classes can strengthen an institution's diversity even more than a cosmetic diversity that congregates similar upper-middle-class people of differing races.[99] Admitting a poor white from a trailer park, says the journalist Jim Sleeper, surely adds more diversity to a college than admitting a middle-class black.[100] Add Dershowitz and Hanft: "The prep school black brought up in a middle-class neighborhood by professional parents might contribute far less diversity than a Hasidic Jew from Brooklyn, a Portuguese fisherman from New Bedford, a coal miner from Kentucky or a recent emigré from the Soviet Union."[101] Professor Clyde Summers of the University of Pennsylvania Law School told the *New York Times* that, while he has black and white students, "I have almost no students whose parents are union members, and very few students who come from what you would call the blue-collar working class. What that means is that no one has any idea what life is like on the other side of the tracks. That leads to a very sterile discussion when it comes to labor law."[102] Berkeley, which has for years employed aggressive racial preferences, added class as a basis for preference, not for reasons of fairness but for reasons of diversity.[103]

Equal Opportunity, Not Equal Result

Finally, and most importantly, the ultimate test of class-based affirmative action is whether it provides individual equality of *opportunity* (including accurate screening devices), not equality of group *results*. Racial diversity is an expected and logical consequence of class-based affirmative action, but it is not the ultimate measure.[104] There is no more efficient way to guarantee racial representation than by mandating it. But if the goal is to provide a fair system of genuine equal opportunity, factoring in class does a much better job than either filling racial quotas or looking solely at academic numbers.

In the end, class preferences, fairly and generously administered, will provide genuine racial and socioeconomic diversity at leading universities. Cultural differences are real, but not enormous. A genuine equal opportunity—something no society has ever tried—may very well yield a rough approximation of equality of group result. But to the extent that it does not, genuine equal opportunity must as a principle prevail over equal group results.

MYTH NO. 3: SHIFTING TO CLASS PREFERENCES IS MARXIST AND WILL SPARK CLASS WARFARE

Any system of class preferences will necessarily decrease race consciousness but increase class consciousness. In chapter 4, reducing race consciousness was seen as a healthy thing, but might not heightening class consciousness cause problems of its own?

Two (somewhat contradictory) arguments are made in this regard. The first is that increasing class consciousness will increase class tensions, enflame class hatred, and promote class warfare. To put it mildly, the twentieth century's failed experiment with totalitarian communism has given class consciousness a bad name. At the extreme, class consciousness results in not only class hatred but a reverse form of classism: the lower classes are presumed to be more pure, more morally worthy, than the decadent middle and upper classes. In China, for example, a system of extreme class preferences was implemented for university admissions following the cultural revolution.[105] China's policy provided for strong preferences for those with "proletarian credentials," even if their academic qualifications were slim. The *New York Times* reported that one coal miner, for example, was admitted to university even though he lacked "a single day of formal schooling." Professors were "reindoctrinated to guard against their influencing students with bourgeois ideas," and students, pledging to "reject blind belief in bourgeois authorities," said, "We are resolved that the true nature of working people will never change."[106]

Of course, the specter of totalitarian communism has been offered as an argument against everything from the progressive income tax, Medicaid, and Medicare to fluoridated water. As the critic Michael Lind points out, class analysis is much older than Marx and was central to the ideas in *The Federalist Papers*.[107] To suggest that a system of class-based affirmative action supported by Antonin Scalia, Clarence Thomas, and Dinesh D'Souza has anything to do with Mao is ridiculous. Class preferences do not imply the moral superiority of the working class or hatred of the rich; they are a way of providing equal opportunity so that the children of the disadvantaged may themselves rise through hard work and effort to become comfortable, or even rich.

Indeed, Marx would oppose class preferences for that very reason. The Marxist focus is on the existence of a class structure, not on the rate of social mobility. To Marxists, even if there were widespread social mobility, with the bottom replacing the top and vice versa each generation, the evil would remain so long as the hierarchical *structure* was replicated.[108] Indeed, if anything, some Marxists see social mobility as counterproductive; it co-opts the smartest members of the working class and undercuts working-class solidarity.[109] Marx himself wrote of the antirevolutionary nature of social mobility: "The more a ruling class is able to assimilate the foremost minds of a ruled-class, the more stable and dangerous becomes its rule."[110] And the class preferences we envision are not meant to ignore traditional academic criteria, as in China, but to supplement them.

Ironically, one also hears the opposite argument about raising class consciousness: not that it will inspire among the poor hatred of the rich or feelings of superiority but rather, feelings of shame and inadequacy. Some are worried about the specter of a child having to betray his parents by arguing, on a college application, that he comes from an inadequate, disadvantaged background.[111] Mickey Kaus argues that class preferences "will still reward those who play the victim."[112] But if universities and employers use objective criteria to define the disadvantaged—rather than relying on whiny application essays—there is no way to "play" the victim. Poor and working-class teenagers are the victims of class inequality not of their own making. But preferences—unlike, say, a welfare check—tell them not that they are helpless victims but that their potential is great and they are going to get a chance (if they work very hard) to prove themselves. As for poor and working-class parents, they are not unaware that their children lack the opportunities of the wealthy; it is insulting to imply they are ignorant of this basic fact. Indeed, most parents want the very best for their children and would be very happy to have their children enjoy a special preference (alumni certainly do).

There is a related argument—that class preferences will be just as stigmatizing as racial preferences. Michael Kinsley says that "any debilitating self-doubt that exists because of affirmative action is not going to be mitigated by being told you got into Harvard because of your 'socioeconomic disadvantage' rather than your race."[113] But class preferences are different from racial preferences in at least two important respects. First, stigma—in one's own eyes and in the eyes of others—is related to the perceived legitimacy of an admissions criterion. Students with good grades are not seen as having gained admittance "just because they're smart." And there appears to be a societal consensus—from Douglas to Scalia—that children from poor backgrounds deserve a leg up. Such a consensus has never existed for class-blind racial preferences. Second, there is no myth in this country about the inferior abilities of poor people comparable to that about African Americans. In America, far from feeling shame, most individuals take pride in humble roots.[114] As we have noted, if racial preferences are purely a matter of compensatory justice, then the question of whether preferences exacerbate white racism is not relevant. But today racial preferences are often justified by the utilitarian benefits of diversity (bringing different racial groups together helps dispel stereotypes), in which case the social consequences are highly relevant. The argument made by proponents of racial preferences—that policies need to be grounded in social reality, not ahistorical theory—cuts in favor of the class category precisely because there is no stubborn historical myth for it to reinforce. In addition, to reduce whatever stigma may exist—and to help prepare underprepared disadvantaged students for the challenge to come—preferences could be made contingent upon attending a rigorous summer program in advance of the school year, making it clear that the preference is not a freebie but an opportunity with reciprocal obligations.[115]

In short, class preferences will neither denigrate nor celebrate the poor and the working class but rather will point up the genuine obstacles to equal opportunity. To the extent that they focus white working-class attention away from race and toward common class interests, that is all for the good. The point is not to stir hatred of the rich but rather hatred of unequal opportunities; not shame in humble origins but pride in having a fighting chance to rise above them.

MYTH NO. 4: SHIFTING TO CLASS PREFERENCES WILL UNDERCUT PRO-FAMILY AND CAPITALIST INCENTIVES

Critics point out that because class, unlike race, is mutable, parents whose children receive benefits for being poor will have an incentive not to succeed. In a capitalist society, where we want to provide workers with incentives to work hard and accumulate wealth, class preferences theoretically provide an incentive to fail.[116] Part of the reason parents work hard is to provide their children with a competitive edge, and taking that away by giving the disadvantaged compensation blunts the incentive for parents to succeed.

The response is fourfold. First, class preferences do not provide the child with an incentive to fail, for the preference provides her not with a check but with an opportunity to prove herself through hard work. Second, the "incentive to fail" argument has not deterred us in the past when important goals were at stake. Any tax provides some disincentive to work and produce, especially a progressive tax. Likewise, even though financial aid programs for students whose parents cannot pay tuition provide a theoretical incentive to fail, the programs have strong and widespread support. Third, the incentive to fail is usually overstated. When marginal tax rates reached up to 90 percent, people continued to work for their marginal gain. Among the wealthy, study after study has shown that the present tax system has no significant impact on work effort, since the "substitution effect" (taxes make leisure more attractive) conflicts with the "income effect" (taxes make people work harder to maintain their living standard).[117] Fourth, a class-based preference for the teenage sons and daughters of poor parents is likely to provide even less of an incentive to fail than a progressive income tax or welfare. If the progressive income tax creates a dual disincentive to earn (by taking away from one's current enjoyment of income and one's desire to help one's children), class preferences affect only the latter.[118] And even if a parent is single-mindedly concerned about his child and would theoretically sacrifice his own well-being for the child, that would still not be an incentive to fail under a class-based affirmative action program. In no case does a parent's success actually disadvantage his child, because preferences are at most meant to correct for disadvantage. Moreover, in practice, the advantages of high socioeconomic status for one's child will almost always outweigh a preference because preferences are limited in size by the requirement that the child be qualified (see chapter 5). The preference will not, in many cases, provide full equality of opportunity. And though a parent's ability to pass on the full economic benefits to his child is diminished, there will be nothing to stop parents—nor should there be—from passing on the strong values and cultural advantages of a loving home.

MYTH NO. 5: CLASS PREFERENCES UNFAIRLY TREAT PEOPLE AS MEMBERS OF GROUPS RATHER THAN AS INDIVIDUALS

It might be said that the class grouping oversimplifies barriers to achievement—replacing a race reductionism with a class reductionism. Just as it was wrong to say that the legacy of past discrimination was the only impediment to equal opportunity, so it is wrong to say that class is the only impediment.

On one level, the criticism has a certain validity. Not all impediments to equal opportunity have to do with class. The son of a wealthy manufacturer may attend the most elite prep school but feel the rejection of having been shipped off to boarding school, causing him to underperform and not reveal his full natural talents.[119] The daughter of an affluent doctor may live with the pain and distraction of her father's alcoholism. Or the son of a black judge may be worn down by repeated racist remarks from his prep school colleagues. Other students have to overcome physical disability or language difficulties. Some even point to evidence that firstborn children tend to have advantages over later siblings.[120] Looking only at class ignores all these more subtle disadvantages.

Ideally, universities would look at some of these criteria, though they would need to be cautious. Since preferences are provided not out of pity but to correct for underprediction of long-run potential, to the extent that, say, a child's physical disability is permanent and will continue to truncate his performance, a preference may make little sense. Schools should also be extremely cautious about criteria like birth order, on which the data are mixed and the "disadvantage" small.[121] And universities may want to avoid providing too much weight to certain impediments (repeated racist remarks, an alcoholic father, being abused as a child) that are difficult to authenticate.[122]

Inevitably, universities and employers do treat people as members of groups, for at some point the tradeoff between fairness and efficiency tips in favor of the latter. Theoretically, universities should not rely on criteria like GPAs and SATs to measure intellectual promise but should interview every teacher who taught each candidate throughout his or her eighteen years of schooling. But we do not expect such thoroughness.[123] Is rejecting those with abysmal scores unfair because it is treating them like members of a group (people with low scores) rather than as individuals?[124]

Moreover, while we hope universities will treat people as individuals to the greatest extent practicable, a public policy that seeks to encourage (or require) universities to employ class-based affirmative action needs a definition of disadvantage that is verifiable and enforceable. If we leave the question to universities entirely, providing total discretion with no bright lines, we are likely to find widespread evasion. We have seen that many universities today claim to give a preference for disadvantage, but most in practice do not do so; their financial incentive is to do the opposite (on the low end, to avoid absorbing financial aid costs and, on the high end, to encourage alumni gifts). If we say universities can "count" as equally disadvantaged the wealthy alumni son who claims to feel alienated by cold parents and the poor student who grew up in the ghetto facing daily challenges, we know which student will be chosen to fill the goal. While universities should count all sorts of disadvantages, the government also needs a workable definition that will not be easily circumvented.

MYTH NO. 6: CLASS PREFERENCES WILL FAIL BECAUSE THEY IGNORE ROOT CAUSES

Finally, some argue that any scheme of preferences in college or employment ignores the root causes of inequality. This is troubling because (a) any form of "zero-sum social engineering"[125] will cause resentment; (b) preferences treat symptoms rather than causes; and (c) giving preferences at age eighteen is "too late" in an individual's life.

Some say class-based affirmative action will cause as much resentment among those left out as race-based affirmative action does. Michael Kinsley argues that the rejected applicant in the infamous Jesse Helms commercial from 1990 would feel just as angry for losing out on a class-based as a race-based preference, since both involve "making up for past injustice."[126] The difference, of course, is that class preferences go to the actual victims of class injury, mooting the whole question of intergenerational justice. In the racial context, this was the type of victim-specificity for which even the Reagan administration approved compensation. Blacks who achieve will be free of the racial stigma and resentment associated with racial preferences.

The larger point in Kinsley's question—that any preference system, whether race- or class-based, is "still a form of zero-sum social engineering"—is more serious. Rather than giving preferences to teenagers, would it not be better to do the job of providing equal opportunity in the first place? Why should liberals push for class preferences, which merely treat symptoms? Shouldn't we provide more funding for education, safer schools, better nutrition? The answer is that we should indeed do these things, but that we must push for class preferences as well, for three reasons.

First, because preferences are less expensive than social programs and go directly to innocent children (rather than to "undeserving" parents), they are likely to be more politically sustainable than providing equal opportunity through social programs and education. On a practical level, preferences are needed to make up for some of the inevitable shortfall in the funding of equal opportunity social programs. While we should continue to push for such funding, we cannot hold our breath for it to happen. These programs are under heavy attack, and even in 1993 and 1994, when all the planets were aligned—a populist Democratic president with majorities in both houses of Congress—they produced what the *New York Times* called "A Budget Worthy of Mr. Bush."[127]

But even if, by some miracle, federal social programs were fully funded and education expenditures equalized, it seems inconceivable that suburban parents would give up the advantage received by their children from going to strong suburban schools, with motivated fellow students, in favor of some type of economic-based school integration.[128] By contrast, class preferences are cheaper than social spending, seem less threatening than public school class–based integration, and solve the conundrum of welfare by providing direct aid to the child without aiding the "undeserving" parent.

Second, preferences are necessary to compensate for our failure to provide substantive equal opportunity owing to our strong and proper attachment to the values of liberty and family. Even if we were somehow to achieve the unprecedented—if social mobility programs were fully funded and schools were integrated economically—we would still not have genuine equal opportunity. Why? Because we (rightly) allow parents the liberty to purchase for their children superior private school education, educational family vacations and computer programs, private tutors, SAT preparation courses, and the rest. No one would advocate limiting the liberty of parents to provide these competitive advantages for their children, unearned though they are. But class preferences can begin to compensate underprivileged children by acknowledging that because they do not have these advantages, their long-run potential as suggested by predictors may be greater than we think.

Third, to the extent that class preferences help change the focus of public discourse from race to class, they help reforge the coalition required to sustain much-needed social programs. There is no contradiction, then, between class preferences and pushing for additional investment in equal opportunity programs; emphasis on the first is likely to make achieving the second more probable. As Bayard Rustin has written: "Today's struggle must be a non-racial program for economic justice that would facilitate the formation of coalitions based on mutual need."[129]

Finally, on a practical level, some argue that preferences are inappropriate for poor teenagers because they lack basic skills. Giving a preference to an unprepared kid from Appalachia or Harlem to go to Harvard does no one any good because these students are woefully unprepared and likely to flunk out. Simply put, preferences work for middle-class minorities with good educations and manners.[130]

There is some truth to this criticism, and that is why class-based affirmative action should apply before age eighteen (to tracking), why preferences should go beyond just the underclass to include the working class, why recipients of university preferences should be required to take a rigorous summer course (to be prepared), and why preferences should apply to entry-level jobs as well as to selective colleges (so that the majority of poor children who do not attend college may benefit).

More important, we should not underestimate the capacity of poor and working-class kids to do well. If some are too quick to underestimate the barriers faced by the poor and believe that everyone could get off welfare if they just tried, neither should we assume that no child of welfare can handle challenging work. Lest we forget, two of our most insightful critics on the issue of poverty—Daniel Patrick Moynihan and William Julius Wilson—are themselves products of it.[131] Given the proper incentives, universities will seek and find talented poor and working-class students who deserve a leg up. Even the authors of *The Bell Curve*, who are among the most pessimistic observers of the poor, argue in favor of class-based preferences.[132]

Part 3

Toward What End?

7. Picking Up the Lost Thread

AFFIRMATIVE ACTION is but the most dramatic example of a larger trend in which American policy makers, particularly progressives, have redefined inequality with a racial lens. Ever since the assassinations of Martin Luther King and Robert Francis Kennedy, the emphasis these men put on class over race has been largely absent from our political discourse. In this chapter, we look at how and why the thread was lost—and why a shift back to class-based affirmative action could be the beginning of a larger effort to pick up the lost thread. This broader move to shift the focus from race to class is imperative if we wish to foster social cohesion, reunite political coalitions for progressive change, and get at the root problems of inequality, which go beyond race to the bedrock issue of class.

THE LOST THREAD: RACE OVER CLASS

In the 1930s and 1940s progressives romanticized the working class, largely to the exclusion of women and racial minorities.[1] But by the late 1960s (and through the present day) the left's important (and long overdue) focus on race and gender had swung so far that class was all but eclipsed. Today when Andrew Hacker entitles a book "Two Nations," he is referring to a racial divide as opposed to the class divisions invoked by Benjamin Disraeli's original use of that phrase.[2] The 1968 Kerner Commission's "two societies, one black, one white," have replaced Michael Harrington's two Americas, one affluent, the other impoverished. Indeed, Hacker's title was criticized not for failing to consider class but for failing to be racially conscious enough—

that is, conscious of Asians, Mexican Americans, Eskimos, and others.[3]

In 1965 Daniel Patrick Moynihan was lambasted for emphasizing the racial component of out-of-wedlock births to the detriment of class, but in 1978 William Julius Wilson was attacked for the opposite reason—emphasizing class over race. In *The Declining Significance of Race*, Wilson argued: "Whereas the old barriers bore the pervasive features of racial oppression, the new barriers indicate an important and emerging form of class subordination."[4] For these thoughts, he was blasted by the Association of Black Sociologists, which was "outraged over the misrepresentation of the black experience." Hunter College's Alphonso Pinkney wrote that black sociologists like Wilson "who support the conservative movement are not unlike government officials in (formerly) South Vietnam who supported American aggression against their own people." And Harvard's Charles V. Willie said, "Wilson is an accomplice to whatever harm is visited upon [the urban poor] in the deadly 'game' of power politics."[5]

The press, following the liberal zeitgeist and in turn feeding it, now sees issues primarily through the prism of race. SAT scores, for instance, are reported broken down by race, with little attention given to the wide class gaps. Infant mortality and high school dropout rates are seen as minority problems even though they afflict poor whites largely to the same degree.[6] The 1992 Los Angeles riots were seen principally as an uprising of African Americans, even though more Latinos were arrested than blacks, and one of seven taken into custody was white.[7] Charles Murray and Richard Herrnstein's *The Bell Curve* was portrayed as a book about racial inferiority even though their central argument, equally frightening and more far-ranging, was about the genetic inferiority of the poor.[8] The Census Bureau feeds the media with racial breakdowns on every conceivable issue, including the proportion of blacks who bike to work.[9]

The declining focus on class parallels the decline of organized labor. There was a time around 1940, the labor lawyer Thomas Geoghegan writes, when labor's John L. Lewis would give a speech "and all three national [radio] networks would carry it live." Today civil rights and women's groups are in the spotlight, and fights over labor laws to protect the working class fail to excite anyone the way civil rights legislation does. "It mystifies me how liberals get worked up over fairly minor blips in [civil rights] law," Geoghegan writes, "and completely ignore the fact that, year after year, blacks are being denied a most basic civil right, the right to join a union without being fired." He adds: "If only we thought of the Wagner Act as a civil rights law, instead of a labor law, then maybe liberals would wake up and do something."[10] Today Democrats have a hard time saying "class," employing a string of euphemisms from "middle income" to "wage earners" to "people who play by the rules."[11]

But nowhere is the shift from class to race and gender more obvious than in the discourse of university intellectuals. We have gone from class as the central intellectual construct, to class sharing a place in a trinity with race and gender, to the new paradigm of race and gender, full stop. Writes the critic Robert Hughes: "The academic left is much more interested in race and gender than in class. And it is *very* much more interested in theorizing about gender and race than actually reporting on them."[12] Dinesh D'Souza's 1991 book on the American university, *Illiberal Education*, was subtitled *The Politics of Race and Sex on Campus.*[13]

Because of the overlap between race, class, and gender, the shift can sometimes be subtle. Where the left used to champion poor and working-class Americans (a disproportionate number of whom were black, Hispanic, and/or female), today the left champions blacks, Hispanics, and females (a disproportionate number of whom are poor and working-class). On many issues, the shift in focus will not make a difference; either way, the left will be for health care reform, a higher minimum wage, and more money for education. But on the issue of preferences, the shift from class to race and gender is anything but subtle; the loyalties are unmistakable, and white working Americans know it.

Sometimes the emphasis on race is plainly misplaced. Was New York City's restriction on smoking in public places really a racial issue, as the New York NAACP charged, simply because 39.6 percent of black males smoke, compared with 31.6 percent of white males?[14] Was Clarence Thomas right to say that those who opposed his nomination were engaged in a high-tech lynching?[15] The problem is not so much that Americans overplay the race card—there are plenty of times when race *is* the issue—but that we have developed a blind spot to class. Even when we had a disgraceful legalized caste system in the 1940s, race was, to Gunnar Myrdal, *An American Dilemma*. That race would become widely seen as *the* American dilemma, overshadowing all others—at the very instant when we moved to dismantle the legalized caste system—makes no sense.[16] The 1964 Civil Rights Act was a landmark in the attack against caste. It should have signaled a move toward class, but in fact the very opposite occurred.

Why did progressives continue to shift their emphasis from class to race even after passage of the Civil Rights Act, when, on the merits, race should have waned in importance? The best explanation is that the very struggle for black freedom and the resistance of many working-class whites to that effort had the lingering legacy of making many progressives fundamentally rethink the old New Deal coalition. First, many progressives concluded that there was nothing natural about a coalition of working-class white and black people. As blacks began to assert their rights as equals, it became clear that the white working class was not the *ally* of the black community, but its chief *competitor*. The history of American labor had always had an element of this competition,[17] but when the civil rights movement began demanding desegregated schooling and housing, the white working class—with whom integration would primarily take place—rebelled.[18]

White workers came to be viewed as among the most conservative and reactionary segments of society. The proletariat disappointed the left. They did not march and they did not rebel.[19] Instead, they provided the country's strongest backlash against the civil rights movement, and later, against the feminist and gay rights movements as well. The most vehement opposition to progressive causes seemed to come not from the educated upper-middle class, which was comparatively tolerant, but from insecure white working-class people whose outlook was said to border on the authoritarian. The romantic Joe Hill, says Mark Shields, became the bigoted Archie Bunker.[20] Electorally, it was the white working class that had provided the bulk of support for a string of racists, the left now said, from Tom Watson and Father Coughlin to Joe McCarthy and George Wallace.[21] Jesse Jackson's effort to appeal to white working voters, by contrast, fell flat on its face because, it was said, they could not stomach voting for a black man; David Duke and Pat Buchanan seemed more to their liking.[22] In the 1970s the white working class violently opposed busing in Boston, Canarsie, and elsewhere. In the 1980s racial hostility in white working-class communities—resulting in the death of blacks in Howard Beach and Bensonhurst—confirmed the fears of blacks and white liberals that white working people were hardly soulmates. In that decade, many white workers deserted the Democratic Party permanently, voting in droves for one of the most anti–civil rights presidents of this century, Ronald Reagan. Even if a voting coalition were possible, it was argued, what common ground would there be for governing with racist, sexist, and homophobic authoritarians?

In addition to the disappointment over the white working-class backlash, there was a growing sense that the old left had been proven wrong about the role of race and ethnicity. Racial and ethnic awareness was not melting away, as predicted; rather, ethnic feelings on both sides (black and white) were on the rise. Identity politics was in. As the ethnic revival sprouted and grew in the 1970s, the notion of building cross-racial class-based coalitions seemed more and more like a pipe dream.[23] In the 1980s, in the battle between class allegiances and ethnic and racial ties, class was trounced, both internationally and domestically.[24] Freud, Moynihan noted, triumphed over Marx.[25]

Finally, there was a sense among some that, given the extreme undesirability of working with reactionary working-class white people, maybe it was possible to build a new coalition between blacks and suburban liberals, especially women. Maybe the conservatives were right: times had changed since the New Deal. The class-based appeal was not relevant anymore. America had become too affluent, too suburban, too middle-class. (In 1994 one poll showed that 93 percent of Americans considered themselves middle-class.)[26] After the 1984 Democratic Convention, George Will quoted a northeastern blue-collar worker turned Republican who was supposed to epitomize the demise of the New Deal coalition: "The Democratic Party has been good to me—Social Security, GI Bill, student loans," he said. "The Democratic Party made me middle class. But perhaps Reagan will keep me middle class."[27] Following Will, some on the left suggested abandoning the attempt to appeal to conservative working-class people. Why not build alliances with the more educated and enlightened suburban middle class instead?[28]

PICKING UP THE LOST THREAD OF CLASS

While the progressive critique of class has held sway for almost thirty years, the liberal decision to reject Kennedy and King has clearly incurred tremendous costs. It is now manifest that emphasizing race in the United States is dangerous to minorities and politically disastrous for progressives, and that it leaves unremedied the larger and more potent injuries that stem from class.

The Dangers of a Racial Emphasis

In the 1960s liberals still realized that to confuse race and class was not only wrong but dangerous. This notion was at the heart of the protest over Daniel Patrick Moynihan's 1965 report, *The Negro Family: The Case for National Action*, in which he described the rising rates of illegitimacy among poor blacks. While Moynihan's critics were wrong to silence discussion of illegitimacy among blacks, they rightly noted that the title of the report, which implicated all blacks, was misleading, and that fairly high rates of illegitimacy also were present among poor whites—a point that Moynihan readily endorses today. In the wake of the second set of Los Angeles riots in 1992, Moynihan rose on the Senate floor to reaffirm that family structure "is not an issue of race but of class. . . . It is class behavior."[29]

If the left was unfair in denouncing the Moynihan report as racist, they were on to something in their concern about racialism: even benign preferences, aimed at remedying past discrimination, run the risk of putting an unhealthy focus on the particular problems of blacks, which would be misinterpreted by racists. Today this insight has been lost. Because the parameters of the affirmative action debate are racial rather than economic, academic studies focusing on racial differences have proliferated. Indeed, a finding of racial disparity supports both sides of the affirmative action argument. Liberals cite studies showing that minorities do worse on certain tests than whites to prove that the legacy of discrimination continues to live with us and requires affirmative measures to counteract. Conservatives cite the same studies to highlight their argument that affirmative action lowers "meritocratic" standards and—as some conservatives have done recently—to "prove" genetic differences. Both sides ignore the fact that minorities do poorly in large part because they come from disproportionately poor populations and lack equal opportunity to develop their talents.

The late Bayard Rustin pointed out in 1987 that there is a new racism afoot that thrives on these studies. "What makes the new form more insidious is its basis in observed sociological data," he wrote.

> The new racist equates the pathology of the poor with race, ignoring the fact that family dissolution, teenage pregnancy, illegitimacy, alcohol and drug abuse, street crime, and idleness are universal problems of the poor. They exist wherever there is economic dislocation and deterioration—in the cities, for example, dotting Britain's devastated industrial north. They are rampant among the white jobless in Liverpool as well as among unemployed blacks in New York.[30]

The lesson, then, is this: while on the surface it would seem that our racist history requires a race-based cure, our very history of racism, and the way in which it continues to be endemic in our culture, is a strong reason to avoid a race-based solution. We live in a frightening racial climate, where social analysts are re-opening issues thought to have been closed — the genetic inferiority of blacks and the soundness of the Civil Rights Act of 1964.[31] These theories must be fought tooth and nail, and certain racial policies, like the Civil Rights Act, should be defended.

But on the issue of preference, where there is a danger that a racial solution will perpetuate racial myths, not only are class-based solutions more sound, they are also safer.

Reuniting the Political Coalition of King and Kennedy

It is also crucial to emphasize class over race because to do so will unite rather than divide King's and Kennedy's coalitions of poor and working-class people across race lines. While the New Left's critique offers some valuable insights into the difficulties of class-based movements, the old coalition, pursued by King in his last years and achieved by Kennedy in his, is possible, necessary, and desirable.[32]

The Black and Blue Coalition Is Possible First, the coalition of blacks and blue-collar whites, though fragile, is clearly still achievable. While it may be utopian to envision loving affection between working-class whites and blacks, that is not what a voting coalition requires.[33] The one thing that runs deeper than fear, hatred, and racism, write Jack Newfield and Jeff Greenfield, is self-interest.[34]

Martin Luther King, who knew well the hatred of certain elements of white working-class America, thought that a coalition of self-interest was possible. As he moved his sights north and faced virulent opposition in white working-class communities like Cicero, Illinois, he might easily have grown pessimistic about the prospects of a class-based coalition. In fact, the opposite occurred. Where he had had no illusions that the white poor in the South would join an alliance to pursue black *civil rights* (that theory "wilted under the heat of fact"),[35] the push for *economic equality* united blacks and whites, offering the potential "for a powerful new alliance."[36] King believed that ultimately underprivileged whites would see their self-interest: "White supremacy can feed their egos but not their stomachs," he wrote.[37] (King realized that the new economic agenda was more expensive than the old civil rights crusade, making the class-based alliance both possible *and* necessary.)[38]

Second, to the extent that some white working-class voters have a reactionary, racist, and anti-Semitic streak in them (and the stereotype is overblown),[39] many of these same voters have a liberal and populist side which can and should be encouraged. Wrote Bayard Rustin: "The question is not whether this group [lower-middle class whites] is conservative or liberal, for it is both, and how it acts will depend upon the way the issues are defined."[40] History teaches that if class anger is not directed "up" by the Democrats, it will be directed "down" by the Republicans.[41] So while the white working class may sometimes be manipulated by the white elites for their own ends, it is not inevitable.[42]

In fact, a number of different analysts have found that while the white working class does clash with blacks and other minorities—and does have a tendency to scapegoat—it reserves its greatest anger for upper-middle and upper-class whites who hold the real power. In Jonathan Rieder's study of lower-middle-class whites in Canarsie, a section in Brooklyn, he found that, while whites were labeled reactionary because of their opposition to busing, another strain was evident as well. "Italian Conservative and Republican leaders in Canarsie did not defend the prerogatives of the country club set or corporate business. A Conservative Party activist who revered Joseph McCarthy and George Wallace complained, 'It's unfair. The rich get richer, that's a fact.' "[43]

Likewise, J. Anthony Lukas, in his book *Common Ground*, found that Alice McGoff and the other white working-class antibusing activists in Boston directed far more anger toward white liberal elites such as Judge Arthur Garrity, who ordered the plan, than toward black families. Says Lukas, "Many of the angriest letters and phone calls emphasized the judge's remoteness from Boston, his long residence in affluent Wellesley, where his family and friends were exempt from his court orders."[44] While Boston's Louise Day Hicks channeled the class anger against busing, Lukas says, it could have been redirected in a more constructive way.[45] "What kind of alliance could be cobbled together from people who feel equally excluded by class, or by some combination of class and race?" he asks. In *Common Ground*, Lukas notes that, ideologically, the busing crisis pit the Harvard-educated liberal Colin Diver and the underclass black

Rachel Twymon against the working-class Irish American Alice McGoff. But, says Lukas, "the McGoffs and the Twymons have far more in common than either of them does with the Divers. And they knew it. . . . Robert Kennedy seemed to be talking about [it] in Indiana [and] Martin Luther King, arguably, with the Poor People's March was moving in that direction. But if an even more serious effort was made by somebody who didn't get himself killed, we don't know what would happen. I would love to see it happen in this country before I die."[46]

Survey research backs up these ethnographic studies. Donald Warren of the University of Michigan found that, though white "Middle Americans" clearly resented blacks and poor people, their resentment "upward" was greater. In a poll of white Americans, Warren found that

> 30 percent of the population thought that the blacks had too much political power; 63 percent said that about the rich. Approximately 30 percent said that poor blacks were getting more than their fair share of government aid; 56 percent said the same thing about the rich. Eighteen percent said that blacks have a better chance than whites to get fair treatment from courts, while 42 percent said that about the rich.[47]

Likewise, studies show that much of George Wallace's appeal among white workers was based on his populist economic program—including guaranteed jobs—rather than on his dark racist message. In fact, when Barry Goldwater made Wallace's racial arguments without his economic ones, Goldwater fell flat in working-class industrial communities.[48]

Most intriguing of all is the way in which many white working-class Wallace supporters were also strongly attracted to Robert F. Kennedy and were willing to support his 1968 campaign for president. The pollster Patrick Caddell was astonished in 1968 when he found that "there were people in Jacksonville, Florida, telling me that they were for either George Wallace or Bobby Kennedy."[49]

Numerous polls, both regional and national, found that many Wallace supporters in the fall of 1968 had backed Kennedy before his assassination.⁵⁰ Polls found that Kennedy ran better than any other Democrat against Wallace.⁵¹ In fact, Wallace's popularity, which had remained constant from the middle of 1967 to the summer of 1968, jumped seven points following RFK's assassination.⁵² The reporter Paul Cowan commented on the overlapping support for the two men after attending a Wallace campaign trip to Massachusetts, the month after Kennedy's death. "The clear majority of Wallace's audiences, day or night, are white working class men," Cowan wrote. "Many of them planned to vote for Robert Kennedy this year. 'He wasn't like the other politicians,' said a television repairman from Framingham. 'I had the feeling he really cared about people like us.'" In fact, Wallace often praised Robert Kennedy as "a great American" in his speeches to working-class audiences. "He was a patriot, unlike those professors on college campuses—pseudo-intellectuals, I call them—who say they long for a victory of the Viet Cong," Wallace said at one rally. "You know," a woman at a Wallace rally in Middleboro, Massachusetts, told Cowan, "Wallace is very much like Kennedy was." Cowan concluded: "I realized for the first time how important Robert Kennedy's candidacy had been. . . . More than Lyndon Johnson or Hubert Humphrey—more even than John Kennedy—[RFK] had sought to help [white working men] understand the confusing period their country had entered."⁵³

The reporter David Halberstam was also intrigued. On the one hand, he wrote, "many of those who were for Kennedy were borderline backlashers, who thought the choice in American politics narrowed to George Wallace or Bob Kennedy." On the other hand, he said, the relationship between blacks and Robert Kennedy "was one of the few remaining love affairs in American politics."⁵⁴

In the Indiana presidential primary, running against Eugene McCarthy and a popular stand-in for Hubert Humphrey, Governor Roger Branigan, Kennedy's appeal to the Wallace constituency was put to its toughest test. Riots were sweeping the nation, and working-class whites, who had shown their allegiance to Wallace in 1964—and would do so again in the 1968 general and 1972 primary campaigns—were more on edge than ever. Nevertheless, on primary day, Kennedy won not only 85 percent of the black vote but also the seven counties where George Wallace had run strongest in 1964.[55] He carried backlash bastions like East Chicago, which was two-thirds white, and Whiting, which was all-white. In Gary, a city near the brink of racial war, Kennedy ran ahead two-to-one in many Polish precincts, while simultaneously sweeping the black vote.[56] A week later Kennedy won the Nebraska primary, garnering 51 percent of the vote. But "of equal significance," writes Jack Newfield, "was the fact that Kennedy's delicate alliance of slum Negroes and low-income whites had worked again; Kennedy received more than 80 percent of all Negro votes and almost 60 percent of the votes cast by low-income white areas."[57]

Kennedy was able to rebuild the coalition in part because of who he was, but also because of what he stood for. He preached an urban populism, which was a blend of liberalism without elitism and populism without racism. Kennedy's private thinking about the primary role of class came through clearly in his public pronouncements.[58] Class inequality, in particular tax equity, was a major theme of Kennedy's campaign. On the stump, Jeff Greenfield notes, Kennedy "would constantly say . . . that 200 people who made $200,000 a year paid no taxes. . . . He kept coming back to those 200 people . . . and then he'd say, 'One year Hunt paid $102. I guess he was feeling generous.' "[59] Business was scared to death of Kennedy and reviled him more than any other candidate.[60]

Always Kennedy emphasized the common ground between poor and working-class blacks and whites. When he called for jobs, he would say, "I want to find jobs for the black people of Watts, and the white people of Eastern Kentucky." When he spoke of hunger, he was always sure to speak of white hunger and poverty as well as black.[61] When he railed against the student draft deferment, as he did at Notre Dame, he attacked it not by pointing out its racial bias but by saying, "You're getting the unfair advantage while poor people are being drafted."[62] Where in 1968 many liberals saw crime as a racial issue—and the call for law and order as racist—Kennedy saw it as a class issue, emphasizing that the victims of crime and lawlessness were in large part the poor and working class, white and black.[63] Though the issue of racial preferences was beginning to be discussed in 1968, Kennedy never endorsed the policy, and his previous statements declared opposition to them.[64] The Harvard psychiatrist Robert Coles said the key to Kennedy's appeal among working-class whites was their feeling that "this guy isn't going to use us to show those rich Harvard-types what a great guy he is. He may be for [the blacks] but he's for us too."[65]

In the end, Kennedy's success showed that even in the most turbulent and racially charged times, a candidate could draw support from both underclass blacks and working-class whites. There was no Great Depression to get poor and working people of all races and origins to see their common interests. The economy was roaring ahead. Indeed, after three years of rioting, race was at the top of everyone's mind. But in the year when American cities were burning and Wallace's backlash campaign did frighteningly well, Kennedy's core of support came from both blacks and the working-class whites who most feared blacks. If George Wallace showed that it is necessary for progressives to come up with a nonracist populism, Robert Kennedy showed that it is possible.

Some have suggested that Robert Kennedy's 1968 campaign was sui generis (because he was the brother of a recently slain president) or ancient history (marking the end of the golden era in which the New Deal coalition had thrived). But a subsequent answer to George Wallace and to Tom Watson (the populist turned race-baiter) is the later George Wallace—the rabid race-baiter turned biracial populist.[66] Wallace's biographer Stephan Lesher records the remarkable transformation. After years as the embodiment of segregation, and then of the white backlash against civil rights, Wallace appeared before the SCLC in 1982 and apologized for the harm he had done to blacks. He garnered 25 percent of the black vote in the Democratic gubernatorial primary that year, and nearly unanimous black support in the general election.[67] He became, says the journalist Roy Reed, "the darling of the Alabama NAACP" and yet continued to draw the strong white support necessary for victory.[68] By July 1987, Wallace would be courted by none other than the Reverend Jesse

Jackson, who was then beginning his presidential campaign. Jackson told Wallace: "You had a message about challenging the rich and the powerful to be fair. It's a message that's going to have a place in this campaign, too. The extremes of wealth and poverty—the billionaires on one end and the dirt poor on the other—[pose] a real threat to our stability now."[69] When Jackson and Wallace joined hands to pray, says Lesher, "the sight of that particular white hand enfolded by that particular black hand created an almost palpable sense of history flowing from that astonishing nexus."[70]

Jesse Jackson's campaigns for president in 1984 and 1988, far from showing the failure of class-based populism, show how crucial it is that class-based rhetoric be matched by class-based policies. Jackson began to strike out in a different direction thematically in a bold effort to move beyond race to class-based populism. He spoke of the need to "leave the racial battle ground and come to the economic common ground."[71] He told his black and white audiences, "When a baby cries at midnight because it has no supper, that baby doesn't cry in black or white or brown or male or female. That baby cries in pain."[72] His campaign literature announced: "Twenty years ago racial violence in the Old South was not only constant, but legal. Today racial violence still occurs but it's illegal, so we can struggle effectively to end it. But economic violence is legal and is devastating the lives of Americans of all races."[73]

Some portion of Jackson's failure to appeal to white working-class voters may stem from a racist distaste for voting for any black candidate.[74] But more important, Jackson's strong support for race-based preferences severely undercut his talk of moving to common ground. At the 1980 Democratic Convention, he told the black caucus: "We have the key to the White House door. And we should hold that key until we get more judgeships. We should hold that key until we have at least three cabinet members."[75] His organization, Operation PUSH, was clear about its goal—"economic justice for Black America," a worthy goal, but hardly inclusive.[76] At the 1984 Democratic National Convention, he pushed hard, against Walter Mondale's objections, to include in the platform a plank that effectively endorsed quotas.[77] Again in 1988, Jackson pushed for, and received, an endorsement for racial set-asides in an otherwise cautious Democratic platform.[78] Logically, all of Jackson's rhetoric about leaving "the racial battleground" for "economic common ground" supports a class-based preference program. His long support for racial preferences made his new economic rhetoric ring hollow. The race appeal explicitly contradicted the class appeal in a way that working Americans understood very plainly.

Finally, in 1992, another southern populist did win the White House, not by emphasizing racial preferences but by focusing directly on economic issues. Bill Clinton had seen what had happened in the 1990 midterm elections when a number of Republicans defeated Democratic opponents by turning the Civil Rights Act of 1990—largely an issue of employers versus employees—into an issue of quotas and employees versus employees.[79] So the candidate Bill Clinton studiously avoided the affirmative action question, even fudging when asked about it directly, much to the dismay of some black supporters.[80] The strategy worked. During the primaries, the *New York Times* compared Clinton's coalition to the one forged in RFK's Indiana primary campaign, and William Julius Wilson said that the media's focus on Clinton's private life had "failed to appreciate the significance of Mr. Clinton's remarkable biracial coalition" of lower- and middle-income whites and blacks.[81] In the general election, one commentator noted that Clinton's victory was based on his "successful wooing of the killer B's—the brothers, the Bubbas and the Archie Bunkers—a coalition of blacks, southern whites and urban ethnic voters."[82] By contrast, Clinton's embrace of racial preferences following the election appears to have hurt him with white male voters in the 1994 elections.[83]

During the 1992 campaign, Clinton relied heavily on Kevin Phillips's *The Politics of Rich and Poor*, a book whose appearance in 1990 represents a transformation almost as stunning as George Wallace's.[84] Phillips, the well-respected Republican commentator, made his name in the late 1960s predicting (in the title of his book) *The Emerging Republican Majority*. His central thesis was that the Democratic Party's identification with blacks and elite liberals would make it fairly easy for Republicans to gain the confidence of the white working-class vote.[85] By 1990 he was making the case in *The Politics of Rich and Poor* that economic populism—"class warfare," in the words of critics—would work for Democrats.[86]

At the core of Phillips's change of heart was the transformation of the American economy in between publication of his two books. Until 1973 there was much truth to George Will's assertion that the Democrats had created Republicans through the GI Bill and other social initiatives. But then stagnation hit. While Will's World War II veteran might have switched from the Democratic to the Republican Party, there has been plenty of incentive for his son or daughter to return to the Democratic fold. The changing economic situation has been accompanied by a growing populist outrage. As Vice President Al Gore noted in 1994, "The percentage of Americans believing [in 1965] that the government favors the rich and powerful was 29 percent. Today it is 80 percent."[87]

The Black and Blue Coalition Is Necessary If the coalition is possible, it is also necessary. A coalition of blacks, Latinos, women, and white liberals will occasionally suffice (especially in three-way races), but in most cases that coalition is unsustainable. While affirmative action theoretically energizes women, in fact the vast majority of women oppose gender preferences.[88] So we are left with the plain fact that there are more poor and working-class people of all races in America than there are people of color.[89]

The simple but fundamental political truth of twentieth-century America is that when white working people vote their class, Democrats win; when they vote their race, Republicans win. Through the middle of this century, Franklin D. Roosevelt's New Deal coalition—largely a class-based coalition of blacks and blue-collar whites—sustained an unparalleled string of Democratic victories. In the 1960s the Republican Party began shrewdly exploiting racial animosity between working-class whites and blacks. The result: white Robert Kennedy Democrats became Wallace Democrats, then Nixon Democrats, then Reagan

Democrats—and then today's "angry white males," whom we no longer even bother calling Democrats. This is politically disastrous for progressives. While emphasizing class threatens to reduce Democratic appeal among well-to-do blacks, that loss of support is more than offset by gains among working-class and poor blacks and whites.[90] (The shift would not be bad for African Americans either, who are now completely shut out when Republicans win.)[91]

The necessity of winning white working-class votes is today so obvious that it is often said almost in passing. In the 1980s, Bob Woodward writes, "The so-called Reagan Democrats . . . held the balance in national elections,"[92] while a *Wall Street Journal* news story declared in 1994, "The working class [constitutes] a block of voters that . . . Mr. Clinton needs if he is to remain in the White House beyond 1996."[93] Five to 10 percent of the electorate—primarily white working-class voters—can cause a "sea change in American presidential politics," argue journalists Thomas and Mary Edsall. "[T]he replacement of a liberal majority with a conservative majority," they write, "involved the conversion of [this] relatively small proportion of voters."[94] As affirmative action is one of the best ways to lose these votes, class preferences may be the best way to win them back.

The Coalition Is Desirable Even if one disagrees that the white working class is necessary for a Democratic victory—that is, even if the numbers of upper-middle-class white liberals equaled the number of working-class whites so that an electoral victory was achievable with either—there are three strong reasons to build a coalition with blacks and working-class whites at the core anyway.

First, because upper-middle-class whites do not have a self-interest in addressing class inequality, some of them prove fair-weather friends on the meat-and-potatoes Democratic issues. As Bayard Rustin pointed out, not only is the affluent/poor coalition politically naive (since "its constituents comprise a distinct minority of the population"), it also poses severe problems of governance, since the affluent "are hardly the undisputed friends of the poor."[95] Jonathan Kozol found this to be true when he spoke to liberals about funding for education. "Many people, even those who view themselves as liberals on other issues, tend to grow indignant, even rather agitated, if invited to look closely at these inequalities," he wrote.[96] Likewise, the labor lawyer Tom Geoghegan argues that white liberals can be unreliable allies on labor issues. It was, he points out, "the 'liberal' Warren Court of the 1960s"—and Earl Warren and William Brennan, in particular—that effectively gutted the Norris–La Guardia Act when, in the *Boys Markets* case, it sharply cut back the instances when unions could strike.[97] Alliances between African Americans and big business can also prove troublesome to progressive interests.[98]

Indeed, some argue that upper-middle-class liberals emphasize race and seek to forge an upper-middle-class white/black coalition precisely so as to eclipse larger issues of class. The columnist Jim Sleeper, for example, asks, is white liberal support for various racial initiatives, like busing and scatter-site housing, in fact designed to create a "way to blame white ethnics for black deprivations really caused by economic and social arrangements that benefited primarily the liberals themselves?"[99] Writing after the Los Angeles riots, University of Southern California Professor Ronald Steel said the "division is usually described as one of race, because it is to the advantage of those who control the levers of power to do so. . . . But the increasingly profound division is one of class."[100]

Second, the failure of progressives to try to win over working-class whites creates a vacuum that is filled in by demagogues, who are not only bad for Democrats electorally but also bad for the country. When the festering wounds of disadvantaged black and white people are left unaddressed, the potential for mischief is great. On the one hand, Cornel West points out, "white ethnic working class . . . anxieties must be spoken to by prophetic figures. One must not write them off or there will be more David Dukes."[101] On the other hand, when liberals fail to emphasize common class interests in the black community, the black poor are likely to turn to hate-mongers like Louis Farrakhan or charlatans like Al Sharpton. When Martin Luther King was threatened by Stokely Carmichael and H. Rap Brown, he countered with the Poor People's Campaign.[102] When Benjamin Chavis tried to make the NAACP more attractive to poor blacks, he took the opposite tack, making overtures to black separatists.

Third, while an alliance of affluent liberals and blacks might in some ways be easier to build, there are reasons to forge ahead with a class-based coalition to preserve peace and reduce the likelihood of more Howard Beaches and Bensonhursts. As Arthur Schlesinger notes, "The more important thing to do, obviously, is to try to bring the low-income whites and low-income blacks together . . . to preserve social cohesion."[103] Because people are inclined on occasion to vote by ethnicity is surely no reason to exacerbate that tendency through public policy and public definition of issues. Adds Jeff Greenfield: "For a Democratic candidate not to appeal to white working-class voters is [not only] a prescription for suicide; it's also wrong if your message is reconciliation."[104]

The key, obviously, is to pursue policies that do not pit black and white working Americans against each other but rather unite them. Jonathan Rieder points out that the blacks in New York clearly have suffered more than the ethnic whites in Canarsie. "The complaints of Canarsians about ghetto culture and reverse discrimination pale before the historic brutalization of black Americans." But, he continues, "the very posing of the question in that fashion, setting up a situation in which black or white interests can be satisfied only at the expense of the other party, symbolizes much of the recent failure of liberalism."[105]

The whole notion of affirmative action—putting the price of remedying past discrimination not on employers and discriminators but on fellow employees—was a tailor-made issue for conservatives. Write Thomas and Mary Edsall: "For a Republican Party seeking to divide the electorate along lines giving the GOP a huge advantage, few issues are as attractive as affirmative action."[106] By contrast, trading race for class preferences would at once eliminate for progressives an obvious albatross and potentially ignite a formidable class-based coalition not fully realized since the New Deal. In recent decades, as the columnist Mark Shields notes, when Democrats and Republicans have fought over working-class and middle-class voters, Democrats generally say, "We have your interests at heart" (worker safety, minimum wage), while Republicans say, "We respect your values" (school prayer, patriotism.)[107]

When Democrats support race-based affirmative action and Republicans oppose it, Democrats lose on both scores. Racial preferences plainly put the interests of minorities above the interests of the white working class. And race preferences contradict the values most white Americans have finally agreed on (do not judge on the basis of skin color, play by the rules). Worse, in recent years some Democrats have told white working-class voters that if they oppose racial preferences, they are racist. As Paul Starr points out, this charge of racism will intimidate some, "but it will succeed in making permanent enemies of many more."[108]

By contrast, shifting to class-based preferences provides Democrats a twin victory on interests and values. The criterion no longer divides the Democratic coalition in two; it unites natural allies, whose numbers are also much greater.[109] At least as important, class preferences respect, rather than conflict with, basic American values. The program is consistent with the antidiscriminatory thrust of the early civil rights movement—no preferences on race—and it is also consistent with the basic Democratic message of helping the underdog. Throughout the darkest days of defeat, the Democratic Party always had the edge on the "fairness" question: even if Democrats were the party of taxes and inflation, they were still more concerned about fairness than the Republicans. The Democratic Party's embrace of racial preferences, which appeared to be tied to its political base in the black community, severely undercut that claim. Class preferences, by contrast, acknowledge that the current rules are unfair to poor and working-class people of all races, and that giving a leg up to those dealt a raw deal is only fair.

While Republican wedge issues will remain, particularly on religiously based questions (gay rights, prayer in school, abortion), these pale in comparison to the old wedge, communism, and to the most potent of all wedge issues, race.[110] And of the various racial issues, says Thomas Edsall, affirmative action is the most divisive.[111] Unlike welfare or crime, which Republicans attempt to racialize with images of welfare queens and Willie Horton, affirmative action is unmistakably an issue of race. But it is possible to turn that issue around, to the advantage of Democrats. More important, it is possible to do so in a way that does not cut back on the Democrats' commitment to fairness but rather is a better fulfillment of that promise.

Race Marginalizes Larger Issues of Class

While the political argument is important, the ultimate reason for emphasizing class over race is that, on the merits, addressing race alone marginalizes larger and more fundamental issues of class.[112] King and Kennedy were driven not only by a political imperative but by a moral imperative. The race problem was real, but following passage of the civil rights legislation, the larger and more difficult issue of class was to take center stage.

King's Poor People's Campaign was not a whimsical notion but the culmination of many years of thinking. His initial call for class remedies in *Why We Can't Wait* grew in intensity as the urban riots of the mid–1960s underlined for him the notion that legal equality and liberation were not sufficient to significantly alter the lives of the black masses.[113] King called Watts "a class revolt of underprivileged against privileged." Poverty was now the most "pressing issue," and King decided, says his biographer David Garrow, to "fundamentally alter the nature of the movement."[114] The day after the 1966 midterm election, King announced that "we must face the fact that we are now in the most difficult phase of the civil rights struggle [involving] the basic class issues between the privileged and underprivileged." Economic issues, Garrow wrote, "increasingly occupied him."[115]

The Poor People's Campaign was King's final, most ambitious call for economic justice, encompassing the disadvantaged of all races. In an article published in April 1968, the month he was shot, King laid out his vision for the campaign: a march on Washington, with "Negro and white participation," seeking "to benefit the poor of both races"; he called it "a Selma-like movement on economic issues." Rejecting SNCC's move toward black separatism, King said he would seek the Economic Bill of Rights

for the Disadvantaged—of which he had spoken four years earlier—including guaranteed jobs for those who could work and a
guaranteed income for those who could not.[116] The Poor
People's Campaign was, according to one observer, "the most
serious effort" to forge a coalition among the poor of various
ethnic groups "since the Depression."[117]

In the years since King's assassination, a few lonely voices
have explained why addressing race alone does not go far
enough.[118] In 1969, when James Forman and others began
demanding reparations for blacks, Michael Harrington was concerned about the misfocused attention. Such a scheme, he argued,
"distracts people from the real battle against poverty" and would
"divert precious political energies."[119] Harrington preferred
King's Poor People's Campaign to Forman's Black Manifesto;
whereas the latter distracted and divided, the Poor People's Campaign's call for full employment had "enormous resonance," Harrington wrote, "among great masses of people in the West."[120]

In 1971, as the question of housing desegregation loomed
large, a young attorney named Mario Cuomo argued that the
issue was really "class before color." When New York City
Mayor John Lindsay tapped Cuomo to settle a dispute over the
placement of a low-income housing project in a white middle-
class community in Queens, Cuomo immediately saw that an
issue commonly defined as racial was in fact rooted in class.
While the press and the public interpreted neighborhood resistance to the project as bigotry, Cuomo saw it as "a clash
between working and nonworking people, many of the unemployed being black." In his book about the controversy, *Forest
Hills Diary*, Cuomo writes: "It's clear to me that the objection is
to crime and deterioration and not color. The coincidence that
most of the lower economic class are black is what produces
confusion. This isn't casuistry, but the black leadership is sure to
say it is."[121] The central proposition of *Forest Hills Diary*,
Cuomo says, "is that the big difference in Forest Hills was not
race, it was class. . . . If the world were all Lena Hornes and Bill
Russells, we'd get past that problem soon enough."[122]

A few years later, as Boston was riled by a federal court
order to desegregate the city's schools, the liberal psychiatrist

and Harvard professor Robert Coles said the larger hidden issue was class. The busing plan involved primarily black and working-class white children within the city limits and did not encompass the affluent white suburbs. Coles was unsparing in his criticism of white suburban liberals, who wrote off the working-class Irish opposition to busing as bigotry. "I think the busing is a scandal," Coles told the *Boston Globe* columnist Mike Barnicle.

> I do not think that busing should be imposed like this on working class people exclusively. It should cross these lines and people in the suburbs should share it. . . . The ultimate reality is the reality of class. . . . That's the real struggle that's going on. And to talk about [busing] only in terms of racism is to miss the point. It's working class people who happened to be white and working class people who happen to be black . . . poor people . . . both of whom are very hard pressed; neither of whom have got much leverage on anything. They are both competing for a very limited piece of the pie, the limits of which are being set by the larger limits of class which allow them damn little, if anything. . . . They've all gotten a raw deal, white and black. Both groups have been ignored. Both of them are looked down upon by the well-to-do white people who pick up the pieces. Because all the laws are being written for the wealthy and powerful. The tax laws, the zoning laws, the laws that have to do with protecting their housing and their education . . . all of this is protected. And no one had been taking anything away from them.[123]

Coles was blasted by the liberal elite he attacked.[124] But his argument also struck a chord among some notable liberals sympathetic to the aspiration of blacks; eleven years later, J. Anthony Lukas published his chronicle of the Boston busing crisis, *Common Ground*, and Coles's thinking was at the center of the Pulitzer Prize–winning volume. Throughout the book, Lukas emphasizes how the judge's desegregation order pitted working-class whites against blacks.[125] But Lukas goes beyond merely saying that there is an injustice in limiting busing to blacks and working-class whites and that the burden of busing should be shared. Like Coles, he appears, too, to yearn for a way to affirmatively advance both groups. When Alice McGoff complains to Lukas—"What did the blacks think they were doing? . . . They acted as though they were the only people who'd ever had it tough in this world. Poor was poor, hungry was hungry."[126]— Lukas appears sympathetic not to the complaint about blacks but about the common class injuries. Or so the book's title, *Common Ground*, suggests.[127]

Jack Beatty, a liberal editor of the *Atlantic Monthly*, echoes these sentiments, arguing that in Boston and elsewhere there will be no real solution until school desegregation efforts address the more basic issue of class segregation. As Beatty argues, the social science evidence supporting *Brown v. Board of Education* "was surely not that the whiteness of the white students would have a beneficial effect upon black students," but rather that "something of the social power, the ease and relatively greater confidence and expectations of the white students, would light a spark of social hope in the blacks." However, Beatty continues, "When segregation by class replaces segregation by race, this premise no longer holds."[128]

For Beatty, school desegregation in Boston was a failure not only in execution—resulting in dramatic white flight—but more important, a failure to recognize the salience of class over race.[129] Even if one could execute busing within the city of Boston without a hitch—desegregate the white working class and blacks perfectly, no strife, no white flight—one would still face the fact that the whites and blacks being bused simply do not have the same life chances as the whites (and occasional blacks) in the good suburban schools. To provide fairer chances, he suggests, the children of wealthy white lawyers need to be mixed with those of working class white janitors and black bus drivers.[130] "A final lesson to be learned from the Boston busing crisis," Beatty writes, "is that while our society has instruments for remedying some of the inequalities stemming from race—often rough and counterproductive instruments, like Judge Garrity's court order—it has neither the public language nor the policy instruments to identify and ameliorate inequalities stemming from class."[131]

In 1975 the journalist James Fallows, later a speechwriter for President Carter, argued that the question of who served in Vietnam involved not just race but deeper issues of class. The charge had frequently been leveled that blacks were being sent to fight in disproportionate numbers, and in 1965 the Department of Defense took steps to alter the racial makeup of the armed forces when it was learned that 25 percent of Americans killed in combat were black.[132] But Fallows made it clear that the injustice was broader, and that to talk about the issue as one affecting racial minorities was to marginalize it. In a seminal article in the *Washington Monthly* titled "What Did You Do in the Class War, Daddy?," Fallows detailed how he and his Harvard classmates employed various tricks to avoid the military draft, while "the boys from Chelsea, thick, dark-haired young men, the white proles of Boston . . . walked through the examination lines like so many cattle off to slaughter." It was, Fallows wrote, a "most brutal form of class discrimination."[133]

In 1978, William Julius Wilson argued in *The Declining Significance of Race* that class is now the greatest impediment for most blacks. While he was labeled a "neoconservative" for that stance, his message is clearly in the tradition of Bayard Rustin—it is not that race-based solutions go too far, but that they do not go far enough.[134] When he was blasted by black intellectuals for essentially betraying his race, Wilson responded with tough rhetoric:

> The group that would have the most to gain by a shift in emphasis from race to economic dislocation, the black lower class, is not the group that is really defining the issues. . . . The issues are being defined by the articulate black intelligentsia—the very group that has benefited the most in recent years from antidiscrimination programs [and that has] a vested interest in keeping race as the single most important issue in developing policies to promote black progress.[135]

In 1993, Cornel West, in his book *Race Matters*, in fact argued that class matters more.[136] One observer writes that,

"While *Race Matters* examines such topics as black conservatism, black-Jewish relations, black 'rage' and taboos surrounding black sexuality, West's prescription for America transcends race." The heart of the matter for West is this: "We never had a public debate in this country about 1 percent of the population owning 37 percent of the wealth . . . or 10 percent owning 86."[137] Unlike some others who preach the importance of class but fight for race-specific preferences, West says that class-based affirmative action is the optimal solution.[138] Likewise, in 1995 Betty Friedan, the mother of modern feminism, had come to the conclusion that while gender is important, it is time to get "beyond identity politics" to economic empowerment.[139]

Race- and gender-based affirmative action contradicts the class principle, particularly when wealthy blacks or women benefit over poor white males. But worse, it confines our definition of the problem in a way that is pleasing to those in power. When economic inequality is presented to white America with a black face, remedial action is much less likely to be forthcoming. It is far more radical, as the *Washington Post* columnist E. J. Dionne suggests, to focus on ensuring "something closer to equality of opportunity—for an inner-city child and [a] white janitor's son alike."[140]

It is clear as we come to the close of the twentieth century that those of us concerned with inequality of opportunity need to embark on a new strategy. Even strong proponents of race-based affirmative action concede that almost all the true progress for equal opportunity—*Brown v. Board of Education*, the Civil Rights Act of 1964, Head Start, the Elementary and Secondary Education Act—came before 1968, and that many of the battles since then have been rearguard actions.[141] When the civil rights movement changed direction after the assassinations of King and Kennedy—insisting on racial remedies in a country trying to move beyond race—it charted a course that has produced, at best, uneven progress. The underclass continues to fester. Race relations remain tense. And we seem further than ever from King's vision of a color-blind society.

But in a strange way, it may be that the very existence of affirmative action, an imperfect and highly unpopular attempt at promoting justice, has laid the groundwork for a triumphant return of the principles of Kennedy and King. If affirmative action has helped conservatives adopt the rhetoric of color blindness, and if racial preferences have prompted the right to champion breaks to the disadvantaged as an alternative, progressives should not disparage these developments but rather should seize upon them.

Class-based affirmative action is a highly radical idea, but radical in the most American way. Americans hold doggedly to notions of family and liberty, but they also believe in a sort of rough equality of opportunity that gives the underdog a real chance in life. Racial preferences do a poor job of advancing that goal. Indeed, they have divided the very people who would naturally champion policies to bring about greater fairness. A system of preferences for the disadvantaged offers a far bolder and more appropriate way of promoting Jefferson's vision of a natural aristocracy—a state in which children, born into all walks of life, can flourish in a way we have never truly allowed.

Notes

Note: *This book crosses several disciplines—law, sociology, philosophy, and political science. Citations employ a social science rather than a legal format, since the former is likely to be more familiar to most readers.*

Introduction

1. Sen. Robb recounted this exchange in an address to the Senate; see *Congressional Record*, October 15, 1991, S14688.

2. By "class," I mean socioeconomic status (SES). See ch. 5.

3. Some object to the use of the word preferences and particularly to using preferences as a synonym for affirmative action; see Dorothy Gilliam, "Damaging, Destructive Doublespeak," *Washington Post*, June 17, 1995, H1 (complaining about the press's use of the word preferences to describe a federal program giving a 10 percent bonus to contractors who use minority subcontractors); Louis Harris, "Affirmative Action and the Voter," *New York Times,* July 31, 1995, A13; and Geneva Overholster, "Preferential Treatments," *Washington Post*, August 13, 1995, C6. But "preferences" are precisely what the controversy over affirmative action is all about, and the two terms will be used interchangeably in this book. Almost everyone favors making sure there is a diverse applicant pool (what I call "old-style affirmative action"), and almost everyone opposes quotas for the unqualified. The nub of the disagreement is over "preferences"—counting race or gender in favor of otherwise less qualified women or people of color.

It is not the use of the term *preference* that makes race- and gender-based decision-making unpopular. When polls ask whether race should be "a factor when deciding who is hired, promoted or admitted to college," the same negative reaction is registered as when the word *preference* is used; see *Washington Post*/Kaiser Family Foundation/Harvard University Survey, *Washington Post*, October 11, 1995, A1, A12. By contrast, veterans' "preferences" are broadly supported. The policy I advocate—class-based affirmative action—will be used interchangeably with class preferences. I argue that class preferences are justified, and therefore do not shrink behind more euphemistic terms like *class-conscious remedies* to describe what is in fact a preference.

4. Richard Morin and Sharon Warden, "Americans Vent Anger at Affirmative Action," *Washington Post*, March 24, 1995, A1, A4.

5. Jeffries, *Justice Powell*, 473.

6. Dershowitz and Hanft, "College Diversity," 383.

7. Jeffries, *Justice Powell*, 469.

8. White House Office of the Press Secretary, *Remarks by the President on Affirmative Action*, July 19, 1995, 5. Northwestern University's Charles Moskos also approvingly cites the army's use of the *Bakke* straddle; see Charles Moskos, "Affirmative Action: The Army's Success . . . ," *Washington Post*, March 15, 1995, A19.

9. The initiative provides: "Neither the State of California nor any of its political subdivisions or agents shall use race, sex, color, or national origin as a criterion for either discriminating against, or granting preferential treatment to, any individual or group in the operation of the State's system of public employment, public education or public contracting"; see Quentin L. Kopp and Bill Leonard, "Take the Initiative on Reverse Discrimination," *Wall Street Journal*, June 6, 1994. Early polls suggest it could pass by a wide margin; see Mona Charney, "Lack of Funds Threatens California Civil Rights Initiative," *Fresno Bee*, November 2, 1995, B7, citing Field poll finding 65 percent support for CCRI; Charles Krauthammer, "Affirmative Action: The Debate Is Over," *Washington Post*, April 14, 1995, A21; and "Affirmative Action on the Edge," *U.S. News and World Report*, February 13, 1995, 32.

10. Scalia, "Commentary: The Disease as Cure," 147.

11. Nathan Glazer, "Race, Not Class," *Wall Street Journal*, April 5, 1995, A12.

12. See UPI, "Dr. King's Group Maps Civil Disobedience Strategy," *New York Times*, November 27, 1967, 53; Oates, *Let the Trumpet Sound*, 434–35.

13. Garrow, *Bearing the Cross*, 607, 616.

14. Fager, *Uncertain Resurrection*, 18.

15. Garrow, *Bearing the Cross*, 598.

16. Fager, *Uncertain Resurrection*, 142; Mitchell Shields, "King in Washington," *Washington Post Magazine* (April 4, 1993); Oates, *Let the Trumpet Sound*, 435, 446, 463.

17. Schlesinger, *Robert Kennedy and His Times*, 875.

18. Halberstam, *Robert Kennedy*, 87.

19. Ibid., 91; Stein and Plimpton, *American Journey*, 261.

20. Schlesinger, *Robert Kennedy and His Times*, 873.

21. Halberstam, *Robert Kennedy*, 128–29.

22. Phillips, *The Emerging Republican Majority*, 350.

23. Jeff Greenfield, interview with the author, New York, N.Y., January 30, 1985. See also Newfield, *Robert Kennedy*, 296.

24. Robert Coles, interview with the author, Cambridge, Mass., February 25, 1985.

25. See *DeFunis v. Odegaard*, 416 US 312, 331 (1974) (Douglas dissenting); Senate Judiciary Committee, *Nomination of Judge Thomas*, 358–60; and Scalia, "Commentary: The Disease as Cure," 153–54. For more details, see ch. 4.

26. See West, *Race Matters*, 64; and D'Souza, *Illiberal Education*, 251–53.

27. D'Souza takes just two pages to outline his proposal (*Illiberal Education*, 251–53); Scalia devotes two paragraphs to it ("Commentary: The Disease as Cure," 153, 156).

Chapter 1

1. See Lyndon B. Johnson, commencement address at Howard University, June 4, 1965, *Public Papers of Presidents: Lyndon B. Johnson*, 1965, 636.

2. See Goodwin, *Remembering America*, 343.

3. King, *Why We Can't Wait*, 134.

4. Moynihan, *The Negro Family*, 3, and Introduction.

5. Moynihan, *Family and Nation*, 27.

6. *Dred Scott v. Sanford*, cited in Kluger, *Simple Justice*, 47.

7. See Prince E. Wilson, "Discrimination Against Blacks," in Blackstone and Heslep, *Social Justice and Preferential Treatment*, 167.

8. Fleming, *The Lengthening Shadow of Slavery*, 1.

9. Kluger, *Simple Justice*, 62.

10. Quoted in ibid., 385.

11. Quoted in Hughes, *Culture of Complaint*, 136.

12. See Juan Williams, "It's a White Thing," *Washington Post*, April 2, 1995, C1.

13. Walzer, *Spheres of Justice*, 151–52.

14. Johnson, Howard commencement address (1965), 636.

15. Daniel P. Moynihan, rough draft of President Lyndon Johnson's Howard University commencement address, June 2, 1965, copy given to author by Moynihan, 7-8.

16. *Regents of University of California v. Bakke*, 438 US 265, 395 (1978).

17. *City of Richmond v. J. A. Croson Co.*, 488 US 469, 532 (1989).

18. *UC v. Bakke*, 324 (from the first sentence in Brennan's opinion). See also Fleming, *The Lengthening Shadow of Slavery*, 125.

19. Johnson, Howard commencement address (1965), 638.

20. *UC v. Bakke*, 396.

21. *Wygant v. Jackson Board of Education*, 476 US 267, 315 (1986) (Stevens dissenting).

22. Tom Wicker's report on the speech in the *New York Times* ("Johnson Pledges to Help Negroes to Full Equality," June 5, 1965) noted that Johnson "did not mention such specific remedies as job quotas or preferential hiring, which some civil rights leaders have advocated."

23. Johnson, Howard commencement address (1965), 639.

24. Editorial, "Freedom Is Not Enough," *Washington Post*, May 6, 1992.

25. Quoted in Rainwater and Yancey, *The Moynihan Report*, 377.

26. Ibid., 278. Later, in 1967, following rioting in Detroit, Johnson continued to avoid race-specific solutions in favor of summer jobs for unemployed young people; see Skrentny, *The Ironies of Affirmative Action*.

27. EO 11246, 3 CFR 339 (1964–65) reprinted in 42 USC, section 2000e, 28–31 (1983). Its significance was largely reorganizational. Indeed, the executive order was if anything meant to be a setback for civil rights because it abolished an existing organization headed by the civil rights champion Vice President Hubert Humphrey; see Nicholas Lemann, "Taking Affirmative Action Apart," *New York Times Magazine* (June 11, 1995): 42.

28. Weir, *Politics and Jobs*, 108. See also Lind, *The Next American Nation*, 108–10.

29. See Graham, *The Civil Rights Era*, 278. The plan was rescinded by the Labor Department in November 1968 (296). The Johnson administration did pursue affirmative action plans in St. Louis, San Francisco, and Cleveland; see Citizens' Commission on Civil Rights, *Affirmative Action*, 40–45. But the Johnson program of goals was seen as "insufficiently specific" (55). And it was not until 1970, with Nixon's order no. 4 and 1971's revised order no. 4, that teeth were added (55–56). James E. Jones, Jr., wrote in 1988 that Nixon's revised Philadelphia plan in 1969 marks "the beginning controversy"; "The Origins of Affirmative Action," 383; see also Mills, *Debating Affirmative Action*, 10; and Laurence H. Silberman, "The Road to Racial Quotas," *Wall Street Journal*, August 11, 1977 ("Prior to 1969, affirmative action was defined in ambiguous procedural terms").

30. Interview with Daniel Patrick Moynihan, Washington, D.C., January 25, 1995. See also Moynihan, *The Negro Family*, 47 ("The object of this study has been to define a problem, rather than propose solutions to it"). At a 1965 conference of the American Academy of Arts and Sciences, Moynihan said in response to a question about racial preferences, "Congressmen vote for everybody more readily than they vote for anyone. Because the poverty program is colorblind, we can do what we could not have done otherwise"; see *Daedalus* 2 (Fall 1965 and Winter 1966): 288–89.

31. Daniel P. Moynihan, commencement address, New School for Social Research, June 4, 1968, copy given to author by Moynihan, 13, 15–16. See also Peter Kihss, "Moynihan Scores Ethnic Quota Idea," *New York Times*, June 5, 1968, 1; and Daniel P. Moynihan, "State vs. Academe," *Harper's* (December 1980): 31, 32.

32. King, *Why We Can't Wait*, 135, 137. King also discussed the Bill of Rights for the Disadvantaged at a retreat at Black Mountain, North Carolina, in January 1964. King told his advisers that calls for compensatory treatment for blacks must include a similar call for compensatory treatment for poor whites; Garrow, *Bearing the Cross*, 311. King also made the argument to the Republican National Convention in July 1964, where he renewed his call for a bill of rights to (in Garrow's words) "compensate both blacks and poor whites for past injuries" (340).

33. Skrentny, "Politics and Possibility," 5. In contrast to King's 1964 book *Why We Can't Wait*, Charles Silberman's best-selling book that year, *Crisis in Black and White*, advocated racial preferences; see Steinberg, *Turning Back*, 72. The issue of compensation was also hotly debated in the *New York Times Magazine* (October 6, 1963, 43ff). Michael Lind, noting the degree to which current civil rights policies have repudiated King's color-blind ideals in favor of policies advocated by rival civil rights leaders, quips, "If today's establishment were honest, Martin Luther King Day would be James Farmer Day" (*The Next American Nation*, 109).

34. Cited in Skrentny, *Ironies*. David Garrow also said King never endorsed race-based affirmative action; David Garrow, telephone interview with the author, January 18, 1995.

35. See Bell, *Faces at the Bottom of the Well*, 27; Dreyfuss and Lawrence, *The Bakke Case*, 139; Days, "Civil Rights at the Crossroads," 272–73, 279; Ansley, "Stirring the Ashes," 1027 n135; and Greenberg, *Crusaders in the Courts*, 432. See also Garrow, *Bearing the Cross*, 311, 340, 439, 455, 537, 607, 616; Paul E. Peterson, "The Urban

Underclass and the Poverty Paradox," in Jencks and Peterson, *The Urban Underclass*, 25; Bloom, *Class, Race, and the Civil Rights Movement*, 212–13; Skocpol, "Race, Liberalism, and Affirmative Action (II)," 87; and Gates, "Heroes, Inc.," 7.

36. Quoted in Steinberg, *Turning Back*, 67, 111.

37. Quoted in Skrentny, *Ironies*.

38. Kerner et al., *Report of the National Advisory Commission*, 12. The report does discuss "affirmative action" in the context of police hiring, but in so doing, it affirms that standards must be maintained, and affirmative action efforts appear to mean widening the net of applicants (166).

39. See Brown, *Minority Party*, 25.

40. Graham, *The Civil Rights Era*, 106–7; Senate Judiciary Committee, *Civil Rights— The President's Program*, 414. While Kennedy might have "evolved" on the issue of affirmative action, as civil rights groups threw their support behind racial preferences, there is some reason to doubt this. First, the case for compensation was, of course, much more powerful in 1963, when the legacy of segregation was much stronger, than it is today. Indeed, Robert Kennedy's son Douglas Harriman Kennedy chairs a group of post-baby boomers, Third Millennium, which argues the time has come for "a new approach to affirmative action that focuses on economic status"; "Third Millennium Declaration," New York, July 1993, 20; see also Michael Grunwald, "Third Millennium," *Boston Globe Magazine* (November 28, 1993): 12ff. Second, we know that Kennedy was not afraid to cross civil rights groups where he disagreed. For example, during his 1964 Senate campaign, Kennedy announced his opposition to busing; Robert Kennedy, address, Binghamton, N.Y., September 9, 1964, cited in Ross, *Robert Kennedy*, 61. Class-based affirmative action, by contrast, comports with Kennedy's political instincts about coalition building; with his moral sense that problems are more rooted in class than race; and with his affirmation of the antidiscrimination principle that people ought not to be burdened by the color of their skin.

41. Newfield, *Robert Kennedy*, 287.

42. None of this is to argue that Johnson, King, and Kennedy would, or that Moynihan does, oppose racial preferences today in the absence of a class-based remedy. Indeed, as a U.S. senator, Moynihan has supported racial set-aside programs precisely because the class-based remedies to our nation's history of discrimination were not forthcoming; Moynihan interview (1995).

43. In the Howard commencement address, Johnson did argue that "Negro poverty is not white poverty" (638). Black poverty is generally more concentrated, he noted, and more likely to be associated with family breakup—both a consequence, he argued, of past discrimination (638–39). But he also said these differences "are not racial differences" (638). While racial in origin, the differences are manifested in economic terms. So while poor blacks are, in the aggregate, more likely to live in concentrated poverty and single-parent homes than poor whites, some poor whites do live under those circumstances, and some poor blacks do not. These differences, in the end, are class differences. As I will argue in ch. 5, these class factors—single-parent home and concentration of poverty—should be factored into a class-based affirmative action program, and their inclusion will disproportionately benefit minorities.

44. Ibid., 637, 1113, 1115.

45. Moynihan, *The Negro Family*, 29.

46. Moynihan, "A Family Policy," 282.

47. King, *Why We Can't Wait*, 138.

48. Kerner et al., *Report of the National Advisory Commission*, 16, 4, 73.

49. Glazer, *Ethnic Dilemmas*, 219.

50. Rainwater and Yancey, *The Moynihan Report*, 182–83, 201–2.

51. Moynihan interview (1995). See also Moynihan's statement on the Senate floor in 1992, 138 *Congressional Record*, May 6, 1992, S6059; and Moynihan, *Pandaemonium*, 171.

52. Quoted in Garrow, *Bearing the Cross*, 312. See also King, *Why We Can't Wait*, 141–42.

53. Rustin, "The King to Come," 21.

Chapter 2

1. The University of California at Davis program, challenged by Allan Bakke, was an exception. Preferences were limited to economically disadvantaged members of minority groups. Most observers, both proponents and opponents of affirmative action, point to the riots as the crucial event that spurred colleges and others on to race-based affirmative action; see Jencks, "Affirmative Action for Blacks," 753; *UC v. Bakke*, 369, n45 (Brennan); Culp, "Diversity, Multiculturalism, and Affirmative Action," 1154; and Liacouras, *Cross Reference*, 158. For example, Harvard, which said it had been seeking "diversity" for years, suddenly tripled its black enrollment in the late 1960s (from 2 percent to 7 percent); see Klitgaard, *Choosing Elites*, 27; see also Dershowitz and Hanft, "College Diversity," 383.

2. Kennedy first suggested the Poor People's Campaign in the summer of 1967 to Marian Wright Edelman, who passed on the idea to King; Lemann, *The Promised Land*, 216. See also Greenberg, *Crusaders in the Court*, 430; and Schlesinger, *Robert Kennedy*, 873.

3. Brief for the National Council of Jewish Women and others as amici curiae, *DeFunis v. Odegaard*, 59.

4. How often this happens in practice is addressed more fully in ch. 3.

5. Rodriguez, *Hunger of Memory*, 151. Likewise, says Andrew Kull, "the color-blind consensus, so long in forming, was abandoned with surprising rapidity"; *The Colorblind Constitution*, 183.

6. *UC v. Bakke*, 365–66.

7. Brennan must have known that Americans would reject the argument that Bakke would probably have lost out on the merits but for past discrimination: in making the point, Brennan's normally eloquent style suddenly yields to unusually tortured syntax.

8. See John Taylor, "The Rosewood Massacre," *Esquire* (July 1994): 46–54. See also, "Florida Seeks Survivors of 1923 Racial Massacre," *Washington Post*, May 31, 1994, A5.

9. Although government payments necessarily translate into increased taxes, taxpayers are often called upon to pay for all sorts of problems not of their own making, such as the savings and loan scandal; Carter, *Affirmative Action Baby*, 18. And because compensation takes the form of cash payments, the relative burden of compensation does not fall disproportionately on certain individuals but rather is progressively distributed.

10. *See* Civil Liberties Act of 1988, 50 USC 1989 et seq. The U.S. Circuit Court for the District of Columbia upheld the Japanese compensation legislation as a "perfect fit between means and ends," citing Justice Scalia's concurrence in *Richmond v. Croson*. See *Jacobs v. Barr* (959 F2d 313, 319 [1992]). The act pays reparations not to all Japanese Americans but to those directly affected by the internment during World War II; see sect. 1989b–7(2).

11. In addition, Germany paid Israel "to alleviate the costs borne by that country of settling refugees after the war"; Goldman, *Justice and Reverse Discrimination*, 100. *See* also Fishkin, *Justice, Equal Opportunity*, 124; and Posner, "The DeFunis Case," 16–17, n33.

12. For example, in *Franks v. Bowman* (424 US 747 [1976]), an employer was found guilty of past discrimination, and the actual victims received compensation. The Court approved the remedy but noted that the compensation—which came in the form of cash (back pay), "priority hiring" (when new slots became available), and "retroactive seniority"—placed the burden not only on the wrongdoer (the employer) but also on the white employee who lost competitive seniority and the new white applicants who might have been hired but for the requirement of compensation. Justice Burger argued, in partial dissent, that innocent employees should not pay the price in lost seniority. Rather than "robbing Peter to pay Paul," he said, monetary damages/front pay should be paid by the employer to the victims of discrimination (781). Likewise, Justice Powell expressed concern that in the case of layoffs, against which competitive seniority is a protection, the burden might fall on "innocent employees hired in the interim" (786).

Even though we have gotten another step away from Aristotle's model, the support for this notion is widespread. We clearly need to do *something* to compensate the victim, to make her "whole"; see *Franks v. Bowman*, 774 (Brennan). And we do not want to fire the white jobholder who got the job unfairly the first time around. To do so would impose a large burden on her (because being fired is worse than not being hired), may be impossible (if the worker is retired or difficult to identify), and is socially undesirable (if she now has built up skills); see Greenawalt, *Discrimination and Reverse Discrimination*, 44. Such a firing would also be excessively punitive, since the employee, while a free-riding beneficiary of discrimination, is not a wrongdoer (the discriminator). Nevertheless, these considerations have been put aside, and even the most conservative justice, Antonin Scalia, supports this type of compensation so long as discrimination is proven and the victim is identifiable.

13. See Glazer, *Ethnic Dilemmas*, 162.

14. The Reagan administration and Justice Scalia refused to cross this line; see, e.g., Mary Thornton, "Top Justice Aide Calls Race Quotas 'Morally Wrong,'" *Washington Post*, April 30, 1983, A1. Justice Scalia argues that backward-looking remedies are con- stitutional only when a "legislature can identify both the particular victims and the par- ticular perpetrators of past discrimination"; *Richmond v. Croson*, 511–12, n1. Even if there is proof of past discrimination against individual black applicant A by individual employer B, it is no remedy to thereby prefer individual black C, Scalia argued; *Rich- mond v. Croson*, 526–27 (Scalia concurring), 515 (Stevens concurring).

But a majority of the Supreme Court has never taken the Reagan/Scalia position; rather, it has said that when there is documented wrongdoing on the part of an employer, compensation shall be provided to individuals of the same race as the victims. And Title VII vests broad authority in the federal courts to order "affirmative action" remedies— including preferential hiring—when there is a documented history of discrimination; see sect. 706(g), 42 USC 2000e(5)(g). See also Taylor, "*Brown*, Equal Protection," 1712, n48 (citing nine cases from 1971 to 1981).

15. Fried, *Order and Law*, 105. Likewise, in practice, victims of discrimination might not be identifiable because, though qualified, they did not apply for a particular job, knowing a firm's reputation of discrimination; see Greenawalt, *Discrimination and Reverse Discrimination*, 45; and Goldman, *Justice and Reverse Discrimination*, 136. Also implicit in the Court's reasoning may be a partial acknowledgment that since the strict requirement of proving documentation is likely to mean blacks are often undercom- pensated in practice, when discrimination is proven, victim-specificity will not be required. This may be a partial bow to Justice Marshall's argument that "for several hun- dred years, Negroes have been discriminated against, not as individuals, but rather solely because of the color of their skins"; *UC v. Bakke*, 400; see also Taylor, "*Brown*, Equal Protection," 1717–18, 1722. Finally, the Court's other requirement—that the rights of whites not be unnecessarily trammeled—helps limit the instances of nonvictims bene- fiting at the expense of innocent whites; see *Metro Broadcasting, Inc. v. FCC*, 497 US 547 (1990), 597.

16. *UC v. Bakke*, 400. See also Justice Brennan's emphasis on slavery and the "unique legal disabilities" faced by Negroes in education (326, 369–73).

17. The four groups chosen for preference were "Negroes, Mexican-Americans, American Indians, and Asians"; *UC v. Bakke*, 309, n45 (Powell). Between 1971 and 1973, the University of California at Davis admitted sixty-three minorities under its spe- cial program: twenty-one blacks, thirty Mexican Americans, and twelve Asians (275). Likewise, in *Richmond v. Croson*, the city of Richmond could cite a long history of dis- crimination against blacks but could not explain the bizarre inclusion of Aleuts and Eskimos as beneficiaries. Justice O'Connor wrote: "It may well be that Richmond has never had an Aleut or Eskimo citizen" (506). See also Days, "*Fullilove*," 482.

Even assuming one could agree on a list of beneficiaries, absent particular findings of discrimination, how will one know how or whether preferences should be calibrated? In *Fullilove*, Justice Stevens asked: "Even if we assume that each of the six racial subclasses has suffered its own special injury at some time in our history, surely it does not neces- sarily follow that each of those subclasses suffered harm of identical magnitude"; *Fullilove v. Klutznick*, 448 US 448, 537–38 (Stevens dissenting). Lyndon Johnson's 1965 Howard University speech, outlining the need for affirmative steps, noted that blacks faced an intense exclusion "matched by no other prejudice in our society" (638).

In addition, it is crucial to define precisely when the wrong occurred, along with its severity. The goal, after all, is not compensation of all historical wrongs, but compensation to root out the *remaining* vestiges of injustice as reflected in *today's* environment. The further back in history you go, the less likely it is that the actual wrongdoers or victims are still alive—and the less likely it is that today's whites continue to unfairly benefit and today's minorities continue to be hurt. The argument for compensating for slavery was certainly powerful following the Civil War because compensation went to the actual victims of slavery—blacks in "the rebel States"—not the descendants several generations removed; see Schnapper, "Affirmative Action," 756–57.

But over time the direct harm of slavery became more diffuse, and, as Borris Bittker notes in *The Case for Black Reparations*, the white profit from slavery "may well have been dissipated" (9). Just as German compensation to Jewish victims of the Nazis makes much more sense than compensation for Jewish enslavement in Egypt, black compensation for Jim Crow makes more sense than for slavery (27). The farther back in time we go, the less likely that the harms will be (to use the language of torts) "direct, clear and measurable," as opposed to "remote, indirect, or speculative"; Goldman, *Justice and Reverse Discrimination*, 69. It is no accident that when Sen. Robert Dole began his attack on affirmative action, he tied its justifications to slavery, an utterly unconvincing argument for most white Americans today. The Court has argued that reference to general "societal discrimination" is "an amorphous concept of injury that may be ageless in its reach into the past" and that can justify race-based decisions that are "essentially limitless in scope and duration"; see *UC v. Bakke*, 307; and *Wygant v. Jackson Board of Education*, 476 US 267 (1986), 276.

18. *Richmond v. Croson*, 510. See also *Fullilove v. Klutznick*, 533–35 (Stevens dissenting).

19. See *Richmond v. Croson*, 511 (O'Connor), citing *Fullilove v. Klutznick*, 539 (Stevens). In practice, smaller governmental units may be run by a "minority" group that constitutes a majority. See, e.g., the Richmond set-aside contested in *Richmond v. Croson*. At the state level, too, minority groups may have strong political clout; see Jeffries, *Justice Powell*, 472–73.

Likewise, at the national level, politics often appears at the core of federal affirmative action efforts. According to Jimmy Carter's secretary of health and human services, Joseph Califano, Carter was a strict bean counter on appointments, not so much because of a "burning conviction" about civil rights but out of a desire "to appease constituencies"; Califano, *Governing America*, 230; see also White, *America in Search of Itself*, 335, quoting Carter aide Hamilton Jordan's memo on the 1980 Democratic Convention: "Recommended Speakers for Tuesday programs are: Blacks: Parren Mitchell, Pat Harris. Hispanics: Mayor Ferre, Cesar Chavez. Catholics: Senator Moynihan. Jews: Phil Klutznick." Given Ronald Reagan's strong philosophical objection to quotas, it is hard to explain his campaign declaration that his first appointment to the Supreme Court would be a woman as anything but political calculation. President Bush, another strong opponent of quotas, set up a quota system while chairman of the Republican National Committee (RNC), designating seats on the RNC's executive council for a black Republican, a Hispanic, and a Jewish American; Editorial, "The Quota Party," *New Republic* (May 11, 1992): 7.

20. Some advocates of affirmative action try to confuse this issue by saying that opponents of proportional representation must believe that certain racial groups are innately inferior. Ronald Fiscus, e.g., says in *Constitutional Logic*: "If there are no relevant differences between a given group of whites and a given group of blacks at birth, then any differences manifested at a later point in their development must be the result of societal factors—i.e. racism. If not nature, then nurture" (24). And Professor Cheryl Harris flatly declares: "If one assumes relative equality of ability among the races at birth, then it is only racial subordination that can explain the fact that Blacks have not secured the proportion of society's benefits that they would be expected to have based on

their numbers in society"; "Whiteness as Property," 1783, n314; see also *UC v. Bakke*, 365–66 (Brennan).

The notion that certain racial groups are genetically inferior, a theory revived by publication of *The Bell Curve* in 1994, has been thoroughly discredited. For a sampling of the mountain of evidence that refutes the Murray-Herrnstein thesis, see generally Fraser, *The Bell Curve Wars*. For particularly trenchant critiques, see Mickey Kaus, "Behind the Curve," *New Republic* (October 31, 1994): 4; Ann Hulbert, "Freedom Is Slavery," *New Republic* (October 31, 1994): 18; Richard Nisbett, "Blue Genes," *New Republic* (October 31, 1994): 15; Stephen Jay Gould, "Curve Ball," *New Yorker* (November 28, 1994): 139–40; Mihaly Csikszentmihalyi, "Scales of Inequality," *Washington Post Book World* (November 6, 1994): 2; Sowell, *Race and Culture*, 107, 160–61, 165–67, 170, and 296, n21; John J. DiIulio, Jr., "The Plain, Ugly Truth about Welfare," *Washington Post*, January 15, 1995, C2; Myron A. Hofer, "Behind the Curve," *New York Times*, December 26, 1994, 39; Douglas J. Besharov, "IQ and Getting Smart," *Washington Post*, October 23, 1994, C4; Barbara Vobejda, "Book Rekindles Emotional Controversy on Intelligence and Race," *Washington Post*, October 21, 1994, A3; Sowell, *Ethnic America*, 281–82; Sowell, *Essays and Data*, 208, 219–22; Fallows, "The Tests and the 'Brightest,'" 39; Davis, *Who Is Black?*, 24; Randall Kennedy, "The Phony War," *New Republic* (October 31, 1994): 19; Alan Ryan, "Apocalypse Now?," *New York Review of Books* (November 17, 1994): 9; and Richard Morin, "An Army from Academe Tries to Straighten Out 'The Bell Curve,'" *Washington Post*, January 16, 1995, A3.

21. Sowell, *Race and Culture*, xii. Median age of marriage and childbirth are both important determinants of educational achievement for parents and vary widely between ethnic groups. One study found that half of all Mexican American wives marry during their teen years, compared with only 10 percent of Japanese American wives; Sowell, *Civil Rights*, 18. Likelihood of teen births varies as well. In 1992 blacks averaged 81.3 live births per 1,000 girls aged 15 to 17; whites averaged 51.8, and Asians just 15.2; see Barbara Vobejda, "Birthrate Among Teenage Girls Declines Slightly," *Washington Post*, October 26, 1994, A5.

A second cultural difference involves family composition. In 1965 Moynihan drew the link between family stability among the Chinese, Japanese, and American Jews and their relative educational and economic success; "A Family Policy," 281. In 1993 the percentage of black children living with two-parent families was only 36 percent—making blacks three times as likely as non-Hispanic whites to have an absent parent; Census Bureau, "Black Children in America—1993," cited in *Washington Post*, September 15, 1994, A14. The impact of family structure on family income is well documented. In 1992, while black married couples earned 80 percent of white family income, the figure for all black families—a disproportionate number of whom are single-parent—was 54 percent; Census Bureau, "Black Children in America." Combining the first two cultural differences—teenage births and unwed mothers—a 1995 Census Bureau report noted that unmarried black teenagers have a birth rate four times higher than that of unmarried teenage whites; see Edward Walsh, "Black Women Are Closing Racial Gap in Employment, Census Data Show," *Washington Post*, February 22, 1995, A3.

Family size also varies by ethnicity and race. The 1992 Current Population Survey found that women age 35–44 had, on average, by race and ethnicity: 1.89 children (whites); 2.23 children (African Americans); and 2.47 children (Hispanics); see Census Bureau, cited in Murray and Herrnstein, *The Bell Curve*, 352. Statistically speaking, children in large families tend to live in households where finances are more thinly stretched, and they have lower academic success; Sowell, *Essays and Data*, 230.

Attitudes toward "success" also vary. There is some evidence that one aspect of black culture (in part, a product of discrimination) is a tendency to denigrate academic achievement. Sowell cites one study that found that while Americans with high IQs are generally happier than average, blacks with high IQs are less happy than blacks with average IQs. Moreover, blacks with high IQs were five times more likely to label their childhoods "extremely unhappy" compared with those blacks with an average IQ; *Black Education*, 288. The black anthropologists Signithia Fordham of Rutgers and John Ogbu of Berkeley found in a study of Washington, D.C., black high school students that "fear of acting white and fear of becoming the other was a motivating factor in underachievement in the school context." Fordham says, "What appears to have emerged in some segments of the black community is a kind of cultural orientation which defines academic learning in schools as 'acting white' and academic successes as the prerogative of white Americans"; "Black Identity vs. Success and Seeming White," *New York Times*, April 25, 1990, B9. More disturbing is the report that even on elite campuses the attitude endures; at MIT, black students call their black classmates who excel "incognegro," (i.e., "You can't really tell he's black"); see Loury, "Why Preferential Admissions Is Not Enough," 100. Asian American culture, by contrast, prizes academic success. According to the Stanford sociologist Stanford M. Dornbush, Asian American students in the San Francisco area work an average of 11.7 hours per week on homework, compared with 8.6 hours for whites, and even less for African Americans and Latinos; cited in D'Souza, *Illiberal Education*, 267, n79.

Finally, linguistic differences often reduce achievement in American culture for immigrants, but language also affects African American achievement as well. Many educators have begun pushing instruction in a "Black English" dialect. "The use of standard English as the only language of instruction aggravates the process of deculturalization," says the black educator Felix Boateng; quoted in Schlesinger, *The Disuniting of America*, 103. But, of course, this movement, as Arthur Schlesinger notes, has the effect of "handicap[ping] black children from infancy" (103). The point is not that standard English is somehow superior to Black English in an absolute moral sense. The point is that unless one wants to be a rap singer (for whom Black English is an advantage), using Black English is likely to hurt one's chances of succeeding in American life (103).

22. Much of what we call "cultural" or "racial" differences may in fact stem not from an ethnic or racial culture but from current economic status—which may, in turn, be traced to past discrimination; Steinberg, *Ethnic Myth*, 107–8; Webster, *The Racialization of America*, 178; and Liebow, *Tally's Corner*, 208, 223–24. And to a degree, cultural differences between ethnic groups may themselves be a direct product of discrimination; see Ellwood, *Poor Support*, 196; and Johnson, Howard commencent address, 638. If African American teenage males are used to applying for jobs and being turned down because of discrimination, their discouraged response is predictable.

23. First, we know that after controlling for economics—the fact that certain minorities are disproportionately poor—there is still a residual impact of culture on achievement. Part of the reason blacks do worse on the SAT than whites is that blacks are disproportionately poor, but within income categories stubborn racial gaps remain. In 1981, e.g., Asian American students from *poor* families (earning less than $6,000) scored higher on the math portion of the SAT than did black, Mexican American, and Native American students from families earning more than $50,000; Sowell, *Race and Culture*, 16, 159; see also ch. 6. The National Research Council's report concluded that cultural differences are central to the explanation for why a residual racial gap remains in test scores after controlling for socioeconomic status; National Research Council, *A Common Destiny*, 370.

Likewise, when controlling for the impact of discrimination on culture, culture still has a residual impact on life chances. As Thomas Sowell notes, the existence of certain successful minority groups throughout the world, who lack the power to discriminate, suggests that not all economic differences between racial and ethnic groups can be attributed to discrimination; *Preferential Policies*, 88–89. For example, the ethnic Chinese minority has suffered widespread, explicit, and unremitting discrimination in a number of Southeast Asian countries, but in Malaysia, Indonesia, Vietnam, Thailand, and the Philippines, the Chinese are wildly overrepresented in various industries, owning "a majority of the nation's total investments in key industries," though they constitute only 5 percent of the population; Sowell, *Civil Rights*, 20–21; see also Sowell, *Race and Culture*, 159.

24. Jencks, *Rethinking Social Policy*, 28.

25. Asian Americans have suffered virulent discrimination, not on the level of that suffered by black Americans, but surely more than whites have, and arguably on the level

of Latinos; see Peter Uhlenberg, "Demographic Correlates of Group Achievement: Contrasting Patterns of Mexican-Americans and Japanese-Americans," in Yin, *Race, Creed, Color*, 86. Uhlenberg writes: "In California in the early 1900's there were laws prohibiting intermarriage with Japanese and segregating Oriental school children. Laws were passed making it impossible for Japanese immigrants to become naturalized citizens, and then legislation in California prohibited 'aliens ineligible for citizenship' from owning agricultural land. Hostility toward Japanese-Americans resulted in the total exclusion of Japanese immigrants to the United States after 1924, and it was not until 1952 that token immigration quotas were again given to Japan" (86). The prohibition against owning land, Stanley Lebergott reminds us, came at a time when "farming constituted the largest single sector in the economy." Asian Americans were also "excluded from schools, neighborhoods, and occupations by legal as well as community pressures"; *The American Economy*, 108. Of course, the ultimate in Asian discrimination came during World War II, when large numbers of Japanese Americans were interned. The impact was pervasive. In 1976, Lebergott estimated, "at least one member in almost every American Japanese family today was raised in a concentration camp. . . . And most heads of these families lived in the camps during the critical years when they could have been developing labor market skills and/or being educated in schools" (108–9).

Nevertheless, Asians have done very well, by any number of measures of success. Academically, Asian Americans score 30 points higher than whites on the math portion of the SAT and, more strikingly, are *twice* as likely to score above 700 on the math SAT; Sowell, *Race and Culture*, 175–76. In 1986 Asian American high school graduates in California were more than twice as likely (32.8 percent) to qualify for the University of California (being among the top one-eighth of graduating California high school seniors) as whites (15.8 percent), and six times as likely as Hispanics (5 percent) and blacks (4.5 percent); Karabel, *Admissions at Berkeley*, 15. Professionally, Asians are overrepresented in high-level occupations and have higher salaries than whites; James R. Flynn, *Asian Americans: Achievement beyond IQ* (Hillsdale, N.J.: Lawrence Erlbaum Associates, 1991), 1, 74, 99. Among certain Asian groups—Pakistanis, Sri Lankans, Burmese, Chinese, Japanese, and Asian Indians—average on-the-job earnings are $25,198—far above the national average of $15,105. When all Asians are considered, the mean on-the-job earnings are $16,928; see Dante Ramos, "Losers," *New Republic* (October 17, 1994): 24–25.

Some critics have pointed out that we must be cautious about overinterpreting Asian Americans as the "model minority." First, they say, the large income of Asians in part reflects the high concentrations of Asians in expensive areas like California, Hawaii, Illinois, New York, and Washington; see, e.g., Deborah Woo, "The Gap Between Striving and Achieving: The Case of Asian American Women," in Asian Women United, *Making Waves*, 187. Indeed, 75 percent of Asian Americans live in New York, California, and Hawaii alone; Webster, *The Racialization of America*, 137. But while geographic dispersion may account for a portion of what appears to be Asian American economic success, it does nothing to explain why Asians, who have been the victims of discrimination, achieve more than whites in both the academic and professional arenas.

Second, some lay the success of Asian Americans at the door of immigration policies, which since 1965 have given priority consideration to highly educated immigrants; see Woo, "The Gap Between Striving and Achieving," 189. But pre-1965 Asian immigrants were not highly skilled and still managed to do quite well. In the early twentieth century, Thomas Sowell notes, Japanese immigrants were domestic servants and field hands in even greater percentages than were blacks; *Race and Culture*, 83. And in 1969—before the large influx of post-1965 immigrants and not far from the time when Asians had suffered blatant discrimination—Asian Americans were already doing better than the average American. As Lebergott points out, Japanese Americans had a lower poverty rate in 1969 (6.4 percent, compared with 8.6 percent for whites), Japanese Americans made 132 percent of the American average income, Chinese Americans made 112 percent; *The American Economy*, 108; Jencks, "Affirmative Action for Blacks," 744. Indeed, in the 1950s Japanese Americans were already represented disproportionately at the University of California; Glazer, *Ethnic Dilemmas*, 60. By 1960 Japanese Americans had a higher occupational level than whites, and by 1970 Chinese Americans were overrepresented among college teachers, physicians, dentists, and engineers (191).

Third, some argue that Asian Americans do better than whites and blacks not because their culture values hard work and education but because they benefited from "selective migration"—only the smartest and most hardworking immigrants from Asia made it to this country. While the theory conceivably explains some of the difference between the performance of Asian Americans and African Americans—most of whom were brought to this country involuntarily in slave ships—it does not explain the difference between Asian and white immigrants, since both groups came voluntarily. For the dubious history of selective migration theory, see Kluger, *Simple Justice*, 397.

26. Hacker, *Two Nations*, 84.

27. See Stephan Thernstrom, "Racial Bias in the Federal Courts?," *Wall Street Journal*, March 22, 1995, A17.

28. Sowell, *Preferential Policies*, 149. See also Jencks, *Rethinking Social Policy*, 28. Between 1972 and 1979, blacks earned 68 percent of the national average income, compared with 64 percent for Mexican Americans and 62 percent for Puerto Ricans.

29. See Associated Press, "High School Graduation Rate Increases for Black Students," *Washington Post*, November 21, 1994, A16; and "Affirmative Action on the Edge," *U.S. News and World Report*, February 13, 1995, 32, 35. The median annual earnings of black men in 1993 was 74 percent that of white men; for Hispanics, the figure was 64.8 percent.

30. See Ramos, "Losers." In the ultimate illustration of the power of culture, Wilson and Herrnstein cite this simple statistic: "During the 1960s, one neighborhood in San Francisco had the lowest income, the highest unemployment rate, the highest proportion of families with incomes under $4,000 per year, the least educational attainment, the highest tuberculosis rate, and the highest proportion of substandard housing of any area of the city. That neighborhood was called Chinatown. Yet in 1965, there were only five persons of Chinese ancestry committed to prison in the entire state of California"; *Crime and Human Nature*, 473.

Indeed, the recognition of distinct cultural differences between ethnic groups—not all individuals, but in the aggregate—is the central insight of the diversity movement. Patricia Williams proudly identifies an African American culture with its own "shared heritage of language patterns, habits, history and experience"; "Comment," 529. If black culture were *only* a product of white racism and discrimination, we would see it as something to extinguish and move beyond rather than as something to celebrate. Black culture is surely not—as Myrdal wrote—"a distorted development, or a pathological condition of American culture"; quoted in Peller, "Race Consciousness," 792, n71. Americans—especially liberals—do recognize a distinctive positive black culture; to deny that such a culture (or subculture) exists is considered silly at best. Nathan Glazer wrote in 1963 that "the Negro is only an American and nothing else. He has no values and culture to guard and protect"; he was denying the very existence of a vibrant culture; *Beyond the Melting Pot*, 53. Alphonso Pinkney says Glazer's statement "is so absurd that further comment on it would only serve to dignify it"; *The Myth of Black Progress*, 9. Glazer himself says he no longer stands by the statement; Nathan Glazer, interview with the author, Cambridge, Mass., January 5, 1995. Indeed, the very switch from the term "black" to "African American," is in part a reflection of the notion that we should spend less time identifying people by skin color and more by their culture; Davis, *Who Is Black?*, 186. It would be very peculiar if this distinct culture did not have an impact on relative group results.

31. See James Webb, "In Defense of Joe Six-Pack," *Wall Street Journal*, June 5, 1995, A14.

32. Glazer, *Ethnic Dilemmas*, 166–67. The Philadelphia Plan contains a loophole for those who make "good faith efforts" to meet racial goals but cannot find qualified minorities. The scheme does, however, require preferences of lesser qualified minorities over more qualified whites. See ch. 5, n.141.

33. The Philadelphia Plan was limited to six trades in the five-county Philadelphia area and was buttressed by a strong factual predicate showing past discrimination. The Philadelphia Plan was upheld by the courts in *Contractors Assn. of Eastern PA v. Sec. of Labor*, 442 F2d 159 (3d Cir. 1971). But not so the Nixon Labor Department's decision to extend the plan—calling for employers to establish racial goals and timetables—nationwide, to all federal contractors, whether guilty of past discrimination or not; see Laurence Silberman, "The Road to Racial Quotas," *Wall Street Journal*, August 11, 1977, 14; see also Taylor, "*Brown*, Equal Protection," 1713. The program was extended to women in 1974; Steven A. Holmes, "Affirmative Action Plans Are Part of Business Life," *New York Times*, November 22, 1991, A20.

34. See Weir, *Politics and Jobs*, 112. Ironically, some advocates of affirmative action today proudly cite Nixon's role as evidence of bipartisan support; see, e.g., President Clinton's National Archives address noting that "a Republican president" launched federal affirmative action effort; White House, Office of the Press Secretary, *Remarks by the President on Affirmative Action*, July 19, 1995, 1.

35. Ehrlichman, *Witness to Power*, 228–29.

36. Citizens' Commission on Civil Rights, *Affirmative Action*, 49 (quoting Shultz).

37. Graham, *The Civil Rights Era*, 340.

38. Ibid., 291.

39. Rustin, "Coalition or Conflict?," 7.

40. Rustin, "The Blacks and the Unions," 79.

41. Quoted in *Congressional Quarterly Weekly Report* 28 (November 27, 1970): 2859–61. See also Mitchell, letter to Speaker of the House John McCormack, December 22, 1969 (*Congressional Record*, December 22, 1969, 40,917–18), expressing support for the Philadelphia Plan but questioning the Nixon administration's motives for "enthusiastically cracking down on discrimination that involves labor unions" but failing to attack discrimination in other arenas.

42. Memo from John Price to John Campbell, December 22, 1969, cited in Skrentny, *Ironies*.

43. Graham, *The Civil Rights Era*, 340.

44. Skrentny, "Politics and Possibilities," 280. Time and again on matters of domestic politics, the Nixon administration sought to draw clear divisions in public opinion. Nixon's attorney general called for "positive polarization," and his speechwriter Pat Buchanan told Nixon, "If we tear the country in half, we can pick up the bigger half"; both quoted in Hughes, *Culture of Complaint*, 44–45; see also West, *Beyond Eurocentrism*, 2:151–52.

Nixon must have been delighted when, throughout the 1970s and 1980s, the issue of affirmative action repeatedly split civil rights groups who favored the practice and some labor groups, like Albert Shanker's American Federation of Teachers, who were staunchly opposed; see U.S. Congress, *Report of the Study Group*, 200; Urofsky, *A Conflict of Rights*, 106; *DeFunis v. Odegaard*, 313 (AFL-CIO and Anti-Defamation League of B'nai B'rith lined up against the Lawyers' Committee for Civil Rights under Law and the NAACP Legal Defense and Education Fund); *Boston v. Beecher*, 679 F2d 965 (1st Cir. 1982) (pitting the Boston Firefighters Union against the Boston Chapter of the NAACP); and Sullivan, Pressman, and Arterton, *Democratic Convention*, 74 (describing the fight between labor and civil rights groups over racial quotas at the 1974 Democratic National Midterm Convention). The New Deal coalition of blacks and ethnic whites split openly on *Bakke*, with major Jewish, Italian, and labor groups siding against affirmative action, and major black and Hispanic groups favoring it.

45. While today it seems obvious that Republicans would want to woo white working-class voters, Thomas Edsall notes that at the time of the Philadelphia Plan it was unclear whether Nixon would have much success with the group. Until 1968 labor had always been pro-Democratic, and there was some talk that George Wallace would run for president again as an independent in 1972, in which case Nixon would have had a tough time carrying even those hard hats who were upset with Democrats on civil rights; Thomas Edsall, telephone interview with the author, January 23, 1995.

46. Skrentny, *Ironies*.

47. Safire, *Before the Fall*, 585.

48. Phillips, "Post-Southern Strategy," *Washington Post*, September 25, 1970, A25. Phillips believed that Republicans ought not to bother pursuing the black vote; see *The Emerging Republican Majority*, 468.

49. Ehrlichman, *Witness to Power*, 218.

50. Secretary of Labor James D. Hodgson, memorandum to "All Heads of Agencies," September 15, 1972, cited in Hill and Jones, *Race in America*, 324–25. The reversal appears to have prompted Assistant Secretary of Labor Arthur A. Fletcher to resign (324–25).

51. Edsall and Edsall, *Chain Reaction*, 97.

52. Richard M. Nixon, "Labor Day Message," September 3, 1972, in *Public Papers of the President, Richard Nixon, 1972*, 832.

53. Richard M. Nixon, "Remarks on Accepting the Presidential Nomination of the Republican National Convention," August 23, 1972, *Public Papers—Nixon, 1972*, 788. See also Bell, "In Defense of Minority Admissions Programs," 369, n13.

54. *DeFunis v. Odegaard*, 331.

55. See *Bakke v. Regents of University of California*, 553 P2d 1152, 1166 (1976), affirmed in part and revised in part, 438 US 265 (1978).

56. *UC v. Bakke*, 362.

57. Ibid., 306; see also ibid. , 311–15.

58. Justices Brennan, White, Marshall, and Blackmun said they would support the diversity rationale to the extent that it was used to remedy "the lingering effects of past discrimination"; *UC v. Bakke*, 326, n1.

59. Ibid., 407. The statement actually originates with Bundy, ("The Issue Before the Court," 54): "To get past racism, we must here take account of race. There is no other present way. In the words of Alexander Heard of Vanderbilt, 'To treat our black students equally, we have to treat them differently.'"

60. See *UC v. Bakke*, 403 (Blackmun). Likewise, Justice Brennan said that while we are not yet a color-blind society, "this is not to denigrate the aspiration"; ibid., 327 (Brennan).

61. *UC v. Bakke*, 401–2. See also Dworkin's assertion that affirmative action is necessary to eventually "reduce the degree to which American society is overall a racially conscious society"; "Why Bakke Has No Case," 11.

62. Thomas Sowell notes that preferences have been termed "temporary" in society after society and inevitably remain on the books; *Preferential Policies*, 15. In India, "temporary" preferences for backward classes were supposed to expire after ten years but have been renewed numerous times; see Witten, " 'Compensatory Discrimination' in India," 356, n17.

63. Quoted in Nieli, *The New Affirmative Action Controversy*, 124.

64. Norton, *A Conversation*, 21.

65. Quoted in Graham, *The Civil Rights Era*, 111.

66. *UC v. Bakke*, 403. Wisely, Blackmun hedged, adding that his hope was "a slim one." Likewise, the NAACP implicitly endorsed a time limit when it argued in *UC v. Bakke* that UC Davis's preference program was an appropriate response to de jure segregation in California; see A. E. Dick Howard, "The High Court's Road in the *Bakke* Case," *Washington Post*, October 9, 1977, C1. The national Law School Admissions Council (LSAC) also noted that in 1976 applicants to medical school had been in public schools from 1954 to 1972, during which period 75 percent of schools were unlawfully segregated. Today, while many American school districts have de facto segregation, de jure segregation has been largely addressed and no longer provides the legal remedial justification cited by the NAACP and LSAC.

67. *UC v. Bakke*, 401 (Marshall).

68. *Richmond v. Croson*, 542. In a striking departure from established doctrine, Judge Ruth Bader Ginsburg endorsed in her confirmation hearings the awarding of preference points as "a safeguard, a check against unconscious bias"; Senate Judiciary Committee, *Nomination of Judge Ginsburg*, 130–31.

69. Laurence Tribe noted in 1988 that all members of the Court applied a "restrictive focus on past discrimination." See Tribe, *American Constitutional Law*, 1537, n74.

70. See Marshall in *UC v. Bakke*, 387, 394, 396, 399, 401, 402; and in *Richmond v. Croson*, 533, n3, 536, 538, 540, 552. See Brennan in *UC v. Bakke*, 324, 328, 341 n17, 344, 352, 353, 362, 369, 373. See O'Connor in *Richmond v. Croson*, 476–77, 486, 488.

71. See 1975 House report cited by Marshall in *Richmond v. Croson*, 531; and 1977 House report cited by Marshall in *Richmond v. Croson*, 532.

72. See, e.g., Johnson, Howard commencement address (1965); and HEW regulations ("to overcome the consequences of prior discrimination"), 36 *Federal Register* 23494 (1971), cited by Brennan in *UC v. Bakke*, 344, n18.

73. Johnson, Howard commencement address (1965), 636.

74. A second new theory, that preferences are necessary to address contemporary and future discrimination, is discussed at length in ch. 6.

75. See Gotanda, " 'Our Constitution Is Color-Blind,' " 59–60.

76. Wilson, "Race-Neutral Programs," 81.

77. *UC v. Bakke*, 325. Brennan made this argument even though internal court documents show that Powell specifically rejected Brennan's characterization, saying in a June 23 letter to Brennan that the "holding could be stated more broadly in one simple sentence as follows: 'Government validly may take race into account in furthering the compelling state interest of achieving a diverse student body.' " Any reference to remedying past discrimination was "dicta," Powell said, not binding as precedent; quoted in Schwartz, *Behind Bakke*, 139–40. For his part, Brennan wrote that the Harvard diversity plan was constitutional, but he added the caveat: "at least so long as the use of race to achieve an integrated student body is necessitated by the lingering effects of past discrimination"; *UC v. Bakke*, 326, n1.

Initially, the diversity theory was pushed not so much by the civil rights groups as by Harvard's Archibald Cox; it was picked up only by the moderate to conservative Justice Powell—described by his biographer as "the Court's lone southerner, a former segregationist and consistent foe of forced busing"; Jeffries, *Justice Powell*, 493. But in recent years, diversity has been embraced most ardently by left commentators in academia, including the critical race theory school; see Delgado and Stefancic, "Critical Race Theory: An Annotated Bibliography" 79 *Virginia Law Review* 461, 463 (1993); Peller, "Race Consciousness"; and Kennedy, "A Cultural Pluralist Case for Affirmative Action." That the likes of Cox and Powell would provide the intellectual underpinnings for today's hottest and most radical legal theory is truly astounding.

78. Compare *UC v. Bakke* (where only Justice Powell relied on diversity) with *Metro Broadcasting v. FCC* (where five members of the Court approved of racial preferences in broadcasting to increase diversity). The two cases are, however, somewhat different. Because Congress had approved of the racial preferences instituted by the FCC in *Metro Broadcasting*, a majority of the Court applied "semi-strict" or "intermediate" scrutiny rather than the "strict scrutiny" test applied in *UC v. Bakke*.

79. The *Adarand* Court explicitly overruled *Metro Broadcasting* insofar as *Metro Broadcasting* applied "intermediate" rather than "strict" scrutiny to federal affirmative action programs. The *Adarand* Court did not specifically address the question of whether diversity is a compelling state interest.

80. *Metro Broadcasting v. FCC*, 546–47.

81. *UC v. Bakke* cited by Brennan in ibid., 568.

82. Quoted in Sullivan, Pressman, and Arterton, *Democratic Convention*, 10.

83. See, e.g., David Broder, "Diversity Was Paramount in Building the Cabinet," *Washington Post*, December 25, 1992, A1.

84. According to a *Washington Post* exit poll, 83 percent of blacks voted for Clinton, compared with 40 percent of whites. And Clinton won 47 percent of the female vote, compared with 41 percent of the male vote; see "Exit Poll," *Washington Post*, November 4, 1992, A24.

85. See *Taxman v. Piscataway*, 832 FSupp 836 (1993). For further discussion of the case, see ch. 3.

86. "Diversity," declares the very first sentence in Harvard University's register, "is the hallmark of the Harvard/Radcliffe experience." The University of Michigan bulletin says, "Diversity is the virtual core of University life"; see Nicolaus Mills, "The Endless Autumn: Universities' Methods of Recruiting Students," *The Nation* (April 16, 1990): 529ff; see also Lynch, *Invisible Victims*, 175; and Kerlow, *Poisoned Ivy*, 148.

The selling of preferences for the socioeconomically disadvantaged at Berkeley is another case in point. The sociologist Jerome Karabel has spent many years arguing the unfairness of economic inequality; see, e.g., Brint and Karabel, *The Diverted Dream*; and Jerome Karabel and David Karen, "Go to Harvard: Give Your Kids a Break" (criticizing legacy preferences), *New York Times*, December 8, 1990. But when Karabel argued for giving poor and working-class students a preference in undergraduate admissions, the basis was not fairness but the promotion of economic diversity: "A genuinely diverse freshman class must be ... socioeconomically as well as racially and ethnically heterogenous," Karabel, *Freshman Admissions*, 43, 45.

87. Susanto Basu and David Barkan, "A View from the Top: An Interview with Derek Bok," *Harvard Political Review* (Spring 1985): 9.

88. Carter, *Affirmative Action Baby*, 74. Elsewhere, he contrasts the compensatory argument of "an earlier era" with today's diversity argument (44). Among academics, the diversity rationale was initially seen as somewhat obscure and "quite uncommon"; Blackstone and Heslep, *Social Justice*, 2. Now academics lead the charge; see, e.g., Williams, "Comment"; Sullivan, "The Supreme Court, 1986 Term"; and Tribe, *American Constitutional Law*, 1537.

89. See Judith H. Dobrzynski, "Some Action, Little Talk," *New York Times*, April 20, 1995, D1, D4.

90. See Andy Lamey, "Do as I Say," *New Republic* (June 26, 1995): 14–16.

91. Some have tried to revive the notion that an employer's decision to discriminate in hiring should be considered private; see Epstein, *Forbidden Grounds*; D'Souza, *The End of Racism*; and (in the context of discrimination involving homosexuals) Andrew Sullivan, *Virtually Normal: An Argument about Homosexuality* (New York: Knopf, 1995). For an argument that the public/private distinction should be resurrected for affirmative action, see Jeffrey Rosen, "Affirmative Action: A Solution," *New Republic* (May 8, 1995): 20–25; Marshall, *From Preferences to Empowerment*; and Robert J. Samuelson, "Affirmative Action: Theatrics," *Washington Post*, August 9, 1995, A19. These arguments were rejected by drafters of the Civil Rights Act of 1964.

92. The former is illegal under 42 USC 3604(c) (1988). See "Note: Racial Steering in the Marketplace" (*Harvard Law Review*); but see discussion of "benign" housing quotas in ch. 3.

93. "Note: Racial Steering in the Marketplace," 878.

94. In *Loving v. Virginia* (388 US 1 [1967]), the Supreme Court struck down Virginia's ban on white intermarriages with other races in part because of its racial basis but also, independently, on the grounds that the state has no right to interfere with people's choice of spouse. An element of the liberty exception was also evident in *UC v. Bakke* when Justice Powell argued that the government must tread carefully, giving universities the discretion necessary in admissions policy to protect academic freedom. Note, however, that Powell did not believe that academic freedom extends to a university's desire to use racial quotas, nor, presumably, to an intention to discriminate against minorities.

95. See *Roberts v. U.S. Jaycees* (468 US 609 [1984]), which delineates the boundary as to when associational rights end and the state interest in antidiscrimination begins. In *Roberts*, the Court held that the Jaycees lacked a constitutional right of association to exclude women. The other major cases are *Board of Directors of Rotary International v. Rotary Club of Duarte*, 481 US 537 (1987), and *New York State Club Assocation v. City of New York*, 487 US 1 (1988).

96. See Glazer and Moynihan, *Ethnicity*, 10.

97. See Citizens' Commission on Civil Rights, *Affirmative Action*, 25–26, 99; Senate Judiciary Committee, *Nomination of Judge Thomas*, 297, 299–301; and Glazer, *Ethnic Dilemmas*, 161.

98. Although disparate impact cases played a highly controversial role in the debate over the Civil Rights Act of 1991, prompting opponents to label the legislation a "quota bill," the controversy centered not on the validity of disparate impact suits per se but rather on the relative distribution of burden between plaintiff and defendant. President Bush said that if it was made too hard for business to prove that an employment practice was valid, employers would throw up their hands and adopt informal quotas in order to avoid the litigation. But Bush, along with the Democrats, pledged allegiance to the notion in *Griggs*; Epstein, *Forbidden Grounds*, 183. The key to the *Griggs* decision is that it sought to remove unintentionally discriminatory barriers to meritocracy but did not cross the line to preferences; see *Griggs v. Duke Power Co.*, 401 US 424 (1971), 431.

99. See Civil Rights Act of 1964, sect. 703(a)(1)(e), 42 USCA sect. 2000e–2(a)(1)(e).

100. See Fishkin, *Justice, Equal Opportunity*, 27; and Goldman, *Justice and Reverse Discrimination*, 54.

101. See Margaret Jacobs, "EEOC Reopens Issue of When Discrimination Is Legal," *Wall Street Journal*, April 19, 1995, B4.

102. *Wygant v. Jackson Board of Education*, 314 (Stevens dissenting). See also *DeFunis v. Odegaard*, 343 (Douglas).

103. *Richmond v. Croson*, 521 (Scalia).

104. In *Lee v. Washington*, the permanent segregation of a prison to reduce the chance of racial turmoil was found unconstitutional; cited in *Richmond v. Croson*, 520 (Scalia).

105. The result in *Korematsu v. United States* (323 US 214 [1944]) is today thoroughly discredited—indeed, Congress has compensated Japanese American victims for the mistake—though the strict scrutiny rule it laid down is central to equal protection clause jurisprudence.

106. See, e.g., John F. Kennedy's address in response to George Wallace: "If an American, because his skin is dark . . . cannot enjoy the full and free life which all of us want, then who among us would be content to have the color of his skin changed and stand in his place?"; quoted in Kluger, *Simple Justice*, 954.

107. See generally Gilligan, *In a Different Voice*.

108. The distinction between diversity in education and employment rests largely on Justice Powell's acceptance of the diversity rationale in college admissions (*UC v. Bakke*) but his rejection of the rationale in the employment of teachers (*Wygant v. Jackson Board of Education*).

109. See Cox, *The Role of the Supreme Court*, 64–65.

110. See Dworkin, *Taking Rights Seriously*, 225.

111. Sandel, *Liberalism*, 140, 142.

112. See Kennedy, "Persuasion and Distrust," 1333. The Supreme Court would generally agree with the analysis that someone with the highest academic credentials has no fundamental constitutional "right" to be admitted to a particular university or hired for a particular job; see, e.g., *San Antonio Independent School Dist. v. Rodriguez*, 411 US 1 (1973). But that issue is a red herring; the key question is not the fundamental nature of the interest at stake (university admissions), but whether the classification (race) is suspect. The issue is not the right to go to college if one has high grades, but the right not to be disadvantaged by one's racial status.

113. Carter, *Affirmative Action Baby*, 32, and 259, n6.

114. Richard Cohen, "Diversity Kick," *Washington Post*, January 13, 1994, A27.

115. Fried, "*Metro Broadcasting v. FCC*," 121.

116. A third argument, sometimes used in the occupational context but made most frequently in the educational context, says minorities bring a distinct viewpoint to the table and ought to be represented in key positions for that reason. Since the argument is made most frequently with respect to the educational context, that issue is discussed under the educational heading.

117. See *Wygant v. Jackson Board of Education*, 314 (Stevens).

118. Michael Isikoff, "Questions of Diversity: White Agents Intervene in FBI Settlement," *Washington Post*, June 10, 1993, A21.

119. Glazer and Moynihan, *Ethnicity*, 11.

120. Dworkin, "Why Bakke Has No Case," 14.

121. Richard Cohen, interview with the author, Washington, D.C., December 13, 1994.

122. *Affirmative Action Review*, 4

123. Bartholet, "Applications of Title VII," 1013–14.

124. See Kennedy, "A Cultural Pluralist Case," 716–17, and 706, n7.

125. Citizens' Commission on Civil Rights, *Affirmative Action*, 15.

126. See *Congressional Record*, September 11, 1991, S12775.

127. See ibid., S12776 (Sen. Kennedy quoting President Reagan). See also Randall Kennedy, "Persuasion and Distrust," 1332.

128. Bush's statement that Thomas was the "most qualified person" in America was rejected by most, including the NAACP Legal Defense Fund, which called him the least qualified nominee in this century; Culp, "Diversity, Multiculturalism," 1146.

129. See *Congressional Record*, September 11, 1991, S12777 (Sen. Kennedy quoting Sen. Hatch).

130. Ogbu, *Minority Education and Caste*, 2, 4, 5, 319. In the next chapter, we will evaluate these arguments, but for now it is important simply to note the dramatic shift from compensation to diversity, and its profound consequences.

131. Stephen Carter notes that the diversity rationale "solves too many problems too neatly," raising the prospect that "it was designed that way"; *Affirmative Action Baby*, 41.

132. See Sullivan, "The Supreme Court—1986 Term," 80; and *UC v. Bakke*, 369. In *Bakke*, Justice Powell dismissed as a "conceptual leap" the Brennan-Marshall argument that Bakke would not have been admitted on the merits but for past discrimination. "The breadth of this hypothesis is unprecedented in our constitutional system," Justice Powell wrote (296). Instead, the Court required some "judicial, legislative, or administrative findings of constitutional or statutory violations" (307). As Kathleen Sullivan says, "Original sin in the garden of history was not enough" (87).

133. *Richmond v. Croson*, 501. Statistics are relevant, but one must know not just the percentage of blacks in Richmond but the percentage of qualified black contractors (501–2). The disparity must be "significant" (509).

134. Ibid., 504, 503, 505. So, too, in *Bakke*, claims of discrimination in primary and secondary schools were deemed too amorphous to justify a preference in medical school (*Richmond v. Croson*, 499).

135. Ibid., 541 (Marshall). Even when proper findings are made, race-neutral alternatives must be considered first, and only "in the extreme case" will "narrowly tailored" preferences be deemed necessary (509). The Court's "onerous" requirements in *Croson*, Justice Marshall said, "will inevitably discourage or prevent government entities, particularly states and localities, from acting to rectify the scourge of past discrimination" (529, 548). The requirement of localized findings, Marshall said, requires localities "to reinvent the evidentiary wheel and engage in unnecessarily duplicative, costly, and time-consuming fact finding" (547). The "daunting standard" imposed by the Court, Marshall wrote, "calls into question the validity of the business set-asides which dozens of municipalities across this Nation have adopted" (555).

Following the Court's decision in *Croson*, a distinguished group of thirty scholars put together a statement of the law in an attempt to ensure municipalities that the *Croson* decision still allowed them to establish and maintain many types of set-aside programs; see "Constitutional Scholars' Statement." Then-Solicitor General Charles Fried responded, noting that the scholars' statement was "strangely at odds with itself and at times quite misleading. It is strange as it adopts the tone at once of Chicken Little and Dr. Pangloss: Something terrible happened, but it's not so bad after all"; see Fried, "Affirmative Action," 155–56. A similar denial occurred following the *Adarand* decision in 1995.

136. See Sullivan, "The Supreme Court—1986 Term," 92. On a continuum, the degree of documentation required is as follows:

SCALIA	O'CONNOR	BRENNAN	BRENNAN
Croson	*Croson*	*Bakke*	*Metro*
Individual Victim	Specific Evidence	Societal Discrimination	None (Diversity)

137. *Metro Broadcasting v. FCC*, 633 (Kennedy). The remedial statute litigated in an earlier case, *Fullilove v. Klutznick*, provided that "minority group members are citizens of the United States who are Negroes, Spanish Speaking, Orientals, Indians, Eskimos, and Aleuts." (454) The FCC program was for stations owned by individuals of "Black, Hispanic Surnamed, American Eskimo, Aleut, American Indian and Asiatic American Extraction"; *Metro Broadcasting v. FCC*, 553. Professor Neal Devins said the FCC preference appeared to be "primarily a remedial measure clothed in the garb of diversity"; "Comment," 129–30. The FCC's subsequent adoption of a preference for licenses for two-way pagers and interactive video—for which viewpoint is clearly irrelevant—adds further suspicion; see Jonathan Rauch, "Color TV," *New Republic* (December 19, 1994): 12; see also Mike Mills, "Women, Minorities to Gain at FCC Wireless Auction," *Washington Post*, June 29, 1994, F3.

138. Robert Dole, appearing on *Meet the Press*, cited in R. Jeffrey Smith, "GOP Senators Begin Studying Repeal of Affirmative Action," *Washington Post*, February 6, 1995, A1.

139. See *Metro Broadcasting v. FCC*, 614 (O'Connor). Racial imbalances have existed throughout history and across cultures, and diversity concerns will continue to operate in perpetuity, particularly as the concept of diversity is applied to finer and finer subcategories in the workforce. In the case of *Taxman v. Piscataway*, e.g., the school faculty was racially balanced throughout the school district, and even at the high school level, but the diversity preference was invoked because the department was not racially balanced; see Jeffrey Rosen, "Is Affirmative Action Doomed?," *New Republic* (October 17, 1994): 26. Duncan Kennedy readily concedes that his proposal of using race as a positive credential for diversity on law faculties "contemplates race-conscious decision making as a routine, non-deviant mode, a more or less permanent norm in distributing legal academic jobs"; "A Cultural Pluralist Case," 720–21.

140. See Sullivan, "The Supreme Court—1986 Term," 97.

141. Quoted in Carter, *Affirmative Action Baby*, 45.

142. Greenberg, *Crusaders in the Courts*, 467. Greenberg says he remains more at home with the notion of preferences to address "past injustices dealt to blacks" than with diversity (467). William Taylor makes the same argument; interview with the author, Washington, D.C., December 15, 1994.

143. Carter, *Affirmative Action Baby*, 44.

144. Indeed, all the evidence suggests that daughters of wealthy families end up wealthy themselves virtually to the same degree as sons; see Brittain, *The Inheritance of Economic Status*, 24. As Nicholas Lemann notes, "13 percent of white women are poor, 16 percent of women, 33 percent of blacks and 37 percent of black women"; "The Lawyer as Hero," *New Republic* (September 13, 1993): 36. In fact, the relative distribution of wealth among women, as compared to blacks, has led some minorities to complain that wealthy white women should not receive the same advantages under affirmative action as people of color; see Fuchs, *The American Kaleidoscope*, 455.

145. In 1994 the gap between men and women on the combined SAT was 45 points. The gap between whites and blacks was almost four and a half times greater—198 points; see College Entrance Examination Board, *1994 Profile of SAT and Achievement Test Takers* (Princeton, N.J.: Educational Testing Service, 1994). And women as a group have higher grades than men; see Richard Marius, "Boys, Girls, and Fairness," *Harvard* (March-April 1994): 99. Most universities, therefore, do not give preferences to women. One of the rare exceptions is MIT, but even there, the preference given to women is quite small, on the order of 20 SAT points; see Elaine Louie, "Unequal Contest," *New York Times* (education supplement) August 6, 1989, 28. Likewise, in the employment context, apart from physical tests, women generally do as well as men; Rutherglen, "After Affirmative Action," 354.

These facts do not stop proponents of preferences from trying to lump the two groups together for political purposes. After the UC Board of Regents vote to repeal race and gender preferences, California State Sen. Diane Watson argued, "If this university reverts to an all-white male and Asian male institution . . . why should we as taxpayers want to support it?"; see Sarah Lubman, "UC Vote to Ban Race Criteria Has Shades of Gray,"

Wall Street Journal, July 24, 1995, A6. For the general attempt by progressives to emphasize the benefits of affirmative action to women, see "What about Women?," *Newsweek*, March 27, 1995, 22–25.

146. Similarly, homosexuals have faced discrimination throughout American history, but without the dynamic among racial minorities of intergenerational transmission of unequal opportunities, since homosexuals are usually the offspring of heterosexuals and in most cases will themselves have "no offspring to transmit class position to"; Rossides, *Social Stratification*, 22. Shifting the basis of preferences from compensation to diversity and ongoing discrimination brings gays and lesbians into the fold. The *Columbia Law Review*'s diversity preference, e.g., includes homosexuals; see Stephen Labaton, "Law Review at Columbia in Dispute on Bias Plan," *New York Times*, May 3, 1989, B1.

In practice, the new alliances are less potent than in theory. For the limited appeal of gender preferences to women, see ch. 4. There is also debate in the gay community as to whether to pursue affirmative action. Unlike women and racial minorities, gays and lesbians do not enjoy basic antidiscriminatory protections. Some believe the call for preferences for homosexuals may backfire, legitimating the antihomosexual lobby's argument that homosexuals seek not just civil rights but special treatment as well; see Dennis Farney, "Have Liberals Ignored 'Have-Less' Whites at Their Own Peril?," *Wall Street Journal*, December 14, 1994, A8. And preferences for gays raise serious questions about privacy that are not present in the racial context; see Byrne, "Affirmative Action for Lesbians and Gay Men," 80.

Chapter 3

1. *UC v. Bakke*, 324 (Brennan). Today, by contrast, one often hears the argument that affirmative action was never meant to be a social program providing greater equal opportunity; see, e.g., Harris, "Whiteness as Property," 1788; Morton, "Class-Based Affirmative Action," 1123; Kennedy, "Race, Liberalism, and Affirmative Action (I)," 118; and Steven Holmes, "Mulling the Idea of Affirmative Action for Poor Whites," *New York Times*, August 18, 1991, Sec. 4, p.3. This is surely a description of today's affirmative action, but as we saw in ch. 1, it is not an accurate reflection of the programs as envisioned by its early backers.

2. *UC v. Bakke*, 276. In 1973, 73 of 297 special applicants were white; in 1974, 172 of 628 were white. None was accepted (275).

3. *UC v. Bakke*, 272, n1, and 377. Likewise, the Small Business Administration's sect. 8(a) program for "socially and economically disadvantaged" is means-tested and theoretically race-blind (*Fullilove v. Klutznick*, 464). In practice, only 40 of the 5,400 participants are not "protected" minorities; see Paul Barrett, "A White Man Is Ruled Eligible for Set-Asides," *Wall Street Journal*, June 13, 1995, B1. Other federal programs, like the one challenged by Adarand Constructors, Inc., use similar schemes and requirements of disadvantage. The fact that many of these programs are—to the untutored eye—completely class-based belies the notion that class has always been irrelevant to affirmative action.

4. The racial diversity theory aims at equality of group result, just as the compensatory theory does, only more obviously, since diversity does not even make the pretense of being concerned with equal opportunity. Under diversity theory, even if the process for selection is completely fair, if, for cultural reasons, groups are not represented at the table proportionately, the process is flawed. And diversity does not just mean a seat at the table, it means the right number of seats. Harvard University, e.g., says if only a small number of minorities are present, they might feel isolated and thereby not provide the benefits of diversity; *UC v. Bakke*, 323 (appendix to Powell opinion). In addition, because the type of diversity sought is racial rather than economic, it does not even provide a backdoor way of approximating genuine equal opportunity. If a university is filled with upper-income blacks, Asians, Latinos, Native Americans, and whites, then racial diversity is satisfied.

5. I agree with the critique that the goal of equal group results also "goes too far" to the extent that it incorrectly assumes that all racial groups have identical cultures and would be proportionately represented in all fields but for discrimination.

6. See Freeman, "Race and Class," 1894–95. See also Ansley, "Stirring the Ashes," 1049.

7. Chang-Lin Tien, "Diversity and Excellence in Higher Education," in Mills, *Debating Affirmative Action*, 244. See also Karabel, "Berkeley and Beyond," 157.

8. Tien, "Diversity and Excellence," in Mills, *Debating Affirmative Action*, 244.

9. Andrew Hacker, *Two Nations*, 142. Accordingly, most affirmative action programs probably provide some net gain in equal opportunity—which is one of the reasons I am marginally in favor of affirmative action over doing nothing. The conservative argument that color blindness is a necessary element of equal opportunity is correct, but color blindness is not sufficient. It is also necessary to recognize different starting points—something many conservatives fail to do. That is why it is possible to say that although affirmative action lacks the necessary condition of color blindness, it actually does a better job at equal opportunity than doing nothing. Of the two necessary conditions—color blindness and equal starting points—the latter is more important.

10. Senate Judiciary Committee, *Nomination of Judge Thomas*, 360.

11. Dershowitz and Hanft, "College Diversity," 416, n114.

12. D'Souza, *Illiberal Education*, 33–34.

13. Adelson, "Living with Quotas," 27.

14. See Richard Cohen, "Affirmative Action under the Gun," *Washington Post*, January 31, 1995, A15.

15. Cohen interview (1994).

16. See Michael Kinsley, "The Spoils of Victimhood: The Case Against the Case Against Affirmative Action," *New Yorker* (March 27, 1995): 66.

17. Smith and Welch, *Closing the Gap*, viii.

18. The median white household income in 1993 was $32,960, and 26.5 percent of African American households made over $35,000. See *Statistical Abstract of the United States, 1995* (Washington, D.C.: US Government Printing Office, 1995), 469.

19. Webster, *The Racialization of America*, 110.

20. Smith and Welch, *Closing the Gap*, 13.

21. See Cose, *The Rage of a Privileged Class*, 36–37; see also National Research Council, *A Common Destiny*, 275; Brown, *Minority Party*, 85–86; Judges, "Bayonets for the Wounded," 646, n205; and Peter Brimelow and Leslie Spencer, "When Quotas Replace Merit, Everybody Suffers," *Forbes* (February 15, 1993): 102.

22. Cose, *The Rage of a Privileged Class*, 36–37.

23. "The Other America," *The Economist*, July 10, 1993, 17. See also Smith and Welch, *Closing the Gap*, vii. Between 1940 and 1980, Smith and Welch report, black male wages increased 52 percent faster than wages for white males.

24. See Sam Roberts, "Where Median Income of Blacks Leads That of White Households," *New York Times*, June 6, 1994, 1.

25. See Henry Louis Gates, Jr., "Why Now?," *New Republic* (October 31, 1994): 10. The expansion of the black middle class is undeniable and has been widely remarked upon by commentators of all political stripes. Cornel West estimates that the black middle class has multiplied by more than five times since before the civil rights era; *Race Matters*, 35; see also Taylor, *Paved with Good Intentions*, 26; Graham, *The Civil Rights Era*, 453; Wilson, *The Truly Disadvantaged*, 109; Taylor, "Brown, Equal Protection," 1704–7; National Urban League, *The State of Black America*, 27; and Williams, "It's a White Thing," *Washington Post*, April 2, 1995, C1, C4 (according to whom, the black middle class has grown from 18 percent to 40 percent of the black population over the past thirty years).

26. See National Research Council, *A Common Destiny*, 312.

27. Wilson, *The Truly Disadvantaged*, 109. See also Kahl and Gilbert, *The American Class Structure* (1987), 75.

28. See Robert Frank and Eleena De Lisser, "Research on Affirmative Action Finds Modest Gains for Blacks over 30 Years," *Wall Street Journal*, February 21, 1995, A6.

29. See, e.g., Wilson, *The Declining Significance of Race*, 16; Wilson, *The Truly Disadvantaged*, 110; Goldman, *Justice and Reverse Discrimination*, 90; Fishkin, *Justice, Equal*

Opportunity, 90; Sandalow, "Racial Preferences in Higher Education," 691; Posner, "The DeFunis Case," 15, n31; Judges, "Bayonets for the Wounded," 645; Nickel, "Preferential Policies in Hiring and Admissions," 538; Kennedy, "Persuasion and Distrust," 1333, n23; Drew S. Days, "Civil Rights at the Crossroads," in Mills, *Debating Affirmative Action*, 276; Steele, *The Content of Our Character*, 124; West, *Race Matters*, 63; and "America's Wasted Blacks," *The Economist*, March 30, 1991, 12.

30. Wilson, *The Truly Disadvantaged*, 110–11.

31. Hacker, *Two Nations*, 131.

32. *Fullilove v. Klutznick*, 538 (Stevens dissenting).

33. Richard B. Freeman, "Black Economic Progress after 1964," in Rosen, *Studies in Labor Markets*, 280.

34. See Lind, *The Next American Nation*, 172. See also Tim Bovee, "Minority Programs Mostly Aid White Areas," *Los Angeles Times*, April 17, 1994, A18; and Rep. David Dreir, "'Disadvantaged' Contractors' Unfair Advantage," *Wall Street Journal*, February 21, 1989, A18.

35. See Bovee, "Minority Programs Mostly Aid White Areas," A1.

36. See Michael Kinsley, "Invidious Distinction," *New Republic* (February 5, 1990): 4. See also Lemann, *The Promised Land*, 290. Preferences may sometimes not even benefit wealthy minorities, but rather wealthy whites; see *Metro Broadcasting v. FCC*, 636, n4 (Kennedy).

37. See Jackie Calmes, "Tax Break Bill Could Affect Viacom Sale," *Wall Street Journal*, February 8, 1995, A3 (citing a Joint Committee on Taxation report).

38. Paul Farhi and Kevin Merida, "House Rejects Tax Break," *Washington Post*, February 22, 1995, A1.

39. See Jackie Calmes and Mark Robichaux, "House Panel Votes to Repeal Tax Law Vital to Viacom's $2.3 Billion Cable Sale," *Wall Street Journal*, February 9, 1995, A3. Normally, of course, Democrats would raise hell about an enormous tax write-off, and Republicans would be forced to defend corporate welfare. But with this legislation, the tables were reversed. The Clinton administration, through Assistant Treasury Secretary Leslie Samuels, initially opposed repeal, calling it a "sledge hammer approach"; see ibid. When faced with defeat, Democrats rallied around a plan to cap the tax certificate at $50 million, but the effort was rejected; the repeal passed the House and Senate overwhelmingly and was signed by the president, who favored other portions of the legislation; see Jackie Calmes, "House Votes to Eliminate Tax Break; Viacom Cable-TV Sale May Be Doomed," *Wall Street Journal*, February 22, 1995, A2. In July 1995, the president's review of affirmative action actually returned to defend the tax certificate program; [Office of the President], *Affirmative Action Review*, 89–96.

40. See U.S. Congress, *Report of the Study Group*, 51–52.

41. Studies by Freeman and by Smith and Welch cited in Heckman and Hoult Verkerke, "Racial Disparity and Employment Discrimination," 284.

42. See Loury, "Moral Quandary," 21. See also Loury, "The Need for Moral Leadership in the Black Community," 19.

43. Smith and Welch, *Closing the Gap*, xxii. The economist Thomas Sowell argues that the well-known bifurcation of the black community into middle-class and poor is directly related to the effects of affirmative action; *Civil Rights*, 51–52.

44. See Fuchs, *The American Kaleidoscope*, 455.

45. See Dirk Johnson, "Minority Contractors Protest Rule That Gives Women Similar Status," *New York Times*, March 5, 1988, 1.

46. Carter, *Affirmative Action Baby*, 7.

47. See Judges, "Bayonets for the Wounded," 603, 629, 644–45.

48. Steele, *The Content of Our Character*, 124. We need to be cautious about overstating this claim. William Taylor points out that in the employment context many of the affirmative action gains have come in blue-collar fields, such as law enforcement and construction; "*Brown*, Equal Protection," 1713–14. He notes, e.g., that the number of black police officers increased from 24,000 in 1970 to 43,500 in 1980 (1713). And the percentage of skilled black construction workers in Philadelphia increased from 1 percent to

12 percent; Taylor and Liss, "Affirmative Action in the 1990s," 34. Taylor notes that in the mid–1970s black medical students were much more likely to be disadvantaged than their white counterparts; "*Brown*, Equal Protection," 1706. But Taylor is a relatively lonely voice in this debate—a large number of affirmative action supporters cite him when making an argument for the broad group of affirmative action beneficiaries; see, e.g., Ronald Brownstein, "Beyond Quotas," *Los Angeles Times Magazine* (July 28, 1991): 18ff; Wilson, "Race-Neutral Programs," 78. His data on medical schools is nearly twenty years old and may be less relevant today in an era when the black middle class is much larger and more likely to dominate the competition for scarce preferences. Taylor says he does not know of new data to support his claim; Taylor interview (1994). Taylor himself returns to the medical school study and law enforcement in "Affirmative Action in the 1990s" (34).

None of this is to say that because a program benefits middle-class blacks and not poor blacks it is necessarily problematic. The same point can be made about the antidiscriminatory mechanism of the Civil Rights Act. Because only middle-class blacks were in a position to use desegregated restaurants and hotels does not mean the laws are flawed. The difference, of course, is that antidiscrimination laws remove barriers rather than creating preference, so there is no comparable clash between class and race.

49. See Fishkin, *Justice, Equal Opportunity*, 90.

50. See Jeffries, *Justice Powell*, 455.

51. See Richard Bernstein, "Racial Discrimination or Righting Past Wrongs?," *New York Times*, July 13, 1994, B8. Likewise, when a white student, Janice Camarera, was excluded from a California community college English 101 class because she was white, opponents of the policy emphasized that "she is a struggling widow who's trying to get an education to provide for her three children"; see Editorial, "Affirmative Reaction," *Wall Street Journal*, April 20, 1995, A12; see also Howard Fineman, "Race and Rage," *Newsweek*, April 3, 1995, 23.

52. Scalia, "Commentary: The Disease as Cure," 152.

53. *Johnson v. Transportation Agency, Santa Clara County*, 480 US 616 (1987), 677 (Scalia dissenting). Likewise, in the 1992 presidential campaign, Patrick Buchanan argued that it was not those who "belong to the Exeter-Yale GOP club" who "lose contracts because of minority set-asides, it is not the scions of Yale and Harvard who apply to become FBI agents and construction workers and civil servants and cops, who bear the onus of this reverse discrimination. It is the sons of middle America who pay the price of reverse discrimination advanced by the Walker's Point GOP to salve their social consciences at other people's expense"; see E. J. Dionne, Jr., "Buchanan Slashes Bush for Civil Rights Action: Law Said to Foster 'Reverse Discrimination,'" *Washington Post*, February 21, 1992, A8; see also Phillips, *Boiling Point*, 242. The columnist George Will wrote in 1985: "It is an unlovely spectacle, white lawyers and editorial writers telling blue-collar whites that promotions or jobs or seniority systems must be sacrificed in the name of racial reparations"; "Battling the Racial Spoils System," *Newsweek*, June 10, 1985, 96; see also *Wygant v. Jackson Board of Education*, 281, n8 (Powell noting that the union's "compromise" to allow racial preferences in firing placed all the burden on the union's most junior members).

54. Bell, *Race, Racism*, 906.

55. See Freeman, "Race and Class," 1895; Fiss, *Equality and Preferential Treatment*, 109; Walzer, *Spheres of Justice*, 154; and Ansley, "Stirring the Ashes," 1055. See also Webb, "In Defense of Joe Six-Pack," A14.

56. Certainly there are some lower-middle-income white victims of affirmative action, like the blue-collar worker in Jesse Helms's 1990 advertisement crumpling his rejection notice, and there are some rich black beneficiaries of affirmative action, like Frank Washington. But, in fact, the wealthy black Frank Washington was competing against unnamed wealthy whites, and Helms's unemployed white worker was competing against working-class blacks. It is only in those contexts where competition truly involves all economic segments of society that the clash between race and class becomes salient.

57. Sullivan, Pressman, and Arterton, *Explorations in Convention Decision Making*, 36–37.

58. Shafer, *Quiet Revolution*, 530; see also Edsall, *The New Politics of Inequality*, 56.

59. Cited in Judges, "Bayonets for the Wounded," 648.

60. Karabel, *Admissions at Berkeley*, 43–44, 45–46. The national median income for blacks is 57 percent that of whites.

61. David Karen, "Who Gets into Harvard?" (Ph.D. diss., Harvard, 1985), cited in Hacker, *Two Nations*, 140 (the quotation is Hacker's).

62. Lind, *The Next American Nation*, 168.

63. *Hopwood v. Texas*, 578, n75.

64. Even so, separatist means inevitably conflict with integrationist ends. Justice Blackmun's exhortation that, to get beyond racism we must take account of race, sticks in the craw, inevitably sounding Orwellian; see Van Alstyne, "Rites of Passage," 809 ("One gets beyond racism by getting beyond it now"); and *Richmond v. Croson*, 520–21 (Scalia). But there is a stronger case to be made that failing to remedy our history will perpetuate its effects long into the future; see ch. 1.

65. See *McDonald v. Santa Fe Trail Transportation Co.*, 427 US 273, 279 (1976), cited in *UC v. Bakke*, 413 (Stevens).

66. Suspect or semisuspect classes are race, gender, and illegitimacy. See *UC v. Bakke*, 360 (Brennan). In addition, alienage is a sometimes suspect category; though mutable, it is included because aliens are a discrete and insular minority. Immutability, as John Ely notes, is stressed in a number of cases, including *Parham v. Hughes*, 99 SCt 1742, 1745 (1979) (plurality opinion), and *Frontiero v. Richardson*, 411 US 677, 686 (1973) (plurality opinion); see Ely, *Democracy and Distrust*, 249, n53. The Civil Rights Act list or prohibited criteria include "race, color, religion, sex or national origin"; see, e.g., sect. 703(a) of the 1964 Civil Rights Act. The Americans with Disabilities Act added disability to the list. Age discrimination is also prohibited under the Age Discrimination in Employment Act of 1967. Although age obviously changes, relentlessly, it is beyond one's control.

67. Gross, *Discrimination in Reverse*, 14.

68. The illegitimacy cases include: *Levy v. Louisiana*, 391 US 68 (1968); *Weber v. Aetna Casualty and Surety Co.*, 406 US 164 (1972); *Parham v. Hughes*, 99 SCt 1742 (1979); *Caban v. Mohammed*, 99 SCt 1760 (1979). See Ely, *Democracy and Distrust*, 150, 249, n55, and 256, n93.

69. *UC v. Bakke*, 360–61 (Brennan), citing *Weber v. Aetna*, 175, and *Frontiero v. Richardson*, 411 US 677, 686 (1973).

70. Ely uses the example of the blind airplane pilot in the context of constitutional adjudication; *Democracy and Distrust*, 154–55.

71. Curiously, some proponents of affirmative action argue that academic record and race are equally immutable. Ronald Dworkin, e.g., argues that while race is beyond one's control, "it is also true that those who score low in aptitude or admissions tests do not choose their levels of intelligence. . . . [Bakke] would have been accepted if he were black. But it is also true, and in exactly the same sense, that he would have been accepted if he had been more intelligent, or made a better impression in his interview, or, in the case of other schools, if he had been younger when he decided to become a doctor. Race is not, in his case, a different matter from these other factors equally beyond his control"; "Why Bakke Has No Case," 14–15; see also Alex Kozinksi, "Color and Caution," *New Republic* (February 1, 1993): 72.

Is it really true that how well Allan Bakke did in an interview and how he performed on tests are "equally beyond his control" as his race? Surely athletic talent, academic performance, even beauty, are more malleable than race: a natural athlete's talent may atrophy through indolence; a born scientist may become an alcoholic; a ravishing beauty may put on a hundred pounds; but a black person remains black, and a white person white, no matter what.

More important, even if intelligence were entirely immutable, the social utility of sorting the highly intelligent into the positions requiring their skills is very high (just as the utility of keeping the blind away from flying airplanes is high)—much higher than in the case of race, where, I will argue, there are pluses and minuses. Even proponents of race-based preferences endorse the social utility of weighing intelligence to the extent that they insist that preferences should go only to those who are otherwise "qualified."

None of this is to say that university admissions should be measured only by test scores and grade point average. Virtually no universities take that tack; see Karen Paget, "Diversity at Berkeley," *American Prospect* (Spring 1992): 110. Letters of recommendation, student essays, student interviews, achievement in extracurricular activities, and other factors such as service, should count as well.

72. The UC Davis Medical School, e.g., gave preference to those who agreed to serve in underserved geographic areas in California; see *Bakke v. UC*, 1157–58. The criterion is of marginal, rather than great, social utility only because such agreements, if binding, are normally temporary. To a large degree, agreeing to serve the poor is within one's control, subject to side economic constraints (e.g., student loans). Note that this arrangement is different from using race as a proxy for likelihood of public service, as UC Davis once argued and as some continue to argue today; see, e.g., Nicholas Lemann, "What Happened to the Case for Affirmative Action?," *New York Times Magazine* (June 11, 1995): 36. Indeed, there is some evidence that law students of color, perhaps because on average they are less advantaged, are less likely to go into public service than whites; D'Souza, *Illiberal Education*, 53.

73. Athletic preferences can be quite large. Even at Harvard, not generally known for its athletic excellence, the preference for athletes is "massive," according to Jerome Karabel and David Karen. One study found that in the 1970s, if verbal SATs had been used as the sole criterion for admission, 80 percent of the athletes at Harvard would not have been admitted; Karabel and Karen, "Go to Harvard," 23.

74. Gross, *Discrimination in Reverse*, 91.

75. Legacy programs are quite widespread. At UC Davis Medical School at the time of the famous *Bakke* dispute over setting aside sixteen seats for minorities, the dean had authority to fill five seats with children of alumni and donors; see Harris, "Whiteness as Property," 1773. John Larew calls Harvard's legacy preference system its "largest affirmative action program"; "Why Are Droves of Unqualified, Unprepared Kids Getting into Our Top Colleges? Because Their Dads Are Alumni," *Washington Monthly* (June 1991): 10. While the size of the legacy preference is smaller than Harvard's racial preferences (36 SAT points on average for alumni children versus 95 for African Americans), the impact is broader; see Murray and Herrnstein, *The Bell Curve*, 756, n21, and 452. If legacies had been admitted at the same rate as other applicants in 1988, there would have been 200 fewer alumni children at Harvard—more than the total number of blacks, Mexican Americans, Puerto Ricans, and Native Americans in Harvard's freshman class; Karabel and Karen, "Go to Harvard," 23. Legacy preferences are not limited to private schools; they are also employed by such public institutions as the University of Virginia, Berkeley, and the University of North Carolina.

The benefit of such preferences to the university comes in the form of increased alumni contributions (both financial and nonfinancial). The Department of Education's Office of Civil Rights (OCR) found that Harvard's legacy preference was justified for this reason, even though it had a negative disparate impact on Asians; see OCR, letter to Derek Bok, President of Harvard University, October 4, 1990; and Scott Jaschik, "Doubts Are Raised about U.S. Inquiry on Harvard Policies," *Chronicle of Higher Education*, February 6, 1991, A22. See also *Rosenstock v. Board of Governors of University of North Carolina*, 423 FSupp 1321 (1976).

Nevertheless, the actual magnitude of the financial benefit is difficult to establish. Harvard's dean of admissions was unable to cite any empirical evidence on the question, leading Asian groups to question why OCR had accepted the justification; see Jaschik, "Doubts Are Raised," A19; Larew, "Why Are Droves . . . ," 14; and Hacker, *Two Nations*, 136. Former Princeton dean James Wickenden told Larew that the parents of legacy applicants who "are denied admission are initially upset. . . . But typically they come back around when they see that what happened was best for the kids"; Larew, "Why Are Droves . . . ," 13. Indeed, Harvard does reject more than half (57 percent) of legacies without suffering financial ruin (14). While Duke's claim that its "survival as an institution" depends on alumni giving may be true, it is not true that giving would stop without preferences; as Larew notes, some alumni would continue to give based on loyalty (13). The threat of alumni reaction has a dubious history. Dworkin notes that the negative reaction of alumni was used as an argument for keeping blacks out of universities in the 1940s; *Taking Rights Seriously*, 230.

On the other hand, the social costs of alumni preferences are fairly clear. First, legacy preferences often have a negative disparate impact on minorities, as they did on Asian American applicants to Harvard. Some argue that the disparate impact may not be wholly unintentional, and that the original intent of legacy preferences was to decrease the number of Jews in the Ivy League; Larew, "Why Are Droves . . . ," 12; see also Dershowitz and Hanft, "College Diversity," 398. Second, as with any preference, legacy preferences lead to a decrease in the intellectual caliber of students admitted. According to Larew, at Harvard legacies are three times as likely to be accepted as nonlegacies, two and a half times more likely at Yale, and twice as likely at Dartmouth and Stanford. Notre Dame sets aside 25 percent of the class for legacies; Larew, "Why Are Droves . . . ," 10, 13. While Harvard has justified the difference by saying that alumni children are generally smarter and deserve to get in—or that they are equally qualified and legacy status is a mere "tiebreaker"—the statistics do not bear out those explanations. According to the OCR investigation, between 1981 and 1988 nonlegacy admits were better qualified than legacy admits in all areas other than athletics (11). At one Ivy League college, says the former dean of Princeton admissions, the average freshman SAT was 1350, while the legacy admits among the freshman averaged 1280 (13). A 1956 study found alumni children at Harvard were concentrated in the bottom of the class; no study has been conducted since (13).

Third, because alumni generally are wealthier than nonalumni—at Harvard, e.g., alumni are "overwhelmingly affluent and white" (10)—the preference undermines efforts to provide equal opportunity and can actually be considered "affirmative action for the privileged"; Karabel and Karen, "Go to Harvard," 23. If, for the reasons outlined in ch. 4, the test scores of wealthy children overpredict their ultimate potential, we should not compound the already unfair advantage of the wealthy with an additional preference for legacies.

Moreover, one's legacy status is immutable. Indeed, as Justice Blackmun noted in *UC v. Bakke*, it is "ironic" that people become "so deeply disturbed" about racial preferences while widely tolerating preferences for children of alumni and the affluent (404); see also Larew, "Why Are Droves . . . ," 11, 14.

The social utility of geographic preferences is probably marginal at best. Geography is not a particularly good proxy for different background since, as Dershowitz and Hanft point out, "the farm boy from rural New York or New Jersey may add more diversity than would the Harvard educated lawyer's son from Des Moines"; "College Diversity," 411. The marginally improved learning experience, weighed against loss in intelligence, surely does not trump the presumption against being judged by a status beyond the applicant's control. While geographic preferences are less likely than legacy preferences to benefit the wealthy, they have a highly dubious origin. Originally they were meant not to broaden diversity but to limit it; see Dershowitz and Hanft, "College Diversity," on the use of geography to limit the number of Jews at Harvard. Michael Lind notes that the percentage of Jews at Columbia declined from 44 percent to 22 percent after geographic preferences were instituted in the 1920s; *The Next American Nation*, 64.

Overall, then, if we set aside the question of class preferences to ensure genuine equal opportunity or race preferences to compensate for past discrimination (that is, if one assumes a society of genuine equal opportunity in which compensation for past discrimination has been addressed), the "forward-looking" reasons to include the following criteria sort out as follows:

CRITERION	SOCIAL UTILITY	INDIVIDUAL CONTROL	WEIGHT ACCORDED
Academic	Great	Moderate	Maximum
Service	Moderate	Large	Large
Athletics	Marginal	Moderate	Minimal
Legacy	Debatable	None	None
Geography	Debatable	None	None
Race	Debatable	None	None

76. See, e.g., *UC v. Bakke*, 404 (Blackmun); Greenberg, *Crusaders in the Courts*, 461, 464.

77. Richard Bernstein, "Black and White on Campus," *New York Times*, May 26, 1988. The sociology professor Troy Duster also observed that Berkeley freshman quickly balkanize by ethnic group. "Students come here expecting to meet people from different backgrounds and have a good experience. What happens is often just the reverse. After their first five or six weeks, what they learn is how to be a member of an ethnic, racial, or political group"; quoted in Takagi, *The Retreat from Race*, 145; see also Mary Jordan, "College Dorms Reflect Trend of Self-Segregation," *Washington Post*, March 6, 1994, A1.

78. To the extent that affirmative action programs today emphasize "different voice" rather than the need to compensate, it is natural that those who are different are told to bond together, apart from the majority. The widely worn T-shirt, "It's a black thing; you wouldn't understand," captures both halves of the phenomenon: the assertion of difference, which would enrich the university experience, but then the more emphatic assertion of separation.

79. See Carter, *Affirmative Action Baby*, 85.

80. When Jesse Choper, dean of Boalt Hall, said racial preferences are necessary to create an environment where "students have different points of view," Dinesh D'Souza asked if that meant Choper believed "that blacks possess, by virtue of being black a certain vision or the world, or to put it differently, do all blacks think alike?" Choper told D'Souza, "No, no. We are simply hoping for diverse points of view"; *Illiberal Education*, 52–53. The Supreme Court was similarly cautious in arguing that there is not a minority viewpoint but rather "empirical evidence" that minorities bring different views to the table "in the aggregate"; *Metro Broadcasting v. FCC*, 579–80. If race is not a perfect proxy for viewpoint, if racial preferences only "indirectly" further the goal (617), then why rely on race, which is a presumptively bad category to use in the first place? The real goal, Justice O'Connor says, is not viewpoint diversity but allocation of licenses by race (625).

81. Carter, *Affirmative Action Baby*, 29, 31.

82. *Metro Broadcasting v. FCC*, 582–83.

83. Kennedy, "Orphans," 41.

84. Hacker, *Two Nations*, 181. See also National Research Council, *A Common Destiny*, 22–23.

85. See Sunstein, "Why Markets Don't Stop Discrimination," 27.

86. Carter, *Affirmative Action Baby*, 38. The Supreme Court has also expressed concern with the government's assumption that minority groups "think alike" in the context of voting; see, e.g., *Shaw v. Reno*, 113 SCt 2816 (1993), and *Miller v. Johnson* 115 SCt 2475 (1995). But the distinction between voting, on the one hand, and hiring and educational admissions, on the other, is that voting is an inherently group-oriented activity, whereas employment and education decisions are not. As Justice Powell has argued: "The concept of 'representation' necessarily applies to groups; groups of voters elect representatives, individual voters do not"; *Davis v. Bandemer*, 478 US 109, 167 (1986) (Powell concurring and dissenting).

When a university or an employer chooses people to admit or hire, it is by definition choosing individuals. If it uses race as a proxy for viewpoint, it is assuming that an individual is likely to act and think a certain way. By contrast, when a legislature draws a voting line around hundreds of thousands of residents, there is no such individualized process. Just as legislatures assume geographic constituencies have common interests, it is fair to say, given our nation's history, that racial groups have basic common interests;

Guinier, *The Tyranny of the Majority*, 119. The analogy to university and employment decisions in the voting context would be to assume that an *individual candidate* running for office will think or act a certain way because of the color of his or her skin, something most of us would see as different from assuming that a *constituency* of several hundred thousand may have some common interests.

Ironically, it was Lani Guinier's recognition of this central distinction that got her into trouble. Guinier was pilloried for saying that certain black officials, like former Virginia Governor Douglas Wilder, are not "authentic blacks" because they represent majority white constituencies; *The Tyranny of the Majority*, 58. The term sounds highly offensive, as if Wilder was not liberal enough to be genuinely black, but, ironically, Guinier seems to have meant precisely the opposite: that you cannot look at the color of an *individual* elected official's skin (Governor Wilder being black) and presume he will act and vote the way other members of his racial *group* may wish. Conversely, Guinier says, a white elected official who represents a majority black district can be an authentically black representative (13, 215, n84). What is important, Guinier says, is not the color of the representative's skin but the voting group to whom the representative (of whatever color) is beholden. She cites Justice Brennan's opinion in *Thornburg v. Gingles* (1986) on this point: it is the "status of the candidate as the chosen representative of a particular racial group, not the race of the candidate, that is important" (13).

87. Quoted in Allport, *The Nature of Prejudice*, 469.

88. Eisenhower quoted in Taylor, "*Brown*, Equal Protection," 1702, n2.

89. Allport quoted in Kluger, *Simple Justice*, 908.

90. Brownstein, "Beyond Quotas," 18ff.

91. David Lamb and Barry Bearak, "Revolution Incomplete; Gains Made But Racism Runs Deep," *Los Angeles Times*, March 8, 1987, pt. 1, p. 1.

92. Taylor, "*Brown*, Equal Protection," 1702.

93. Allport, *The Nature of Prejudice*, 477. Conversely, Allport noted, it was the legal system of Jim Crow that partly created backward racial attitudes in the South in the first place (470–71).

94. Carter, *Affirmative Action Baby*, 41, 227. "The unfortunate logical corollary" of diversity theory, writes Carter, "is that if the perspective a particular person of color can offer is *not* distinctive, if it is more like the 'white' perspective than the 'black' one, then that person is not speaking in an authentically black voice—an accusation that has become all too common" (6). At George Washington University, one of my law students told me that he was admitted to the law review because he had stated in his "diversity" essay that he would add a special ethnic perspective, and that subsequently he felt guilty about writing an article unrelated to race.

The racial box that the viewpoint rationale perpetuates was nowhere more clear than in the reaction of the civil rights community to the Supreme Court nomination of Clarence Thomas. Whatever one thought of the Thomas nomination (I was strongly opposed), the comments attacking his authenticity as a black were chilling. Arch Puddington, a former aide to Bayard Rustin, summarizes the charges:

> At the core of the anti-Thomas strategy was an attempt by his black opponents to deny the nominee the right to call himself black. According to Ronald Walters, blackness "ultimately means more than color; it also means a set of values from which Thomas is apparently estranged." Derrick Bell, a Harvard law professor, claimed that Thomas "doesn't think like a black." Judge Bruce Wright of New York called Thomas "emotionally white." Others took note of Thomas's marriage to a white woman; Russell Adams, chairman of Howard University's department of Afro-American studies, saw this as "a sign of his rejection of the black community." Indeed, declared New York Congressman Charles Rangel, Thomas "goes against the grain of everything black people believe in." ("Thomas and the Blacks," 29)

Puddington notes that black support for Thomas at the time of the confirmation vote reached nearly 70 percent (30).

Professor Derrick Bell's famous statement about Randall Kennedy—"the ends of diversity are not served by people who look black and think white"—is at once repellent and a logical consequence of the legitimation of an accepted "black" way of thinking; Carter, *Affirmative Action Baby*, 33; and Kerlow, *Poisoned Ivy*, 78. By contrast, Carter notes that the old compensatory justification for affirmative action imposed no requirement on beneficiaries that they think a certain way; *Affirmative Action Baby*, 33–34.

95. Recall that the idea behind subjecting racial classifications to "strict scrutiny" is that, while we should never say "never," we should say "almost never" and require a compelling interest to justify a state's use of racial classifications. The danger in allowing racial classifications when the social benefit is marginal is that arguments can and have been made for marginal benefits for a number of educational theories, including segregation. Through the years, many have said blacks and whites learn marginally better when separated (because they feel more secure in homogenous environments); see Cox, *The Role of the Supreme Court*, 60. Today the view is increasingly popular in the black community; see "The Other America," *The Economist*, July 10, 1993, 17ff (citing school districts in Milwaukee, Detroit, and New York). Advocates cite, among other factors, the higher graduation rates among blacks at historically black colleges. If this view were to become any more fashionable, then predominantly white universities would be justified in providing a preference for white students; Greenawalt, *Discrimination and Reverse Discrimination*, 82. If one believes a white preference sounds fantastic, consider the September 1992 decision of the University of California to accept funds from Margaret F. Hornbeck for "very poor American Caucasian academic scholars"; see Charles Krauthammer, "Bitter Fruit of Racial Set-Asides," *Washington Post*, September 25, 1992, A25.

96. For the argument that diversity is good for customer relations, see Anne B. Fisher, "Businessmen Like to Hire by the Numbers," *Fortune* (September 16, 1985): 26ff.

97. See Kahlenberg, *Broken Contract*, 194.

98. This argument was made in opposition to Ron Brown's bid to be chairman of the Democratic National Committee.

99. Sowell, *Race and Culture*, 84. See also Epstein, arguing that diversity can be bad for business because it increases transaction costs; *Forbidden Grounds*, 59–79.

100. See Sunstein, "Why Markets Don't Stop Discrimination," 25.

101. The trial court actually sided with the airlines, noting that female flight attendants were superior at "making flights as pleasurable as possible"; 442 F2d 385, 387 (1971) (citing district court opinion). But the appeals court held that "it would be totally anomalous if we were to allow the preferences and prejudices of customers to determine whether sex discrimination was valid" (389). Moreover, it is interesting to note that Congress did not even explicitly provide a bona fide occupational qualification exception for race, as it did for religion, sex, and national origin; see sect. 703(e), quoted in *Diaz v. Pan American*, 386.

102. Even then, black officers may be seen as part of the white establishment and be written off as "Uncle Toms"; see Lamb and Bearak, "Revolution Incomplete," *Los Angeles Times*, March 8, 1987, pt. 1, p. 1.

103. See Don J. DeBenedictis, "The Lineup," *ABA Journal* (October 1994): 63.

104. Ellis Cose, "Rage of the Privileged," *Newsweek*, November 15, 1993, 61.

105. Schlesinger, *The Disuniting of America*, 106.

106. In 1995 a Jewish lawyer alleged in federal court that he was fired by a direct-marketing firm because the client said it was bad for the firm to be represented by "a New York Jew"; see Constance Johnson, "Lawyer Says He Was Fired over Religion," *Wall Street Journal*, May 15, 1995, B8.

107. See Amy Stevens, "Minority Lawyers Tapped in Strategic Moves to Win," *Wall Street Journal*, April 24, 1995, B1 (describing such a case in Chicago).

108. Robert Coles notes that Ralph Ellison "insisted that he be considered a novelist, not a black or Afro-American novelist ... to him, *Invisible Man* was written by an

American novelist"; Robert Coles, telephone interview with the author, February 3, 1995. Thus, we come full circle, back to the situation Gunnar Myrdal decried: "The Negro leader, the Negro social scientist, the Negro man of art and letters . . . can grow to a degree of distinction, but always as a representative of 'his people,' not as an ordinary American or an individual in humanity"; *An American Dilemma*, 28; see also Cose, *The Rage of a Privileged Class*, 1, 5.

There are practical complications as well. We know that tensions often run high between black police officers and Hispanic citizens; it is no answer to lump all "people of color" together; Tamara Jones, "A New Taped Confrontation Stretches California Tension," *Washington Post*, August 24, 1994, A1. Glazer and Moynihan ridiculed the drug counselor law: "In other words, the federal government . . . was to match the therapist with the patients: Azerbaijani junky, Azerbaijani counsellor"; *Ethnicity*, 11.

109. As late at the Carter administration, it was still the goal of the federal government to promote teacher desegregation, "to eliminate the concentration of black teachers in black schools and white teachers in white schools"; Califano, *Governing America*, 222. In addition, the Court noted that the role model theory justifies preferences that are limitless in scope and duration; *Wygant v. Jackson Board of Education*, 276, and *Richmond v. Croson*, 498. It was not a narrowly tailored remedy for past discrimination because the "remedy" was keyed not to the pool of qualified black teachers but to the number of black students.

110. See, e.g., Owen Fiss, "Groups and the Equal Protection Clause," in Cohen, Nagel, and Scanlon, *Equality and Preferential Treatment*, 140.

111. Kluger, *Simple Justice*, 553.

112. Carter, *Affirmative Action Baby*, 41–42.

113. Both quoted in Greenberg, *Crusaders in the Courts*, 502.

114. Carter, *Affirmative Action Baby*, 42.

115. All quoted in Greenberg, *Crusaders in the Courts*, 294, 296–98, 503.

116. Ibid., 504.

117. Nelson Mandela, "The Oneness of the Human Race," reprinted in *Washington Post*, October 9, 1994, C7.

118. Charles Krauthammer, ". . . Secrecy and Conformity," *Washington Post*, April 26, 1991, A23.

119. While there may appear to be a tension between the viewpoint rationale (minorities and whites are different) and the integration rationale (minorities and whites are alike), the two can be easily reconciled. It is clearly true both that minorities may, in the aggregate, add to viewpoint diversity and that they are, of course, intellectually and emotionally the same as whites. Still, there is an irony here, especially in the language Stevens uses—color is only "skin deep," and America is a "melting pot." These images will strike many diversity proponents as obsolete.

120. See *UC v. Bakke*, 298 (Powell); *DeFunis v. Odegaard*, 343 (Douglas); and *UC v. Bakke*, 360 (Brennan). Empirical studies affirm that when evaluators or subordinates believe minorities and women have been admitted under affirmative action programs, the beneficiaries are judged to be less qualified; see John F. Dovidio, Jeffrey Mann, and Samuel L. Gaertner, "Resistance to Affirmative Action: The Implications of Aversive Racism," in Blanchard and Crosby, *Affirmative Action in Perspective*, 84.

In addition, some argue that at least as damaging is the message that preferences send to blacks; see Sowell, *Black Education*, 292. Again, some empirical evidence supports the allegation that, among beneficiaries, a perception that a preference contributed to a hiring or promotion could lead to "low job satisfaction, low job commitment, and higher role stress"; see Dovidio, Mann, and Gaertner, "Resistance to Affirmative Action," in Blanchard and Crosby, *Affirmative Action in Perspective*, 84.

121. Cornel West is right to say a certain number of whites held negative views of the qualifications of blacks long before quotas; *Beyond Eurocentrism*, 29. See also Williams, "Comment," 542; and Wilkins, "In Ivory Towers," 10. But preferences may nevertheless increase the numbers.

122. Many commentators assume that tie-breaking is the paradigm. In polls, e.g.,

questions are usually worded in terms of two equally qualified candidates, one black, one white; see, e.g., the *Newsweek* poll cited in Carter, *Affirmative Action Baby*, 266. Likewise, Harvard's fall 1989 *Affirmative Action Newsletter* argued: "Myth: Affirmative action means applying a double standard—one for white males and a somewhat lower standard for women and minorities. Reality: Double standards are inconsistent with the principle and spirit of affirmative action"; Harvard University, Office of the Assistant to the President, Fall 1989, cited in D'Souza, *Illiberal Education*, 220.

123. When, in the spring of 1991, a white Georgetown Law student, Timothy Maguire, leaked documents from the admissions office suggesting that blacks had been admitted with substantially lower scores than whites, the law school did three things. The dean, Judith Areen, issued a statement suggesting that Georgetown did not practice race-conscious affirmative action. She refused to release records to support the claim. And the law school sought to punish Maguire for violating student confidentiality.

The outright denial of racial preferences struck those on both the left and the right as silly and mendacious. From the left, see Peller, "Race Consciousness," B1; from the right, see Graglia, "What's to Be Done." As to the refusal to release records, Richard Cohen wrote, "If affirmative action is worth having, it's worth defending—and acknowledging in candid terms what's entailed. The general refusal to do so leaves a distinct impression that a powerful elite, which never has to pay a penalty, has something to hide"; "At Georgetown: Taboos," *Washington Post*, April 26, 1991, A23; see also Stephen Carter, "Racial Preferences? So What?," in Mills, *Debating Affirmative Action*, 153–54. Charles Krauthammer noted the irony of Dean Areen, who had once worked for Ralph Nader, refusing to disclose data and punishing the student who did. "It is a sign of the moral decline of contemporary liberalism," he wrote, "that a former Nader's Raider should not only see nothing wrong with keeping admissions policy secret but should go after a person who dares to reveal it"; ". . . Secrecy and Conformity," A23.

124. Murray and Herrnstein, *The Bell Curve*, 451. Murray and Herrnstein put the gap between black and white SAT scores as follows: Rice—271; Berkeley—288; University of Virginia—246; Dartmouth—218; Oberlin—206; University of Rochester—219; Wesleyan—219; University of Chicago—207; Stanford—171; Columbia—182; Duke—184; Trinity—188; Williams—181; Northwestern—180; Johns Hopkins—155; Wellesley—175; Swarthmore—200; Amherst—178; Princeton—150; Brown—150; Cornell—162; University of Pennsylvania—150; Harvard—95; Georgetown—147; MIT—122; and Washington—120. Their data come primarily from the Consortium on Financing Higher Education.

125. According to the record in the *DeFunis* case, at the University of Washington Law School, thirty of thirty-seven minorities who were admitted in 1977 would have been summarily rejected if they were white; thirty-six of thirty-seven had benchmark scores lower than that of the rejected white applicant Marco DeFunis; *DeFunis v. Odegaard*, 324. At oral argument, the law school said none of the minority applicants who enrolled at the University of Washington would have been admitted under the general criteria (325).

In the *Bakke* case, admissions data at the UC Davis Medical School showed that while the regular admits had MCAT scores in the 81st percentile (verbal), 76th percentile (quantitative), and 83rd percentile (science), the special admits had scores in the 46th percentile (verbal), 24th percentile (quantitative), and 35th percentile (science). The overwhelming number of blacks and Chicanos admitted in 1973 and 1974 came in under the special admissions program; *UC v. Bakke*, 276–77. While Bakke had MCATs above the 90th percentile and a 3.5 GPA, blacks were admitted with MCATs below the 30th percentile and with GPAs as low as 2.1; Graglia, "What's to Be Done," 40.

In the more recent case of *Hopwood v. Texas*, it was revealed that at the University of Texas Law School, in the fall of 1992, the median LSAT score for nonminorities was at the 93rd percentile, for blacks at the 78th percentile, and for Mexican Americans at the 75th percentile. Median GPAs were also lower for blacks (3.30) and Mexican Americans (3.24) than for nonminorities (3.56); *Hopwood v. Texas*, 563, n32.

At the University of Virginia, African American applicants have on average lower academic indicators but are twice as likely to be admitted. According to a report in the *Washington Post*, the gap in SAT scores between black and white UVA students in 1988 was 246 points (1250 vs. 1004); Lawrence Feinberg, "Black Freshman Enrollment Rises 46% at U-Va.," *Washington Post*, December 26, 1988, C1, C8.

At Harvard, data were made public for admissions to the class of 1975. At the academic extremes, applicants were admitted or rejected at rates close to automatic; if an applicant landed in the middle group, he had on average a 30 percent chance of admission. Of the preferences, race counted the most (black applicants in the middle group had a 73 percent chance of admission), followed by athletes (64 percent chance), alumni sons (60 percent chance), private school alumnus (37 percent chance). Put differently, being black increased one's chances of acceptance over others in the same academic group by 45 percent, being an athlete by 38 percent, being an alumni son by 33 percent, and being a private school alumnus by 10 percent; Klitgaard, *Choosing Elites*, 28.

In a study of applicants to Williams, Colgate, and Bucknell, being a member of a minority group was the most decisive preference, outranking preferences given for alumni children, local residents, and athletes. Assuming comparable high school grades and test scores, being a member of a minority group increased one's chances of acceptance 53 percent at Williams, 46 percent at Colgate, and 51 percent at Bucknell; Klitgaard, *Choosing Elites*, 46. A 1981 study found that at Stanford being black was worth up to 310 SAT points in admissions (175). At MIT, black students score in the 90th percentile of students nationwide but are in the 10th percentile of MIT's entering class; D'Souza, *Illiberal Education*, 41.

At Berkeley, according to Professor Ernest Koenigsberg, an architect of the school's admissions policy, if a student has a 3.5 GPA and 1200 SAT, she has a 100 percent probability of admission if she is black, and less than a 5 percent probability if she is Asian American; D'Souza, *Illiberal Education*, 3. Because nearly 30 percent of Asian American high school graduates are academically qualified for Berkeley, compared with 15 percent of whites, 6 percent of Hispanics, and 4 percent of blacks, to reach the stated goal of proportional representation, Berkeley had to "consistently admit" blacks in 1986 with an academic index score of 4800 out of 8000; "white students needed at least 7000 to get in, while Asians with scores of 7000 had only a 50 percent chance of admission"; D'Souza, *Illiberal Education*, 36. See also Hughes, *Culture of Complaint*, 63. The academic index score weighs grades, SAT scores, and honors achievements; see also Bunzel, "Affirmative Action," 20; D'Souza, *Illiberal Education*, 232; Jerome Karabel, "Berkeley and Beyond," *American Prospect* (Winter 1993): 157; and Lind, *The Next American Nation*, 166. Berkeley has since modified its affirmative action program to add socioeconomically disadvantaged students, but those preferences supplement rather than replace the race-based preferences. In 1994, according to Berkeley's own statistics, the gap between Asian and black SATs among enrolled freshmen was 199 points. There was also a sizable gap in GPA; Peter Applebome, "Gains in Diversity Face Attack in California," *New York Times*, June 4, 1995, 22. In 1997 the racial preference system is slated to be discontinued.

In law school admissions, in the late 1970s only 18 percent of black law students would have been admitted on race-blind criteria; Klitgaard, *Choosing Elites*, 155. At ten top law schools, blacks as a group had GPAs 0.5 points lower than those of whites and LSATs 144 points lower (162–63). In the 1988–89 cycle, for law school applicants nationwide, if an applicant had a GPA between 3.25 and 3.49 and an LSAT score between 30 and 39, she had a 46 percent chance of being admitted if white, but a 76 percent chance of being admitted if black; see Beer, [review of *Invisible Forces* by Lynch], 303.

Preferences can also be quite large at selective high schools. San Francisco's public magnet, Lowell High School, in order to meet a court-ordered quota in 1993, had to make its cutoff for Chinese American students 66 out of a possible 69 points (based on grades and standardized tests), while blacks and Hispanics are admitted with scores of 56; see Lawrence J. Siskind, "San Francisco's Separate and Unusual Public Schools," *Wall Street Journal*, July 13, 1994, A15.

126. *Hopwood v. Texas*, 562. See also Graglia, "What's to Be Done," 40.

127. Graglia, "What's to Be Done," 42–43. The argument that test scores are culturally biased is addressed in ch. 6.

128. D'Souza, *Illiberal Education*, 267, n66. Between 1978 and 1988, black and Hispanic attrition rates increased; see Foster, "Difference and Equality," 106.

129. National Center for Educational Statistics, *The Condition of Education 1992* (Washington, D.C.: Government Printing Office, 1992), tables 170, 249.

130. Steele, *The Content of Our Character*, 118.

131. In 1979, at Cornell, one-half of the school's black students were on academic probation; Scalia, "Commentary: The Disease as Cure," 155. At MIT the dropout rate among blacks is 24 percent versus 14 percent for whites; A. Hu, "Minorities Need More Support," *The Tech*, March 17, 1987, 1. At the University of Wisconsin at Madison, the dropout rate is 28 percent for all students, but 43 percent for minorities; at Oberlin, the dropout figures are 30 percent for all students, and 50 percent for African Americans; and at Ohio State University, 47 percent of students failed to graduate within six years, but the figure for African Americans was 79 percent; D'Souza, *Illiberal Education*, 266, n64. At San Jose State University, 70 percent of black students drop out before graduation; Steele, *The Content of Our Character*, 16.

At Berkeley, which has relied heavily on racial preferences, white and Asian graduation rates have been between 65 and 75 percent; Hispanics graduate at under 50 percent, and African Americans at under 40 percent; D'Souza, *Illiberal Education*, 39; see also James S. Gibney, "The Berkeley Squeeze: The Future of Affirmative Action," *New Republic* (April 11, 1988); Paget, "Diversity at Berkeley," 111; and Hacker, *Two Nations*, 137, 140. James S. Gibney, writing in the late 1980s in the *New Republic*, noted: "If the current black graduation rate remains constant, more blacks will fail to get a diploma in the next three years than the number who earned degrees in the last decade"; "The Berkeley Squeeze," 15ff. Berkeley officials have quibbled with some of these statistics, but the numbers Chancellor Tien boasts of are hardly much better: for students entering in 1986, five years later, the graduation rates are: African American— 46 percent; American Indian—47 percent; Chicanos—56 percent; Latinos—59 percent; Filipinos—63 percent; whites—76 percent; and Asians other than Filipinos—78 percent; see Tien, "Diversity and Excellence," in Mill, *Debating Affirmative Action*, 245. After six years, black graduation rates are 51 percent; Hispanic, 53 percent; Asian, 75 percent; and white, 77 percent; see Karabel, "Berkeley and Beyond," 157.

132. See, e.g., Paget, "Diversity at Berkeley," 111.

133. Linda Chavez, *Out of the Barrio*, 120.

134. Hacker, *Two Nations*, 140.

135. Klitgaard, *Choosing Elites*, 162.

136. Glenn C. Loury, "Beyond Civil Rights," in Nieli, *The New Affirmative Action Controversy*, 443–44.

137. D'Souza, *Illiberal Education*, 49.

138. James Alan McPherson, "The Black Law Student: A Problem of Fidelities," *Atlantic* (April 1970): 99.

139. See Kerlow, *Poisoned Ivy*, 22.

140. Anne C. Roark, "UCLA Stiffens Requirements for Law School," *Los Angeles Times*, May 3, 1987, pt. 2, p. 1, cited in D'Souza, *Illiberal Education*, 49.

141. See Mark Curriden, "Bar Scholarships for Blacks Cause Stir," *ABA Journal* (February 1994): 34.

142. A Rand study of nine representative medical schools found that minority graduates had NBME grades averaging at the 19th percentile of majority scores on part 1, and at the 21st percentile on part 2; cited in Klitgaard, *Choosing Elites*, 165. In 1988, 89.9 percent of white men and 84.1 percent of white women passed part 1 of the medical exam, while 53.9 percent of black men and 44 percent of black women passed; see Associated Press, "White Men Outscore All Women on Medical Exam," *Washington Post*, September 7, 1994, A13 (citing research of Southern Illinois University School of Medicine's Beth Dawson).

143. Hacker, *Two Nations*, 173.

144. See Kennedy, "Persuasion and Distrust," 1331.

145. Klitgaard, *Choosing Elites*, 174–75. Note that the stereotyping problem works both ways. To the extent that minorities, given racial preferences, end up in the bottom of the class, groups that may be peculiarly hurt by affirmative action, such as Asian Americans, will then overperform, again, reinforcing a different set of stereotypes.

146. Jencks, *Rethinking Social Policy*, 62–63.

147. Even if many Africans Americans discount poor performance, blaming it on racism, there are other self-destructive tendencies that follow from initially poor performance. As Jencks points out:

> Most of us will do almost anything to preserve our self-respect. This means we avoid competitions in which we expect to do badly. . . . If we are poor students, we often quit school. If we stay in school, we usually do as little work as possible, because we find it easier to maintain our self-respect if we get a C- after doing very little work than if we get a C+ after weeks of hard work. Colleges that admit large numbers of academically marginal black students should not, therefore, be surprised when these students create a subculture in which working hard is devalued. (Ibid., 63)

148. Steele, *The Content of Our Character*, 112, 49 ("When a white fails, he fails alone"). Others extend the unfairness argument, saying it is fine to admit or hire mediocre minority candidates because there have always been mediocre white candidates. Thus, the columnist Sheryl McCarthy argues, "Mediocrity is a common characteristic of white male academics. . . . Let's hire women and people of color who are as ordinary as the white males who already dominate academia"; quoted in Sleeper, *Debating Affirmative Action*, 317. According to John H. Bunzel, the Department of Health, Education, and Welfare actually went so far as to propose a rule that in faculty hiring, minority and female candidates should not "be required to possess qualifications better than the least qualified member presently employed by the department"; quoted in Bunzel, "In Democracy's Shadow," 752ff. The order was withdrawn.

There are three problems with this argument. First is its obviously lackluster tone, remindful of Sen. Roman Hruska's defense of Fifth Circuit Judge G. Harrold Carswell, President Nixon's nominee to the Supreme Court: "There are a lot of mediocre judges and people and lawyers and they are entitled to a little representation, aren't they?" Second, while all would concede that there are mediocre white male academics, hiring "women and people of color who are as ordinary as the white males," as McCarthy argues, is not a system of preferences; it is a system of antidiscrimination. Alternatively, any system that employs *preferences* will, by definition, result in a *greater* proportion of the preferred being mediocre (or worse). Upholding the normal standards is no guarantee that some mediocre blacks, whites, and purples will not slide through, but when the deck is stacked in favor of certain groups, the chances go way up. Third, a central insight of civil rights activists supporting affirmative action has been the plea for context; the call for color blindness, they say, ignores our nation's history. But the argument that policies need to be grounded in social reality, not ahistorical theory, is precisely the reason to be very careful about policies that reinforce historical myths.

149. The sudden concern of some conservatives for the well-being of black recipients of preferences recalls Harvard's President Lowell and his compassion for Jews. In explaining the imposition of an anti-Jewish quota, Lowell said he had Jewish interests at heart: if the school had too many Jews, it would encourage anti-Semitism; Steinberg, *The Ethnic Myth*, 240.

150. See Sigelman, *Black Americans' Views*, 128.

151. See Sniderman and Piazza, *The Scar of Race*, 130, on the significance of this distinction.

244 • NOTES TO CHAPTER 3

152. For a sampling, see Urofsky, *A Conflict of Rights*, 247. Proponents and opponents vary in their emphasis, but all agree that the support for preferential treatment is not strong; see, e.g., Cose, *The Rage of a Privileged Class*, 143; Sowell, *Knowledge and Decisions*, 253; Graham, The Civil Rights Era, 1059; Glazer, Ethnic Dilemmas, 177; and Brownstein, "Beyond Quotas," 18ff.

153. Sniderman and Piazza, *The Scar of Race*, 133–34.

154. J. Anthony Lukas, "Why I Can't 'Bork' Clarence Thomas," *Wall Street Journal*, September 15, 1991, A15.

155. Isabel Wilkerson, "Discordant Notes in Detroit: Music and Affirmative Action," *New York Times*, March 5, 1989, 1. See also William Raspberry, "Affirmative Action That Hurts Blacks," in Nieli, *The New Affirmative Action Controversy*, 433, on the stigmatizing impact of the *Virginia Law Review*'s affirmative action program.

156. Quoted in John J. Goldman, "*Charlotte Observer* Tops Pulitzer List for PTL Coverage," *Los Angeles Times*, April 1, 1988, 1. The forty-eight writers wrote a letter to the *New York Times Book Review* after Morrison's novel *Beloved* was passed over for two other prizes; see also *Richmond v. Croson*, 493 (O'Connor), cited in *Metro Broadcasting v. FCC*, 613.

157. See D'Souza, *Illiberal Education*, 49, 242. See also Brown, *Minority Party*, 318.

158. Lynne Duke, "'Perception Gap' Is Revealed in Study of Racial Attitudes," *Washington Post*, March 17, 1992, A3. See ch. 4 for more details on the study.

159. Sniderman and Piazza, *The Scar of Race*, 103.

160. See, e.g., White House, Office of the Press Secretary, *Remarks by the President on Affirmative Action*, July 19, 1995, 6.

161. Under *UC v. Bakke*, e.g., it is legal to provide racial preferences to create a diverse student body. See also *United Steelworkers v. Weber*, 443 US 193 (1979), for the difficulty white males have in proving reverse discrimination in the private employment sector.

162. Greenawalt, *Discrimination and Reverse Discrimination*, 65–66.

163. See Rosen, "Is Affirmative Action Doomed?," 35.

164. Ellis Cose called affirmative action a wonderful "tonic for the white male ego"; "To the Victor, Few Spoils," *Newsweek*, March 29, 1993, 54.

165. Cited in D'Souza, *Illiberal Education*, 131.

166. See Lawrence Harrison, "A Dream Not Really Deferred," *Washington Post*, January 17, 1993, C5.

167. Quoted in Edsall and Edsall, *Chain Reaction*, 182.

168. Distress sale preferences were involved in only 0.2 percent of renewal applications; *Metro Broadcasting v. FCC*, 600.

169. This is especially true when nonminorities may be major beneficiaries. In *Metro Broadcasting*, Astroline Communications Company benefited from a distress sale quota as a Hispanic firm because one principal was Hispanic American. His cash contribution in a firm capitalized at $24 million was $210; *Metro Broadcasting v. FCC*, 636, n4 (Kennedy).

170. See Woodward, *The Agenda*, 15–16, listing the "Cast of Characters." Of course, one could just as easily look at these statistics and say the White House did not go far enough on diversity. My point is only that those who back diversity must make a strategic decision about whether the marginal gains are worth all the flak.

In theory, one way to address the issue of racial antagonism is to combine any racial preference program with an increase in the number of seats available. Thus, e.g., a law review that institutes an affirmative action program could simultaneously expand the size of its staff, or an employer could set up a new training program in which a certain percentage of seats are reserved for minorities. As the Citizens' Commission on Civil Rights points out, the training program litigated in the *Weber* case, setting aside 50 percent of the seats in a new training program for minorities, had, strictly speaking, "no adverse effect on white males" and actually "expand[ed] opportunities" for whites because none of the whites in the training program would have had the opportunity "if implementation of affirmative action had not brought about establishment of the program"; see Citizens'

Commission on Civil Rights, *Affirmative Action*, 153. But in practice, most whites appear to see the *Weber* glass half empty, not half full, and want to compete for all the openings, whether they are newly established or not.

171. See Kennedy, "Persuasion and Distrust," 1330. See also "Note: Racial Steering in the Marketplace," 889, citing *Cooper v. Aaron*, 358 US 1, 16 (1958) ("Law and order are not here to be preserved by depriving the Negro children of their constitutional rights"); and *Buchanan v. Warley*, 245 US 60, 81 (1917) ("Rejecting the argument that a law that forbade blacks to occupy homes on predominantly white blocks would 'promote the public peace by preventing race conflicts'").

172. Patricia Williams argues that affirmative action did not create David Duke; "Comment," 541.

173. See Sniderman and Piazza, *The Scar of Race*, 19.

174. On *The McNeil/Lehrer NewsHour*, January 16, 1995, Norton said affirmative action should not be on the ballot in California, noting that if school desegregation had been on the ballot in 1954, it would have lost, too.

175. Sniderman and Piazza, *The Scar of Race*, 23. See also James Kuklinski, testimony before the House Judiciary Subcommittee on the Constitution, October 25, 1995.

176. Wilson, "Race-Neutral Programs," 74.

177. Cose, *The Rage of a Privileged Class*, 6–7.

178. The alienation is so deep that when presented with a miscarriage of justice (Simpson) or a bigoted leader (Farrakhan), many blacks put racial unity above all else. By contrast, the white community can afford to denounce its miscarriages of justice (Rodney King) and its bigoted leaders (David Duke).

179. Sniderman and Piazza, *The Scar of Race*, 8.

180. Even if it is true that proportional representation is not a good remedy for discrimination—given cultural differences—might a "cultural preference" make sense under equal opportunity theory? The argument would go like this: equal opportunity principles attempt to correct for the disadvantages faced by people who happen to have been born poor. Why not correct for the fact that some people are born into a culture that tends, in the aggregate, to prepare people less well for competition in America? As Sowell points out, "It is not personal merit but simply good fortune to be born into a group whose values and skills make life easier to cope with"; *Ethnic America*, 274.

The very idea of "cultural preferences" seems absurd and outrageous, but since it is implicit in some white liberal arguments for affirmative action, we will address it forthrightly. First, and most basically, race is biological, not cultural. Race obviously does not cause culture, because culture is not genetically transmitted. As F. James Davis notes, "A Korean orphan child raised from infancy in Iowa has the racial traits of its biological parents but learns English and Midwest American culture"; *Who Is Black?*, 24. For other discussions of the relationship between race, ethnicity, and culture, see Webster, *The Racialization of America*, 37; van den Berghe, "The Benign Quota," 41; Carter, *Affirmative Action Baby*, 40; Glazer, *Ethnic Dilemmas*, 234; and Williams, "Comment," 535.

Just as it is objectionable to say that looking at a person's skin color can give a good idea of how they think, it is obviously racist to say skin color can tell us an individual's attitude toward hard work, education, or out-of-wedlock birth. Because, statistically speaking, certain ethnic groups have certain cultural traits does not mean that individual members of the group adhere to all aspects of the culture. And where some found (positive) "viewpoint" preferences insulting, (negative) "cultural" preferences are all the worse, since they would necessarily involve a ranking of cultures and an assumption that skin color connotes cultural disadvantage. Conversely, just because many Asian American kids benefit from a strong cultural heritage, do we really want to penalize all Asian Americans on the assumption that they benefited from a stronger culture than that of WASPs?

Second, even if one could stomach the notion of having the government rank cultures and give preferences to those decreed "backward," most of us do not want the government in the business of eradicating ethnic cultures deemed less "successful." Because a culture tends to be less successful as defined by the majority culture says nothing about its intrinsic moral worth. Without going to the extreme of saying all cultural practices (e.g., female genital mutilation) are morally equivalent, we surely do not want the government determining which ethnic cultures fail to stress work enough. In my book on Harvard Law School, I was highly critical of the culture of law firms, in part because of their emphasis on working extremely long hours and leaving little time for family. The larger economy is already penalizing me for disagreeing with that culture and so there is economic pressure on me to adapt. For the government to provide a cultural preference to my child with the stated purpose of reforming the cultural values I impart is clearly objectionable. If, in the aggregate, certain ethnic groups disagree with the ethic of what it takes to get ahead in America, the government should not actively try to change that. To do so would validate the fears of those who worry about "cultural genocide"; see, e.g., Gotanda, " 'Our Constitution Is Color-Blind,' " 60.

Third, to the extent that cultural differences among adults translate into actual economic disadvantages for the child, not of the child's own doing, then class-based affirmative action will include those factors. As we shall see in ch. 5, a child raised by a single mother or a teenage parent is therefore disadvantaged and deserves a preference. However, to the extent that cultural traits—de-emphasis on education and hard work, present-day orientation, linguistic patterns—are adopted by the child and become a part of her being, it makes no sense to provide a preference because adoption of those traits will itself limit the child's potential. While a parent's wealth provides unfair advantages to a child, adoption of a parent's strong values is different to the extent that there is an element of choice (one can reject a parent's appeal to work hard) and it is tied up in personal effort.

181. Justin Blum, "Courting Foreign Students: Colleges Go Abroad for Diversity, Dollars," *Washington Post*, October 29, 1994, A1.

182. See "Press Conference with President Clinton," Federal News Service, October 21, 1994. This was not just an off-the-cuff response, but one that was repeated several months later by Abner J. Mikva, counsel to the president; see Abner J. Mikva, "Deval Patrick Editorial Was a Disappointment," *The New Democrat* (May-June 1995): 3.

183. See Cox, *The Role of the Supreme Court*, 64–65.

184. This factor helps explain Brennan's and Marshall's hesitation to sign on to Justice Powell's unlimited diversity rationale in *UC v. Bakke*, 326, n1.

185. One poll showed Harvard Law students supporting Michael Dukakis over George Bush by a 73–23 margin; see Kahlenberg, *Broken Contract*, 166–67.

186. In theory, racial quota floors for underrepresented groups (blacks and Hispanics) could come out of seats that would otherwise have gone to WASPs—without imposing ceiling quotas on Asians and Jews. But in practice, proportional representation is often the covert goal, and sometimes the overt goal as well. In California the legislature was quite explicit on this point in 1974 when it adopted Assembly Concurrent Resolution 151: "Each segment of California public higher education shall strive to approximate by 1980 the general ethnic, sexual and economic composition of the recent high school graduates"; Karabel, *Freshman Admissions at Berkeley*, 13. Karabel said the notion was reaffirmed by Assembly Concurrent Resolution 83 in 1983.

187. There is strong evidence that the Harvard diversity model, to which Justice Powell referred so favorably in *Bakke*, had the effect (indeed, purpose) of helping WASPs and hurting Jewish Americans. In the 1920s, Harvard President A. Lawrence Lowell discussed placing a cap on Jewish students; see Dershowitz, *Chutzpah*, 67–68; and Dershowitz and Hanft, "College Diversity," 393. When faced with an uproar over the anti-Jewish quota, Harvard turned to more subtle means: a preference for students from geographically underrepresented areas. Says Dershowitz, "It was Harvard hypocrisy at its worst: out of one side of its mouth it repudiated an anti-Jewish quota, while out of the other side it established geographic preferences expressly designed to limit the number of Jews"; *Chutzpah*, 68; see also, generally, Steinberg, "How Jewish Quotas Began," 67–76. By giving a preference to those from geographically remote areas, Harvard was able to achieve its purpose of limiting the number of Jewish students and replenishing the numbers of white Protestants—hardly an act of remedial justice.

None of this is to argue that today's diversity policies are motivated by a desire to exclude Jews. But it is clear that whatever the motivation, since different ethnic groups respond differently to discrimination, proportional representation will hurt one of history's most victimized groups. As Thomas Sowell points out, the whole notion of proportional representation as "natural," and of any deviation as evidence of "sinister goings on," feeds feelings of anti-Semitism. "If fields where men usually outnumber women are called 'male-dominated,' why is it surprising that fields in which Jews are particularly prominent are said to be 'dominated' by Jews?"; "Lucrative Bigotry," *Forbes* (May 9, 1994): 117.

At Yale there is a more modern tale of diversity being used as an argument for limiting the numbers of another historically subjugated group: homosexuals. In the late 1980s, a number of stories appeared in the press about the heavy presence of gays at Yale; D'Souza, *Illiberal Education*, 12. Reacting to a story in the *Wall Street Journal* entitled, "Lipsticks and Lords: Yale's New Look," then-President Benno Schmidt wrote to fund-raisers, "If I thought there were any truth to the article, I'd be concerned too." Gay students at Yale understandably took umbrage, and Schmidt explained that he only meant that Yale needed a proportionate number of heterosexuals to promote diversity; Jerry Adler, "Have Gays Taken over Yale?," *Newsweek*, October 12, 1987, 96.

188. For 1988 data, see D'Souza, *Illiberal Education*, 262, citing the California Postsecondary Education Commission. Gardner quoted in *San Diego Union*, cited in Takagi, *The Retreat from Race*, 72.

189. Cited in Takagi, "From Discrimination to Affirmative Action," 582.

190. D'Souza, *Illiberal Education*, 27, 30. See also Karabel, "Berkeley and Beyond," 157.

191. Applebome, "Gains in Diversity," *New York Times*, June 4, 1995, 22. See also Sarah Lubman, "Campuses Mull Admissions without Affirmative Action," *Wall Street Journal*, May 16, 1995, B1.

192. Quoted in Gibney, "The Berkeley Squeeze," 15ff.

193. See Jay Mathews, "Bias Against Asians Found in Admissions to UCLA; U.S. Says Whites Were Favored for Math," *Washington Post*, October 2, 1990, A5.

194. See Siskind, "San Francisco's Separate and Unequal Public Schools," A15. Chinese Americans needed a score of 66—out of 69 points—to be admitted, compared with a white cutoff of 59 and a black and Spanish-surnamed cutoff of 56. The tests were subsequently tinkered with, and in 1995, Siskind reported, Chinese Americans needed 62 out of 69 to be admitted, whites and other Asians 58, and blacks and Hispanics 53; "A Year Later in San Francisco, the Schools Are Still Segregated," *Wall Street Journal*, July 12, 1995, A15.

195. At Brown in the early 1980s, Asian applicants were on average better qualified but had a lower acceptance rate (14 percent) than non-Asians (20 percent); Brown University, report of the Corporation Committee on Minority Affairs, February 1984, cited in D'Souza, *Illiberal Education*, 263, n25. Brown saw a 430 percent increase in Asian American applicants between 1978 and 1986, but the percentage of students remained constant; Grace Tsuang, "Equal Access of Asian-Americans," *Yale Law Journal* (January 1989): 659–78. Brown's initial response was to declare that Asians were "overrepresented" at the university, but it eventually conceded that Asians had been "treated unfairly"; see Takagi, "From Discrimination to Affirmative Action," 582, 578.

At Stanford, the Committee on Undergraduate Admissions and Financial Aid (CUAFA) found that between 1982 and 1985 Asian Americans were on average better prepared academically than whites, yet one-third less likely to be offered admission; CUAFA annual report, 1986. At Yale the Asian American admission rate fell from 39 percent to 17 percent in the 1980s; see Bell, *And We Are Not Saved*, 268, n2.

Overall, for the classes entering in 1991 and 1992 at the most elite schools, the Consortium on Financing Higher Education data show that admitted Asian students scored 30 SAT points above whites, putting them at the 60th percentile of white SATs; Murray and Herrnstein, *The Bell Curve*, 451. The U.S. Commission on Civil Rights found that at Princeton, Yale, Stanford, Berkeley, and UCLA, Asians were comparably qualified but admitted at lower rates; see Lind, *The Next American Nation*, 167–68.

196. While some try to explain disparities in Asian admission rates as a reflection of the fact that test scores are not all that matters—the underlying stereotype being that Asians are compulsive grinds who are not "well-rounded" Americans—John Bunzel found that nonacademic criteria do not let universities off the hook. One study of some 58,000 high school students found that 30 percent of Asians participated in varsity athletics, compared with 34 percent of whites, and in band and orchestra at a rate of 13 percent, compared with 14 percent for whites; Asians also had a higher participation rate in "intellectual activities" such as school newspapers; John H. Bunzel and Jeffrey K. D. Au, "The Asian Difference," in Nieli, *The New Affirmative Action Controversy*, 464. The slur that "they're all pre-meds" is also not true. James Rogers, the admissions director at Brown, told Bunzel and Au, "The vast majority of Asian Americans applying here—70 to 75 percent are premedical students. . . . The question is not one of race, it's academic balance." But, in fact, the figure for Asian applicants to Brown in 1982 was 39 percent; ibid., 466.

197. Brown, *Minority Party*, 286–87. Outside college admissions, Asian Americans may be hurt by proportional representation as well. In 1974 Democratic Party officials gave a preference to white delegates over Japanese Americans from Hawaii in order to meet the delegation's ethnic goal; see Fuchs, *The American Kaleidoscope*, 453.

198. Peter Schrag, "Regents' Exam," *New Republic* (August 14, 1995): 12. Likewise, in an apparent bid to emphasize the common interests of WASPS, white Catholics, and blacks, Mary Frances Berry, chairman of the U.S. Commission on Civil Rights, said in congressional testimony that basing job hiring on test scores would mean "Asians and Jews would hold the best jobs everywhere"; see Nancy E. Roman, "Affirmative Action Spurs Exchanges Tinged with Rancor," *Washington Times*, April 4, 1995, A10.

199. The theoretical concern was outlined by members of the Supreme Court in *Wygant v. Jackson Board of Education*, 276. See also *Metro Broadcasting v. FCC*, 280.

200. See Bill McAllister, "Postal Official: Too Many Blacks Hired, Lack of Hispanics in Big Cities Cited," *Washington Post*, August 3, 1994, A1, A5. In Los Angeles, blacks accounted for 63 percent of postal workers, compared with 9.6 percent of the nonmilitary labor force; in Chicago, the figures were 79.7 percent of the postal workers, but 18.2 percent of the general labor force. Hispanics were underrepresented in each of those cities.

201. Jones, "A New Taped Confrontation," A16. See also Ramirez, "Multicultural Empowerment," 968.

202. See Jonathan Tilove, "It's Latino vs. Black in LA," *Cleveland Plain Dealer*, December 19, 1993, 25A.

203. See Jonathan Tilove, "Immigration Is Undoing Blacks' Job Gains," *Cleveland Plain Dealer*, December 19, 1993, 25A.

204. Linda Chavez, "Just Say Latino," *New Republic* (March 22, 1993): 18.

205. The commission's report came in response to the Mt. Pleasant riot, which occurred when a black police officer shot a Salvadoran man.

206. Tilove, "Immigration Undoing Blacks' Job Gains," 25A.

207. Ibid.

208. In Washington, D.C., e.g., Chavez says "most" Latinos are recent immigrants; "Just Say Latino," 18.

209. Mark Krikorian, "Affirmative Action and Immigration," in Mills, *Debating Affirmative Action*, 300, 301. See also Fuchs, *The American Kaleidoscope*, 454.

210. Marvin Dunn, *Anatomy of a Riot*, cited in Krikorian, "Affirmative Action and Immigration," 302.

211. The call for diversity can hurt blacks and help whites when it is used to limit the number of African Americans in a housing complex. Given the well-known phenomenon of racial tipping ("too much" black influx threatens white flight), those seeking integration have approved of "benign quotas" to keep that from happening. In 1984, e.g., a federal court approved a 40 percent quota in a federally subsidized, middle-class

housing project in Brooklyn known as Starrett City. As a result of the quota, white families were able to secure apartments in two months, while blacks had to wait twenty months; Sleeper, *The Closest of Strangers*, 178. Whites with $15,000 in annual income were given preference over blacks making $17,000; Jefferson Morley, "Double Reverse Discrimination," *New Republic* (July 9, 1984): 14ff. Black applicants sued and settled out of court for a small increase in the quota and more housing assistance to blacks at other projects. In May 1984, a federal district court approved the settlement, though it was overturned on appeal; ibid. "Benign" housing quotas have been implemented in other cases as well; see, e.g., Hacker, *Two Nations*, 36 (Atrium Village in Chicago); and Bell, *And We Are Not Saved*, 152 (citing *Otero v. New York City Housing Authority*, 484 F2d 1122, 1140 [2d Cir. 1973]).

Likewise, when historically black universities attempt to make their student bodies more diverse, blacks are required to make room for whites. At Florida Agricultural and Mechanical University's, e.g., the university president's "commitment to diversity" (including a call to double the representation of white students from just under 8 percent to 15 percent) has drawn black student anger; Dorothy J. Gaiter, "White Teacher's Use of a Racial Pejorative Roils a Black Campus," *Wall Street Journal*, September 26, 1994, A1. And the 1994–95 bulletin of the North Carolina Central University School of Law, a historically black institution, indicates that it "actively seeks to promote racial integration by recruiting and enrolling a larger number of white students."

Finally, there is the well-worn argument about African Americans and the National Basketball Association. For years, conservatives have said that accepting the theory of proportional representation would mean requiring preferences for whites in the NBA; see, e.g., Koch, *Citizen Koch*, 165; see also Juan Williams, "A Question of Fairness," *Atlantic* (February 1987), citing Clarence Thomas's testimony before a congressional committee asking whether the all-black Georgetown basketball team represented Georgetown's discrimination against white basketball players. Blacks represented approximately 80 percent of NBA players in 1985; National Research Council, *A Common Destiny*, 96.

Liberals have rightly dismissed the argument, since there is no evidence of discrimination by blacks against whites in basketball—and indeed, the overrepresentation of blacks probably results in part from discrimination *against* blacks in other fields, discrimination that channels young black men away from academics and onto the basketball court. If one applied a "reverse" disparate impact analysis to the case, one would surely find that the disproportionate hiring of blacks is justified by a business necessity—the desire to hire the best players who will help the team win the most games. To my mind, under the old set of rules, liberals win.

But the forward-looking diversity argument throws in a new curve. One could plausibly make the argument that there are strong utilitarian reasons for supporting an increase in the number of white players. One could say that professional basketball is watched by millions of fans, and the sight of significant numbers of black and white players cooperating in a highly visible way would help promote racial harmony in a way that a team not thoroughly integrated does not. Moreover, a number of black leaders have stressed that the predominance of African Americans in professional basketball is not an entirely healthy thing for blacks; see Frank Deford, "Barkley's Last Shot," *Vanity Fair* (February 1995): 125. Sound farfetched? Preferences for whites were proposed by a Cleveland school official, who suggested requiring that two of five first-team players in Cleveland's high schools be white, a move bitterly opposed by black players; *DeRonde v. Regents of University of California*, 625 P2d 220, 237, n7 (Mosk dissenting).

Chapter 4

1. Fishkin, *Justice, Equal Opportunity*, 1.
2. Fishkin, *Justice, Equal Opportunity*, 4.
3. Some on the left argue that equal opportunity allows too much inequality, and some on the right that it imposes too great a price on liberty. Both critiques have some legitimacy, but they do not fundamentally challenge the validity of equal opportunity as a desirable social goal.

OBJECTIONS FROM THE LEFT

The left raises a serious and essentially moral objection: even when discrimination is ended and equal economic starting places provided, luck still plays an enormous role in who gets ahead.

For one thing, a system that allows natural talents to flourish, even from environmentally fair starting places, allows the accident of birth—the genetic lottery—to determine distributions of wealth and power, a basis, says John Rawls, that is "arbitrary from a moral perspective"; A Theory of Justice, 74. Even if all race, gender, and class barriers are removed—something no society has ever done—the system, he says, "still appears defective" (73). He explains: "Equality of opportunity means an equal chance to leave the less fortunate behind in the personal quest for influence and position" (106–7). Or as Thomas Nagel puts it, we are "left with the great injustice of the smart and the dumb, who are so differently rewarded for comparable effort"; "Equal Treatment and Compensatory Discrimination," in Cohen, Nagel, and Scanlon, Equality and Preferential Treatment, 17. Genetic endowment is arbitrary; those who are naturally talented are, after all, merely "gifted."

Second, luck continues to intervene throughout life. One farmer works hard for years only to have her property destroyed in a tornado; her indolent neighbor's farm is left untouched. Luck even plays a major role in the celebrated Horatio Alger stories; see Weiss, The American Myth of Success, 53. Third, there is the luck of what the market happens to value. Talent and merit are meaningless in the abstract; each society and culture defines what is to be valued; Sandel, Liberalism, 137. As the conservative economist Milton Friedman points out, "Frank Sinatra's voice was highly valued in twentieth-century United States. Would it have been highly valued in twentieth-century India, if he had happened to be born and to live there?"; Friedman and Friedman, Free to Choose, 21–22.

This critique is valid but should not change our view of how people should be sorted on the front end (e.g., who gets into college, who gets what jobs). It does, however, profoundly affect our view of how material rewards are to be distributed on the back end (e.g., how much more should a doctor make than a sales clerk). As far as social utility goes, the arbitrariness of natural talent makes no difference in continuing to use equal opportunity as a sorting device. The social utilitarian cares less about effort than product, particularly in the distribution of jobs (as opposed to income). He does not want a quadriplegic trying to play professional football, no matter how valiant the effort. If half the reason for equal opportunity is the desire to "stimulate the productive performance of the contestants by awarding the biggest prizes to the most productive," it would make no sense—at least in the sorting of jobs and education—to handicap for natural talent; Brittain, The Inheritance of Economic Status, 30–31. As Arthur Okun notes, "In real track meets, no official has ever disqualified a runner for having 'fast genes'"; Equality and Efficiency, 43–44.

Even assuming that intelligence and athletic ability are completely beyond one's control, an individual who is part of a group trying to set up the rules for society (Rawls's original contractors behind the veil of ignorance) would want jobs and schooling opportunities distributed based on ability. If one turns out to be naturally intelligent, one has the chance for self-fulfillment, which Rawls calls "one of the main forms of human good"; A Theory of Justice, 84. If one turns out to be dull, one would not want to be frustrated at a university (or in a job) that is beyond one's ability; see Goldman, Justice and Reverse Discrimination, 30.

If one does not sort offices by talent and performance, what is the alternative? As Alan Goldman points out, jobs could be assigned randomly. But that alternative decreases social utility (to the extent someone retarded is randomly assigned to do nuclear physics), negates the value of effort (since one cannot be promoted for hard work), and is no more fair than the natural lottery; Goldman, Justice and Reverse Discrimination, 44–45. And, of course, forcing people to rotate jobs is totalitarian; see Bell, The Coming of Post Industrial Society, 425. See also Friedman and Friedman, Free to Choose, 135, on who decides who should be a doctor and who should be a street sweeper. A lottery system takes away the freedom to choose one's career—again, something Rawls clearly sees as valuable; *A Theory of Justice*, 272.

On the back end, some differential rewards are necessary to motivate and sort people, and some differential reward can also said to be deserved, for talent (whether intellectual, physical, or artistic) is something one can improve by hard work and study—and is therefore at least moderately within one's control. Even if Edison's estimation was high on one end—"Genius is 1 percent inspiration and 99 percent perspiration"—Rawls overemphasizes natural talent, as Robert Nozick notes, giving "no mention *at all* of how persons have chosen to develop their own natural assets"; *Anarchy, State, and Utopia*, 214.

Rawls argues that effort and motivation are *themselves* influenced by social position and natural factors. An individual's effort and character depend "in large part upon fortunate family and social circumstances for which he can claim no credit"; *A Theory of Justice*, 104. Likewise, an individual's initial endowment of natural assets influences effort, since "the better endowed are more likely, other things being equal, to strive conscientiously" (311–12). But surely there is some residual element of choice that is not predetermined, that leads some to study harder for one more hour while others flip on *Beavis and Butthead*. Ultimately, if humans are but vessels for social and natural factors, then we lack all moral autonomy and cannot be blamed or praised for any sort of behavior. If one goes along with Rawls's point that effort is not our own doing, then, as Nozick points out, there is not much left—no autonomy, no moral responsibility, just sums of our genes and environment, where "everything noteworthy about the person" is attributable to "external factors"; *Anarchy, State, and Utopia*, 214. Because there is no neat way to separate "effort" and "natural talent," we need to use an individual's productivity as a certain measure of her effort.

Having said all that, Rawls's insight on the arbitrariness of natural talent is important in helping to determine the material shares that individuals are entitled to on the back end. Balancing against the social need to provide incentives to work hard and to steer the naturally talented into the most demanding positions, the moral argument for some degree of redistribution is a powerful one. No less a conservative than George Will has written that progressive taxation makes sense because "those who make the most money get the most from society not merely in terms of money but also in terms of 'faculties' and thus owe a proportionately larger debt"; George F. Will, "Taxation Isn't Tyranny," *Washington Post*, April 13, 1989, A31. Even if we achieve the genuine equal opportunity of the Great Society, some would need the economic security of the New Deal; Jencks, *Rethinking Social Policy*, 3. Even if the distribution is according to perfect equal opportunity, we still retain some notion of distribution based on need; see Walzer, *Spheres of Justice*, 25–26. And we wish to support the disabled irrespective of social product. As Arthur Okun has written, "The presumption that gladiatorial contests were fair made it no less barbaric to feed the losers to the lions"; *Equality and Efficiency*, 84; see also DeLone, *Small Futures*, 24.

In sum, then, even after the left critique, it makes sense to provide genuine equal opportunity on the front end (education and employment, the issues in affirmative action). On the back end, to make up for chance and the arbitrariness of natural talent, there may be some redistribution, subject to the limitation that we wish to maintain strong incentives for hard work and accomplishment. Surely there is room to maneuver here. The ratio today between the salary of a typical American CEO and his average wage worker is 150 to 1; see Steven Rattner, "GOP Ignores Income Inequality," *Wall Street Journal*, May 23, 1995, A22; see also Phillips, *Boiling Point*, 63. Japan has a 30-to-1 ratio, has, overall, about half the inequality of the United States, and manages to run a strong and efficient economy; see Thurow, "A Surge in Inequality," 30, 35.

OBJECTIONS FROM THE RIGHT

If the left is concerned that substantive equal opportunity worries too little about equality, the right believes it is concerned too little about liberty. Taken literally, substantive equal opportunity, with its requirement that everyone live up to her God-given (i.e., natural) potential, drives a stake in the heart of the family unit. Even if liberals are given everything they want—Head Start, equal school funding, school integration, redistribution of wealth—one is inexorably faced with the inequalities inherent in family. Some parents provide loving, nurturing, educational environments; others provide sterile homes that stunt even the greatest potential. Plato understood this and argued that children should be ripped from their families and raised communally. In his Ideal Commonwealth, Plato suggested a law: "That the wives of our guardians are to be in common, and their children are to be in common, and no parent is to know his own child, nor any child his parent"; cited in *Meyer v. Nebraska*, 262 US 390, 401–2 (1923). Since we reject the Platonic nightmare, we do not want to take substantive equal opportunity literally. (On the left, Rawls, too, notes that equal opportunity runs up against the family unit; *A Theory of Justice*, 74, 301, 511.)

But most of us would go further than the family itself and say that a parent has the right not only to raise a child but also to purchase a superior education. Though the public school is the embodiment of democratic America and equal opportunity, we say that parents have the right, if they choose, to send their children to private schools; *see Meyer v. Nebraska*, 390. Dinesh D'Souza once asked students at a prep school, "How many people in this room believe in equal opportunity?" Every hand went up. D'Souza said, "Well, look, none of your parents do. That's why you're here"; Dinesh D'Souza, interview with the author, Washington, D.C., December 19, 1994. In this sense, James Fishkin is right when he says that equal opportunity—which attempts to reconcile liberty and equality in a way that equality of result can not—does not completely elide the conflict. Our revised definition of substantive equal opportunity, then, would ensure that protections are built in for the family, and for the family's right to pursue private education.

BIPARTISAN OBJECTIONS

A third objection to equal opportunity, bipartisan in nature, says, watch out, if you seek equal opportunity, you may get what you ask for. The specter, raised by Michael Young and Mickey Kaus on the left and by Richard Herrnstein and Charles Murray on the right, is that as society approaches genuine equal opportunity and life's race becomes a fair one, the losers will rightfully feel bad, the winners will feel good, and society will become even more stratified as it divides into genetically superior and genetically inferior factions.

The phrase "meritocracy," which in this country is taken on faith as a positive ideal, in fact originated with Young's 1958 satirical essay *The Rise of the Meritocracy*. Young noted that in a nonmeritocratic society, the upper-class man knew that "his social inferiors were sometimes his biological superiors," that his butler might in fact be more intelligent or witty than he; *The Rise of the Meritocracy*, 104–5. Likewise, the average worker could console himself by saying, "Had I had a proper chance I would have shown the world" (106). In a genuinely meritocratic system, by contrast, differences are seen as fully deserved. "The distribution of rewards has become far more unequal and yet with less strife than before" (152). The rich know full well they are more deserving and lose any trace of self-doubt.

Richard Herrnstein and Mickey Kaus take Michael Young one step further and say that, as we make life increasingly fair, and as we equalize environments (as liberals want), genetic differences become more important: as the very bright marry the very bright, and the very dull the very dull, the genetic gap will widen, as will the gap between rich and poor; *see* Kaus, *The End of Equality*, 43, and Richard Herrnstein, "I.Q.," 63. What is "most troubling," Herrnstein wrote, is that social equality will be lost; ibid., 64.

In practice, the concern is a tiny one. As we shall see later in the chapter, we are in no danger of closing in on Michael Young's meritocracy, Herrnstein's predictions notwithstanding. Genetically similar people do not start life's race in anything resembling equal starting positions, and as even Kaus argues, in addition to genetics, success is also due to "(a) luck, (b) acts of will, and (c) social, cultural, and environmental influences"; *The End of Equality*, 45.

The theoretical concern is somewhat larger: because the whole point of pursuing equal opportunity is to minimize all but the genetic differences, we *hope* meritocracy (including its downside) becomes a reality. Kaus calls this the Fairness Trap: "The more the economy's implicit judgements are seen as being fair and based on true 'merit' (and 'equal opportunity'), the more the losers will tend to feel they deserve to lose, the easier it will be to equate economic success with individual worth, and the greater the threat to social equality"; *The End of Equality*, 47–48.

But even here, the downside seems small. With respect to Young's concern—that in a fair race, losers will feel bad—the answer is not to continue to rig the race but rather to teach people precisely what everyone from John Rawls to George Will acknowledges: natural endowment is an unearned gift that says not a thing about an individual's moral worth. A society that teaches the disabled they should feel bad about a condition over which they have no control is a society badly in need of moral rethinking. Indeed, would it really be preferable to maximize unfairness so that losers feel completely let off the hook? Besides, winners already feel superior, and curiously enough, "old money" winners, who by definition did not earn their own way, feel the most superior of all.

As to Herrnstein's genetic nightmare, where the gulf between the genetically gifted and the genetically inferior widens and widens, one must ask, where does this concern lead us? Does it mean we should give up trying to equalize educational opportunity because achieving that goal—raising the bright poor—only hastens the inevitable biological caste system? For Kaus, the lesson seems to be that we should emphasize the importance of civic equality; that is a good idea, but not one that requires that we let up on the drive for equal opportunity.

Taken together, after considering the criticisms from the left and right, the tentative working definition of equality of opportunity comes out substantially intact, with two modifications: (1) in response to the legitimate arguments of the right, we must respect the family; and (2) in response to the legitimate arguments of the left, we must provide for some redistribution not in front-end opportunities but in back-end rewards.

4. Gary Wills, *Nixon Agonistes: The Crisis of the Self-Made Man* (Boston: Houghton Mifflin, 1969), 236.

5. *UC v. Bakke*, 324 (Brennan). For a more recent example, see White House, Office of the Press Secretary, *Remarks by the President on Affirmative Action*, July 19, 1995.

6. Abram, "Commentaries," 1312.

7. Fishkin distinguishes between procedural fairness and background unfairness; *Justice, Equal Opportunity*, 22.

8. Tawney, *Equality*, 109.

9. The question of whether antidiscrimination laws in fact work is addressed in detail in ch. 6.

10. Moynihan called the Civil Rights Act's removal of race barriers, without removing the barriers of class, "the high-water mark of Social Darwinism in America"; "Toward a National Urban Policy," 4.

11. Davis and Moore, "Some Principles of Stratification," 242, 243.

12. The obvious critique is that less talented people will work more and produce less, so they are more morally deserving but rewarded less. For a response, see note 3 above.

13. Tawney, *Equality*, 104–5. Tawney himself does not endorse this view.

14. Thomas Jefferson, letter to John Adams, October 28, 1813, in Peterson, *Portable Thomas Jefferson*, 534, 537. See also Hartz, *The Liberal Tradition in America*, 71; and Kahl and Gilbert, *The American Class Structure* (1987), 169.

15. Jefferson letter to Adams, October 28, 1813, 537.

16. Quoted in Kahl and Gilbert, *The American Class Structure* (1987), 168.

17. Quoted in Christopher F. Armstrong, "On the Making of Good Men," in Kingston and Lewis, *High Status Track*, 6.

18. Tawney, *Equality*, 115.

19. Quoted in Kozol, *Savage Inequalities*, 206.

20. There might be other ways to measure effort, but most would be difficult to administer. And since the functional approach is concerned with product, not effort, we tend to measure effort by the proxy of product.

21. See Theodore Roosevelt, message to Congress, December 3, 1906, in Chester, *Inheritance, Wealth, and Society*, 60.

22. Paul Glastris, "Life among the 'Meritocrats,'" *U.S. News and World Report*, September 6, 1993, 30.

23. Tocqueville, *Democracy in America*, 507.

24. William Angoff, quoted in Fallows, "The Tests and the 'Brightest,'" 43.

25. Abigail Thernstrom, "A Class Backwards Idea: Why Affirmative Action for the Needy Won't Work," *Washington Post*, June 11, 1995, C1, C2.

26. The genetic argument, revived by publication of *The Bell Curve* in 1994, says that relative social mobility is small, not because there is inequality of opportunity, but because poor people are, in the aggregate, less innately intelligent and pass on their genetic deficiencies to their children. Michael Young's meritocratic nightmare is upon us, the argument says; see Murray and Herrnstein, *The Bell Curve*, 51. In the 1940s, Murray and Herrnstein argue, to say someone was poor did not say much about them; today, however, given the advances toward meritocracy, the poor "are likely to be disproportionately those who suffer not only bad luck but also a lack of energy, thrift, farsightedness, determination—and brains" (129). The "powerful trend toward meritocracy," which Herrnstein saw coming back in 1971, has made Young look very "prescient"; Herrnstein, "I.Q.," 44–45, 63. Murray and Herrnstein say the chief concern is not achieving meritocracy but coming to terms with the "merging of the cognitive elite with the affluent"; *The Bell Curve*, 509.

To buy the argument that social mobility levels are simply a reflection of genetic differences—a claim even Murray and Herrnstein do not fully make—one must believe that (a) we live in a perfect meritocracy, so that rich parents are rich because they are smarter; (b) rich children do well because they have their parents' smart genes, as opposed to having superior chances to develop their talents; and (c) children succeed in replicating their parents' positions, again, based on the perfect workings of the meritocracy in the next generation. Most of the evidence points in the opposite direction.

The first and third assumptions—that a meritocracy exists in both generations—is at least as weak as the argument that intelligence is based on nature, not nurture. Studies by Christopher Jencks and by Bowles, Gintis, and Nelson suggest that IQ plays a fairly small role in who gets ahead; see Jencks, *Inequality*, 7–8 ("there is almost as much economic inequality among those who score high on standardized tests as in the general population"); see also Jencks, *Who Gets Ahead*, 121, but see 73–75; Bowles and Nelson, "The 'Inheritance of IQ,'" 44 (arguing that while a child's IQ does matter, a child's socioeconomic background matters more in predicting ultimate adulthood status). In all, Bowles and Nelson found that "the genetic inheritance of IQ plays a minor role in the process of intergenerational educational and economic status transmission" (40). Likewise, in 1984 Hunter and Hunter found that cognitive test scores fail to explain 72 percent of the variance in job ratings; see Ira T. Kaplan, "Hugging the Middle of the Bell Curve," *Wall Street Journal*, November 7, 1994, A15.

Indeed, while Murray and Herrnstein worry about the rise of the meritocracy, there is evidence that in some areas we are becoming *less* meritocratic—that young Americans are becoming, in Kevin Phillips's words, "the first generation to receive—or not to receive—much of their economic opportunity from family inheritance, not personal achievement"; *Boiling Point*, 190–92 (noting that among individuals ages 35–39, an astounding 86 percent of net worth in 1986 came from their parents, up from 56 percent in 1973). In the area of college admissions, as Steven Waldman notes, between 1982 and 1989 the percentage of students at private colleges and universities hailing from well-to-do families increased from 50 percent to 63 percent; "How Washington Tries to Strangle Even the Best Ideas," *Washington Monthly* (January-February 1995): 28. This could be a stunningly rapid, genetically driven convergence of the wealthy and the cognitive elite, but it looks more like old-fashioned unequal opportunity at work.

The second assumption—rich kids do well for genetic reasons—is also highly problematic. There has been a broad debate for centuries on the question of the heritability of intelligence; the debate is unresolved to this day. Today most studies say intelligence among individuals is 50 percent hereditary, Murray and Herrnstein say 60 percent, while other studies indicate 70 percent; see Gina Kolata, "Study Raises the Estimate of Inherited Intelligence," *New York Times*, October 12, 1990, A22 (reporting that the Minnesota twins study found 70 percent genetic differences, while "previous studies had suggested that about 50 percent of the differences in scores were inherited").

Two factors work against the creation of genetic castes. First, setting aside the role of environment, the genetic transmission of intelligence is itself complicated. As Adrian Woolridge, author of *Measuring the Mind*, points out, "The random element in Mendelian inheritance combined with regression to the mean insured that children would differ in significant ways from their parents"; "Bell Curve Liberals," *New Republic* (February 27, 1995): 22. Herrnstein himself conceded the existence of "regression toward the mean," a genetic phenomenon in which there is a "tendency for children to be closer to the general population average (in this case, IQ 100) than their parents. And in fact, *very bright* parents have children who tend to be merely *bright*, while *very dull* parents tend to have them merely *dull*"; "I.Q.," 58. And we all know marriages (say, Marilyn and Dan Quayle) in which partners may be of different IQs.

Second, even if we agree with Murray and Herrnstein's estimate that 60 percent of intelligence is inherited, that leaves an enormous role to environment. "Forty percent variability based on environment would make intelligence an exceptionally pliant trait," notes the former Harvard evolutionary biology professor Evan Balaban; quoted in Gregg Easterbrook, "The Case against the Bell Curve," *Washington Monthly* (December 1994): 25. "If IQ swings by 40 percent owing to circumstances and life experiences," adds Gregg Easterbrook, "then human society has more control over intelligence than virtually anything else in its genetic inheritance" (25). Arthur Jensen, a leading proponent of the genetic school, concedes that there are "great and relatively untapped reservoirs of mental ability in the disadvantaged"; quoted in Sowell, *Race and Culture*, 169.

In sum, then, both links in the argument that genetics accounts for the reproduction of economic inequality are weak. Even Murray and Herrnstein concede that (a) we are not a pure meritocracy, so that the socioeconomic status a child is born into has an impact on his life chances separate from IQ (*The Bell Curve*, 135), and (b) IQ is not a pure measure of raw genetic ability, because IQ itself is affected by socioeconomic background. Thus, they argue, "improvements in the economic circumstances of blacks, in the quality of the schools they attend, in better public health, and perhaps also diminishing racism," may explain the closing gap between black and white IQ observed over the past few decades (270–71). Indeed, for these reasons, Murray and Herrnstein themselves argue for a form of class preference for disadvantaged students (475). As we shall see, the environmental differences based on wealth are quite dramatic; far from proving the genetic superiority of the rich, the scores merely confirm what we would expect.

27. See Rossides, *Social Stratification*, 20.

28. Jencks, *Who Gets Ahead?*, 82–83, 82, 81.

29. Brittain, *The Inheritance of Economic Status*, 16.

30. See Blau and Duncan, *The American Occupational Structure*, 28. Blau and Duncan were generally fairly sanguine about occupational mobility in the United States, but they noted that short-distance mobility was more common than long-distance mobility, and that much of the occupational gain was due to an expansion in the higher professions (36–37). In 1972, Duncan, teaming up this time with David L. Featherman and Beverly Duncan, wrote: "The absolute number of able young men and women of lower socioeconomic origins who are 'wasted' is striking"; Duncan, Featherman, and Duncan, *Socioeconomic Background and Achievement*, 257.

31. Bowles and Gintis, "IQ in the United States Class Structure," cited in DeLone, *Small Futures*, 209.

32. Zimmerman study cited in Frances Ann Burns, "Income Study Says, Like Father, Like Son," *Los Angeles Times*, March 17, 1991, A34. See also Zimmerman, "Regression Toward Mediocrity in Economic Status," 409.

33. Solon, "Intergenerational Income Mobility," 404, 403.

34. Historians have made several findings. Edward Pessen of the City University of

New York argues that Tocqueville and others who claimed to see great social mobility in America "mistook appearances for reality"; *Social Mobility*, 57. Pessen's study found that "only about 2 percent of the Jacksonian era's urban economic elite appear to have actually been born poor, with no more than about 6 percent of middling social and economic status" (112). In New York, Pessen found that 95 percent of the city's wealthiest one hundred were born into families of wealth or high status, 3 percent were from middling families, and 2 percent were born poor. Pessen found the same pattern in Boston and Philadelphia (113).

In his study of lawyers in early nineteenth-century America, Gary B. Nash found that most were born to wealth. Between 1800 and 1805, 72 percent were from upper-class backgrounds, 16 percent were middle-class, and only 12 percent were lower-class; "The Social Origins of Antebellum Lawyers," in Pessen, *Social Mobility*, 108.

Harvard's Stephen Thernstrom found in his study of Bostonians from 1880 to 1970 that "all in all, it was very helpful indeed to a man's career to come from a family headed by a professional or a prosperous businessman." Offspring of upper white-collar workers "were overrepresented in upper white-collar jobs by about 400 percent as compared with lower white-collar sons, 650 percent as compared with skilled sons, and 1200 percent as compared with the sons of unskilled or semiskilled fathers"; *The Other Bostonians*, 89–90.

Even the hallowed notion that some of our presidents were born in log cabins turns out to be largely mythical. In Pessen's study of American presidents, he found that only one, Andrew Johnson, came from the bottom 50 percent of the economic strata; *Log Cabin Myth*, 69–70; see also Michael Kelly, "The President's Past," *New York Times Magazine* (July 31, 1994): 20ff, on President Clinton's "comfortable" background.

35. See Lipset and Bendix, *Social Mobility*, 12–13.

36. The correlation in the United States was 0.4, while the correlation in Britain was 0.45, "only slightly more"; Zimmerman quoted in Burns, "Income Study," A34. Kahl and Gilbert cite seven different studies finding similar rates of social mobility in the United States and other advanced industrial societies, all of "which contradicts the myth that the United States has a society much more open than others"; *The American Class Structure* (1987), 161.

37. National Research Council, *A Common Destiny*, 4.

38. Poor children who grow up to be successful businesspeople, said one economist, "have always been more conspicuous in American history books than in American history"; Pessen, *Log Cabin Myth*, 172–73. We hear more about success partly because our culture is attuned to it. As the writer Katherine Newman points out, "No one ever talks about the Pilgrims who gave up and headed back to England"; *Falling from Grace*, 8. Just as African Americans are rightly annoyed when whites cite Colin Powell as evidence that racism has been eradicated, so the poor and working class are rightly annoyed when Ross Perot is cited as proof that anyone can rise from humble origins to be a billionaire.

39. The end of World War II, says Jeff Greenfield, "triggered the swiftest, broadest rise in living standards any society has ever known": median family income doubled between 1947 and 1973; quoted in Phillips, *Boiling Point*, 223; see also Barry Bluestone, "The Inequality Express," *American Prospect* (Winter 1994): 82. Occupationally, progress was also largely a result of absolute mobility. Stephan Thernstrom found that "32 percent of Boston's males held white-collar jobs of some kind in 1880, 51 percent in 1970; the proportion of professionals, a mere 3 percent in 1880 increased sevenfold during the period, while unskilled-labor jobs shrank from 15 percent of the total to 5 percent"; *The Other Bostonians*, 49–51. Nationally, between 1940 and 1970 the number of professional and technical jobs for men increased 192 percent, while the jobs for nonfarm laborers declined 32 percent; Census Bureau statistics cited in Kahl and Gilbert, *The American Class Structure* (1987), 163. The average level of education also rose astronomically as the proportion of people earning college degrees increased fifteen times between 1900 and 1990; Census Bureau statistics cited in Murray and Herrnstein, *The Bell Curve*, 29–33.

All this absolute mobility is good and important, but it tells us little about equal opportunity and, indeed, obscures the question of whether people have equal life chances. Because the standard of living has until recently risen swiftly, a child born into the 25th percentile of income could do twice as well as his parents (having, say, two cars instead of one) but would not have moved up in relative terms and still be in the 25th percentile. For our purposes—knowing the degree to which people are handicapped or advantaged by their social origins—absolute mobility merely confuses the issue. So how much mobility is relative as opposed to absolute? When controlling for absolute mobility, the researcher Joseph Kahl found that only 20 percent of American males exceed the status of their fathers by individual effort; See Kahl, *The American Class Structure* (1957). And most of these do not climb very far; see Chester, *Inheritance, Wealth, and Society*, 8.

40. Tocqueville, *Democracy in America*, 9.

41. Quoted in Spencer Rich, "Number of Poor Americans Increases to 39.3 Million," *Washington Post*, October 7, 1994, A1.

42. See Census Bureau statistics cited in ibid., A18. The upper 20 percent took home 48.2 percent of income. The bottom fifth took in 3.6 percent.

43. Labor Department statistics cited in Rick Wartzman, "A Clinton Potion to Restore Middle Class Love, Brewed by Labor Secretary, Stresses Job Training," *Wall Street Journal*, January 11, 1995, A16.

44. Rattner, "GOP Ignores Income Inequality," A22.

45. Phillips, *The Politics of Rich and Poor*, 179–80.

46. Phillips, *Boiling Point*, 63; and Rattner, "GOP Ignores Income Inequality," A22.

47. Revised JEC figures cited in Phillips, *The Politics of Rich and Poor*, 11.

48. Rose, *Social Stratification*, 21–22. See also Mishel and Simon, *The State of Working America*, iii–iv.

49. Cited in Lapham, *Money and Class*, 22.

50. See, e.g., Rep. Richard K. Armey, "Income Mobility and the U.S. Economy: Open Society or Caste System?," Joint Economic Committee of Congress, January 1992.

51. Kotlowitz, *There Are No Children Here*, 18, x.

52. Kozol, *Savage Inequalities*, 182, 20–21.

53. See Kahl and Gilbert, *The American Class Structure* (1987), summarizing Kohn, 118–21.

54. Rubin, *Worlds of Pain*, 18, 23, 93–94.

55. Ibid., 38.

56. Olson, *The Rise and Decline of Nations*, 86–87.

57. Brittain, *The Inheritance of Economic Status*, 6.

58. Thurow, *The Zero Sum Society*, 155–56, 172.

59. Quoted in Johnson, *Divided We Fall*, 36–37.

60. Rattner, "GOP Ignores Income Inequality," A22.

61. See David S. Broder, "Are We Really Overtaxed?," *Washington Post*, April 23, 1995, C7, citing statistics of the Organization for Economic Cooperation and Development.

62. See Alwin and Thornton, "Family Origins and the Schooling Process," 784.

63. Kaus, *The End of Equality*, 52. Kaus cites Ira Katznelson and Margaret Weir, *Schooling for All: Class, Race, and the Decline of the Democratic Ideal* (New York: Basic Books, 1985), 214.

64. In the 1973 case of *San Antonio v. Rodriguez*, the Supreme Court upheld disparate public school spending: a wealthy district in Texas spent more than one and a half times what a poorer district did (counting state, local, and federal contributions)—$356 versus $594 per pupil; see *San Antonio v. Rodriguez*, 12–13. Fifteen years later, when lawyers for the poor brought suit under the Texas state constitution, the gap between the richest and poorest per pupil expenditure had grown to $2,112 versus $19,333. The 100 poorest districts averaged $2,978 per student, and the 100 richest averaged $7,233; *Edgewood Independent School District v. Kirby*, 777 SW2d 391, 392–93 (Tex. 1989) (*Edgewood I*); see also Taylor, "The Continuing Struggle," 1705. On Long Island, New York, where a similar suit was tried in 1991, the spending disparity ranged from $17,435 per pupil to $7,305 per pupil; see Judges, "Bayonets for the Wounded," 699. In New

Jersey, the site of ongoing lawsuits, Camden spent $4,184 per pupil, and Princeton spent $8,344; see John B. Judis, " A Taxing Governor," *New Republic* (October 15, 1990): 24; see also Valerie Strauss, "Disparity Between City, Suburban Schools: Almost $440 a Student," *Washington Post*, September 28, 1994, A20.

State courts have begun to strike down unequal funding as violative of state constitutions in Texas, California, New Jersey, Kentucky, Montana, and elsewhere; see, e.g., *Serrano v. Priest*, 18 Cal. 3d 728, 557 P2d 929, 135 *Cal. Rptr.* 345 (1976); see also Taylor, "The Continuing Struggle," 1704, 1707. But the progress is uneven; as of 1994, fourteen states had struck down funding mechanisms, but fourteen had seen mechanisms upheld; see Curriden, "Unequal Education at Issue," *ABA Journal*, May 1994, 36. And even where legal victories are claimed, the progress is often very slow. In New Jersey, legal wrangling over equal funding has gone on for a quarter-century. Strong voter resistance to Governor Jim Florio's attempt to equalize funding has given governors in other states ample reason to delay and circumvent court orders as long as possible.

65. Taylor, "The Continuing Struggle," 1706. See also David Broder, "Getting Serious about Schools," *Washington Post*, February 20, 1994, C7.

66. See Broder, "Getting Serious about Schools."

67. See Kenneth J. Cooper, "$13 Billion Education Bill Clears House; Senate Is Likely to Vote on It Next Week," *Washington Post*, October 1, 1994, A4; Associated Press, "Senate Passes $12 Billion in Federal Education Aid," *Washington Post*, August 3, 1994, A3; and Broder, "Getting Serious about Schools." Forty-three percent of funds now go to the bottom 25 percent of school districts. Clinton wanted them to get 50 percent. In the *San Antonio v. Rodriguez* case, the federal grant did reduce the spending disparity somewhat, but a substantial gap remained: from $310 per pupil before federal aid to $238 afterwards; *San Antonio v. Rodriguez*, 12–13.

68. Conservatives are partially right to cite Coleman for the proposition that there is a weak correlation between school spending and test scores; see Mosteller and Moynihan, *Educational Opportunity*, 15–16; see also George F. Will, "Meaningless Money Factor," *Washington Post*, September 12, 1993, C7. But there is empirical support in the academic literature for the commonsense notion that spending money does matter; see Ogbu, *Minority Education and Caste*, 52–53 (citing review of seventeen studies); see also *San Antonio v. Rodriguez*, 83 (Marshall dissenting) (citing two studies conflicting with the Coleman report.) The Texas Supreme Court also found that money mattered. "The amount of money spent on a student's education has a real and meaningful impact on the educational opportunity offered that student," the court found; *Edgewood I*, 393. It is obvious, the court said, that money can purchase better equipment and more books, provide lower teacher-student ratios and dropout prevention services, and attract and retain better teachers.

If it were true that money made no difference in the quality of education, why would wealthy school districts fight so much to keep their edge? Why in the *San Antonio* case did we see amicus briefs filed by the nation's wealthiest school districts, from Beverly Hills to Bloomfield Hills and Grosse Pointe?; see *San Antonio v. Rodriguez*, 85 (Marshall dissenting). During the litigation over equal expenditure in New Jersey, the superintendent in the wealthy South Brunswick area was asked what he would do if he had to live on the budget of the low-income Trenton area. Kozol reports: "The superintendent tells the court that such a cut would be an 'absolute disaster.' He says that he 'would quit' before he would accept it. If such a cut were made, he says, class size would increase about 17 percent; nursing, custodial and other staff would have to be reduced; the district would stop purchasing computers and new software; it would be unable to paint the high school, would cut back sports, drop Latin and German, and reduce supplies to every school"; *Savage Inequalities*, 168.

69. See Edmund Gordon, "Toward Defining Equality of Educational Opportunity," in Mosteller and Moynihan, *Educational Opportunity*, 427; see also Kozol, *Savage Inequalities*, 2–5, 205. We do not insist that firefighters spend equal amounts of time on a house that is burning and a neighboring house that is not; nor do we argue that a doctor must provide equal attention to two patients, one with a cold, the other in critical

condition in the emergency room; see Gross, *Discrimination in Reverse*, 19. As William Taylor points out, the object of Chapter 1 was to have federal money supplement, not equalize; the extra money was needed for disadvantaged students; "The Continuing Struggle," 1706.

70. Christopher S. Jencks, "The Coleman Report and the Conventional Wisdom," in Mosteller and Moynihan, *Educational Opportunity*, 87. And the relationship was linear: poor students in working-class schools "fell neatly in between"; ibid.

71. Coleman, quoted in Mosteller and Moynihan, *Educational Opportunity*, 20.

72. See "Note: Teaching Inequality" (*Harvard Law Review*), 1318.

73. Friedman and Friedman, *Free to Choose*, 151.

74. Summarized in Kahl and Gilbert, *The American Class Structure* (1987), 170.

75. Kingston and Lewis, *High Status Track*, xi.

76. Caroline Hodges Persell and Peter W. Cookson, Jr., "Chartering and Bartering: Elite Education and Social Reproduction," in ibid., 30, 42.

77. Fallows, "The Tests and the 'Brightest,' " 46.

78. See Fallows, "The Tests and the 'Brightest,' " 43.

79. Mary Jordan, "SAT Changes Name, but It Won't Score 1600 with Critics," *Washington Post*, March 27, 1993, A7.

80. According to the *New York Times*, ETS officials "now concede that their previous public posture that tests are not coachable was less than accurate"; Edward B. Fiske, "Nader's Challenge to Testing," *New York Times*, January 15, 1980, C4. For a summary of ETS's internal study by Pike and Evans, see Owen, *None of the Above*, 96–97, finding a 33-point increase from a coaching course above and beyond increases attributable to practice and growth. Nancy Cole reviews five studies and finds an average combined gain of 47 points on the SAT; "The Implications of Coaching for Ability Testing," in NAS, *Ability Testing II*, 402–10. See also Slack and Porter's review of studies, which found a combined mean gain of 62 points; "The Scholastic Aptitude Test," 161.

81. A Federal Trade Commission study found that those who were coached "were heavily concentrated in the upper income brackets"; Nairn and Associates, *The Reign of ETS*, 98. And the founder of the Princeton Review SAT preparation course, John Katzman, readily acknowledges, "Most of our kids are wealthy." His students "have an advantage to begin with. And we're moving them up another level"; quoted in Owen, *None of the Above*, 138–39. While the National Academy of Sciences says it has no evidence that commercial coaching is more effective than "free coaching" in schools, it notes that even the latter retains a class bias, since "school-based coaching is more generally available in schools with many college-bound students than it is in those with fewer such students"; see Nancy Cole, "The Implications of Coaching for Ability Testing," 402–10.

82. College Board, *College Bound Seniors, 1973–74*, Table 21, 27, cited in Nairn and Associates, *The Reign of ETS*, 201. See also Fallows, "The Tests and the 'Brightest,' " 47; and Fallows, *More Like Us*, 163–64.

83. See College Board, *College Bound Seniors: 1994 Profile of SAT and Achievement Test Takers*, 7.

84. Fallows, "The Tests and the 'Brightest,' " 47.

85. Robert Linn, "Ability Testing: Individual Differences, Prediction, and Differential Prediction," in NAS, *Ability Testing II*, 363.

86. The College Board likes to argue that its own test is not that important: the SAT is only one factor used in admissions, they argue, and on average public four-year colleges accept 80 percent of applicants and private four-year colleges accept 70 percent. At elite colleges, however, acceptance rates can go below 20 percent; Rodney Skager, "On the Use and Importance of Tests of Ability in Admission to Postsecondary School," in NAS, *Ability Testing II*, 292–93, 294, 307. Only two selective institutions nationwide— Bates and Bowdoin—do not consider the SAT at all; see Michael Kirst and Henry Rowen, "Scrap the SATs for Achievement Tests," *Washington Post*, September 16, 1994, A27. And an NAS study found that the SAT ranks second only to grades as an admis-

sions criteria. In law school, the LSAT is often more important than grades; Skager, "On the Use and Importance of Tests of Ability," 307. Moreover, the College Board's general figures on acceptance rates ignore the powerful indirect impact of the SATs. Many students with low scores will assume their scores are a valid indicator of their long-run potential (if not their very self-worth) and, with the help of a high school guidance counselor, will "face the facts of life" and adjust their aspirations. As the NAS study points out, applicant self-selection can play a major role in acceptance rates; the academy notes that "one distinguished private institution accepts 80 percent of its applicants because mainly academically outstanding students choose to apply" (293). Relying on the SAT, high school counselors across the country guide poor and working-class students away from selective colleges, predicting, accurately, that they would simply be rejected if they applied.

The result is that the wealthy—who score better and do not face uncertainties about financial aid—are dramatically more likely to attend high-status schools. In 1984, 13.7 percent of freshman nationwide came from families with income exceeding $50,000, while among the twenty-eight most selective colleges and universities, the figure was over 50 percent. While 4 percent of freshman nationwide came from families with incomes exceeding $100,000, more than 20 percent of freshman at the elite colleges came from that background; Kingston and Lewis, *High Status Track*, xii. In 1986, while less than 20 percent of American families made $50,000 or more, 31 percent of families of freshman students did, as did more than 60 percent of families with freshman at highly selective private colleges. Only one in twelve students at highly selective private universities came from families with incomes below $20,000 (at a time when the national median income was $28,000) (111). At Berkeley, for example, in the fall of 1987 only 22 percent of the freshman class came from families with income at or below the national median. The median income for freshman families was $53,500, compared with $30,000 for the national population; Karabel, *Freshman Admissions at Berkeley*, 53.

Moreover, attendance at selective universities matters greatly in determining who gets ahead. While it is true that many bright students may attend nonselective public universities and go on to do quite well, the evidence confirms that going to a high-prestige college brings a greater return. Kingston and Lewis found that the lay wisdom is right: where one goes does matter; *High Status Track*, 148. Forty-three percent of the Harvard class of 1940, for example, are now worth more than $1 million; Larew "Why Are Droves . . . ," 12. The median family income of the Harvard class of 1968 is $135,000 and the median net worth is $500,000; James K. Glassman, "Crimson and Closure," *New Republic* (July 11, 1994): 14. Almost 30 percent of the Harvard-Radcliffe class of 1970 had become millionaires by 1995; see Jonathan D. Canter, " 'Stock of the Puritans': 1970 Issue," *Harvard* (September-October 1995): 26. A 1992 study by Duke University's Philip Cook and Cornell's Robert Frank says the commonsense notion that students from elite universities get the best-paying jobs is more true than ever; Reuters, "Graduates of Elite Schools Increasingly Get Top Jobs," *Chicago Tribune*, August 19, 1992, C1. They cite a *Fortune* survey of CEOs that found that one in ten had attended just seven elite schools (ibid., C1). In Yale Professor George W. Pierson's exhaustive study, *The Education of American Leaders: Comparative Contributions of U.S. Colleges and Universities*, graduates of elite universities were heavily overrepresented among "elder statesmen" in the professions, in scholarship, in politics, and in business. Looking at *Who's Who*, Pierson found that one of twenty-five graduates of Harvard, Yale, and Princeton were recognized, compared with one in 145 for state universities as a whole; cited in Klitgaard, *Choosing Elites*, 123–24.

87. Nozick, *Anarchy, State, and Utopia*, 236.

88. See David K. Shipler, "My Equal Opportunity, Your Free Lunch," *New York Times*, March 5, 1995, sect. 4, pp. 1, 16. See also Hugh Price, "Affirmative Action: Quality, Not Quotas," *Wall Street Journal*, August 18, 1995, A10.

89. As Derek Bok points out, the case for racial preferences in faculty hiring is weaker than in student admissions because "we can make better judgements about who is better than whom when he hire people for jobs. They are older, they have track records. . . . We

really are guessing with students"; Derek Bok, interview with *Harvard Political Review* (Spring 1985): 9.

90. As an individual grows older, she may, with effort, attempt to improve her economic position so that over time class becomes more mutable than race. But even Charles Murray concedes, "There is no such thing as an undeserving five-year-old"; *Losing Ground*, 223. In constitutional terms, the Court has recognized that illegitimacy is a semisuspect class precisely because children are not themselves to blame for their status; see *Trimble v. Gordon*, 430 US 762, 770 (1977)—illegitimate children "can affect neither their parent's conduct nor their own status"—and *Weber v. Aetna* 164, 175: "Imposing disabilities on the . . . child is contrary to the basic concept of our system that legal burdens should bear some direct relationship to individual responsibility and wrongdoing."

91. See Hacker, *Two Nations*, 94, 100. See also Steinberg, *Turning Back*, 213.

92. In 1987, for example, while 20 percent of all American children lived in poverty, the figure for black children was 45 percent, and for Hispanic children it was 39 percent; see National Research Council, *A Common Destiny*, 8.

93. Rose, *Social Stratification*, 23.

94. *Statistical Abstract of the United States*, no. 705 (1992), 450, cited in Munro, "The Continuing Evolution," 603.

95. See Fleming, *The Lengthening Shadow of Slavery*, 98.

96. Cyrena N. Pondrom, "The Carrot and the Stick: Twin Approaches to Achieving Minority Employment Equality," in Van Horne, *Ethnicity, Law, and the Social Good*, 76. Margaret Weir notes that in 1966 one-half of individuals in poverty programs were racial minorities even though only 30 percent of the poor were black; *Jobs and Politics*, 84–86.

97. See Liz Spayd, "Montgomery School Chief Attacks Racial Balance Study," *Washington Post*, July 12, 1994, A1, A10.

98. Koch, *Citizen Koch*, 164. See also Koch, "Equal Opportunity—Without Minority Set-Asides," *New York Times*, February 20, 1989, A19.

99. See Carter, *Affirmative Action Baby*, 87; and Edsall and Edsall, *Chain Reaction*, 247–48.

100. Where, in 1976, grants accounted for 80 percent of all financial aid, by 1995 two-thirds of all financial aid came in the form of loans; see Steven Waldman, "How Washington Tries to Strangle Even the Best Ideas," *Washington Monthly* (January–February 1995): 28.

101. National Research Council, *A Common Destiny*, 343, 338–39.

102. Starr, "Civil Reconstruction," 12. Class preferences will also disproportionately help blacks in college admissions, an issue we take up in ch. 6.

103. Fishkin, *Justice, Equal Opportunity*, 91.

104. Roger Wilkins, "The Black Poor Are Different," *New York Times*, August 22, 1989, A23.

105. See Goldman, *Justice and Reverse Discrimination*, 90.

106. Wilson, *The Truly Disadvantaged*, 117–18.

107. Robert Penn Warren said that any notion of "debt" was "fraught with mischief"; [review of *Why We Can't Wait*], *New York Review of Books*, cited in Oates, *Let the Trumpet Sound*, 296.

108. I would go further than King and supplement class remedies with temporary, carefully circumscribed racial preferences in narrow circumstances that satisfy the strictures laid down by the Supreme Court in *Croson* and *Adarand* (see ch. 5). By applying the strict rules of *Croson* to affirmative action across the board—state, federal, and private programs—proper racial compensation would be given where, and only where, it is clearly justified. To address broader past societal discrimination, class-based preferences would provide the remedy.

109. After thirty years of race-based affirmative action, the dearth of minority and female role models is not as severe as it once was. Ogbu notes that providing equal opportunity—antidiscrimination laws that forbid discrimination based on race (but do not take the next step to preferences)—will by itself do a great deal to end the vicious cycle by which lack of opportunity leads to underperformance. Under Ogbu's theory, by

removing barriers and "giving educationally qualified minorities new opportunities," a society will improve "minority efforts in school and thereby [increase] the number qualified"; *Minority Education and Caste*, 348–49. This process will be slow, however, to the extent that past discrimination against a caste minority has a hangover effect. Class-based affirmative action will accelerate the process above and beyond the use of antidiscriminatory mechanisms.

110. In 1995 the Court also let stand a Fourth Circuit decision striking down a blacks-only scholarship program at the University of Maryland; see *Podberesky v. Kirwan*, 38 F3d 147 (4th Cir. 1994) cert. denied, 115 SCt 2001 (1995).

111. See Richard D. Kahlenberg, *California Law Review* (forthcoming, July 1996).

112. See Walter Dellinger, memorandum to "General Counsels," June 28, 1995, 6, reprinted in *Affirmative Action Review*, appendix B. Even more provocatively, Assistant Attorney General for Civil Rights Deval Patrick said the administration would not be "intimidated" by *Adarand*; see Nat Hentoff, ". . . And Double Talk," *Washington Post*, August 9, 1995, A19.

113. See Jeffrey Rosen, "The Colorblind Court," *New Republic* (July 31, 1995): 19, 23. The Court came close in *United States v. Paradise*, 480 US 149 (1987), when four justices held that a racial preference scheme involving Alabama state troopers survived strict scrutiny.

114. Paul Gewirtz, "Affirmative Action: Don't Forget the Courts," *Wall Street Journal*, August 2, 1995, A11.

115. See Ralston, "Courts vs. Congress," 206.

116. Stuart Taylor, "A Case for Class-Based Affirmative Action," *Connecticut Law Tribune* (September 30, 1991): 23.

117. In a series of cases, the Court has held that classifications that negatively impact the poor are unconstitutional; see, e.g., *Harper v. Virginia State Board of Elections*, 383 US 663 (1966) (voting); *Douglas v. California*, 372 US 353 (criminal justice); *Zablocki v. Redhail*, 434 US 374 (1978) (marriage); and *Shapiro v. Thompson*, 394 US 618 (1969) (travel). However, these cases are now read to stand, not for the proposition that class is a suspect category, but that the pieces of legislation in question required heightened judicial scrutiny because they involved the exercise of fundamental rights or interests.

118. Ely, *Democracy and Distrust*, 148.

119. See, e.g., *James v. Valtierra*, 402 US 137 (1971); and *Harris v. McRae*, 448 US 297, 316–17 (1980).

120. Although the Court in *Rodriguez* argued that the legislative classification involved children in property-poor areas and those in property-rich areas (rather than poor and rich children per se), William Taylor points out that the issue was indeed poor versus rich because only the poor cannot vote with their feet and move to property-rich school districts; "*Brown*, Equal Protection," 1730.

121. When feminist groups failed to have gender added to the list of fully suspect classifications and received only semisuspect status, it was seen as a setback for progressives; see, e.g., *Craig v. Boren*, 429 US 190 (1976) (gender discrimination receives an "intermediate" level of scrutiny). Today, however, courts have upheld gender-based affirmative action, where similar race-based preferences are struck down, precisely because gender is not fully suspect; see Dellinger, memorandum to "General Counsels," 8 (citing five circuit court opinions, four of which applied the more lenient intermediate scrutiny to gender preferences). See also Judith Hessler, "Beneath the Glass Ceiling," in Mills, *Debating Affirmative Action*, 137–38.

122. Koch, *Citizen Koch*, 164.

123. See Sniderman and Piazza, *The Scar of Race*, 130. A 1988 Harris poll, e.g., found that 55 percent of whites favored "affirmative action programs for blacks and other minorities, which do not have rigid quotas"; ibid.

124. See, e.g., polls cited in Brownstein, "Racial Politics," 122; William R. Beer, "Unaffirmative Answers," *New Republic* (August 8 and 15, 1988): 6; Sniderman and Piazza, *The Scar of Race*, 133–34; Graham, *The Civil Rights Era*, 565; Munro, "The Continuing Evolution," 566; Urofsky, *A Conflict of Rights*, 247, n61; Congressional

Research Service, *Race Issues in the United States*, May 9, 1992, 57; and Rick Wartzman, "Clinton Is Still Struggling to Get Message Across to 'Angry White Males' Who Have Tuned Out," *Wall Street Journal*, January 24, 1995, A24.

125. A 1995 *Newsweek* poll found that 75 percent oppose preferences for qualified blacks over equally qualified whites in college admissions and employment; see Howard Fineman, "Race and Rage," *Newsweek*, April 3, 1995, 25; see also Brownstein, "Beyond Quotas."

126. See Steven A. Holmes, "Affirmative Action Plans Are Part of Business Life," *New York Times*, November 22, 1991, A20: 60 percent of whites oppose racial preferences even when an employer is guilty of past discrimination.

127. For example, a March 1995 *ABC News* poll showed that women oppose gender preferences (69 percent) at almost the same rate as men (76 percent); see Morin and Warden, "Americans Vent Anger at Affirmative Action," A1.

128. Cited in Graham, *The Civil Rights Era*, 565. See also Sidney Hook, foreword, in Gross, *Discrimination in Reverse*, viii.

129. See Lamb and Bearak, "Revolution Incomplete," 1. More recently, see Stanley B. Greenberg, "The President—and I—Support Affirmative Action," *Washington Post*, March 14, 1995, A16.

130. Quoted in Brown, *Minority Party*, 145–46.

131. Sniderman and Piazza, *The Scar of Race*, 144–45. Forty-two percent will change their minds after a "rhetorical nudge" on social welfare issues, compared with 20 percent on questions involving affirmative action.

132. In 1989, thirty-six states and almost two hundred local governments had minority set-aside programs for nonwhites and women; Linda Greenhouse, "Court Bars a Plan Set up to Provide Jobs to Minorities," *New York Times*, January 24, 1989, 1; see also Hill and Jones, *Race in America*, 352–53; and Days, "*Fullilove*," 453, 453–54, n10. In university admissions, race is "the most influential personal credential in determining admissions preference"; College Entrance Examination Board and ETS study, cited in Lynch, *Invisible Victims*, 33. On the federal level, a 1995 Congressional Research Service review of statutes yielded a list of 160 laws and government policies favoring women and minorities; "Affirmative Action Assault Is Being Prepared by GOP," *Wall Street Journal*, February 22, 1995, A4; see also Days, "*Fullilove*," 454, 465; Kellough, *Goal and Timetables*, 41; and *Metro Broadcasting v. FCC*, 560, 575, 578.

133. The conventional wisdom is that affirmative action has survived for procedural reasons: programs were instituted, in large part, by bureaucratic, university, and judicial entities largely unaccountable to the people; see, e.g., Brownstein, "Beyond Quotas." But this is not the entire answer, for it is always possible for Congress, responding to political currents, to attempt to modify that which the executive, and in some cases the judiciary, has decreed. Bill Clinton learned this lesson shortly after his election when he saw his policy on gays in the military attacked by Congress. (William Taylor made this point in my seminar at George Washington University, October 31, 1994.)

Taking stock of affirmative action in 1988, thirteen years after publication of his book *Affirmative Discrimination*, Nathan Glazer noted the growth and resiliency of preferential programs through the presidencies of Nixon, Ford, Carter, and Reagan; "The Affirmative Action Stalemate," 100. This is the central political paradox of affirmative action: while it is politically disastrous for those who advocate it, it is also politically correct. Until recently, almost every effort by Congress or the executive branch to retrench on affirmative action has been beaten back. In 1969 an attempt to kill President Nixon's Philadelphia Plan for quotas in the construction industry was adopted by the Senate 52–37 but then defeated in the House 208–156; see Graham, *The Civil Rights Era*, 339–40. In 1972 Sen. Sam Ervin's effort to repeal the Nixon administration's imposition of goals and timetables on federal contractors failed on a vote of 44–22; see *Congressional Record*, January 28, 1972, 1662–76; see also Days, "Turning Back the Clock," 317, n45; Citizens' Commission on Civil Rights, *Affirmative Action*, 51–52; and *UC v. Bakke*, 354, n28 (Brennan). In 1977 an effort by Rep. Ashbrook to bar HEW from requiring racial preferences passed the House as an amendment to the FY1978 Labor/HEW bill but was stripped out in the conference with the Senate (347).

Other attempts to outlaw affirmative action in the 1980s—such as Sen. Orrin Hatch's proposed constitutional amendment to forbid racial preferences and Rep. Robert Walker's bill outlawing racial quotas in education and employment—never saw the light of day; Robert M. O'Neil, "Ethnicity and the Law: Of Policy and the Constitution," in Van Horne, *Ethnicity, Law, and the Social Good*, 26. Whereas in 1980 Hatch proclaimed confidently, "I will outlaw affirmative action," fifteen years later racial preferences had multiplied in number (26).

During the Reagan administration, one might have expected a broad retrenchment of affirmative action, but in three major attempts the administration was unsuccessful. Following a favorable Supreme Court decision in *Firefighters v. Stotts* (1984), the Reagan Justice Department sought to release fifty-one cities, states, and counties from court orders requiring goals and timetables. But the localities—many of which had originally opposed imposition of quotas—actually opposed the effort to lift them; Glazer, "The Affirmative Action Stalemate," 107. In August 1985, when President Reagan's Justice Department proposed to modify Johnson's executive order requiring goals and timetables for federal contractors, the effort was opposed within the administration by the Labor Department and certain members of Congress and was never implemented (106); see also Howard Kurtz, "Civil Rights Lobby Plays Defense but Wins," *Washington Post*, June 8, 1986, A1; Fuchs, *The American Kaleidoscope*, 386; and Citizens' Commission on Civil Rights, *Affirmative Action*, 91–92. And when the Reagan administration sought to study and potentially revise the FCC's minority preference program for broadcast ownership, Congress passed a rider on the FY1988 appropriations bill for the FCC, forbidding the expenditure of funds for review of the preference program; Continuing Appropriations Act for FY1988, Publ L. 100–202, 101 Stat. 1329–31, cited in *Metro Broadcasting v. FCC*, 560.

134. In December 1990, President Bush's assistant secretary of education for civil rights, Michael Williams, created a flap when he told the organizers of the Fiesta Bowl that their plan to set up minority scholarships at the University of Louisville and Auburn would violate Title VI of the Civil Rights Act; see Days, "Civil Rights at the Crossroads," 261–62. A firestorm ensued, with Chief of Staff John Sununu, no liberal he, ordering a reversal (and then suspension) of the "politically damaging decision"; Andrew Rosenthal, "White House Retreats on Ruling That Curbs Minortiy Scholarships," *New York Times*, December 18, 1990, A1. The debate within the administration was not about whether to let the decision stand but about whether to go for outright reversal or a more subtle retreat. The policy was suspended for a year. In December 1991, the Justice Department proposed guidelines with enormous loopholes, including the famous "*Bakke* straddle": race may be a factor in awarding scholarships to create diversity but do not openly set aside a fixed number. Education Secretary Lamar Alexander declared: "A college president with a warm heart and a little common sense and a minimum amount of good legal advice can make a special effort to grant scholarships to minority students and can use financial aid to create diversity on his campus"; see Kenneth J. Cooper, "Limits on Race Scholarships Proposed," *Washington Post*, December 5, 1991, A3.

The second political flap came on November 20, 1991. As Bush was preparing to sign the Civil Rights Act, the White House legal counsel, C. Boyden Gray, drafted an order to abolish racial preferences among both federal agencies and federal contractors. In the written statement, the president called for the elimination, "as soon as is legally feasible," of "any regulation, rule, enforcement practice, or other aspect of these [equal opportunity in employment] programs that mandates, encourages, or otherwise involves the use of quotas, preferences, set-asides, or other similar devices, on the basis of race, color, religion, sex, or national origin"; quoted in American Law Institute (ALI), *Civil Rights Act of 1991*, 37; see also Ann Devroy and Sharon LaFraniere, "U.S. Moves to End Hiring Preferences: Affirmative Action Policies Targeted," *Washington Post*, November 21, 1991, A1. After an uproar, Bush did not sign the statement and instead declared: "I support affirmative action. Nothing in the bill overturns the Government's affirmative action programs"; cited in ALI, *Civil Rights Act of 1991*, 37. Similar attempts to eliminate preferences in legislative amendments sponsored by Sen. Jesse Helms were overwhelmingly defeated in the Senate during the Bush era, by votes of 71–28 and 67–33; see *Congressional Record*, June 16, 1991, S8732, and September 11, 1991, S12,779.

135. Support for racial preferences may not be broad, but it is intense among civil rights groups. By contrast, there is no organized lobby for opposition to quotas. For Democrats, crossing the line with civil rights groups risks the ire of the Democratic Party's most loyal constituency. And while civil rights groups are unlikely to actually advise African Americans to vote Republican, they may signal their displeasure, resulting in a fatally low black voter turnout.

In addition to providing an intense and organized voice in favor of preferences, civil rights groups can tar opponents as racist. When California Gov. Pete Wilson endorsed the effort to repeal affirmative action in California, Jesse Jackson said, "Pete Wilson is liken unto George Wallace of Alabama. He wants to stand in front of the schoolhouse door"; see B. Drummond Ayres, Jr., "Conservatives Forge New Strategy to Challenge Affirmative Action," *New York Times*, February 16, 1995, A22. And being a Democrat does not make one immune to the charge; if anything, questioning affirmative action is seen as more traitorous. When liberal Democratic Sen. John Kerry of Massachusetts gave a speech in March 1992 at Yale saying he had some concerns with affirmative action, he "touched off an explosive chain reaction," as the *Boston Globe* noted. Twenty-five articles and op-eds later, after Kerry had been accused of "race baiting" by the Boston NAACP, employing "racially divisive code words" by the *Globe* editorial board, and leaving blacks feeling "stabbed in the back" according to another observer, it was hard to remember that in the speech Kerry acknowledged legitimate white criticism but in the end said he favored affirmative action. For his sentiments, one columnist noted, Kerry was "scorched," "flogged," and "whiplashed"; David Nyhan, "Affirmative Action: Should We Stay the Course or Rethink It?," *Boston Globe*, April 9, 1992, 21.

But affirmative action is unlikely to have survived with the support of civil rights groups alone. What has made the defense particularly strong is their alliance with the educational and business establishment. When the lines were drawn in the *Bakke* case, John Jeffries notes, "establishment opinion lined up behind the university"—including the American Bar Association, the Association of American Law Schools, and the Association of American Medical Colleges; *Justice Powell*, 462. UC Davis had Archibald Cox arguing in court, McGeorge Bundy arguing in the *Atlantic*, and Dean Rusk arguing at policy conferences; see McGeorge Bundy, "The Issue Before the Court"; and Dean Rusk, "Preferential Treatment: Some Reflections," in Blackstone and Heslep, *Social Justice and Preferential Treatment*, 154–60.

Universities like race-based affirmative action because they wish to have the ability to create a racially diverse class and, more fundamentally, the right to do as they wish without governmental interference. Race-based affirmative action, as currently practiced, is fairly easy to administer, and not being means-tested, it allows universities to advertise themselves as diverse while filling the minority slots with upper-middle-class people of color who easily fit in and often can pay full tuition. Only a few universities employ class preferences; they require more time to administer and often universities must pick up the financial slack for disadvantaged students; Robert Reinstein, telephone interview with the author, December 14, 1994.

Many businesses also support affirmative action, and, in fact, the National Association of Manufacturers and the Business Roundtable opposed President Reagan's 1985 proposal to amend the requirement that federal contractors employ affirmative action goals and timetables; Shulman and Darity, *The Question of Discrimination*, 32–33; see also "Note: Rethinking Weber" (*Harvard Law Review*), 658, 662. In 1987, when the Supreme Court reaffirmed the legality of voluntary efforts to employ gender-based affirmative action under Title VII in the case of *Johnson v. Santa Clara*, the U.S. Chamber of Commerce applauded the decision as "very positive for business"; Alice Kessler-Harris, "Feminism and Affirmative Action," in Mills, *Debating Affirmative Action*, 68–69. For an explanation of why business supports affirmative action, see n.170 below.

136. Joe Klein, "The End of Affirmative Action," *Newsweek*, February 13, 1995, 37.

137. Rosen, "Is Affirmative Action Doomed?"

138. For the easy adoption of the 1977 10 percent minority construction set-aside, see *Congressional Record*, February 24, 1977, 5327–32, and *Congressional Record*, March 10, 1977, 7155–56. In 1995 the House overwhelmingly passed legislation repealing the FCC's minority tax certificate program, and the Senate approved the bill by voice vote; see Helen Dewar, "Senate Votes to Repeal Tax Break Encouraging Minority-Owned Broadcast Stations," *Washington Post*, March 25, 1995, A13. Clinton subsequently signed the legislation, despite his opposition to the repeal, because it also included a popular health insurance deduction for the self-employed; see Ann Devroy, "Clinton Signs Self-Employed Insurance Deduction," *Washington Post*, April 12, 1995, A9.

139. Cooper, "Limits on Race Scholarship Proposed"; Lamar Alexander, "Where I Come from Has Everything to Do with Where I Stand" (excerpts of February 28, 1995, presidential announcement speech, Maryville, Tennessee), *Washington Post*, March 1, 1995, A7; for Alexander's endorsement of the California initiative, see George F. Will, "A Spoils System with a Constituency," *Washington Post*, March 2, 1995, A21.

140. See Kevin Merida, "Dole Takes 180-Degree Turn on Affirmative Action," *Washington Post*, March 17, 1995, A4. During the mid-1980s, Dole actually fought Reagan administration officials who sought to repeal the executive order on affirmative action; see also Colbert I. King, "Dole's Lurch to the Right," *Washington Post*, July 22, 1995, A21.

141. See John F. Harris and Dan Balz, "Affirmative Action Divides Democrats," *Washington Post*, March 10, 1995, A15.

142. See William Claiborne, "Affirmative Action Curbed in California," *Washington Post*, June 2, 1995, A1, A20 (citing initiative campaigns in Washington, Florida, Illinois, Oregon, Colorado, and Nevada).

143. See Carter, *Affirmative Action Baby*, 71. See also Wilson, *The Declining Significance of Race*, 19; and Wilson, *The Truly Disadvantaged*, 109–10.

144. Hacker, *Two Nations*, 98.

145. Population Reference Bureau figures, cited in Holmes, "Mulling the Idea of Affirmative Action for Poor Whites."

146. In his first interview with the *New York Times*, Califano squarely backed racial quotas to address past discrimination; see David Rosenbaum and Nancy Hicks, "Califano Says Quotas Are Necessary to Reduce Bias in Jobs and Schools," *New York Times*, March 18, 1977, A1; and Califano, *Governing America*, 232. He was widely denounced and forty-four educators from leading universities called on Carter to repudiate Califano's comments; Califano, *Governing America*, 233.

Califano then hedged, saying he was for "goals," not "quotas," but what practical difference that made was unclear; by his own account, he continued to be a vigorous champion of the UC Davis goal/quota admission system challenged by Allan Bakke. (While Attorney General Griffin Bell wanted to take a neutral stance, Califano lobbied heavily in favor of the UC Davis position.) When the Carter administration's initial draft in the *Bakke* case did not come down on the university's side, Califano wrote a memo to the president that began, "The draft Justice Department brief in the *Bakke* case is bad law, and pernicious social policy"; *Governing America*, 238. He sent a handwritten note to the president, saying it would be "the most serious mistake of your administration in domestic policy" to let Justice's *Bakke* brief go forward (239). Califano urged that the "rational relationship" test of equal protection review be applied to affirmative action— a position, as it turns out, to the left of Justices Brennan and Marshall and the entire Supreme Court (240). (Brennan and Marshall argued for "intermediate" review, while Justice Powell—and a majority of the Court today—apply "strict scrutiny" to government programs.)

147. Califano, *Governing America*, 239. Califano says, "Giving minorities preference was a temporary remedy, not a permanent fixture of America's quest for racial equality, and time would someday run out" (235).

148. Joseph Califano, "Tough Talk for Democrats," *New York Times Magazine* (January 8, 1989): 28ff. See also Wilson, "Race-Neutral Programs," 79–80.

149. In the late 1970s, Eizenstat argued that an early Justice Department draft brief on the *Bakke* was too critical of racial preferences; Schwartz, *Behind Bakke*, 46. Califano

said Eizenstat was "sympathetic" to Califano's criticism of the original Justice Department brief; *Governing America*, 239. Greenberg also says Eizenstat urged Carter and Mondale to become personally involved in the *Bakke* case and to prevent the filing of an anti–affirmative action brief; *Crusaders in the Court*, 466. By 1991 Eizenstat was arguing, "Affirmative action, as envisioned by President Johnson in his famous Howard University speech in 1965 where he first put forward the idea, was a transition program. It was not a permanent program. There is always a question of how long does that last"; Holmes, "Mulling the Idea of Affirmative Action for Poor Whites." Eizenstat favors moving away from race preferences to a system of class-based preferences.

In 1995 the liberal stalwart Susan Estrich, a law professor and campaign manager to Gov. Michael Dukakis in 1988, came out for an end to affirmative action. "Affirmative action was never meant to be permanent," she told the *New York Times*, "and now is truly the time to move on to some other approach"; see Ayres, "Conservatives Forge New Strategy," A22.

150. Dorothy J. Gaiter, "Mr. Fletcher's Plan: Lights, Camera, Affirmative Action," *Wall Street Journal*, April 5, 1995, A1.

151. See Lynn Duke, " 'Perception Gap,' Is Revealed," A3. The poll was administered by Peter D. Hart Research Associates for People for the American Way. See also Cose, *The Rage of a Privileged Class*, 9, 142.

152. See "Third Millennium Declaration," New York, July 1993, 20; and K. L. Billingsley, "Student Revolution on Affirmative Action," *Wall Street Journal*, October 12, 1995, A22.

153. W. E. B. Du Bois spoke of the twentieth century's greatest issue being the color line—not lines. The 1965 Moynihan report had to rely on some census data that categorized people as white or nonwhite. Nonwhite was seen as a relatively good proxy for black because, as Moynihan pointed out, in 1960 blacks constituted 92.1 percent of nonwhites; *The Negro Family*, 4. LBJ's Howard University speech was followed up by a conference with "men of both races"; Johnson, Howard commencement address (1965), 639.

154. Hacker, *Two Nations*, 15.

155. Barbara Vobejda, "Births, Immigration Revise Census View of 21st Century U.S.," *Washington Post*, December 4, 1992, A10.

156. Ramirez, "Multicultural Empowerment," 960.

157. Vobejda, "Births, Immigration," A10. See also Webster, *The Racialization of America*, 103.

158. Ramirez, "Multicultural Empowerment," 963.

159. Arthur Schlesinger points out, "In 1910 nearly 90 percent of immigrants came from Europe. In the 1980s more than 80 percent came from Asia and Latin America"; *The Disuniting of America*, 120. See also D'Souza, *Illiberal Education*, 13, 260.

160. See Ely, "The Constitutionality of Reverse Racial Discrimination," 723, 727. See also Ely, *Democracy and Distrust*, 170; and Ramirez, "Multicultural Empowerment," 961–62.

161. Felicity Barringer, "Census Shows Profound Change in Racial Makeup of the Nation," *New York Times*, March 11, 1991, A1, B8.

162. In 1990 non-Hispanic whites constituted 31.4 percent of the population in Hawaii, 50.3 percent in New Mexico, 57.3 percent in California, and 60.7 percent in Texas; see Hacker, *Two Nations*, 228. Blacks constituted in 1990 a majority of the population in a number of cities, including Detroit, Atlanta, Washington, D.C., Birmingham, New Orleans, Baltimore, Newark, Jackson, Richmond, and Wilmington (229).

163. Wilson, "Race-Neutral Programs," 79–80.

164. Mishel and Simon, *The State of Working America*, 1.

165. Goldthorpe, *Social Mobility in Britain*, 328–29.

166. See Jack Beatty, "Who Speaks for the Middle Class?," *Atlantic* (May 1994): 65ff.

167. Moynihan, "The Family and the Nation—1986," *America* (March 22, 1986).

168. Quoted in Phillips, *Boiling Point*, 3.

169. The annual number of hours the average worker puts in increased by ninety-

five hours between 1979 and 1987, "the equivalent," Phillips notes, "of three and a half extra weeks"; *Boiling Point*, 24.

170. Many businesses support pro–affirmative action court decisions, and even government regulations, for two reasons that have nothing to do with moral commitment to racial equality and everything to do with the bottom line. First, to fend off statistically based disparate impact suits, many businesses do hire by the numbers—not because it is impossible to defend imbalances with reference to business necessity, but because corporations are risk-averse and may not wish to go through the review process necessary to make sure its procedures are truly fair. Because Title VII of the Civil Rights Act of 1964 is theoretically meant to protect white males from discrimination, too, and disparate impact law does not itself *require* preferences, corporations worry about reverse discrimination suits from white males. Accordingly, business applauds decisions like *Weber*, which allowed the use of racial preferences to create racial balance; if the government tells federal contractors they must hire by the numbers, businesses are further insulated; see Anne B. Fisher, "Businessmen Like to Hire by the Numbers," *Fortune* (September 16, 1985): 26. In January 1979, the Equal Employment Opportunity Commission (EEOC) issued "Guidelines on Affirmative Action Appropriate under Title VII," specifically designed to insulate employers from reverse discrimination claims. The guidelines allow employers to "consider race, sex, and/or national origin in making selections among qualified or qualifiable applicants" in order to meet affirmative action goals; *Federal Register*, January 19, 1979, 4425; see also Citizens' Commission on Civil Rights, *Affirmative Action*, 64. Professor Blumrosen says that the 1979 guidelines "point out a legitimate way of doing affirmative action. They also immunize the businesses against financial liability"; Holmes, "Affirmative Action Plans," A20.

President Reagan's draft executive order weakened this assurance. Not only did it provide that the secretary of labor shall revoke regulations requiring companies to "use numerical quotas, goals, ratios, or objectives"—thus making goals and timetables voluntary—it went further, stating, in what *Fortune* called "incendiary language": "Nothing in this executive order shall be interpreted to require or provide a legal basis for a government contractor or subcontractor to utilize any numerical quota, goal, or ratio, or otherwise discriminate against, or grant any preference to, any individual or group on the basis of race, color, religion, sex, or national origin with respect to any aspect of employment"; quoted in Fisher, "Businessmen Like to Hire by the Numbers."

According to one labor lawyer, "Getting rid of the Johnson executive order would turn the corporation into a battlefield. Again"; quoted in Fisher, "Businessmen Like to Hire by the Numbers"; see also Taylor, *Paved with Good Intentions*, 157. The concern also was felt within the administration; Attorney General Ed Meese, says Charles Fried, was "worried that businesses might be squeezed between lawsuits by blacks and women over unbalanced work forces and a new class of lawsuits by white males hurt by voluntary affirmative-action programs"; *Order and Law*, 27. Later in the book, Fried elaborates: "Employers who had reason to fear the *Griggs* overhang welcomed *Weber*. If your work force is not racially balanced you may get sued (*Griggs*). If you use quotas and preferences to make the numbers come out right, you are in the clear (*Weber*)" (98).

Second, business supported court decisions approving of voluntary affirmative action because such programs can be an effective way to elude back-pay liability. In *United Steelworkers of America v. Weber*, the Supreme Court approved such a scheme: a private employer, without explicitly admitting past discrimination, conceded that certain employment categories were "racially imbalanced" and set up a preferential program to eliminate that imbalance; see *USWA v. Weber*, 205. The Court said that as long as the preferences were temporary and did not unnecessarily trammel the interests of innocent whites, private wrongdoing employers could entirely shift the burden of compensation to innocent employees. (The Court held in *Weber*, and reaffirmed in *Johnson*, that Title VII requires much less proof of past discrimination than a public entity requires to engage in a program of race preferences.)

In the *Weber* case, as Jack Greenberg notes, the NAACP Legal Defense and Education Fund had successfully sued the employer, Kaiser Aluminum, at one of its plants in

Louisiana and settled for $300,000 in back pay, "leaving Kaiser and the union facing more of the same at the other two plants." When Kaiser adopted a "voluntary" program to set aside 50 percent of training slots for blacks, LDF backed off; Greenberg, *Crusaders in the Courts*, 468; see also Days, "*Fullilove*," 461 (Kaiser's program was motivated in part to "divert attention from the fact that it had long been engaged in discriminatory employment practices that violated federal law.") Everyone is happy (LDF and Kaiser) except, as Clarence Thomas notes, the actual victims of discrimination, who lose out on back pay, and the white male applicants, who lose out because of preferential treatment; see "Commentary: Affirmative Action Goals and Timetables," 404. Thomas, while director of the EEOC, found that this practice was quite common: employers often pushed for affirmative action settlements *before* the commission had identified actual victims of discrimination. "The reason for this is obvious," Thomas writes. "Giving back pay to each actual victim can be quite expensive, but the cost of agreeing to hire a certain number of blacks or women is generally *de minimis*." (406). Being able to shift the burden is part of the reason business groups like the National Association of Manufacturers applaud Court decisions favorable to affirmative action (406–7); see also Nathan Glazer, *Ethnic Dilemmas*, 172. Businesses also sometimes use affirmative action to weaken unions; see Ansley, "Stirring the Ashes," 1068, citing *W. R. Grace & Co. v. Local Union 759*, 461 US 757 (1983).

In these cases, liberal justices find themselves in the strange position of arguing that a prohibition against voluntary racial preferences "would augment the powers of the Federal Government and diminish traditional management prerogatives"—"values," the conservative critic Charles Fried noted, "that did not often move" the author, Justice Brennan; *Weber*, cited in Fried, *Order and Law*, 93; see also ibid., 92; and Ansley, "Stirring the Ashes," 1072, citing management prerogative as an argument "we would rather not make."

171. See Kahlenberg, California Law Review.

172. See Munro, "The Continuing Evolution," 602, 610.

173. Businesses will also want to ensure that current law, under which retreating from a race-based affirmative action program could be cited as evidence of intent to discriminate, is modified; see Holmes, "Affirmative Action Plans."

174. Newt Gingrich, appearing on *Face the Nation*, April 9, 1995, 6 [transcript]. Likewise, in Maryland, Republican state legislators have indicated that they may "try to strip the contracting program of its racial preferences and replace them with provisions to give preference to economically disadvantaged business regardless of race"; see Michael Abramowitz, "Glendening Pushes Rise in Minority Contracting," *Washington Post*, March 4, 1995, B1.

175. See Lubman, "UC Vote to Ban Race Criterion Has Shades of Gray," A6. The Regents' vote allowed preference for the economically or socially disadvantaged, such as those from "an abusive and otherwise dysfunctional home or a neighborhood of unwholesome or antisocial influences." Originally, Regent Ward Connerly, who led the fight against racial preferences, favored a "total academic meritocracy" with no consideration given to socioeconomic status or obstacles overcome. He then modified his position; see "Regent Softens Stance on Affirmative Action," *New York Times*, June 21, 1995, A14.

176. See Steven A. Holmes, "Affirmative Action Passes Test in Senate's Vote," *New York Times*, July 20, 1995, 7. The measure failed 61–36. Holmes also notes that presidential politics were a factor: supporters of Gramm's rival for the Republican nomination, Sen. Robert Dole, voted against Gramm's amendment. The measure was also seen as a fairly dramatic step to take during consideration of appropriations legislation.

177. See Thernstrom, "A Class Backwards Idea," C1, C2. A Capitol Hill staffer described affirmative action alternatives as "an inoculation strategy."

178. Sowell, *Preferential Policies*, 168.

179. Massachusetts State Sen. Bill Owens, chair of the legislature's Black Caucus, told the *Boston Globe*: "He has to establish alternatives. If he is not posing alternatives, then he's just adding to the fire that already exists"; John Aloysius Farrell, "Kerry Stands by Yale Speech," *Boston Globe*, April 19, 1992, A17.

180. Reagan opposed all the grand hallmarks of progress—the original Civil Rights Act of 1964, the Voting Rights Act of 1965, and the Fair Housing Act of 1968; Mills, *Debating Affirmative Action*, 18; see also Kennedy, "Persuasion and Distrust," 1342. Reagan continued to call the Civil Rights Act unconstitutional following its passage; see Higgenbotham, "An Open Letter to Justice Thomas," 1019. Reagan began his presidential campaign in 1980 in Neshoba County, Mississippi, telling a white southern audience—not far from the site where three civil rights workers had been killed in 1964—that he endorsed "states' rights"; see White, *American in Search of Itself*, 384. At the outset of his administration, he changed sides in the *Bob Jones University* case, arguing that a private school, denied a tax-exempt status since 1970 because it forbade interracial dating, should have its exempt status reinstated—a position rejected in a 8–1 ruling by the Supreme Court; see Guinier, *The Tyranny of the Majority*, 23; Greenberg, *Crusaders in the Courts*, 397–98; and Mills, *Debating Affirmative Action*, 18. Reagan vetoed the Civil Rights Restoration Act of 1987, only to see his veto repudiated by an overwhelming bipartisan vote. (The Civil Rights Restoration Act overturned the Supreme Court's 1984 decision in the *Grove City College* case, which had given an extremely narrow interpretation to sex discrimination law.)

Likewise, in 1985 Congress overrode Reagan's veto of legislation applying sanctions against South Africa; Fuchs, *The American Kaleidoscope*, 388; see also Kennedy, "Persuasion and Distrust," 1343. Reagan signed the Voting Rights Act amendments of 1982, but only after fighting for amendments that would have "substantially weakened" the legislation; Days, "Turning back the Clock." If there was a consistent pattern to Reagan's stances, it was not color blindness but hostility to black interests. Reagan's repeal of affirmative action was about as easy as McGovern going to China. The same can be said even more emphatically of Jesse Helms's attempts to roll back affirmative action. Even George Bush, thought of as more moderate on civil rights, had, as a senatorial candidate, opposed the Civil Rights Act of 1964, and stood by as vice president while Reagan attempted to roll back civil rights advances; Higgenbotham, "An Open Letter to Justice Thomas," 1019.

181. See Puddington, "Thomas and the Blacks," 31; Sen. Orrin G. Hatch, remarks on the confirmation of the nomination of Judge Clarence Thomas to the Supreme Court, *Federal News Service*, October 3, 1991; and Senate Judiciary Committee, *Nomination of Thomas* (views of Sens. Thurmond, Hatch, Simpson, Grassley, and Brown).

182. See Dershowitz and Hanft, "College Diversity"; Dershowitz, *Chutzpah*, 76; West, *Race Matters*, 64 ("I would have favored—as I do now—a class-based affirmative action in principle"); Mark Shields, appearing on *The McNeil/Lehrer NewsHour*, July 21, 1995; Clint Bolick, "Racial Affirmative Action Is on the Way Out: Should Income-Based Preferences Replace It?," *American Enterprise* (July-August 1995): 19–20; and Murray and Herrnstein, *The Bell Curve*, 475 ("In the case of two candidates who are fairly closely matched otherwise, universities should give the nod to the applicant from the disadvantaged background").

A number of other commentators have made supportive statements about class-based affirmative action, broadly defined, including: Peter Brown (*Minority Party*, 318); John Bunzel (quoted in Steven V. Roberts, "Temple Law School Offers Unusual Affirmative Action Plan for Deprived Students," *New York Times*, February 7, 1978, 25); Richard Cohen ("More Important Than Affirmative Action," *Washington Post*, August 6, 1991, A15); Benjamin DeMott ("Legally Sanctioned Special Advantages Are a Way of Life in the United States," *Chronicle of Higher Education* [February 27, 1991]: A40); Dinesh D'Souza (*Illiberal Education*, 251–53); James Fishkin (*Justice, Equal Opportunity*, 89); Eugene Genovese ([review of *Illiberal Education* by Dinesh D'Souza], *New Republic* [April 15, 1991]: 30ff); Alan Goldman (*Justice and Reverse Discrimination*, 202); Nat Hentoff ("Coming: Class-Based Affirmative Action," *Village Voice*, December 6, 1994, 22); Tamar Jacoby ("An Integrationist Manifesto," *Wall Street Journal*, October 4, 1994, A18); Will Marshall (Michael K. Frisby, "President and Advisers Are Struggling to Find Position on Affirmative Action," *Wall Street Journal*, February 17, 1995, A19, and Marshall, "Rebuilding America's Civil Rights Consensus," *New Democrat* [May-June 1995]:

30–31); Brian Mikulak ("Classism and Equal Opportunity"); Don Munro ("The Continuing Evolution," 610); Albert Shanker ("Help for Disadvantaged, but Not Quotas," *New York Times*, March 27, 1977); Jim Sleeper ("Race and Affirmative Action," 91); and Stuart Taylor ("A Case for Class-Based Affirmative Action").

And we have noted that, among the judiciary, proponents of class-based affirmative action have included both liberals and conservatives, such as: Justice William O. Douglas (*DeFunis v. Odegaard*, 331); Justice Stanley Mosk (California) (*Bakke v. Regents of UC*, 1166); Justice Antonin Scalia ("Commentary: The Disease as Cure," 153–54 and 156, and *Richmond v. Croson*, 526–28); Justice Clarence Thomas (Senate Judiciary Committee, *Nomination of Judge Thomas*, 358–60); and Justice Sandra Day O'Connor (*Richmond v. Croson*, 509–10).

Other proponents of class-based affirmative action have been cited. A *New York Times* article (Holmes, "Mulling Affirmative Action") lists Cohen, Scalia, Sleeper, William Julius Wilson, Stuart Eizenstat, and Michael Williams. Dana Takagi says that the list of conservatives who "have argued that class-based affirmative action is fairer social policy than race-based affirmative action" includes Allan Bloom, John Bunzel, Richard Ramirez, Thomas Sowell, and Shelby Steele; *The Retreat from Race*, 171. Kimberly Paap Taylor lists Steele, Wilson, Donald P. Judges, and Robert Greenstein; "Note: Affirmative Action for the Poor," 807. D'Souza lists Sleeper, Wilson, Gingrich, Kemp, Randall Kennedy, and Clarence Page; *The End of Racism*, 542. The Anti-Defamation League also says it "supports special initiatives to assist the economically disadvantaged on a race-neutral basis"; see its newsletter, *Frontline*, May-June 1995, 10.

In addition, there is a much larger group of people who speak generally about the need to move from race- to class-based remedies. In a 1991 article in the *Los Angeles Times Magazine*, Ronald Brownstein identified a "synthesis school"—those who agree that the problems of blacks are more a function of class than race. It includes Greenstein, Sleeper, Steele, West, Wilson, William Raspberry, David Garrow, and Jonathan Rieder; "Beyond Quotas."

183. On *Face the Nation* on April 9, 1995, Gingrich said: "I want to help people who work hard, who come out of poor neighborhoods, who come out of poor backgrounds, who go to school in poor counties. I want to see us find ways to reach out and help individuals, but I am against any kind of quota structure of set-aside that is based purely and simply on some kind of background, genetic definition"; transcript, 5. See also John F. Harris, "President May Appoint Panel to Study Preference Programs," *Washington Post*, April 10, 1995, A9; and Newt Gingrich, "Newt Gingrich on Affirmative Action," *Washington Post*, August 2, 1995, A24.

On Kemp, see Mickey Kaus, "Class Is In," *New Republic* (March 27, 1995): 6; and D'Souza, *The End of Racism*, 697, n25. See also Kemp, "Affirmative Action: The 'Radical Republican' Example," *Washington Post*, August 6, 1995, C9 ("The time has definitely come for a new approach, an 'affirmative action' based not just on gender or race or ethnicity but ultimately based on need").

184. Pataki told the *Washington Post* that his staff is researching "whether we should shift [the criterion for] some programs from race to economically disadvantaged"; see David S. Broder and Robert A. Barnes, "Few Governors Join Attack on Racial Policies," *Washington Post*, August 2, 1995, A1. Whitman was quoted in the *Bergen Record* as saying: "It may be that there's a better way, that you can set economic triggers that will reach the people who need the help but that will stop defining everybody in terms of sex or race"; Kelly Richmond, "Whitman Looking to Forge Affirmative Action Accord," *Bergen Record*, July 27, 1995, A3.

It has been widely reported in the media that Gen. Colin Powell supports racial preferences, but what he supports may be closer to class-based affirmative action. He has said that schools should "take a look at the total background of these youngsters, regardless of race"; Howard Kurtz, "Powell Explains Positions at Odds with Conservatives," *Washington Post*, September 12, 1995, A6.

185. Ann Devroy, "Clinton Cites GOP 'Hostility': In Shift, President Supports Affirmative Action Based on Needs," *Washington Post*, March 4, 1995, A1.

186. See "Democratic Senator [Lieberman] Calls for a Phaseout of Race Prefer-ences," *Wall Street Journal*, August 4, 1995, A10. See remarks of Sen. Charles S. Robb, *Congressional Record*, October 15, 1991, S14, 688. I worked on Sen. Robb's staff at the time but had no role in the drafting of this speech.

Likewise, aides to former Boston Mayor Ray Flynn and former Massachusetts Gov. Michael Dukakis have urged the switch. Ray Flynn's policy director, David Cortiella, told the *New York Times* that affirmative action "should embrace all poor people—black, Hispanic, Asian and white"; Susan Diesenhouse, "In Affirmative Action, a Question of Truth in Labeling," *New York Times*, December 11, 1988, sect. 5, p. 26. The former Dukakis aide Jack Corrigan backs class-based preferences over racial preferences; Jack Corrigan, telephone interview with the author, February 23, 1995.

187. See Paul M. Barrett and G. Pascal Zachary, "Race, Sex Preferences Could Become Target in Voter Shift to Right," *Wall Street Journal*, January 11, 1995, A1, A11 ("Mr. [Tom] Wood says he favors some alternative to affirmative action based solely on need and ignoring sex and race—at least for entry-level jobs and college admissions"); see also John Boudreau, "Effort to Outlaw Affirmative Action Promoted in California," *Washington Post*, December 27, 1994, A3 ("Assemblyman Bernie Richter, a Republican from Chico, intro-duced a similar anti-affirmative action amendment in the state Assembly in early December. His legislation would support preferences only for economically disadvantaged people applying for entry-level positions"). In addition, UC Regent Ward Connerly, who has led the fight against racial preferences, says, "I would support programs aimed at specific high schools that don't have many graduates, and if the students at one happen to be black, that's fine"; see Lubman, "Campuses Mull Admissions Without Affirmative Action," B1, B10.

For the Democratic side, see William Claiborne, "Chipping at a Democratic Corner-stone: California Party Leaders Consider Compromise on Affirmative Action," *Wash-ington Post*, February 4, 1995, A1 (State Democratic chairman Bill Press is considering "a counter ballot initiative that would allow remedies to discrimination based more on 'socioeconomic considerations' than race, ethnicity and gender").

188. None of this is to say that there would be unanimous agreement on the partic-ular *shape* of the deal to trade race- for class-based affirmative action. Many conserva-tives probably envision a very modest program that will be unsatisfying to many liberals. Dinesh D'Souza, for example, backs a voluntary program of class-based affirmative action, limited to universities, and providing a break to only the very poorest applicants; D'Souza interview (1994).

After all, addressing class inequality has never been a top priority of conservatives. As Michael Walzer points out, "At the very center of conservative thought lies this idea: that the present division of wealth and power corresponds to some deeper reality of human nature"; "In Defense of Equality," 399; see also Kaus, *The End of Equality*, 6; and Rattner, "GOP Ignores Income Inequality," A22. And the fact that conservatives normally argue for class-based affirmative action in the last portion of a long attack on affirmative action, with little room to elaborate, suggests a lack of seriousness, if not sincerity. D'Souza devotes two full pages of *Illiberal Education* to the subject (251–53). Scalia devotes two paragraphs to it; "Commentary: The Disease as Cure," 153, 156. Stuart Taylor, Jr., notes that the lack of specificity raises questions about the seriousness of conservatives; "A Case for Class-Based Affirmative Action."

Conservatives have every reason to advance the least aggressive class-based affirma-tive action policy possible. As affirmative action is further weakened, conservatives will have less and less reason to bargain, and the deal that conservatives cut on the shape of class-based affirmative action will grow less and less satisfying to those concerned about social justice. It is therefore crucial to call the conservatives' bluff while they still have some reason to follow through with their program.

Rather than standing as a roadblock to class-based affirmative action, proponents of the status quo should try to negotiate the best deal they can. Universities will want to negotiate to ensure that if they are to be required (as a condition for receiving federal aid) to admit poor and working-class students, the federal government will pick up some por-tion of the associated costs.

It will be important for civil rights groups to begin the negotiations soon so that their interests are protected. First, if civil rights groups are seen as fighting a losing battle for racial preferences—which primarily benefit the middle class—and opposing the chance to help poor blacks (and whites), they will further alienate the community of poor and working-class blacks, whom they are forever trying to reach. Backing class preferences could signal a much more constructive way of reaching out to poor blacks than cozying up to Louis Farrakhan. Second, while some civil rights leaders will decry the shift from race to class preferences as splitting the black community in two and driving some affluent blacks into the Republican Party (see, e.g., Wilkins, "In Ivory Towers," 10), other civil rights leaders may realize that nothing could be healthier for the black community. Today, Jack Beatty notes, blacks have voice and leverage in only one party, and when Democrats lose, it can leave blacks high and dry; Jack Beatty, interview with the author, Boston, January 6, 1995. After the 1994 election, which rendered the Congressional Black Caucus impotent, Juan Williams noted that "the most influential black American in government today is Republican-appointed Supreme Court Justice Clarence Thomas"; "Blacked out in the Newt Congress," *Washington Post*, November 20, 1994, C1. If civil rights groups insist that all Democrats fall in line on racial preferences, they vastly increase the likelihood of Republican victories.

Third, civil rights groups want to be in the bargaining process to ensure that the structure of class-based affirmative action is fair and will benefit large numbers of minorities. As we will see in ch. 6, the more generous the program, the more likely it is that the net number of people of color benefiting will be the same as under race-based programs. And civil rights groups will want to push for a fair and sophisticated definition of class, where possible, one that reflects the relative disadvantage of blacks compared with whites in the same income category (lower net worth, disadvantageous family structure, lower quality schools and neighborhoods).

New York City's public works preference program should serve as a cautionary tale. In the 1980s, Mayor Edward Koch instituted a class-based public contracting set-aside, which provided some benefit to blacks. Following his election, Mayor David Dinkins instituted a 20 percent set-aside for businesses owned by minorities and women, providing, in the short term, even more benefit to blacks; see Calvin Simms, "Dinkins Plan Gives Minority Concerns More in Contracts," *New York Times*, February 11, 1992, A1. When Mayor Rudolph Giuliani came to power, however, he eliminated parts of the Dinkins program, leaving minorities worse off than under the Koch plan; see Jonathan P. Hicks, "Giuliani Is Altering Minority Contract Program," *New York Times*, January 25, 1994, A1; see also Jim Sleeper, "Apple Juice," *New Republic* (May 9, 1994): 17.

Civil rights groups must strike the deal with conservatives *before* affirmative action is officially killed. Only while the future is uncertain will both sides come to the table. Race-based affirmative action provides the leverage necessary to get conservatives even to talk about class preferences. For the moment, class preferences unite Cornel West and Clarence Thomas, but the moment may pass.

189. *Newsweek* poll cited in James D. Besser, "Tug of War," *The Jewish Week*, March 31, 1995, 28, 29.

190. Cathleen Decker, "Most Back Anti-Bias Policy but Spurn Racial Preferences," *Los Angeles Times*, March 30, 1995, A1.

191. See Kevin Merida, "Worry, Frustration Build for Many in Black Middle Class," *Washington Post*, October 9, 1995, A1, A22.

192. After Clinton's March 4, 1995, statement, civil rights and feminist groups strongly denounced any wavering. In fact, Rep. Dick Gephardt (D-Mo.), whose populist presidential campaign in 1988 made him a natural supporter of class preferences, came out against them ten days after Clinton's statement; see David S. Broder, "Gephardt Defends Affirmative Action," *Washington Post*, March 14, 1995, A6.

193. Albert Shanker, interview with the author, Washington, D.C., September 20, 1995.

194. Although passage of both bills came only after hard work and the overcoming of obstinate opposition, eventually the Civil Rights Act of 1964 was passed by more than

two to one in the House (290–130) and almost three to one in the Senate (73–27); Califano, *Governing America*, 226–27.

For Clinton's continued support for class-based preferences, despite strong opposition from organized civil rights and feminist groups, see Michael K. Frisby, "Black Executives Are Showing Increasing Clout with White House on Issue of Affirmative Action," *Wall Street Journal*, June 6, 1995, A20 ("Mr. Clinton also asserted that affirmative action programs needed to be broader and made more inclusive so that poor whites could also take advantage of them. He said, according to participants, 'We need to find ways to broaden them so they won't be subject to so much criticism'").

195. Quoted in Peter Applebome, "Rights Movement in Struggle for Image as Well as a Bill," *New York Times*, April 3, 1991, A1. As Bayard Rustin notes, King's use of nonviolence and moral suasion to bring about social change was even more remarkable than Gandhi's, for Gandhi had a majority in India who would materially benefit, whereas King did not; "The King to Come," 20.

196. Though class-based and color-blind, welfare is among the programs most reviled by the American public. Its unpopularity may stem in part from its disproportionate benefit to blacks, but more so from its tension with the American work ethnic. Lyndon Johnson, deeply attuned to this attitude, personally directed that before the Council of Economic Advisers' final *Economic Report of the President* was released, all references to "welfare" and "income transfer payments" be deleted; Thurow, *The Zero Sum Society*, 112–13. "When Jesse Jackson wants to move a national audience, he doesn't talk about race or poverty," writes Mickey Kaus. "He talks about maids and janitors who 'work every day'"; *The End of Equality*, 176.

Likewise, funding for education has always been popular because it is not seen as rewarding idleness. A June 1994 *Wall Street Journal*/NBC poll found that 75 percent of Americans were willing to pay higher taxes to improve the quality of education; see Albert R. Hunt, "Dick Darman's Field of Dreams," *Wall Street Journal*, June 16, 1994, A17. While many Americans do blame poverty on the poor, Lee Sigelman notes, there is "a conspicuous exception": Americans also believe that "inadequate access to good schools is a prime cause of poverty," and that better efforts should be made in this area; *Black Americans' Views*, 86.

197. Rustin, "The King to Come," 21.

198. See Glazer, *Public Interest*, 108 ("the actual condition of blacks . . . the mass of misery characterizing the poor stands as the greatest argument for affirmative action").

199. One might think of the political matrix as follows:

PROGRAM	MORAL FORCE	PRICE	DEGREE OF SUCCESS
Early Civil Rights	High	Low	Great
Affirmative Action	Low	Low	Mixed
Welfare	Mixed	High	Mixed
Education	High	High	Mixed
Class Preferences	High	Low	Great

200. Bell begins by citing Tocqueville, for the argument that, "in the United States people abolish slavery for the sake not of the Negroes but of the white men"; *Race, Racism, and American Law*, 13–14. Slavery was abolished in the North, Tocqueville wrote, only because it was unprofitable. Likewise, the Fourteenth Amendment, guaranteeing equal protection under the law, was passed in large part because it was in the interests of white northern Republicans to have blacks vote, Bell says. "If the Southern states could rejoin the union, bar blacks from voting, and regain control of state government, they might soon become the dominant power in the federal government as well"; *Faces at the Bottom of the Well*, 53–54. So, too, says Bell, the Supreme Court's decision in *Brown v. Board of Education* "has proved of greater value to whites than blacks." Dismantling apartheid helped the United States in its cold war struggle "to win the hearts and minds of emerging Third World peoples"; it helped ensure that American blacks would fight in a war with Russia; and it was part of the effort to industrialize and modernize the rural South; *Race, Racism, and American Law*, 640–41.

201. The ex-labor organizer Marshall Gans points out that there is a serious ques-

tion about what organized constituency would lobby for class preferences, particularly since labor has largely signed on to affirmative action; Marshall Gans, interview with the author, Cambridge, Mass., January 5, 1995. But this may be an issue—like term limits— that is so charged, and so well understood, that no formal organized lobby is necessary. In any event, as the DLC's Al From has argued, "to get a new coalition, you have to jettison your reliance on interest group politics and focus on issue politics"; Gerald Sieb, "At a Crossroads, Democrats Ask: Fight or Switch?," *Wall Street Journal*, June 21, 1995, A20.

Chapter 5

1. Citizens' Commission on Civil Rights, *Affirmative Action*, 160.

2. National Women's Law Center, "Need-Based Programs Are No Substitute for Affirmative Action," (April 1995): 2. The NWLC says it is dedicated to promoting the legal rights of women, "with special attention to the concerns of low-income women."

3. Michael Kinsley, "Class, Not Race: It's a Poor Basis for Affirmative Action," *Washington Post*, August 1, 1991, A15.

4. Taylor, "A Case for Class-Based Affirmative Action," 23.

5. "This idea of basing affirmative action on social class rather than race has gotten little of the serious exploration it deserves," writes Stuart Taylor, Jr. "Conservatives like Thomas and Scalia have not offered the kind of detailed proposal that would evidence real enthusiasm for class-based affirmative action"; ibid.; see also Holmes, "Mulling," 3.

6. Thernstrom, "A Class Backwards Idea," C1, C2.

7. Kinsley, "Class, Not Race," A15 (for the phrase "meritocratic crisis points").

8. Karabel, *Freshman Admissions at Berkeley*, 43. Adopted in 1989, the program was first implemented in 1991; Robert Laird, telephone interview with the author, July 18, 1995; see also Takagi, *The Retreat from Race*, 154.

9. Laird interview (1995).

10. See Temple University Law School admissions brochure (1994–95), 45.

11. Dean Robert J. Reinstein, telephone interview with the author, December 14, 1994. SPACE gives special consideration to six groups; see Temple brochure (1994–95), 45. Dean Reinstein said that categories 1 (minority status) and 4 (economically disadvantaged) are the two dominant criteria. He further explained that while race is a separate plus in the admissions process, all other things being equal, a disadvantaged white candidate normally has a better chance of admissions than an advantaged minority applicant. A majority of those admitted under SPACE are white; Reinstein interview (1994).

12. Assistant LEOP Director Algera Tucker, telephone interview with the author, November 4, 1994. According to Tucker, race is considered a plus in LEOP admissions, but advantaged people of color do not qualify for LEOP.

13. See 1993–94 HEOP annual report summary. For example, at Bard College, according to HEOP official Gabriel N. Mendes, students not normally admissible are given a break if they are educationally disadvantaged. Mendes, unpublished letter to the editor of the *New Republic*, April 12, 1995.

14. See *UC v. Bakke*, 275. In addition, Harvard has no trouble designating Asian applicants as either blue-collar or non-blue-collar; see Department of Education, "Statement of Finding, Compliance Review 01–88–6009," October 4, 1990, 16.

15. Although less well publicized than alumni preferences, there is evidence that some colleges currently give prep school applicants preference in admissions. At Harvard, notes David Karen, "going to prep school almost doubles the chances that a white applicant will be admitted"; quoted in Takagi, *The Retreat from Race*, 30–31.

16. While class preferences are often discussed in the context of university admissions, there is a strong case for applying preferences to admission to selective public and private primary and secondary schools, and to tracking within primary and secondary schools. Under current tracking procedures, low SES (socioeconomic status) children are generally tracked low, and high SES children high. A quarter-century ago, Ray Rist argued that tracking provides a central explanation for the reproduction of class status over generations; "Student Social Class and Teacher Expectations." Rist spoke of the "self-fulfilling

prophesy" of low SES kids, placed in low tracks and expected to do little, doing about as much as expected, while high SES–high track kids, being continually challenged, perform to their natural limits. For a more recent assessment of the literature confirming much of Rist's observations, see Shannon, "Reading Instruction and Social Class."

Whatever one thinks of tracking pedagogically (and there are strong arguments for it), it is likely to continue, for it is popular among teachers. Moreover, tracking by social class is likely to continue, not because teachers are malevolent, but because social class *is* highly correlated with educational preparedness, even in kindergarten. What I am arguing for is a marginal preference. When a lower-class student does well—not as well as her middle-class peers *but better than we would expect given her obstacles*—then bump her up, in the hope that the self-fulfilling prophecy is a brighter one.

The phrase "better than we would expect" underlines why it is crucial that such programs be class- rather than race-based. While it is reasonable to have low expectations for poor people because of the obstacles they face, it can be racist to have low expectations for upper-middle-class blacks. According to Stephen Carter, Harvard Law School initially rejected him, then phoned him to offer a slot, indicating that the school had "assumed from your record that you were white"; *Affirmative Action Baby*, 15. Carter noted that "Stephen Carter, the white male, was not good enough for the Harvard Law School; Stephen Carter, the black male, not only was good enough, but rated agonized phone calls urging him to attend. And Stephen Carter, color unknown, must have been white: How else could he have achieved what he did in college?" (16).

The tracking preference cannot be a large one, for a substantial preference would defeat the whole idea of tracking, but on the margins, a small preference could make a genuine difference in the lives of thousands of disadvantaged kids. The problem is that once a child is placed in a lower track, her aspirations often decline, and even students who are misplaced in a low track often end up remaining there; NAS, *Ability Testing II*, 174–75.

In addition, selective public and private schools should provide class preferences so that highly talented and motivated students from poor backgrounds will develop their skills to the point where they can apply to, be accepted at, and succeed in rigorous university programs. In May and September 1994, the *Wall Street Journal* ran two heartbreaking stories about Cedric Jennings, a hardworking, intelligent black student at decrepit and dangerous Frank W. Ballou Senior High School in Washington, D.C. Jennings hid in the chemistry lab and avoided gangs—but also avoided student assemblies where bright students were jeered for winning academic prizes. He dreamed of going to MIT and attended a summer session for minority students, where he could not keep up with affluent black students, who ridiculed his Washington street slang. His SAT was 910, and he was told by a white MIT professor, "I don't think you're MIT material." Jennings blamed the professor, saying he was racist. But the professor was, of course, right: it does no one any good to admit a student to a university he is likely to flunk out of. The answer is to reach students like Jennings earlier. Jennings was offered a scholarship at a private school and inexplicably turned it down, but there are many other Cedric Jennings who do not have that opportunity; see Ron Suskind, "In Rough City School, Top Students Struggle to Learn—and Escape," *Wall Street Journal*, May 26, 1994, A1; and Suskind, "Poor, Black and Smart: An Inner-City Teen Tries to Survive MIT," *Wall Street Journal*, September 22, 1994, A1.

17. See 12 USC 1701u, and *Federal Register*, June 30, 1994, 33866–95. Sect. 1701u(b) provides: "Employment and other economic opportunities generated by federal financial assistance for housing and community development programs shall, to the greatest extent feasible, be directed toward low- and very low-income persons, particularly those who are recipients of general assistance for housing." Sect. 1701u(d)(1)(A) provides: "The Secretary shall require . . . contractors and subcontractors . . . to award contracts . . . to business concerns that provide economic opportunities for low- and very low-income persons." Paul Sonn of the NAACP Legal Defense and Education Fund brought this program to my attention.

18. Preferences are especially appropriate for the many entry-level positions that

require applicants to take tests as a screening device. The Educational Testing Service, which administers the SAT, also provides tests for fifty different occupations, including firefighting and police work; Nairn and Associates, *The Reign of ETS*, 32. One study found that among employers with over a thousand employees, more than 50 percent used testing in hiring; NAS, *Ability Testing II*, 110. The federal government is a heavy user of testing, both in civilian and military positions, and state and local governments employ written tests for between 65 and 88 percent of skilled positions (135); see also D'Souza, *The End of Racism*, 309.

19. See American Council on Education, *Higher Education and National Affairs*, January 25, 1993, 3. See also Fox Butterfield, "Colleges Luring Black Students with Incentives," *New York Times*, February 28, 1993, 26.

20. See Tim W. Ferguson, "Income Disparity and Democrats," *Wall Street Journal*, August 30, 1994, A11.

21. India has been running a hybrid caste-class form of affirmative action for employment for decades; see Witten, "Note: 'Compensatory Discrimination' in India."

22. Jeffrey Rosen notes, correctly, that it would be ridiculous for a sharecropper's son, ten years into his job, to receive a preference in promotion to office manager over a peer with a more advantaged childhood; "Affirmative Action: A Solution" *New Republic* (May 8, 1995): 22.

23. See Carter, *Affirmative Action Baby*, 89.

24. Duncan, Featherman, and Duncan, *Socioeconomic Background and Achievement*, 252.

25. See, e.g. Glazer, "Race, Not Class," *Wall Street Journal*, April 5, 1995, A12.

26. *Richmond v. Croson*, 526, 509–10.

27. See Mike Mills, "FCC May Drop Race, Sex Preferences," *Washington Post*, June 22, 1995, A1, A20. See also "FCC Chooses August 29 for the Next Auction of Its PCS Licenses," *Wall Street Journal*, June 26, 1995, C15; and Daniel Pearl, "Women, Blacks Back FCC Plan to Hold Wireless Auction without Preferences," *Wall Street Journal*, June 23, 1995, B9. The FCC reserved the right to reinsert race and gender preferences in subsequent auctions.

28. See "Setback for Set-Asides," *Washington Post*, December 31, 1992, A26. (Interestingly, this *Post* editorial endorsed the program as "fairer" than the previous race-based program.) Some have said the District's program is a shell for a race-based preference scheme; Rosen calls the newly revamped program a cover for the old race-based system; "Affirmative Action: A Solution," 25. But if the allegation is true, then the new program, too, may be litigated and struck down in the courts.

29. See Koch, "Equal Opportunity—Without Minority Set-Asides," *New York Times*, February 20, 1989, A19; see also Koch, *Citizen Koch*, 164–65.

30. See Thomas B. Edsall, "City Tax Credits, Set-Asides Urged: Mayor Rendell Calls for Affirmative Urban Economic Action," *Washington Post*, April 16, 1994, A2.

31. See White House, Office of the Press Secretary, *Remarks by the President on Affirmative Action*, July 19, 1995, 10; see also Michael Frisby, "Clinton Sees Need for Affirmative Action Plans, but May Open Set-Aside Programs to Whites," *Wall Street Journal*, July 14, 1995, A14. At the time, the Labor Department already was earmarking contracts for 1,528 counties defined as labor-surplus areas; see Michael Frisby, "Labor Surplus Preferences Endangered by Clinton's Affirmative Action Review," *Wall Street Journal*, June 2, 1995, A10. In addition, the Empowerment Zone and Enterprise Communities Act of 1993 designated nine geographical empowerment zones and ninety-four enterprise communities for special breaks; see Sen. Joseph I. Lieberman, testimony before Senate Small Business Committee, October 19, 1995.

As currently structured, these programs and proposals do not limit beneficiaries to young entry-level employees, though in practice many of the beneficiaries may be young, and almost all will fill entry-level rather than high-skilled or supervisory positions. Class-based affirmative action programs benefiting the poor of all ages are justified on two bases. First, even conservatives concede that not all middle-aged poor people are entirely to blame for their economic position. Second, whether or not they are "to blame," a social good is accomplished by providing the poor with special opportunities that will empower them. Companies that take on the burden of training and employing the hard-core unemployed or of locating in a poor neighborhood are performing a public service for which the government may properly reward them.

32. See Sen. Christopher S. Bond, Senate Small Business Committee, opening statement, October 19, 1995. See also Paul Barrett and Michael Frisby, "'Place, Not Race' Could Be Next Catch Phrase in Government's Affirmative Action Programs," *Wall Street Journal*, October 18, 1995, A24. HUBZones are similar to enterprise zones, but less costly. To the extent that HUBZone set-asides replace existing racial set-asides, there is no additional cost to the federal government. Enterprise zones, which grant tax breaks to businesses that locate in distressed areas, lose revenue.

33. See, e.g., Erik Wright, *Class Structure*, 8.

34. Cited in Clay Chandler, "It's Getting Awfully Crowded in the Middle," *Washington Post*, December 18, 1994, H1, H7.

35. Max Weber, "Class, Status, Party," in *Max Weber: Essays in Sociology*, 181.

36. Simply dividing family income by the number of family members (to come up with a per capita income figure) seems to overstate the impact of family size, since some living expenses (like heating a home) can be efficiently shared. On the other hand, ignoring family size altogether would be unfair (and as we will see in ch. 6, would negatively impact people of color). In determining the poverty line, officials have applied a one-to-two ratio, so that the needs of a single individual are one-half that of a family of four; Rose, *Social Stratification*, 9.

37. Phillips notes that to match the living standard that an income of $100,000 buys in Minneapolis, an individual would need to earn $112,700 in New York City, $111,600 in San Francisco, $110,000 in Los Angeles, $106,200 in Boston, $93,300 in Miami, and $90,000 in New Orleans; *Boiling Point*, 29.

38. Using data provided by the Bureau of Labor Statistics, the government pays its employees a supplemental "locality pay" in twenty-seven areas in the nation; see Stephen Barr, "U.S. Workers Here to Get 3.21% Raise," *Washington Post*, November 8, 1994, A1.

39. In the college admissions context, more than half the student population already discloses family income on financial aid forms; see Associated Press, "More Than Half of All Students Need Financial Help after High School," *Washington Post*, October 26, 1994, A16. At elite schools like Harvard, the figure receiving aid can reach up to 70 percent; see "Tuition Rises 5.4%," *Harvard* (May-June 1994): 66.

40. See Mayer and Jencks, who conclude, in a review of numerous studies, that three factors are the "standard" indicators of SES; "Growing Up in Poor Neighborhoods," 1441ff; and Derek Bok, who notes that "academic achievement and persistence depend in some significant part on the parents' education, income and occupation"; "Admitting Success: The Case for Racial Preference," *New Republic* (February 4, 1985), 14; see also Jonathan Crane, "Effects of Neighborhoods on Dropping Out of School and Teenage Childbearing," in Jencks and Peterson, *The Urban Underclass*, 303–4.

41. Laird interview (1995).

42. See, e.g., S. M. Miller and Pamela Roby, "Poverty: Changing Social Stratification," in Moynihan, *On Understanding Poverty*, 71–72. Likewise, the University of California found that father's and mother's education correlates more highly with student SATs and GPAs than does parental income; see University of California, "The Use of Socio-Economic Status in Place of Ethnicity in Admissions" (May 1995): 15.

43. Karabel, *Freshman Admissions at Berkeley*, 43–45.

44. Clearly, all American graduate schools already have ways of evaluating the quality of undergraduate institutions. Two semiobjective ways to broadly evaluate colleges are by selectivity and mean board scores. This is helpful only for very broad categories (e.g., most selective, highly selective, selective; mean SAT above 1100, and below). Note also that applicants already provide information to colleges on their parents' education.

45. Laird interview (1995).

46. Thernstrom, *The Other Bostonians*, 102.

47. Indeed, the Duncan Index, described below, ranks occupations based on education required and income received.

48. Melvin Kohn of the National Institute of Mental Health has argued that parental occupation serves as a fairly good proxy for the transmission of certain values that play "an important role in the perpetuation of the existing class order"; paraphrased in Kahl and Gilbert, *The American Class Structure* (1987), 118. Kohn found that parents of lower occupational status tend to emphasize obedience, where higher-status parents emphasize self-direction (119–21). Likewise, the Johnson O'Connor Research Foundation has established a direct correlation between English vocabulary skills and professional status.

49. See Ehrenreich, *Fear of Falling*, 12–13.

50. See Davis and Moore, "Some Principles of Social Stratification," 243.

51. Kahl and Gilbert, *The American Class Structure* (1987), 155.

52. See also Blau and Duncan, *The American Occupational Structure*, 26 (ranking seventeen occupational groupings by a composite of median income and education—noting that in only five of twenty-seven instances do the education and income measures diverge). Among other indicators is the Hollingshead Index of Social Position, which incorporates both education and occupation. See Kahl and Gilbert, *The American Class Structure* (1987), 119.

53. Duncan, Featherman and Duncan, *Socioeconomic Background and Achievement*, 77; see also Blau and Duncan, *The American Occupational Structure*, 119–20; and Kahl and Gilbert, *The American Class Structure* (1987), 41–42 (noting that "the correlation between the two sets of scores [1963 and 1947] were nearly perfect [0.97]," and that there have been "virtually no changes in the rankings of occupational prestige since 1925" [42]). The correlation between the NORC studies and the Duncan Index is 0.91 (43).

54. Sennett and Cobb, *The Hidden Injuries of Class*, 221, 226–27. In a somewhat different context, the government of India uses occupation as one of the major factors in determining which groups will receive the "backward" status necessary for preferential treatment; see Witten, "Note: 'Compensatory Discrimination' in India," 377.

55. Cited in Kahl and Gilbert, *The American Class Structure* (1987), 42.

56. Paul Fussell, *Class*, 9. Civil service occupations range from grade 1 (messenger) to 2 (mail clerk), 5 (secretary), 9 (chemist), and 14 (legal administrator).

57. There are ten major occupational groupings under Census Bureau guidelines. See Blau and Duncan, *The American Occupational Structure*, 23.

58. See Kahl and Gilbert, *The American Class Structure* (1987), 67–69.

59. Rose, *Social Stratification*, 19. Rose states that the categories are "managers, professional and technical, administrative support and sales, skilled blue-collar, less skilled blue-collar, service, and farmers/farm laborers. Implicitly, the structure of this list reflects ideas of status. Various experts have examined the nature of various types of work and have conducted surveys on public attitudes toward different jobs. By looking at salary levels, whether the work is primarily manual or mental, how much control one has over one's work situation, and how much opportunity there is for advancement, each occupation is ranked according to its desirability."

The Fair Labor Standards Act also makes a distinction between professional and non-professional positions with respect to the requirement of paying overtime; see Toni Lacy, "Judge Rules for the *Post* on Overtime," *Washington Post*, January 4, 1995, D3. In addition, various court decisions carefully define who is a "supervisor"; see Frank Swoboda, "Ruling Could Narrow Labor Protections: High Court, in Nurses' Case, Expands 'Supervisory' Roles," *Washington Post*, May 24, 1994, D1.

60. Laird interview (1995).

61. Robert D. Reischauer, "The Welfare Reform Legislation: Directions for the Future," in Cottingham and Ellwood, *Welfare Policies for the 1990s*, 14.

62. Williams, "It's a White Thing"; D'Souza, *Illiberal Education*, 252. While wealth by itself is not a good indicator—in 1983 the financial assets of more than half of all families was zero or negative—to ignore it altogether would be wrong; George Will, "What Dukakis Should Be Saying," *Washington Post*, September 15, 1988, A25.

63. Holly Holland, "Schools Worried by Clusters of Poverty," *Louisville Courier Journal*, December 11, 1993, A16.

64. Cited in Taylor, "The Continuing Struggle," 1702.

65. Marshall Smith and Jennifer O'Day, cited in Taylor, "The Continuing Struggle," 1704.

66. See Owen, *None of the Above*, 267–68.

67. D'Souza, *Illiberal Education*, 251–52.

68. See Lubman, "Campuses Mull Admissions Without Affirmative Action," B1.

69. William Julius Wilson is especially noted for this hypothesis; see, e.g., "Another Look at the Truly Disadvantaged," 642, on the effects of social isolation. See also Paul E. Peterson, "The Urban Underclass and the Poverty Paradox," in Jencks and Peterson, *The Urban Underclass*, 20 (citing Jonathan Crane and Susan Mayer's separate studies); and Crane, "Effects of Neighborhood," in ibid., 317.

70. In 1980, according to Mickey Kaus, there were 31 million poor, of which only 1.8 million lived in census tracts with 40 percent or more residents in poverty; *The End of Equality*, 105–6.

71. In addition, participants in the so-called Gautreaux program are more likely to attend a four-year college (27 percent versus 4 percent) and, if not in college, are more likely to be employed full-time (75 percent versus 41 percent); see "From Ghetto to Suburb," *The Economist*, October 7, 1995, 33; see also Douglas J. Besharov, "IQ and Getting Smart," *Washington Post*, October 23, 1994, C4.

72. See, e.g., Mayer and Jencks, "Growing Up in Poor Neighborhoods," arguing that the impact may not be as large as Wilson and others believe.

73. See Wilson, "Another Look at the Truly Disadvantaged," 651, citing four studies that support the negative effects of concentrated poverty.

74. Corcoran, et al. used this methodology for zip codes; see "The Association Between Men's Economic Status. . . ." One widely used definition of underclass census tracts looks at such factors as the "proportion of high school dropouts; young males outside the labor force; welfare recipients; and female-headed households"; see Erol R. Ricketts and Isabel V. Sawhill, "Defining and Measuring the Underclass," *Journal of Policy Analysis and Management* 7 (1988): 321–22.

75. See Lubman, "UC Vote to Ban Race Criteria Has Shades of Gray," A6.

76. See Marc Bendick, Jr., testimony before Senate Small Business Committee, October 19, 1995 (describing S. 1184, Urban Regulatory Relief Act of 1995).

77. Census Bureau statistic, cited in Murray and Herrnstein, *The Bell Curve*, 137. For families headed by single women, the poverty rate in 1991 was 36 percent, compared with 6 percent for all other American families.

78. Moynihan, *The Negro Family*, 36–37. This section of the report dealt specifically with black children; see also Moynihan, *America*, 281.

79. See Sara McLanahan and Gary Sandefur, *Growing up with a Single Parent: What Hurts, What Helps* (Cambridge, Mass.: Harvard University Press, 1994), 1–2.

80. See Dan Balz, "Quayle Revisits Old Themes in Speech about U.S. Values," *Washington Post*, September 9, 1994, A4 (citing Shalala's testimony before Congress). See also Barbara Dafoe Whitehead, "Dan Quayle Was Right," *Atlantic* (April 1993): 47ff.

81. See E. J. Dionne, Jr., "Bill and Dan and Murphy Brown," *Washington Post*, September 13, 1994, A21.

82. See Douglas J. Besharov, "Broken Family Values," *Washington Post Book World* (January 18, 1995): 4; and Ellwood, *Poor Support*, 45–46. Seven in ten children live in some arrangement that includes two parents, married or unmarried, biological or nonbiological; see Barbara Vobejda, "Study Alters Image of 'Typical' Family: Half of U.S. Children Live in Nontraditional Settings, Census Bureau Says," *Washington Post*, August 30, 1994, A3.

83. See Valerie Strauss, "Maret School Gets Lesson in Modern Times," *Washington Post*, October 24, 1994, D5.

84. "More Children Being Born to Unwed Parents, Study Says," *Washington Post*, July 20, 1994, A3.

85. D'Souza interview (1994); Kinsley, "The Spoils of Victimhood," 66.

86. High school graduates earn 59 percent of the income of four-year college gradu-ates; Larew, "Why Are Droves . . . ," 12; see also Thernstrom on the correlation between occupation, income, education, and neighborhood: "To know that John Jones is a banker, a bartender, or a bootblack is to know a good deal about him. It not only tells us what he does to earn a living, but enables us, with varying degrees of accuracy, to make inferences about how good a living he earns, how much education he had before leaving school, what kind of dwelling and what kind of neighborhood he lives in"; *The Other Bostonians*, 46. See also Rossides, *Social Stratification*, 405.

87. An analysis of pro- and anti-Bakke editorials found that those supporting Bakke talked about his specific case, while those supporting the Davis program spoke at the macro level; Susan D. Clayton And Sandra S. Tangri, "The Justice of Affirmative Action," in Blanchard and Crosby, *Affirmative Action in Perspective*, 186. New Jersey Gov. Jim Florio told Peter Brown that he would not discuss specific applications of affir-mative action. "I'm inclined to not want to deal with it on a micro-level because it's a trap"; quoted in Brown, *Minority Party*, 148. It is indeed much easier to argue in the abstract for "more black law professors at Harvard law school" than to say Jack Green-berg should not teach civil rights because he is white.

88. See, e.g., Holmes, "Mulling," an article on class-based affirmative action that ends with the thought, "Programs based on race or sex could have one big advantage—simplicity" (sect. 4, p. 3).

89. The principle for most governmental programs, the Citizens' Commission on Civil Rights explains, is that blacks, Hispanics, Asians, and Native Americans "have been subjected to *official, governmentally-sanctioned* discrimination"; *Affirmative Action*, 159. However, the Arab American Institute argues that Arab Americans should be taken out of the white box and included as beneficiaries; Lawrence Wright, "One Drop of Blood," *New Yorker* (July 25, 1994): 47. Italian Americans receive a preference at the City University of New York for faculty hiring; see Hacker, *Two Nations*, 135. In 1976 a HUD regional office announced plans to make Polish Americans beneficiaries of its affir-mative action employment program; Glazer, Ethnic Dilemmas, 349. In 1988 legislation was introduced in the Louisiana House of Representatives to extend minority status to Cajuns—a move strongly opposed by blacks; see Associated Press, "Cajuns Ask Minority Status," *New York Times*, May 23, 1988, A14.

90. Sowell, *Race and Culture*, 144.

91. Glazer, *Affirmative Discrimination*, 198.

92. Richard Cohen, "Suddenly Hispanic," *Washington Post*, December 11, 1990, A23. In 1979 an agency of the D.C. government, recognizing these intricacies, proposed eliminating minority status (and minority contracting preferences) for Hispanics born in Europe and South and Central America—reserving special status for Mexican Americans and Puerto Rican Americans only; see Vernon C. Thompson, "City Minority Contract Restrictions Considered," *Washington Post*, May 22, 1979, A1. In San Francisco, Mex-ican American firefighters challenged the promotion of a Spanish firefighter, recom-mending that a panel of twelve Hispanics determine who qualified and who did not; see Chavez, *Out of the Barrio*, 170. Berkeley has removed Spaniards from its list of those who qualify as Hispanic, and Williams College stopped counting Spaniards as Hispanic after students protested; see D'Souza, *Illiberal Education*, 55, 170, and 270–71, n121. Carnegie-Mellon University gives a preference for Latin Americans but not Spaniards; see Ramos, "Losers," 24. When José Cabranes was considered for the Supreme Court, Clinton found out that adding a Puerto Rican would not carry much weight with Mexican Ameri-cans; see Ruth Marcus, "Ideal Supreme Court Candidate May Exist Only in Clinton's Mind," *Washington Post*, April 19, 1994, A7. And when the Commission on Civil Rights suggested that the District hire more Hispanic police officers to make social peace, it over-looked the fact that when Puerto Rican Officer Craig Melendez was accused of beating the Salvadoran Carlos Sanchez, the long-standing antipathy between Puerto Ricans and Sal-vadorans was reignited; see Pamela Constable, "Scapegoat or Villain? Arrest, Beating of Salvadoran Costs Latino Officer His Job," *Washington Post*, October 21, 1994, D1.

93. The Lowell Magnet School in San Francisco entered into a consent decree that includes nine racial and ethnic groups, including four Asian subcategories: Chinese, Japanese, Korean, and Filipino; see Siskind, "San Francisco's Separate and Unequal Public Schools," A15. Berkeley divides Asians into Filipino and non-Filipino Asians; see, e.g., Chang-Lin Tien, "Diversity and Excellence for Higher Education," in Mills, *Debating Affirmative Action*, 245. In 1975 the director of the Office of Federal Contract Compliance Program said that Asian Americans include those "whose appearance reveals oriental, Polynesian origin," but not those of "Indo-European descent, e.g. Pakistan and East Indian as well as Malayans, Thais"—all of whom are to be regarded as "white"; OFCCP Director Phil J. Davis, memorandum, February 18, 1975, cited in Glazer, *Ethnic Dilemmas*, 199. Glazer says the memorandum has been superseded. In 1982 the Reagan administration added Asian Indians to the Small Business Administration's sect. 8(a) set-aside program. Ironically, the Reagan administration, which strongly opposed racial preferences, took credit for adding Asian Indians to the list of beneficiaries (10). See also Felicity Barringer, "Ethnic Pride Confounds the Census," *New York Times*, May 9, 1993, sect. 4, p. 3.

94. Reginald Wilson of the American Council on Education says that West Indians and Caribbeans should not count; D'Souza, *Illiberal Education*, 170.

95. As Stephan Thernstrom notes, there are 106 ethnic groups in the American labor force; cited in William Raspberry, "Critics of Diversity," *Washington Post*, December 23, 1992, A17.

96. As noted previously, most recent immigrants to the United States are people of color who can instantly benefit from racial preference programs designed to remedy past discrimination. In 1979 the D.C. Minority Business Opportunity Commission proposed eliminating minority status for persons born in Vietnam, India, Korea, and Africa; Thompson, "City Minority Contract Restrictions," A1.

97. Writes Prof. Deborah Ramirez: "Uniform remedies for all people of color threaten to dilute benefits historically intended for black Americans: affirmative action programs may fill their ranks with Asians and Latinos, leaving blacks once again out in the cold"; "Multicultural Empowerment," 967–68.

Likewise, critics of affirmative action have suggested that, to be fair, programs should calibrate not only the degree to which each minority group suffered but the degree to which each white group benefited. As Justice Scalia notes, the ethnic white immigrant of the twentieth century "not only took no part in, and derived no profit from, the major historic suppression of the currently acknowledged minority groups, but were in fact themselves the object of discrimination by the dominant Anglo-Saxon majority." To be fair, Scalia sarcastically proposed the Restorative Justice Handicapping System (RJHS), with the Aryans (northern Europeans) paying the most and, within that category, the English paying more than the Germans, who in turn pay more than the Irish; "Commentary: The Disease as Cure," 152–53.

On one level, a policy of proportional representation should address the question of calibrating preferences, but as we have seen, since there is no precise link between discrimination and representation, an actual calibration of benefits is more equitable.

98. Critics note that sometimes it is difficult to tell by sight whether a person is black or white. When Vanessa Williams was crowned the first black Miss America in 1984, many viewers thought she was white; Davis, *Who Is Black?*, 2. Adam Clayton Powell, Jr., the black congressman from New York, says in his autobiography that his freshman roommate at Colgate did not know he was black until his father came to campus, at which time the roommate declared an end to their friendship (2). In 1984 in Stockton, California, Ralph White, a black businessman, accused a competing candidate for the city election, Mark Stebbins, of saying he was a black candidate when in fact he was white; see Gotanda, " 'Our Constitution Is Colorblind,' " 24. The very notion of "passing"—or today, "reverse passing"—would not be possible if race were not, on the margins, mutable; see Harris, "Whiteness as Property," 1712, n6.

99. Both studies cited in Wright, "One Drop of Blood," 53. Furthermore, critics point out, in the close cases, if pushed to its ultimate logic, we have to return to identi-

fying people by genetic origin—as in Nazi Germany, South Africa, or the American South; *Fullilove v. Klutznick*, 534–35 (Stevens dissenting) (citing Nazi guidelines defining Jews); *Metro Broadcasting v. FCC*, 633, n1 (Kennedy) (citing South African Regulations); and *UC v. Bakke*, 297, n37 (Powell) (citing *Plessy*, 549, 552). Critics point to the absurdity of our historical rules of racial identification: from North Carolina's rule that "any visible admixture of black blood" makes one black to Ohio's use of a "preponderance of blood" measure, to the requirement in Michigan and Virginia that three-quarters white blood was necessary to qualify as white; all cited in *Plessy*, 552. As Yehudi Webster points out, "One's race could be changed by crossing state lines"; *The Racialization of America*, 34.

Louisiana employed the "one drop" rule until 1970, when it changed the law in response to a lawsuit brought on behalf of a child said to be 1/256th black; Davis, *Who Is Black?*, 9. Then in the early 1980s, when one Susie Phipps, the great-great-great-great-granddaughter of a mixed union, sued to declare herself white, the Louisiana courts held that, although she was less than 10 percent (3/32) black and had never held herself out to be black, she was by law black (10). The Supreme Court declined to disturb the ruling, "for want of a substantial federal question"; 107 SCt 638 (1986), cited in Davis, *Who Is Black?*, 11; see also Ramirez, "Multicultural Empowerment," 964–65, n36. Interestingly, one of the early affirmative action programs, employed by the University of Washington Law School in the program contested by Marcus DeFunis, appeared to use a sort of blood quantum test—whether the applicant had a "dominant" ethnic origin of black, Chicano, American Indian, or Filipino; *DeFunis v. Odegaard*, 320.

100. Leo Grebler, Joan W. Moore, and Ralph C. Guzman, "Mexican Americans and the U.S. Census," in Yin, *Race, Creed, Color, or National Origin*, 192. In 1990 Lawrence Giovacchini, whose mother was Hispanic and father was Italian, changed his designation from Italian to Hispanic and was promoted to captain in the San Francisco Fire Department; see Cohen, "Suddenly Hispanic." When Hispanics are not Spanish-surnamed, lengthy investigations may be required. In 1981 the FCC had to trace back to 1492 the origins of a non-Spanish-surnamed applicant seeking a minority tax credit; see *Storer Broadcasting Co.*, 89 FCC 2d 1980 (1981), cited in *Metro Broadcasting v. FCC*, 633, n1.

101. Since race is itself a scientifically questionable construct, self-identification is usually the appropriate measure. This is the preferred method outlined by the Office of Management and Budget (OMB) in its 1980 statistical directive no. 15; Ramirez, "Multicultural Empowerment," 965. But in the rare cases when ethnicity or race is questioned, further evidence must be evaluated. When the Boston firefighters Philip and Paul Malone switched their racial designations from white to black after failing to meet the white cutoff for a promotion exam, the city of Boston resolved the matter by turning to state and federal authorities for guidance. The state of Massachusetts employed a three-part test: (1) "Visual identification"; (2) "Documentary evidence—birth or marriage certificate, military record"; and (3) "Evidence that individuals hold themselves out to be black in the community"; see Steven Marantz and Peggy Hernandez, "Defining Race a Sensitive Elusive Task," *Boston Globe*, October 23, 1988, 33. Boston used the first two parts of the test.

102. In a literal sense, mixed *births* are, of course, nothing new in this country. Today between 75 percent and 90 percent of "blacks" are of mixed racial heritage; Wright, "One Drop of Blood," 47. Between 21 percent and 31 percent of the genes of black people are white; Davis, *Who Is Black?*, 21. To the extent that mixed births resulted from white men raping black women or forcing them to be concubines, the offspring received no financial benefit from being part white, and to the extent that white society treated the offspring as "black," the compensatory argument for treating today's mixed-heritage blacks the same as "full-blooded" blacks is just as strong; see Wright, "One Drop of Blood," 48.

But the compensatory case for preferences for the legitimate offspring of interracial marriages, a fairly recent phenomenon, becomes muddled. When affirmative action was first proposed, this was not much of an issue. Thirty of forty-eight states prohibited interracial marriage as late as World War II, and in 1967 miscegenation was still illegal in several states; see *Loving v. Virginia*, and Lind, *The Next American Nation*, 95. But according to the Census Bureau, the number of black-white marriages increased 378 percent between 1970 to 1992 (from 65,000 to 246,000); Lise Funderburg, *Black, White, Other*, 26. Between 1980 and 1992, the number of interracial marriages rose from 651,000 to 1.2 million, according to Census Bureau statistics; see Gabrielle Sandor, "The 'Other' Americans," *American Demographics* (June 1994): 36ff; and Hanna Rosin, "Boxed In," *New Republic* (January 3, 1994): 12. In the 1980s, outside the South, 10 percent of black men and 5 percent of black women had white spouses; Wright, "One Drop of Blood," 49. According to the National Center for Health Statistics (NCHS), the number of births involving one black and one white parent increased 596 percent between 1968 and 1991. The NCHS says its figures probably underestimate the true numbers since the race of the father is often unspecified; NCHS statistics cited in Funderburg, *Black, White, Other*, 11–12.

Other groups receiving racial preferences have even higher intermarriage rates than blacks: 70 percent of American Indians, 38 percent of Japanese American women, and 18 percent of Japanese American males intermarry; Wright, "One Drop of Blood," 49. For native-born Asians, the intermarriage rate is 50 percent, and for Hispanics it is 30 percent; Irving Kristol, "The Tragic Error of Affirmative Action," *Wall Street Journal*, August 1, 1994, A14. Overall, the percentage of children born to parents of different races increased from 1 percent of all births in 1968 to 3 percent in 1990, according to the NCHS; see Sandor, "The 'Other' Americans," 36ff. While the percentages are small, this translates into some one million children of mixed-race marriages; Rosin, "Boxed In," 12.

103. Diversity was supposed to solve all this by shifting the focus to viewpoint, not compensation. But again, if universities are genuinely seeking diversity of viewpoints and not just using diversity as a cover for equality of group results, they clearly should make sure the minority applicant has the "minority viewpoint" being sought. And in theory, we need some assurance from the applicant that she will in fact interact with students of different backgrounds, lest the cosmetic diversity of the freshman yearbook be lost to the reality of ethnic theme houses.

104. *DeFunis v. Odegaard*, 341 (Douglas dissenting).

105. Liacouras, "Toward a Fair and Simple Policy," 162.

106. Ellwood, *Poor Support*, 82.

107. Karabel, *Freshman Admissions at Berkeley*, 45.

108. Laird interview (1995).

109. Nairn and Associates, *The Reign of ETS*, 200.

110. See DeLone, *Small Futures*, 210.

111. Theda Skocpol, "Targeting Within Universalism," in Jencks and Peterson, *The Urban Underclass*, 414. Paul Starr notes that measures "for minority groups or the poor alone" tend to be poorly funded; "Civil Reconstruction," 8.

112. Robert Greenstein, "Universal and Targeted Approaches to Relieving Poverty," in Jencks and Peterson, *The Urban Underclass*, 438.

113. In academic parlance, the measure is known as the "Fuchs" criterion, named for its author, Victor Fuchs; Rawls, *A Theory of Justice*, 98. See also Bell, *Post Industrial Society*, 446, citing Victor Fuchs, "Redefining Poverty," *The Public Interest*, no. 8 (Summer 1967).

114. Okun, *Equality and Efficiency*, 95.

115. Jencks, *Inequality*, 4–5. This is true even though mean income doubled over thirty years. Indeed, when drawing up the federal poverty line, Jencks says the Johnson administration deliberately set the poverty line lower than one-half the average income so that "even conservatives would admit that those below the line were poor" (4–5).

116. Adjustments are made for smaller and larger families; see U.S. Housing Act of 1937 (as amended), 42 USC sect. 1437a(b)(2); and *Federal Register*, June 30, 1994, 33882.

117. See Barbara Vobejda, "U.S. Reports Decline in Number of Poor," *Washington Post*, October 6, 1995, A1, A10.

118. Geoghegan, *Which Side Are You On?*, 212.

119. See Thurow, *The Zero Sum Society*, 110.

120. Hughes, *Culture of Complaint*, 103; and Hal Crawther, "In a Dying Culture, Thank God for Snobs," *Washington Post*, August 27, 1995, G1, G7.

121. Bluestone, "The Inequality Express," 83–84.

122. See IRS, "1995 1040," 5; James Bovard, "Clinton's Biggest Welfare Fraud," *Wall Street Journal*, April 10, 1994, A18; and Michael Kinsley, "Let Them Eat Laptops," *New Yorker* (January 23, 1995): 7. In the 1994 tax year, the figure was $25,296. The 1996 level is slated to be $28,524; see Steven Pearlstein and Edward Walsh, "Tax Credit for Poor Comes under Attack," *Washington Post*, July 30, 1995, A1, A8.

123. See David Rogers, "Senate Moderates Move to the Right, Scaling Back Compromise Health Plan," *Wall Street Journal*, August 19, 1994, A12.

124. The poverty line in 1994 for a family of four was $15,141; see Vobejda, "U.S. Reports Decline in Number of Poor," A1.

125. In the racial context, Richard Kluger notes that the passage of federal funding for schools through the Elementary and Secondary Education Act of 1965 provided "the government with a mighty financial club to enforce compliance with the desegregation orders of federal courts"; *Simple Justice*, 958–59.

126. Title VI is the mechanism through which institutions like Harvard and UCLA had to open up their admissions processes to federal investigators looking at the question of discrimination against Asian Americans. And in *Bakke*, four members of the Court said Title VI also forbade racial discrimination against whites; a majority said Title VI prohibited quotas.

127. See Goldman, *Justice and Reverse Discrimination*, 204.

128. *UC v. Bakke*, 322.

129. Schwartz, *Behind Bakke*, 155.

130. Cookson and Persell, cited in Kingston and Lewis, *High Status Track*, xii, 33.

131. Karabel and Karen, "Go to Harvard," 23.

132. Klitgaard, *Choosing Elites*, 28.

133. At Williams being disadvantaged boosted chances 18 percent, being a minority boosted chances 53 percent, and being an alumni child boosted chances 36 percent. At Colgate the numbers were 6 percent for disadvantage, 46 percent for minority status, and 31 percent for alumni status. At Bucknell being disadvantaged decreased an applicant's chance of acceptance by 1 percent, being a minority boosted chances 51 percent, and being a legacy boosted chances 47 percent; ibid., 46.

134. Franklin, *Shadows of Race and Class*, 64. See also Mikulak, "Classism and Equal Opportunity," 118–19.

135. James C. Hearn, "Pathways to Attendance at the Elite Colleges," in Kingston and Lewis, *High Status Track*, 130.

136. Kingston and Lewis, *High Status Track*, 11.

137. As James Fallows points out, after World War II educators at elite universities were horrified at the idea of accepting masses of students under the GI Bill, but the 2.3 million veterans "turned out to be phenomenally successful"; *More Like Us*, 158–59.

138. See Albert B. Crenshaw, "The New College Criteria: Savings Rank with SATs," *Washington Post*, June 26, 1994, H1, H4.

139. Many believe that figure is too high; ibid.

140. For evidence of the degree to which colleges aspire to high median SAT scores, see Steve Stecklow, "Colleges Inflate SATs and Graduation Rates in Popular Guidebooks," *Wall Street Journal*, April 5, 1995, A1.

141. Although executive order 11246 and revised order 4 do not explicitly require preferential hiring, they do in practice. The government requires federal contractors to set goals and timetables for hiring "underutilized" minorities, and contractors must make "good faith efforts" to meet the goals. The Citizens' Commission on Civil Rights, a group that strongly endorses affirmative action, notes that, in implementing the order, if "the white candidates are significantly better qualified than the minority candidates, an employer may fail to meet its goal with impunity"; *Affirmative Action*, 68. In other words, "good faith efforts" do require preferences, just not "significant" preferences.

Indeed, in upholding the legality of the Philadelphia Plan, the Third Circuit Court of Appeals specifically noted that Title VII's prohibition against preferences (sect. 703[j]) to achieve a balanced workforce did not apply to the executive order; 442 F2d, 172. See also Steinberg, *Turning Back*, 165–66.

The difference, then, between what is required under Title VII and EO 11246 is subtle, but very important. Both look at results, and both allow an escape hatch if the numbers do not work out right. But Title VII's escape hatch is larger: so long as the employer's hiring is justified by business necessity, no preferences are required. Under EO 11246, the "good faith" exception in effect requires preferences, just not "significant" ones. This distinction parallels President Clinton's distinction between preferences for the unqualified (bad) and preferences for the less qualified (good).

142. See Peter Brimelow and Leslie Spencer, "When Quotas Replace Merit, Everybody Suffers," *Forbes*, February 15, 1993, 82. See also Edsall and Edsall, *Chain Reaction*, 188.

143. While those failing to meet goals could continue doing business with the federal government, if they made good faith efforts, those efforts would be judged with reference to the availability of qualified applicants, not the most qualified applicants.

144. The form of such incentives has been thoroughly debated; see Guy Gugliotta, "Subsidy for Hiring Poor under Review," *Washington Post*, November 28, 1993, A6; and Frank Swoboda, "Reich Targets Several Job Programs," *Washington Post*, January 28, 1994, A1 (a report on Labor Secretary Robert Reich targeting for extinction tax credits for employers who hire disadvantaged workers).

145. See Brimelow and Spencer, "When Quotas Replace Merit," 82.

146. *Griggs* is still necessary to combat ongoing racial and gender discrimination. By contrast, a *Griggs*-style disparate impact cause of action for hiring procedures that negatively impact the poor does *not* make sense. The point of implementing class preferences is not so much to overcome prejudice against poor people—as though they were being screened out even though they are just as qualified. The point is to give the poor an extra chance—a preference—because they may have a lot to offer in the long run.

147. See Munro, "The Continuing Evolution," 602, 610.

148. *DeFunis v. Odegaard*, 331.

149. See Linn, "Ability Testing," in NAS, *Ability Testing II*, 378. It is notable, however, that Linn does not make the claim that the scores of the poor are overpredictive, as he does say about the scores of blacks. In general, the issue of class receives much less attention than the issue of race. Linn cites a study involving the prediction of the ACT for GPA at nineteen colleges and finds that "a combined equation did not consistently over- or underpredict the mean GPA of either income group" (378).

150. Quoted in Klitgaard, *Choosing Elites*, 59. Rosovsky advocated a trial period to "give students from lower-status backgrounds a greater opportunity to demonstrate their talents."

151. An astounding number of highly talented students do not attend college at all. Arthur Okun notes: "Among high school graduates with equal academic ability, the proportion going on to college averages nearly 25 percentage points lower for males (and nearly 35 for females) in the bottom socioeconomic quarter of the population than in the top quarter"; *Equality and Efficiency*, 81.

152. William Raspberry, "High Expectations at Georgia Tech," *Washington Post*, July 1, 1994, A25.

153. Espinoza, "Empowerment and Achievement," 294. On the success of CLEO, see also Simien, "The Law School Admission Test," 383–84; and Nairn and Associates, *The Reign of ETS*, 113. Whether applied to class-based or race-based affirmative action, CLEO programs make sense as a way of increasing chances of success and reducing stigma.

154. Espinoza cites four schools with this policy; "Empowerment and Achievement," 285.

155. Ibid., 284.

156. Pondrom, "The Carrot and the Stick," 83–84.

157. Lemann, *The Promised Land*, 219.

158. This arrangement would not be meaningless for opponents of affirmative action, since preferences based on diversity have no end in sight. Likewise, to ensure that the trade is a good one, proponents of racial affirmative action might negotiate for a legislative hammer: if a shortfall in funding of class-based affirmative action occurs, universities and employers would be able to go back to race-based decision-making. This would help to reassure proponents of affirmative action that the deal is a real one, not an unfunded shell, and that the programs would in fact be funded lest the appropriators incur the wrath of voters who do not want to see a return to race-based preferences.

159. On the other hand, as Justice Douglas noted in *DeFunis v. Odegaard*, proven and egregious racial discrimination against an *individual*, influencing performance, might properly be considered a relevant disadvantage (341).

160. In addition, race would not be permitted as a bona fide occupational qualification except in very narrow circumstances, such as when an all-white police force hires a minority officer to do undercover work in a racially homogeneous gang.

161. Existing voluntary consent decrees negotiated under *Weber* would be reopened to see whether the new tougher standard is met. Drew Days has argued that, even in the absence of class-based affirmative action, the *Weber* standard is far too weak; employers and unions should be required to make "a showing of past discrimination"; "*Fullilove*," 462.

The same rule could apply to universities in the sixteen states that agreed to preferences under the *Adams* litigation; see *Adams v. Richardson*, 356 FSupp 92 (DDC), modified and aff'd, 156 US App DC 267, 480 F2d 1159 (DC Cir. 1973), dismissed sub nom. *Women's Equity Action League v. Cavazos*, 285 US App DC 48, 906 F2d 742 (DC Cir. 1990). Universities would no longer be permitted to simply incorporate the provisions of consent decrees adopted by other universities (as Duke has done with the University of North Carolina's consent decree) without their own findings of discrimination; see D'Souza, *Illiberal Education*, 158, 163.

162. When affirmative action is used to remedy a specific employer's past discrimination, Americans still oppose preferences 60–20 percent; see Starr, "Civil Reconstruction," 9; and Holmes, "Affirmative Action Plans," A20.

163. In those narrow cases, then, the effect of this policy in the short run would be one preference for race and one for class, so that wealthy whites would receive no preferences, wealthy minorities would receive one preference, poor whites would receive one preference, and poor minorities would receive a double preference.

164. See, e.g., Bell, *Race, Racism, and American Law*, 906, and Bell, "Race, Class, and the Contradictions of Affirmative Action," 281; *Franks v. Bowman*, 780–81 (Burger); Thomas, "Affirmative Action Goals and Timetables," 406; Citizens' Commission on Civil Rights, *Affirmative Action*, 155; Ansley, "Stirring the Ashes," 1023, 1055; and J. Hoult Verkerke, "Compensating Victims of Preferential Remedies," 1480.

165. This is precisely what District Court Judge Gerhard A. Gesell did in *McLeer v. AT&T* (416 FSupp 435 [1976]). Unfortunately, as Verkerke notes, "curiously, the use of the trial court's equitable powers to mitigate the effects of preferential relief on dispreferred has largely disappeared from the doctrinal landscape of employment discrimination law"; "Compensating Victims of Preferential Remedies," 1486.

Chapter 6

1. Michael K. Frisby, "President and Advisers Are Struggling to Find Position on Affirmative Action," *Wall Street Journal*, February 27, 1995, A14; see also Brown quoted in Brown, *Minority Party*, 147.

2. Jencks, *Rethinking Social Policy*, 61. See also Wilkins, "In Ivory Towers," 10; Tribe, *American Constitutional Law*, 1521; West, *Race Matters*, 64; Alexander Aleinikoff, quoted in D'Souza, *Illiberal Education*, 151; and Taylor and Liss, "Affirmative Action in the 1990s," 37.

3. White House, Office of the Press Secretary, *Remarks by the President on Affirmative Action*, July 19, 1995, 10.

4. This issue is nevertheless somewhat confusing: some vocal opponents of racial preferences *do* argue that racism has largely dissipated and it is time to move on; see, e.g., Taylor, *Paved with Good Intentions*, 29 ("Hunting for Racism"). That, emphatically, is not my argument.

5. Title VII does allow for preferences as a prophylactic against future discrimination in the narrow cases when an employer or union has been recalcitrant in obeying a court injunction to cease and desist from future discrimination. Even in these extremely rare and egregious cases of ongoing discrimination, the preferences must be temporary; see, e.g., *Sheet Metal Workers v. EEOC*, 478 US 421, 448–49 ("In most cases, the court need only order the employer or union to cease engaging in discriminatory practices, and award make-whole relief to the individuals victimized by those practices. In some instances, however . . . where an employer or union has engaged in particularly long-standing or egregious discrimination . . . requiring recalcitrant employers or unions to hire and to admit qualified minorities roughly in proportion to the number of qualified minorities in the work force may be the only effective way to ensure the full enjoyment of the rights protected by Title VII").

6. Taylor interview (1994).

7. There is a somewhat stronger argument for using preferences as a prophylactic against ongoing and future discrimination in the context of contracting set-asides, because antidiscriminatory laws largely exempt racial discrimination between two private firms; see Robert E. Suggs, "*Adarand* Ignores Unique Role of Contract Set-Asides," *Legal Times*, July 3, 1995, 26. But even in the contracting context, creative antidiscriminatory strategies should be the first weapon, not racial preferences.

8. According to the University of Chicago's National Opinion Research Center, 62 percent of whites polled in 1990 believed that African Americans are "lazier" than whites, and 53 percent said blacks are "less intelligent"; cited in Cose, *The Rage of a Privileged Class*, 118. The poll found similar views of Hispanics; Stephen Carter, "Foreword" to Guinier, *The Tyranny of the Majority*, xviii; see also Richard Morin, "Racism on the Left and Right," *Washington Post*, March 6, 1994, C5.

While most whites no longer tell pollsters that they oppose integrated schools, hotels, or restaurants, an amazing number still oppose integrated housing. According to Stephen Carter, fewer than 50 percent of white Americans favor fair housing laws; "Foreword" to Guinier, *The Tyranny of the Majority*, xviii. And we know that white parents are more likely to resist adopting a healthy black infant (74 percent will not) than an Asian, Chicano, or Native American infant (27 percent); Shulman and Darity, *The Question of Discrimination*, 304.

9. See Epstein, *Forbidden Grounds*, 9; and D'Souza, *The End of Racism*, 544.

10. See, e.g., the Urban Institute study cited in Steinberg, *Turning Back*, 151–52.

11. Wilson, *The Declining Significance of Race*, x–xi, 1.

12. De facto segregation of schools remains, a product of residential housing patterns that are often themselves the products of discrimination. But the message sent to children by de facto segregation is quite different from that sent by state-imposed segregation. And it is usually disadvantageous to go to a predominantly black high school today not because it is bad to go to school with other black children but because such schools are often underfunded and populated by large numbers of children from poor backgrounds. A class-based preference system would factor in this phenomenon.

13. Some state constitutions do make funding inequalities potentially unconstitutional, but as we saw in chapter 4, these rulings have often been fairly ineffective.

14. See *Larry P. v. Riles*, 793 F2d 969 (9th Cir. 1984) (applying a disparate impact analysis to tracking, requiring tests to be justified by a Title VI analogue to the Title VII business necessity defense).

15. Steele, *The Content of Our Character*, 120.

16. Starr, "Civil Reconstruction," 9.

17. Says Andrew Hacker, "No colleges today turn down black applicants who meet their academic criteria"; *Two Nations*, 135.

18. National Research Council, *A Common Destiny*, 370.

19. See Stephen Jay Gould, "Curveball," *New Yorker* (November 28, 1994): 145.

20. NAS, *Ability Testing II*, 77. The National Research Council found that the over-prediction for African Americans is 100 points on the SAT; see Linn, in ibid., 377. Another study found that subtracting 200 points on the old MCAT, 110 points on the old LSAT, and 240 points on the SAT would correct for the overprediction of African American scores; Klitgaard, *Choosing Elites*, 163–64. The overprediction for blacks applies not only to college and professional schools but to job performance as well, according to studies by the Civil Service Commission, the U.S. Air Force, the National Research Council, and AT&T (161–64).

21. Robert Linn, a key defender of ability testing, readily acknowledges that "tests are indeed culture dependent . . . a mean difference between groups on a test provides no basis for inferring that one group is inherently inferior to another"; NAS, *Ability Testing II*, 366.

22. Consider the criticism put forth by Catholic University's James Loewen. He says that whites would have difficulty with the following multiple-choice question (cited in Fallows, "The Tests and the 'Brightest,' " 46):

Saturday Ajax for an LD:
(a) He had smoked too much grass
(b) He tripped out on drugs
(c) He brought her to his apartment
(d) He showed it off to his fox
(d) He became wised up.

But as Dinesh D'Souza points out, this argument is flawed on two grounds: it stereotypes blacks (assuming "that blacks are most at home in the world of slang, womanizing, and drugs"), and it suggests—to the grave detriment of people of color—that academic success and success in life require no mastering of mainstream American culture; *Illiberal Education*, 45.

23. Bickel, *The Morality of Consent*, 132. Though grades are culture-bound, we do not generally hear the call for racial preferences in grading.

24. Sowell, *Race and Culture*, 179. How would one construct a culture-free test? Perhaps one would stick with math and cut out the questions about Faust and regattas. But there is an even greater disparity among blacks and whites on abstract tests than on the more overtly culture-bound ones; see Sowell, *Essays and Data*, 205. Tests designed to be completely culture-free, the National Academy of Sciences found, "have not proven to be as good predictors" and often have group differences of magnitudes similar to those of the culture-bound tests; *Ability Testing II*, 74.

25. In *Lau v. Nichols* 414 US 563 (1974), the Supreme Court made it clear that institutions receiving federal aid (such as universities) are subject to a *Griggs*-style effects test under Title VI of the Civil Rights Act: unjustified disparate impact can establish a violation even without a showing of discriminatory purpose. If the NAACP believes that a test is racially biased, then it may sue under the disparate impact theory. Such suits have been successfully waged in other contexts. Women prevailed against New York State's use of the SAT to award Regents and Empire State scholarships; see D'Souza, *Illiberal Education*, 45, and 267–68, n80. We have noted that tracking procedures with disparate racial impact were struck down in California; see *Larry P. v. Riles*, 343 Fsupp 1306 (1972). The Court ruled that the practice, which resulted in a disproportionate assignment of minorities to special education programs, violated the equal protection and due process clauses of the Constitution. In *Larry P. v. Riles* 495 FSupp 926 (*Larry P. II*) (1979), the Court applied the decision to the entire state of California. In 1984 the Ninth Circuit upheld the district court decision; see *Larry P. v. Riles*, 793 F2d 969 (9th Cir. 1984).

On the national level, the ACLU filed a complaint with the Clinton Education Department charging that the PSAT, on which National Merit scholarships are based, discriminates against women (women receive about 40 percent of the scholarships); see Associated Press, "Anti-Female Bias Alleged in Merit Scholarships: Qualifying Test Is Called Discriminatory," *Washington Post*, February 17, 1994, A11. And in Florida, opponents of standardized testing successfully challenged a statute withholding diplomas from those high school graduates who failed a basic literacy exam—a disproportionate percentage of whom were black; see *Debra P. v. Turlington*, cited in Barbara Lerner, "The War on Testing: David, Goliath, and Gallop," *The Public Interest* (Summer 1980): 119, 144.

The issue of the racial disparate impact of the SAT, LSAT, and the like has not been pushed by proponents of affirmative action, in part because some affirmative action supporters, such as members of the Council on Legal Education, feared that an in-depth study would show that standardized tests overpredict the potential of minorities; see White, "Culturally Biased Testing and Predictive Invalidity," 124–26. White himself discounts the notion of overprediction (127). Certainly, the schools that employed racial preferences in *DeFunis* and *Bakke* did not argue that racial preferences were a necessary correction for racial bias in entrance exams; see *UC v. Bakke*, 306, n43 ("Nothing in this record . . . suggests either that any of the quantitative factors considered by the Medical School were culturally biased or that petitioner's special admissions program was formulated to correct for any such bias"); and *DeFunis v. Odegaard*, 326 ("Although it may be speculated that the Committee sought to rectify what it perceived to be cultural or racial biases in the LSAT or in the candidates' undergraduate records, the record in this case is devoid of any evidence of such bias, and the school has not sought to justify its procedures on this basis").

Ironically, in the 1994 case of *Missouri v. Jenkins*, civil rights groups (and the Clinton administration) argued that racial disparity in scores on standardized tests was relevant evidence supporting the proposition that the Kansas City School District needed to do more to eradicate the past effects of segregation; see National Urban League et al., amicus brief, *Missouri v. Jenkins*, 115 SCt 2038 (1995), 14–17; see also Paul M. Barrett, "Clinton to Seek More Court Supervision of Formerly Segregated Public Schools," *Wall Street Journal*, November 25, 1994, B8. While achievement tests are different from aptitude tests, the cultural bias in the former should be even greater than in the latter. Likewise, supporters of Afrocentric education in the District of Columbia have cited a rise on standardized tests as evidence of the program's success; see Sari Horwitz, "Specialist Favors Expansion of District's Afrocentric Curriculum," *Washington Post*, September 22, 1994, A17. If tests were biased toward white middle-class values, presumably a strong dose of Afrocentric education would depress scores rather than raise them.

If we were to junk standardized tests altogether, would we get a better prediction? According to the National Academy of Sciences, the answer is no. Standardized tests, it concludes, predict more accurately than almost all alternatives. The one exception is "records of past performances in similar situations"; see NAS, *Ability Testing II*, 19. Interviews in particular are "notoriously lower in validity" (22–23).

26. See Bell, "*Bakke*, Minority Admissions, and the Usual Price of Racial Remedies," 8. Elizabeth Bartholet says it would be better to apply *Griggs* to professional positions and expose the hiring practices for their unmeritocratic nature than to keep the standards in place and employ "condescending" preferential treatment; "Applications of Title VII," 959.

27. Kluger, *Simple Justice*, 368; and Michael K. Frisby, "Black Family Is Divided on Affirmative Action as Father Backs It, Daughter Seeks Alternatives," *Wall Street Journal*, April 17, 1995, A14.

28. Cited in D'Souza, *The End of Racism*, 318.

29. *Griggs v. Duke Power*, 431.

30. See Uniform Guidelines on Employee Selection Procedures (1978) 29 CFR sect. 1607.4D (1989).

31. Fried, *Order and Law*, 122.

32. See, e.g., Koch, *Citizen Koch*, 164.

33. In *Griggs*, the Court noted, "discriminatory preference for any group, minority or majority, is precisely and only what Congress has proscribed" (431). An employer whose imbalance may be explained in neutral and justified terms is free of liability. For example, in *Spurlock v. United Airlines*, the Tenth Circuit upheld a requirement that airline pilots have college degrees, even though it conceded the rule had a disparate impact on black appli-

cants. (At the time of the case, only nine of United's fifty-nine hundred flight officers were black.) While the plaintiff established a prima facie case of racial discrimination in hiring, the court held that the college degree requirement was job-related, and that United met the "business necessity" test. Pilots must go through intensive training and refresher courses, the court explained, making a college degree an important element of a pilot's background; *Spurlock v. United Airlines, Inc.*, 457 F2d 216, 218–19 (10th Cir. 1972). Likewise, in *New York Transit Authority v. Beazer*, the Supreme Court upheld a requirement that the New York City Transit Authority could bar anyone using narcotics from its employ—including those on a methadone maintenance program—even though the rule had a disparate impact on minority applicants; *New York Transit Authority v. Beazer*, 440 US 568 (1979). In *Townsend v. Nassau County Medical Center*, the Second Circuit upheld the requirement of a B.S. degree to be a technician in a blood bank, though the practice had a disparate impact; *Townsend v. Nassau County Medical Center*, 558 F2d 117 (2d Cir. 1977), cert denied, 434 US 1015 (1978). And in *National Education Association v. South Carolina*, a district court upheld (and the Supreme Court affirmed) the use of the National Teachers Examination for hiring, though the test had a disparate impact; *United States v. South Carolina*, 445 FSupp 1094 (DSC 1977) aff'd mem. sub nom. *National Education Association v. South Carolina*, 434 US 1026 (1978).

34. *Congressional Record*, October 31, 1991, S15503. The five senators opposed were all conservative: Coats, Helms, Smith, Symms, and Wallop.

35. Barbara Vobejda, "Black-White Income Gap Widens over Two Decades," *Washington Post*, September 15, 1994, A14.

36. Asra Q. Nomani, "Clinton Proposes Plan to Seek Data on Women's Pay," *Wall Street Journal*, April 11, 1995, B6.

37. See Frank Swoboda, " 'Glass Ceiling' Firmly in Place, Panel Finds," *Washington Post*, March 16, 1995, A1. For a critique of the Glass Ceiling Commission report, see "Holes in the Glass Ceiling Theory," *Newsweek*, March 27, 1995, 24–25.

38. Sowell, *Civil Rights: Rhetoric or Reality?*, 72–79. According to Sowell, West Indians are represented in professional occupations at a slightly higher level than the average American, and at twice the rate of other blacks; *Civil Rights: Rhetoric or Reality?*, 77. Foreign-born blacks, most of whom are West Indian, constitute 10 percent of New York City's black population but own half the black businesses. The unemployment rate of foreign-born blacks is lower than the national average; Taylor, *Paved with Good Intentions*, 25.

39. The leading cultural explanation for income differences between ethnic groups is family structure. Between 1969 and 1992, median black family income as a percentage of white income actually fell from 61 percent to 54 percent. Few would blame this decline on a rise in discrimination; most attribute the widening gap instead to the breakdown of the black family; Vobejda, "Black-White Income Gap," A14. Indeed, the ratio of black/white income for two-parent families improved between 1969 and 1992, from 72 percent to 80 percent; ibid., A14; see also Cose, *The Rage of a Privileged Class*, 3. Second, we have seen that age of marriage and size of family can have a great impact on aggregate income, both because younger parents have a harder time completing their education and because large young families can depress the average age of an ethnic group, skewing income statistics downward. African Americans have a median age of twenty-eight, while the figure for American Jews is over forty; see D'Souza, *The End of Racism*, 301; and Sowell, *Civil Rights: Rhetoric or Reality?*, 42–43. Third, language and linguistic differences can have an enormous impact on income. Sowell notes that third-generation Mexican Americans make 20 percent more than first-generation Mexican Americans when controlling for age. Since the two groups are physically indistinguishable, it is clear that current racism is not the determining factor; ibid., 116. Finally, different cultures place different value on the pursuit of education, accounting for some of the income discrepancy among groups. The gap between median black and median white family income shrinks somewhat—though not completely—when controlling for education; Hacker, *Two Nations*, 95.

Some argue that these residual differences reflect in part differences in the quality of

292 • NOTES TO CHAPTER 6

education received. The conservative critic Jared Taylor argues that when controlling for the quality of education, "blacks earn *more* than the whites"; *Paved with Good Intentions*, 27; see also Sowell, *Preferential Policies*, 135. Meanwhile, liberals also argue that many predominantly black high schools are of lower quality and, at the college level, that historically black colleges have traditionally been underfunded. It is therefore not insignificant to note, as Kenneth Tollett does, that "until the early 1970s black colleges educated the overwhelming majority of blacks who received post-secondary education. Even today, while they barely enroll one-fifth of blacks attending post-secondary institutions, they graduate approximately 40 percent of blacks who receive baccalaureate degrees"; See Kenneth S. Tollett, "The Liberals' Loss of Nerve," *American Prospect* (Spring 1992): 126.

For overall pay differentials between men and women, the obvious cultural difference is that many women, unlike most men, take time off from their careers when they have children. In 1992 only 36.8 percent of married women with children under eighteen worked full-time all year round; see Martha M. Hamilton, "Women at Work: The Gap in Wages Is a Function of Ages," *Washington Post*, April 14, 1994, D11. Since most women are physically able to return to work almost immediately after childbirth, the central reason they stay home is cultural. That reason is different from discrimination; to say that the many highly intelligent women who choose to stay home with their children are victims of subtle discrimination is highly insulting to them. Indeed, some economists argue that controlling for education and experience, "women now earn essentially as much as men"; Herbert Stein, "White Male Rage Sweeps America," *Wall Street Journal*, February 9, 1995, A14; see also Hamilton, "Women at Work" (citing Census Bureau statistics that "young women now entering the work force make almost as much as their male counterparts"—some 92.5 cents for every dollar earned by a man in 1992); and Elisabeth Fox-Genovese, "For Women Only," *Washington Post*, March 26, 1995, C7 ("Entry-level, full-time women workers now make about 95 cents on the male dollar, up from 63 cents only a couple of decades ago").

40. First, consider the impact of past discrimination on the degree to which blacks are disproportionately affected by economic change. We know that when considering the total money income of year-round, full-time male workers, black earnings increased from 62 percent of white earnings in 1964 to 72 percent in 1975, but then fell again to 69 percent in 1987. Was this because discrimination grew between 1975 and 1987? That seems unlikely. Donahue and Heckman offer a better explanation: the improvement between 1964 and 1975 was due to the federal enforcement of antidiscrimination laws, but the decline since 1975 has been due to black workers being disproportionately affected by the general decline in unskilled wages since then; "Continuous Versus Episodic Change," 1604, 1607–8, 1641. This is also, broadly speaking, Wilson's thesis; see, e.g. "Another Look at the Truly Disadvantaged," 640. Wilson notes that the black/white unemployment ratio in 1980 was worse than it was in 1948, though few would argue that discrimination was greater; *The Truly Disadvantaged*, 30. Note that this explanation does not let discrimination off the hook altogether: a major reason blacks are concentrated in the low-skilled jobs and are more vulnerable to recession in the first place is the legacy of past discrimination. But an increase in present-day discrimination is not itself the cause of the decline in wages between 1975 and 1987 or the worsening unemployment ratio between 1948 and 1980.

The legacy of discrimination may impact current earnings in a second way: older workers, while subject to less discrimination today, still carry the wounds of past discrimination. When controlling for quantity of education, we know that in 1979 and 1980, the average weekly wage of black men with sixteen years of schooling and one to five years of experience was 92.3 percent of the wage earned by white men with comparable education and experience. But for black and white men with the same level of education (sixteen years) but thirty-one to forty years of experience, the percentage dropped to 64.5 percent; "Continuous versus Episodic Change," 1611. Presumably much of this difference stems from the fact that black men with forty years of experience finished college in 1939 and faced a great deal more discrimination than do today's black college graduates.

A statistic that averages these numbers (92 percent and 64 percent) would suggest that current discrimination is much worse than it in fact is; see Smith and Welch, "Black Economic Progress," 522, for the same phenomenon. Black male wages as a percentage of white male wages in 1980 were 72.6 percent (without controlling for education). For younger blacks (with one to five years' experience), the wage was 84.2 percent, while for those with thirty-six to forty years' experience it was 68.5 percent. Likewise, blacks earn dramatically less than whites in the same occupational categories, partly because past discrimination effectively barred blacks from certain occupations so that the blacks in those occupations today are younger and less senior and therefore not earning the same income as whites; Wilson, *The Declining Significance of Rage*, xi.

So, too, the Glass Ceiling Commission reported that only 5 percent of top managers at the Fortune 2000 industrial and service companies are women, a finding that surely reflects, in part, the fact that top corporate executives in 1995 were born mostly in the 1930s, long before civil rights protections were formally put in place (and three decades before *The Feminine Mystique*). The fruits of civil rights laws and changes in societal attitudes took time to filter up to the very top levels, though we are beginning to see evidence of it already. An update of one of the Glass Ceiling studies showed that women now hold 10 percent of top executive positions, up from 1.5 percent in the 1980s; Ellen Ladowsky, "That's No White Male . . . ," *Wall Street Journal*, March 27, 1995, A20.

When controlling for both the legacy of past discrimination (by looking at younger women) and cultural differences (by looking at women who do not take time out for child rearing), the economist June O'Neill of the General Accounting Office found that women age twenty-seven to thirty-three who do not take time off to rear children make 98 percent of what men make; Ladowsky, "That's No White Male . . ." A20. On the racial side, O'Neill found: "Overall, black men earned 82.9 percent of the white wage. Adjusting for black-white differences in geographic region, schooling and age raises the ratio to 87.7 percent; adding differences in [standardized] test scores to this list of characteristics raises the ratio to 95.5 percent, and adding differences in years of work experience raises the ratio to 99.1 percent"; cited in D'Souza, *The End of Racism*, 302. One need not fully accept O'Neill's conclusion to see that when additional factors are considered, the gap between black and white earnings shrinks considerably.

41. Where once the great mass of blacks were poor, today there is a large and solid black middle class, but also a large, festering underclass. Conservatives tend to emphasize the good news and liberals the bad news; both, paradoxically, are right. The financial profile has been "transformed from a pyramid to an hourglass"; Dreyfuss and Lawrence, *The Bakke Case*, 145–46. On the one hand, according to a 1986 Rand study, "the real story of the last forty years has been the emergence of the black middle class," whose growth has been "so spectacular that as a group it outnumbers the black poor"; Smith and Welch, *Closing the Gap*, ix. On the other hand, the National Research Council notes, "the increase in well-to-do families was matched by an increase in low-income families"; National Research Council, *A Common Destiny*, 23–25.

In the 1940s and 1950s, class divisions in the black community were much smaller than among whites; see, e.g., Richard B. Freeman, "Black Economic Progress after 1964," in Rosen, *Studies in Labor Markets*, 265. All blacks were held back; as a result, according to one study, discrimination accounted for 73 percent of the gap between black and white income; Otis Dudley Duncan, "Inheritance of Poverty or Inheritance of Race?," in Moynihan, *On Understanding Poverty*, 100. But in recent years, as racism has moderated and antidiscrimination efforts have been put into place, the black community has gone from being less to more stratified than the white community. In 1988 the ratio of income for whites in the top fifth to the lowest fifth was 8.6:1, but for blacks it was 13.8:1; Graham, *The Civil Rights Era*, 453–54; see also Wilson, "Race-Neutral Programs," 75. By 1991 the ratio for whites remained at 8.6:1, but for blacks it had grown to 14.9:1; National Urban League, *The State of Black America*, 161.

42. Wilson, *The Declining Significance of Race*, x. Likewise, the Harvard economist Richard Freeman argues that, whereas before 1964 race was the primary determinant of black success, by the late 1960s family background and socioeconomic status (partly a

legacy of discrimination) had become more important than contemporary discrimination; "Black Economic Progress after 1964," 248, in Rosen, *Studies in Labor Markets*. While Wilson was vehemently attacked for making this argument in *The Declining Significance of Race*, now even such left activists as Derrick Bell argue that the "race-related disadvantaged" are "now as likely to be a result as much of social class as of color"; *And We Are Not Saved*, 5. None of this argues that a remedy is unnecessary to combat the legacy of past discrimination, but it appears that the case for preferences based on *current* discrimination is very weak.

Of course, some black progress may be attributable to affirmative action programs themselves, so reforming such programs to be class- rather than race-based may result in some decline in the favorable numbers we have been reviewing. A vast literature on the effects of antidiscrimination laws (Title VII) and affirmative action (for federal contractors) tries to disentangle the separate effects of each. Freeman attributes the "marked improvement in the economic status of employed black workers"—and indeed, "the marked acceleration" after 1964—to Title VII of the Civil Rights Act of 1964. Title VII, Freeman writes, "contributed substantially and directly to improving the economic position of employed blacks at a given level of education"; quoted in U.S. Congress, *A Report of the Study Group*, 287. Likewise, Jonathan Leonard's 1985 study, "using data on more than 1,700 class-action suits under Title VII, presented evidence that litigation under Title VII played an important and independent role in advancing the employment of blacks and had a relatively greater impact than affirmative action"; see National Research Council, *A Common Destiny*, 318; see also Glazer, "The Affirmative Action Stalemate," 110.

Having said this, racial preferences do play some role in offsetting discrimination, so it is important that the trade of race for class preferences be accompanied by an increase in funding for antidiscriminatory enforcement agencies. In 1995 the Civil Rights Commission found that the number of federal employees enforcing civil rights laws had declined 19 percent between FY1981 and FY1994. Funding must be increased; see Associated Press, "Federal Commission Criticizes Slow Enforcement of Civil Rights," *Washington Post*, June 24, 1995, A5.

43. Even after controlling for cultural differences, the legacy of past discrimination, and the demonstrable success of the antidiscriminatory measures already on the books, there still appears to be a residue of ongoing discrimination that accounts for part of the income gap between blacks and whites, and between men and women. A widely cited 1991 Urban Institute Study, for example, found very different treatment of black and white job seekers; Urban Institute, "Testing for Discrimination in America," September 26, 1991, cited in Taylor and Liss, "Affirmative Action in the 1990s," 36. But before we resort to preferences, there are two steps that can be taken.

First, Congress and the executive branch should boost funding of agencies and departments responsible for enforcing existing statutes. In the 1980s the Citizens' Commission on Civil Rights reported that the major problem was not with the statutes; "the issue is vigorous enforcement of federal statutes and court decisions by the Executive Branch"; Citizens' Commission, *One Nation*, 24; see also Neas, "Interview," 378. Courts also should employ tougher sanctions against employers that discriminate. Clarence Thomas has suggested that if an employer defies a court injunction against further discrimination, it should be subject to "heavy fines and even jail sentences." Thomas adds, "I am not aware of any case where a court has resorted to such measures, and I must wonder why they are so reluctant"; Thomas, "Affirmative Action Goals and Timetables," 408–9.

Mary Becker of the University of Chicago has suggested providing for full compensatory and punitive damages for women in cases of intentional discrimination; "Needed in the Nineties." Under the Civil Rights Act of 1991, damages were capped for intentional discrimination against women.

Robert Belton of Vanderbilt has argued for outlawing the increasingly popular practice by which employers, as a condition of employment, require employees to give up their right to jury trials and submit all employment discrimination claims to an alternative dispute mechanism; "The Unfinished Agenda of the Civil Rights Act of 1991"; see also Steven A. Holmes, "Some Employees Lose Right to Sue for Bias at Work," *New York Times*, March 18, 1994, A1. The EEOC is also challenging the practice administratively.

Derrick Bell has argued for more vigorous use of "testers"—two individuals nearly identical except for race—to expose discrimination in employment; *Faces at the Bottom of the Well*, 48; see also Jonathan Leonard, testimony before the House Judiciary Subcommittee on the Constitution, October 25, 1995.

Overall, then, when conservatives say that the answer is not more affirmative action but better antidiscriminatory action (through enforcement or enhanced penalties), progressives should take them up on it. When Morris Abram says that if civil rights litigators were really concerned about stopping discrimination they would not seek quotas but would be "jailing and firing discriminators," proponents of civil rights should ask him to lobby on behalf of this reform; Abram, "Commentary: Affirmative Action," 1324, n47; see also Shelby Steele, "Affirmative Action Must Go," *New York Times*, March 1, 1995 (arguing that discrimination by race, gender, or ethnicity should be a criminal offense). Another possibility is ensuring that superiors who engage in blatant discrimination are held personally liable; see Frances A. McMorris, "Boss May Be Personally Liable If Firing Violates Disability Law," *Wall Street Journal*, May 2, 1995, B1.

44. It is important to remember that Wilson's thesis about the declining significance of race was limited to the economic realm, as distinguished from the social realm (e.g., social clubs, housing); *The Declining Significance of Race*, 2.

45. See, e.g., West, *Race Matters*, x.

46. See Ayres, "Fair Driving," 817, 828. Likewise, in 1991, the ABC newsmagazine *Primetime Live* sent two testers, one black and one white, out into the streets of St. Louis to see how much discrimination continues to exist. According to Ellis Cose, the black tester ran into discrimination every day during the two-and-a-half week test. Writes Cose: "The white tester, John, got instant service at an electronics counter; the black one, Glenn, was ignored. Glenn was tailed, not helped, by the salesman in a record store, while John was allowed to shop on his own. Passersby totally ignored Glenn when he was locked out of his car; John was showered with offers of help. In an automobile showroom, Glenn was quoted a price of $9,500 (with a 20 to 25 percent down payment) for the same red convertible offered to John for $9,000 (with a 10 to 20 percent down payment). In an apartment complex, John was given the keys to look around, while Glenn was told that the apartment was rented"; *The Rage of a Privileged Class*, 4. Cose also said the black tester was subject to employment discrimination, confirming the Urban Institute study cited above.

47. See, e.g., ibid., 39–40, citing studies by Queens College of City University of New York and the Urban Institute; National Research Council, *A Common Destiny*, 27, 144; and Massey and Denton, *American Apartheid*, 85–87. The studies confirm not only that racial segregation remains high but that it occurs at all income levels. They also note that segregation is lower for Hispanics and Asians than for African Americans.

48. While some argue that residential patterns reflect a benign form of self-segregation, polls suggest that 85 percent of blacks want to live in integrated neighborhoods; Hacker, *Two Nations*, 35. White flight is the major cause of segregation; it begins when a predominantly white neighborhood becomes just 8 percent black (36). In addition, a 1991 HUD study documents differential treatment by real estate agents of black and white house seekers; see Taylor and Liss, "Affirmative Action in the 1990s," 37.

49. In applications of the death penalty, studies indicate that defendants are much more likely to receive capital punishment (four times as likely in Georgia, for example) if the victim was white rather than black; see *McCleskey v. Kemp*, 481 US 279 (1987). Likewise, racially motivated police brutality, caught on videotape in the famous Rodney King case, was found by a 1991 independent commisssion chaired by Warren M. Christopher to be routine in Los Angeles and, indeed, a "national problem"; see Robert Reinhold, "Violence and Racism Are Routine in Los Angeles Police, Study Says," *New York Times*, July 10, 1991, A1.

50. Ayres, "Fair Driving," 857.

51. When Massey and Denton suggest concrete ways to decrease residential segregation, they do not argue for some sort of racial preference in the private housing market but suggest primarily (1) increased financial assistance to local fair housing organizations; (2) a permanent testing program; (3) a new staff to investigate lending discrimination; and (4) prompt judicial action in enforcing the Fair Housing Act; *American Apartheid*, 230–31.

52. Proponents of the Racial Justice Act argue instead for an analogue to the Title VII disparate impact case: if the numbers do not work out, there is reason to believe something is awry—a suspicion that the prosecution may rebut with race-neutral reasoning. For example, as George Will notes, part of the reason for a higher death penalty rate for white victims may be that 85 percent of murdered police officers are white; "Race, Death, and Democracy," *Washington Post*, May 19, 1994, A21. This would be a race-neutral reason for a disparity.

53. See White House, Office of the Press Secretary, *Remarks By the President on Affirmative Action*, July 19, 1995, 6.

54. Queens College Professor Andrew Hacker asks his white students how much "financial recompense" they would request if a hypothetical visitor told them they were to become black at midnight. White students often say $1 million a year for fifty years; *Two Nations*, 32. White liberals argue that such an answer proves that, despite affirmative action, whites concede that they still have the upper hand. This suggests to some that racial preferences are necessary as a counterweight to current discrimination—indeed, the students' response proves that racial preferences do not go far enough to even the score. Moreover, their response seems to support the idea that race is a greater impediment than class, because students believe it is worse to be black with $999,999 annual income than to be white with no income.

Hacker's game, however, does nothing of the sort. On one level, his question does not even prove that whites face more discrimination than blacks (though I think they do). Hacker says the reason for the $1 million annual payment is obvious. "Surely this needs no detailing. The money would be used as best it could to buy protection from discrimination and the dangers white people know they would face once they were perceived to be black"; *Two Nations*, 32. But is this so obvious? If Hacker wanted to check this, wouldn't he ask his black students the inverted question—what they would pay to become white? If he did, Hacker might very well find that, taking a proper pride in their heritage, black students would not want to be white and, indeed, would themselves have to *be* paid some amount to become white. And if they said $1 million a year would be adequate compensation, surely that would not "prove" that whites are discriminated against more than blacks.

Hacker does not ask the question of blacks, he told me after his July 5, 1993, speech at Chautauqua Institution, because "there are so few black students in my class and I don't want to embarrass them." This is a thoroughly bizarre response. Is it not embarrassing for black students to hear that their white classmates value not having black skin to the tune of $1 million a year? Is it not embarrassing that they are not even asked whether they would have to be paid to be white—that it is assumed that they would want to be?

55. In a less violent context, Thurgood Marshall told William O. Douglas, "You guys have been practicing discrimination for years. Now it's our turn"; Douglas, *The Court Years*, 149.

56. This issue is often confused. See, e.g., Pinkney, *The Myth of Black Progress*, 52 ("Class prejudice is also widespread, but in most cases racial prejudice is more penetrating"). If that is the framework, then proponents of affirmative action are surely right to say, as Dick Gephardt did, that "discrimination against people who are in poverty" is not at all comparable to that against women and minorities; see David S. Broder, "Gephardt Defends Affirmative Action," *Washington Post*, March 14, 1995, A6.

There are, however, interesting exceptions to this rule that illustrate how much racial progress we have made. Consider, for example, the parallel cases of Anita Hill and Paula Jones. It is generally agreed that the Hill allegations were taken much more seriously by the press than the Jones allegations. This might have been because Hill's case was stronger on the merits. (Each case is, of course, distinct.) Another theory is that the liberal press was more likely to believe a charge against the conservative Clarence Thomas than against the liberal Bill Clinton. But another theory emphasizes the class dynamic. In the first case, a professional black woman, a law professor and Yale Law graduate, made accusations of sexual harassment. In the second case, in the words of the Bush aide Mary Matalin, the accuser was "a woman who has big hair and only made $10,000 a year and has an accent"; quoted in Howard Kurtz, "The Plunge into Paulagate," *Washington Post*, May 14, 1994, D7. Whom did the press see as more credible? The upper-middle-class black or the poor white? Class prejudice triumphed over race.

57. In addition, as Christopher Jencks points out, class differences are greater in magnitude than race differences. "There is," Jencks writes, "always far more inequality between individuals than between groups. . . . It seems quite shocking, for example, that white workers earn 50 percent more than black workers. But we are even more disturbed by the fact that the best-paid fifth of all white workers earns 600 percent more than the worst-paid fifth"; *Inequality*, 14.

58. Edelman, *Guide My Feet*, 88.

59. Ralph Neas of the Leadership Conference on Civil Rights, for example, emphasizes, "Civil rights leaders have never said it was either [antidiscrimination law] or [economic opportunity]"; Neas, "Interview," 375–76. Neas told Ronald Brownstein that the class versus race debate sets up a false choice: "This is a multifront war. And they all have to be addressed"; "Beyond Quotas." In the context of preferences, civil rights groups have generally supported racial preferences only, but if class preferences were to be considered, says the Citizens' Commission on Civil Rights, those preferences "must be used as a supplement to, not a substitute for affirmative action"; *Affirmative Action*, 161. Anthony Lukas also argues for affirmative action based on both race and class; Anthony Lukas, interview with the author, New York, January 3, 1995.

60. See John F. Harris, "Clinton Wants Set-Asides to Boost Poor Areas," *Washington Post*, July 15, 1995, A1.

61. There is also a prudential concern. Practically speaking, "doing both" often translates into preferring almost exclusively by race. Many universities say they provide both class and race preferences, but in practice we have seen racial considerations dwarf preferences for the disadvantaged. Likewise, Elizabeth Bartholet argues against allowing race to be a factor in adoption because in practice, once you open the door, it becomes the predominant factor; see, e.g., *Drummond v. Fulton County Department of Family and Child Services*, 547 F2d 835, at 837 (5th Cir. 1977) (where race was just one factor but enough of a factor to keep white foster parents deemed "excellent," "loving," and "extremely competent" from adopting their black foster child).

62. See, e.g., Glazer interview (1995); Thernstrom, "A Class Backwards Idea," C1, C2 (warning against the possibility that "new [class-based] preferences will be piled on top of those we already have").

63. One poll asked whether "affirmative action should be broadened to include disadvantaged people of whatever race or gender." The response was fairly negative, and interestingly enough, nonwhites were more supportive of the idea (approximately half agreed) than whites (one-quarter agreed). This is probably true because majorities of whites believe that "affirmative action helps many who do not need help," and adding another category (poor) does not solve the problem of overinclusion the way a complete shift to class would; Taylor, *Affirmative Action at Work*, 145. Thomas Edsall believes that white working-class people will be "suspicious" of a class plus race preference system; interview with the author, January 23, 1995. The implications are important because, as Sniderman and Piazza note, hostility to race-based affirmative action influences the way whites feel about the general social welfare agenda; *The Scar of Race*, 103.

64. University of California President David Gardner, quoted in Takagi, *The Retreat from Race*, 72. Ironically, others argue the opposite: that switching from race to class preferences is a cosmetic change, a "Trojan Horse"; that blacks and Latinos will continue to disproportionately benefit; and that the program will be seen politically as similar to

welfare—on its face race-neutral but in practice a program for minorities; see Frederick Lynch, appearing on *The Diane Rehm Show* (Washington D.C.), April 3, 1995 (for "Trojan Horse" quote). In fact, class preferences are hardly a Trojan Horse: even if minorities continue to benefit disproportionately, the beneficiaries will be quite different from those who currently benefit.

65. A widely quoted study of Harvard University admissions for the class of 1975 found that if SAT verbal scores had been the basis for admission, the freshman class would have been 1.1 percent black (rather than 7.1 percent); Klitgaard, *Choosing Elites*, 155; see also Derek Bok, "Admitting Success: The Case for Racial Preferences," *New Republic* (February 4, 1985): 14. At Berkeley, one study found that admissions by the numbers (no racial or class preferences) would yield a class with a combined black, Hispanic, and Native American student body of 4 percent; Karabel, *Freshman Admissions at Berkeley*, 22. Likewise, at the University of Washington Law School, the class admitted in 1971 would have had no minorities if applicants had gone through the general admissions process; *DeFunis v. Odegaard*, 325. And UC Davis Medical School, prior to adoption of its special admissions program, had, in 1968, no black, Mexican American, or Indian students in its class of fifty; *UC v. Bakke*, 272.

In the mid–1970s, Boalt Hall Law School found that class-based preferences would yield small numbers of minorities: while blacks and Chicanos were 67 percent of the disadvantaged poor applicants, with whites and Asians the balance, under a class-based preference blacks and Chicanos were only 32 percent of the pool with the highest academic criteria. School of Law (Boalt Hall), University of California at Berkeley, "Report on Special Admissions at Boalt Hall after *Bakke*," cited in Dershowitz and Hanft, "College Diversity," 418.

Relying on these statistics and others, proponents of racial preferences at the time of the *Bakke* case said flatly that any race-neutral method, even one that took class into account (and in theory would disproportionately help minorities) would not recruit sufficient numbers of minorities, raising the specter of Derek Bok's almost all-white Harvard freshman class; see *UC v. Bakke*, 376–77 (Brennan), and 407 (Blackmun); and Dworkin, "Why Bakke Has No Case," 12. At oral argument in *Bakke*, Archibald Cox stressed again and again, "There is no racially blind method of selection which will enroll today more than a trickle of minority students in the nation's colleges and universities"; quoted in Jeffries, *Justice Powell*, 481.

66. Looking at 1994 data, D'Souza found a 150-point gap between blacks and whites with families earning less than $10,000 a year; *The End of Racism*, 456. For similar findings, see Hacker, *Two Nations*, 138, 141–43; Takagi, *The Retreat from Race*, 200; and Jeff Howard and Ray Hammond, "Rumors of Inferiority," in Nieli, *The New Affirmative Action Controversy*, 371. For a similar gap in law school, see *Hopwood v. Texas*, 571.

67. It is important to keep this issue in context. Preference programs, whether race- or class-based, have their greatest impact at elite colleges, which are truly selective. D'Souza notes that a change in affirmative action programs simply means a black student headed for Columbia now will attend Temple instead; *Illiberal Education*, 252. But this switch obviously matters to D'Souza and other critics of affirmative action, who do not tolerate racial preferences on the basis that white students will still go to some college.

68. The black/white gap shrunk 60 points between 1976 and 1994 and now stands at 198 points; see College Board, *College Bound Seniors: 1994 Profile of SAT and Achievement Test Takers*, iv.

If, after twenty-five years of desegregation and affirmative action, improvements had not been made, it would be a major indictment of the efforts. But we *are* beginning to see the fruits of desegregation, and there is promising evidence from the affirmative action era. Whereas many black students applying to colleges and graduate schools in the early 1970s went to officially de jure segregated schools and had depressed test scores, "striking gains" were seen in reading test scores of later black students as a result of the desegregation of the 1970s. (The 1954 *Brown* decision was not truly implemented until the early 1970s; see Taylor, "*Brown*, Equal Protection," 1710.) The figure for Harvard— only 1.1 percent of the student body would be black if Harvard admitted students based on the verbal SAT—comes from the last time Harvard made its data public, for the class of 1975; Klitgaard, *Choosing Elites*, 29, 155. These students entered Harvard in the fall of 1971 and took the SAT in 1970, prior to adoption of many features of today's antidiscriminatory regime: genuine enforcement of *Brown* (*Swann*), enforcement outside the South (*Keyes*), and for their parents, adoption of the disparate impact analysis in employment (*Griggs*).

Taylor notes that black students attending desegregated schools were more likely to complete high school, to enroll in and graduate from four-year colleges, and to major in areas not traditionally associated with blacks, and that they were less likely to become involved in teenage pregnancy or crime; "*Brown*, Equal Protection," 1711. According to one study, black IQ has risen to "eras[e] nearly half the gap between blacks' predesegregation . . . scores and the national norm"; see Greenberg, *Crusaders in the Courts*, 399. The National Assessment of Education Progress notes that the gap between seventeen-year-old blacks and whites has declined in the last twenty years by 50 percent in reading, 25–40 percent in math, and 15–25 percent in science (399); see also National Research Council, *A Common Destiny*, 348.

Moreover, as the children of "affirmative action babies"—affirmative action grandchildren—continue to come of age, we will see increasing numbers of minorities who have grown up with the benefits of having parents who received excellent educations. This was always the goal of affirmative action—to take account of race for a transition period and help create a sizable, educated black middle class; after that, things would take care of themselves; see Bok, "Admitting Success," 14ff.

SAT scores of African Americans have risen in recent years in absolute terms and compared to whites; National Research Council, *A Common Destiny*, 350. Between 1970 and 1980, not only did the black/white gap in SAT scores shrink, but black youth made larger gains than whites did; Taylor, "*Brown*, Equal Protection," 1706–7. There were further gains in the 1980s for blacks, Mexican Americans, American Indians, and Asians; see Sowell, *Race and Culture*, 296, n24; Takagi, *The Retreat from Race*, 211; and Hughes, *Culture of Complaint*, 62. In all, the average black score on the verbal portion of the SAT moved up from the 74th percentile of whites in 1976 to the 80th percentile by 1990, and similar gains were seen on the math portion; see Bluestone, "Inequality Express," 89.

Even Murray and Herrnstein concede the gains, though it undercuts their allegation that scores are largely genetic and fixed among groups; *The Bell Curve*, 289, 292–94. They note also that the rise in African American scores is not due to a more self-selective group of test takers, but quite the opposite: the percentage of black seventeen-year-olds taking the SAT has increased from 10 percent in 1976 to 20 percent in 1993 (720, n56). And similarly promising trends are found for the ACT and the GRE (640–41). The gap between black and white students from low-income backgrounds ($10,000 and $20,000) remained at 169 points in 1991; Takagi, *The Retreat from Race*, 200. But this gap is substantially smaller than the 245-point black/white gap among low-income students in 1976—the period in which the university establishment was rallying for preferences in admissions; see ibid., 184.

Statistics released by the University of California at Berkeley in May 1995—to "prove" that racial preferences must be retained—indicated that if academics alone are considered in admissions, Hispanics would constitute 3.0–6.9 percent of the class, and African Americans 0.5–1.9 percent. When socioeconomic status (parents' income and education) is considered, the numbers rise to 5.6–10 percent Hispanic and 1.4–2.3 percent African American; UC Berkeley Office of Undergraduate Admissions, cited in Lubman, "Campuses Mull Admissions Without Affirmative Action," B1. As we shall see, this study defines class narrowly as income and education, and underestimates the degree to which minorities could benefit from a properly constructed class-based affirmative action program.

69. Lubman, "Campuses Mull Admissions Without Affirmative Action," B1. While most opponents of repeal said the move would have catastrophic effects on the number of minority admits, independent observers noted after the vote that it "could turn out to be more smoke than fire," because "social disadvantage could easily serve as a subtle

proxy for race"; see Lubman, "UC Vote to Ban Race Criteria Has Shades of Gray," A6; see also Rene Sanchez, "California Regents Aren't the Last Word: Diversity Can Be Ensured without Race-Based Admissions, Officials Say," *Washington Post*, July 24, 1995, A1. Note that if the purpose of a facially neutral practice is to discriminate based on race, the practice may be considered unconstitutional; see *Washington v. Davis*, 426 US 339 (1976); *Arlington Heights v. Metropolitan Housing Development Corporation*, 429 US 252 (1977). Our purpose in devising a class-based affirmative action program is to construct a fair policy. The positive disparate impact is a bonus, not its raison d'être.

70. We have noted, for example, the Education Department's finding that legacy preferences were responsible for lower admission rates of Asian Americans at Harvard; "Statement of Findings, Compliance Review No. 01-88-6009," October 4, 1990. There is also evidence that since white Protestants are distributed more evenly throughout the country than other groups, they are the main beneficiaries of geographic preferences. As a result, such preferences tend to pit Jews, Catholics, and blacks more clearly against one another; see Dershowitz and Hanft, "College Diversity," 410-14. Laird confirms that at Berkeley the lion's share of preferences for rural Californians go to whites; Laird interview (1995). Accordingly, under a race-neutral system, eliminating geographical preferences should tend to help non-WASPs disproportionately.

71. Such preferences will beef up the number of minority students above and beyond the numbers indicated by studies using verbal SATs as a measure. Although blacks make up less than 10 percent of undergraduate students, they constitute 49 percent of male college basketball players; National Research Council, *A Common Destiny*, 96. Takagi notes that in the debate over college athletics, "the terms of discourse might have easily translated so that 'college athlete' meant 'black' "; *The Retreat from Race*, 179.

72. Recall that the Boalt Hall Law School study found that 32 percent of the beneficiaries of a program based on disadvantage would be black and Chicano. Since poor and working-class people of all races constitute a larger group than minorities (black, Hispanic, and Native American) of all classes, the informal set-aside should be correspondingly larger. Laird says that Berkeley minority numbers could be boosted by increasing the class-based preference above the weight provided in the May 1995 simulation; Laird interview (1995).

73. When the statistic is left lingering, some commentators jump to dangerous and unwarranted conclusions. Ted Koppel, for example, after noting that blacks and Hispanics do worse than whites and Asians, even when controlling for class, stated to his guest Julian Bond: "That, Mr. Bond, sounds a lot like the theory put forward in *The Bell Curve*"; *Nightline*, June 16, 1995.

74. Roger Wilkins, "The Black Poor Are Different," *New York Times*, August 22, 1989, A23.

75. If we do not address the real aggregate differences between blacks and whites of the same income level, we are likely to see Thomas Sowell's Rule Number Two about preferential programs come into play: programs tend to benefit the most advantaged segment of the preferred group; *Preferential Policies*, 15-16.

76. National Research Council, *A Common Destiny*, 276. In 1984 the median household net worth for blacks was $3,397, compared with $39,135 for whites, a ratio of 11:1 (276). Even holding income and family size constant—comparing whites and blacks with identical incomes—the wealth differential has been estimated at 5:1; Franklin, *Shadows of Race and Class*, 124.

77. Starr, "Civil Reconstruction," 12. See also Melvin L. Oliver and Thomas M. Shapiro, *Black Wealth, White Wealth* (New York: Routledge, 1995), 197.

78. See William D. Bradford, "Money Matters: Lending Discrimination in African American Communities," in National Urban League, *The State of Black America*, 109ff.

79. Franklin, *Shadows of Race and Class*, 124.

80. Smith, "Racial and Ethnic Differences in Wealth," 176.

81. Zena Smith Blau, "The Social Structure, Socialization Process, and School Competence of Black and White Children," in Shulman and Darity, *The Question of Discrimination*, 319-20.

82. See Ellwood and Cottingham, *Welfare Policies for the 1990s*, 3; Rose, *Social Stratification*, 23; and Steinberg, *Turning Back*, 213.

83. Ellwood, *Poor Support*, 200.

84. See Mishel and Simon, *The State of Working America*, 33, table 58.

85. National Urban League, *The State of Black America*, 254.

86. Hacker, *Two Nations*, 68, 230, 231. Likewise, in 1990, 51.2 percent of black children lived only with their mothers, compared with 14.2 percent of white children—a multiple of 3.6 (231).

87. Wilkins, "The Black Poor Are Different," A23.

88. Barbara Vobejda, "Birthrate Among Teenage Girls Declines Slightly," *Washington Post*, October 26, 1994, A5; see also ch. 2.

89. Edward Walsh, "Black Women Are Closing Race Gap in Employment, Census Data Show," *Washington Post*, February 22, 1995, A3.

90. Loic J. D. Wacquant and William Julius Wilson, "Poverty, Joblessness and the Social Transformation of the Inner City," in Cottingham and Ellwood, *Welfare Policy for the 1990s*, 75. See also Peterson, "The Urban Underclass and the Poverty Paradox," in Jencks and Peterson, *The Urban Underclass*, 22; and National Research Council, *A Common Destiny*, 286.

91. National Research Council, *A Common Destiny*, 283–84.

92. Quoted in Wilson, *The Truly Disadvantaged*, 58–60. In addition, if one counts the higher occupation of an applicant's parents, the white occupation is likely to rank higher, even among the same income groups, because among black and white middle-class families, blacks are more likely to be middle-class because two parents are working in lower-level jobs; in white families, the father more frequently has a higher-status job and the mother can afford to stay at home.

93. In the context of IQ gaps, "the socioeconomic class indices commonly employed conceal the fact that a significant portion of blacks categorized as middle class are in fact similar to white working-class adults," Franklin writes. "When adjustments are made for this error, measured IQ differences between children of different races with genuine middle-class backgrounds disappear"; *Shadows of Race and Class*, 64. Likewise, in a study of 180 Latino and 180 non-Latino white elementary school students in Riverside, California, the sociologist Jane Mercer found that when controlling for eight sociocultural variables, the residual IQ gap between ethnic groups disappears; "Ethnic Differences in IQ scores: What Do They Mean? (A Response to Lloyd Dunn)," *Hispanic Journal of Behavioral Sciences* 10 (1988): 199–218. Finally, a 1995 New Orleans study found that looking only at income and education had led previous researchers to the erroneous conclusion that race was a factor in domestic homicides. The University of Washington's Brandon S. Centerwall found that crowded living conditions, not race, explained differences in domestic homicide rates between whites and blacks of the same income and education. Education and income, Centerwall said, "don't completely control for economic differences"; See Heidi Evans, "Poverty, Not Race, Is Critical Factor in Domestic Homicides, Study Finds," *Wall Street Journal*, June 15, 1995, B6.

94. LBJ, Howard commencement address (1965), 638.

95. Wilkins, "The Black Poor Are Different," A23.

96. See David Whitman et al., "The White Underclass," *U.S. News and World Report*, October 17, 1994, 40ff.

97. Quoted in ibid.

98. See Wilson, "Race-Neutral Programs," 81.

99. Graglia, "Racially Discriminatory Admission to Public Institutions," 589.

100. See Sleeper, "Race and Affirmative Action," 91.

101. Dershowitz and Hanft, "College Diversity," 419.

102. Quoted in Holmes, "Mulling," sect. 4, p. 3.

103. See Karabel, *Freshman Admissions at Berkeley*. In fact, failing to take class into account can create a false sense of diversity. Each time the Democratic National Convention issues statistics on the percentages of female and minority delegates, press reports invariably point to the elite makeup of those delegates, whose average income and educa-

tion levels far exceed the national averages. Likewise, in the context of the newsroom, the veteran *Washington Post* editor Richard Harwood says the current definition of diversity, based on race and gender, is "rather narrow"; what is missing are the views of "the nonprivileged"; "An America of Niches," *Washington Post*, September 10, 1994, A23. Similarly, President Clinton's commitment to diversity in appointments was clearly less focused on class than on gender and race. Asserting that his administration should "look" like America (though not necessarily live like it), Clinton appointed a higher percentage of women, blacks, and Hispanics to the judiciary in his first year of office than his predecessors had, prompting Nan Aron of the Alliance for Justice to say, "They should have a much greater understanding of problems confronting ordinary Americans." But the reporter was skeptical. "Despite Aron's claim," Henry J. Reske wrote in the *ABA Journal*, the Clinton appointees did "better than or on a par with their predecessors in terms of personal wealth": only 28 percent of appointees had a net worth below half a million dollars; "A Report Card on Clinton's Judges," *ABA Journal* (April 1994): 16. Aron conceded to Reske that she preferred more of a spread of incomes, with more judges from smaller firms or public interest organizations; ibid.

104. This notion is hard to accept, because a racially imbalanced university seems unacceptable for three reasons: (1) diversity is important as a matter of social utility; (2) lack of diversity suggests the process is unfair; and (3) to some, lack of diversity raises the embarrassing suggestion of genetic inferiority. These conclusions are unwarranted.

First, we saw in ch. 4 that while diversity is a positive social good, when achieved through racial preferences the social utility becomes mixed and surely is not strong enough to justify racial discrimination. Second, the process we have laid out to correct for disadvantage is the fairest one we could devise. If we employ tests that do not underpredict minority performance; if we try our best to correct for social circumstances into which individuals are born; and if, at the end of the day, we do not have the perfect "ethnic mix," if there are "too many" Jews and Asians and "too few" blacks and Hispanics, that is the price of our society's decision to choose equal opportunity over equal group results. If the numbers are vastly askew, that suggests we may need to look closer to ensure that the procedures are all fair, but it does not argue for rigging the procedure at the last moment to ensure equality of group result. When McGeorge Bundy said, "If you want to enlarge the numbers of minority students in selective colleges and professional schools you simply *must* make race a factor in your work" (Bundy, "The Issue Before the Court," 45), he never fully defended the first proposition. Note that he does not argue: "If you want the system to be truly *fair*, you simply *must* make race a factor in your work."

Indeed, to the extent that proponents of racial preferences argue that class preferences will *not* yield a racially diverse class, they unwittingly underline the unfairness of the current system: in fact, many of the preferences and benefits are going to advantaged people of color who would not qualify for preferences under a class system. Say Dershowitz and Hanft: "The fact that certain *advantaged* minority persons who benefit under race-specific programs would no longer receive windfall benefits under a race-neutral program should not be cause for distress; these are precisely the persons who do not—under any principle of morality—*deserve* to be given any special advantage"; "College Diversity," 418–19.

A third, darker force is pushing for proportional representation by implying that underrepresentation of certain groups and overrepresentation of others is "embarrassing"—even if the process itself is fair. But it is only embarrassing if one harbors deep in one's psyche the notion that blacks are innately inferior—a ludicrous idea that has been disproved time and time again but that appears to be at the root of the thinking of a few proponents of affirmative action. After President Francis Lawrence of Rutgers University was taped saying that blacks are genetically inferior, he defended himself by saying that he garbled his words, and that he is a strong supporter of affirmative action. Roger E. Hernandez responded that support for affirmative action and a belief in genetic inferiority are "perfectly consistent"; "Skirting the Real Issue—Racism," *Washington Post*, February 10, 1995, A23. Likewise, Albert Shanker, a strong opponent of racial preferences, says he actually might support them if he believed in genetic inferiority, because quotas might buy social peace; Shanker interview (1995).

105. Michael Kinsley notes: "In Communist societies, such as Mao's China, they have produced hierarchies of reverse social discrimination that match the most rigidly stratified traditional society"; "Class, Not Race," A15; see also Kinsley, "The Spoils of Victimhood," *New Yorker* (March 27, 1995): 62, 66.

106. Tillman Durdin, "China Reopens Universities, Shut Four Years," *New York Times*, September 25, 1970, 10.

107. Lind, *The Next American Nation*, 99.

108. See Robinson, "Reproducing Class Relations," 183.

109. See Taylor, *Affirmative Action at Work*, 61–62.

110. Karl Marx, *Capital*, vol. 3 (Moscow: Forent Publishing House, 1959), 587.

111. The UC Board of Regents made the mistake of permitting fuzzy criteria, such as "an abusive or otherwise dysfunctional home, or a neighborhood of unwholesome or anti-social influences"; see William H. Honan, "College Admissions Policy Change Heightens Debate on Impact," *New York Times*, July 22, 1995, 7. In doing so, the Regents opened themselves up to the criticism of Paul Brest, Dean of Stanford Law School: asking applicants to describe their abusive upbringing "strikes me as an awful idea. It will just encourage them to state what victims they are on their application essays"; Lubman, "UC Vote to Ban Racial Criteria Has Shades of Gray," A6.

112. Kaus, "Class Is In," 6.

113. Kinsley, "Class, Not Race," A15.

114. See Lipset and Bendix, *Social Mobility*, 82 ("British corporation directors are less likely than American executives to report the first menial jobs of their careers"). Compare the attempts to hide humble origins in Charles Dickens's *Great Expectations* with the desire of American presidential candidates to claim log cabin origins.

115. David Halberstam suggests that Robert Kennedy would have supported affirmative action only if a price had to be paid; David Halberstam, telephone interview with the author, December 15, 1994.

116. This is part of Mickey Kaus's more general point that there is a contradiction between capitalism and money egalitarianism; *The End of Equality*, 78.

117. See Okun, *Equality and Efficiency*, 96–97. Okun also notes that savings and investment in 1929, at a time of low and barely progressive income taxes, was 16 percent of GNP, precisely the same figure as in 1973, when higher and much more progressive taxes prevailed (98).

118. Moreover, there is suggestive evidence that, rhetoric aside, many parents are motivated to accumulate wealth primarily for themselves rather than for their children; see Chester, *Inheritance, Wealth, and Society*, 6, 54, 192.

119. Some even argue that those with inherited wealth lose their drive; see, e.g., William Vanderbilt, quoted in Lapham, *Money and Class*, 14. For the general proposition that the affluent have their problems, too; see Coles, *Privileged Ones*, vol. 5 of *Children of Crisis*.

120. Sowell, *Preferential Policies*, 155–56.

121. See National Research Council, *A Common Destiny*, 369 ("net of family size effects, birth order and spacing do not have important consequences for schooling outcomes"). Certainly, there is no question that the seventh child in a wealthy family has greater life chances than the first child in a poor family. Note also that class serves as a very rough proxy for birth order since upper-middle-class people are more likely to have small families; see Rossides, *Social Stratification*, 109–10.

122. To a certain extent, class also serves as a rough proxy for alcoholism and child abuse. Some 94 percent of cases of neglect and abuse take place in families with income below the national median. The 1986 National Incidence Study found that abuse and neglect in families with incomes below $15,000 occurred at five times the rate of families above $15,000; see Murray and Herrnstein, *The Bell Curve*, 209–10. To draw the link between class and abuse is not condescending; it is an empirical fact. As Benjamin DeMott points out, what is condescending is to excuse child abuse among the lower class

and to consider it newsworthy only when a Lisa Steinberg is beaten because we hold the white middle class to a higher standard; *The Imperial Middle*, ch. 6.

123. See Ronald Dworkin, "Are Quotas Unfair?," in Nieli, *The New Affirmative Action Controversy*, 185–86; see also Dworkin, "Why Bakke Has No Case," 14.

124. The UC Davis Medical School summarily rejected all with GPAs below 2.5 in its regular admissions program; *UC v. Bakke*, 273. This type of cutoff is, if anything, more common today. See, e.g., University of Texas Law School admissions as delineated in *Hopwood*. Conversely, universities frequently admit all students above a certain benchmark. The University of Washington Law School, for example, admitted fifty-six of fifty-six applicants above a 78 benchmark score in 1971; *DeFunis v. Odegaard*, 322, and 325, n6. Likewise, legislators rarely treat people as individuals. All fourteen-year-olds are forbidden to drive, even though some are more responsible and could handle driving well. As John Hart Ely notes, "We all order our lives on the basis of such generalizations: without them life would be impossible. Thus a storekeeper may not accept checks drawn on out-of-town banks, even though he or she knows most of them are good, just as an airline may not hire overweight pilots, though it knows most of them will never suffer heart attacks"; *Democracy and Distrust*, 30–31.

125. Kinsley, "Class, Not Race," A15.

126. Ibid.; see also Glazer, "Race, Not Class," A12.

127. Editorial, "A Budget Worthy of Mr. Bush," *New York Times*, July 26, 1993. Two things happened. First, Clinton cut back on his strong campaign commitments to "investments" in job training, education, and infrastructure. He told his economic team, "I hope you're all aware we're all Eisenhower Republicans"; Woodward, *The Agenda*, 165. Second, the Democrat-controlled Congress took Clinton's pared-down investments and slashed them further (162). In some senses, Bush's budget was better on investments than Clinton's. As Jack Beatty notes, President Bush's last budget increased spending on public investments (education, training, and infrastructure) by 8 percent, while Clinton actually cut spending in these areas in his first budget by 1 percent; see "Who Speaks for the Middle Class?"

Even the victories are often hollow. The day President Clinton signed legislation authorizing a major expansion of Head Start, Sen. Tom Harkin (D-Iowa) noted that Congress could afford to appropriate only eighteen cents of every dollar Clinton proposed; see Helen Dewar and Barbara Vobejda, "Clinton Signs Head Start Expansion: President's $700 Million Promise on Crash Course with Budget Caps," *Washington Post*, May 19, 1994, A1. A strong argument can be made that failure to invest on the front end (prenatal care, education, job training) costs much more on the back end (unemployment insurance, lost tax revenues, jails), but that logic does not seem to sway enough legislators.

128. Recall that the Coleman report found that academic performance, demonstrated through test scores, depends "far more on students' family background and the background of their classmates than on the resources that school boards devoted to the students' education"; Jencks, *Rethinking Social Policy*, 4. The report concluded that racial desegregation improved scores of blacks, not because black students performed better when they went to school with whites, but because poor students (disproportionately black) did better when they went to school with wealthier students (disproportionately white); see Mosteller and Moynihan, *Educational Opportunity*, 344. William Taylor reports that "the most dramatic gains" in black student scores following desegregation came in districts where there was "substantial desegregation across socioeconomic class as well as race lines"; "*Brown*, Equal Protection," 1710. If part of the massive white resistance to racial integration in public schools was due to a prejudiced sense that the social pathologies and tendencies of the poor (classroom disruption, gun toting, lower motivation) were race-related, being required to participate in socioeconomic integration may be met with rational objection by parents whose children now enjoy superior educations because of socioeconomic advantage. Says Kaus: "All it takes is a single drive-by shooting, or the sight of metal-detectors in the school hallways, to make the virtues of class-mixing seem fairly theoretical"; *The End of Equality*, 109. In addition, resistance to economic desegregation is likely to be larger than to racial desegregation since, unlike racial busing, economic busing would affect de facto school segregation as well as de jure, reaching across school boundary lines.

129. Rustin, "The King to Come," 21.

130. Says Stuart Taylor, Jr.: "No form of affirmative action can help the underclass"; "A Case for Class-Based Affirmative Action," 23; see also Steele, *The Content of Our Character*, 124. In fact, writes Joseph Adelson, one reason universities moved away from preferences for the disadvantaged to preferences for middle-class people of color was their discovery that middle-class students are less likely to fail; see "Living with Quotas," 28; but see also Howard, "The High Court's Road in the *Bakke* Case" ("Several members of major law faculties say they can think of no law school that has tried the disadvantage approach. Several medical educators say the same of medical schools." [Quoting a 1976 Boalt Hall study that surveyed law schools across the country], "There is no real body of experience in dealing with a disadvantagement approach to special admissions in law schools—and, for that matter, in other schools as well").

131. At age ten, Moynihan fell out of the middle class when his father abandoned the family, sending them into Hell's Kitchen. In fact, Moynihan "learned about Pearl Harbor from a man whose shoes he was shining on Central Park West"; Jim Sleeper, "The Clash: Moynihan vs. Sharpton," *New Republic* (September 19 and 26, 1994): 22. William Julius Wilson, writes Ronald Brownstein, "grew up in rural poverty"; "Beyond Quotas," 18ff.

132. Murray and Herrnstein, *The Bell Curve*, 475–76.

Chapter 7

1. Stephen Steinberg notes that in the 1940s leading liberal journals like the *New Republic* and *The Nation* subsumed race to class and even depicted lynching as having more to do with class than race; *Turning Back*, 55.

2. Hacker cites Disraeli in his preface; *Two Nations*, vii.

3. See Kerner et al., *Report of the National Advisory Commission*, 1; and Harrington, *The Other America*, 9. For criticism of Hacker's title, see, e.g., Ronald Takagi, lecture, Chautauqua Institution, Chautauqua, N.Y., July 8, 1993.

4. Wilson, *The Declining Significance of Race*, 2. Ironically, it was Moynihan's fate that by the 1970s he, too, was emphasizing class, and found himself unpopular with the left once again.

5. All quoted in Edsall and Edsall, *Chain Reaction*, 120.

6. National Research Council, *A Common Destiny*, 10–11.

7. National Urban League, *The State of Black America*, 3. See also Johnson, *Divided We Fall*, 229–30.

8. One of the few commentators to notice this was Charles Krauthammer; see "IQ: What's the Fuss?," *Washington Post*, October 21, 1994, A25. Having said that, Murray, not unaware of the publicity value of the racial angle, chose to emphasize that aspect in excerpts in the *New Republic*; see Charles Murray and Richard J. Herrnstein, "Race, Genes, and IQ: An Apologia," *New Republic* (October 31, 1994): 27–37. And the book flap highlights the authors' attention to the "taboo fact: that intelligence levels differ among ethnic groups."

9. Hacker, *Two Nations*, ix.

10. Geoghegan, *Which Side Are You On?*, 49, 269. Even when Democrats appear to get worked up about labor and class—as they do invariably in the last few days of each campaign—they may in fact be up to something else. When Michael Dukakis in the last weeks of his presidential campaign finally made an overtly populist appeal, "I'm on your side," his campaign manager Susan Estrich told me that the campaign was not going after working Americans but making an appeal to working women.

11. Bill Clinton told Peter Brown, "If we lead with class warfare, we lose"; *Minority Party*, 31. In 1992 Clinton declared his loyalty to "the middle class," not much of a line in the sand, since virtually all Americans consider themselves members of that class. In his acceptance speech at the Democratic Convention, he spoke for the "forgotten middle class," not, as Nelson Lichtenstein notes, the "working class" or "working people," and certainly not "American labor"; see "What Happened to the Working Class?," *New York Times*, September 7, 1992, 19.

12. Hughes, *Culture of Complaint*, 76.

13. For Andrew Hacker, who does write about the real world, class does not merit mention: "As a social and human division, [race] surpasses all others—even gender—in intensity and subordination"; *Two Nations*, 3.

In the field of law, the critical legal studies (CLS) movement, which was supposed to be neo-Marxist and concerned with class, is now overshadowed by critical feminist theory and by critical race theory; proponents of the latter blast CLS for reducing issues of race to class and argue that the original critics were too concerned with building cross-racial alliances; see Ansley, "Stirring the Ashes," 1041; and Barnes, "Race Consciousness," 1868. With the emphasis not so much on solving problems but on having a particular "voice," the poor lose out, since law professors may be black or female or both, but they are rarely poor.

14. Carter, *Affirmative Action Baby*, 218.

15. West, *Race Matters*, 27.

16. For example, the Duke historian John Hope Franklin says that W. E. B. Du Bois's argument that "the problem of the color line will be the problem of the twentieth century" was too optimistic: "It's going to be the problem of the twenty-first century, too. It's still the most powerful force in our national thinking"; quoted in Johnson, *Divided We Fall*, 172.

17. In the late 1960s, as leftists, newly (and properly) sensitive to race, began to take a closer look at history, they saw that competition between white labor and blacks had always been a source of division, and that white workers had often been a negative force in the lives of black people. Going all the way back to slavery, some northern working-class whites, including members of the Democratic Party in New York City, opposed abolition "on the ground that emancipation would result in the migration of thousands of blacks to northern states, increasing competition for jobs and reducing wages"; Wilson, *The Declining Significance of Race*, 50. It was white northern workers' fear of black labor that led to Lincoln's bizarre proposal in 1862 to colonize emancipated slaves in the Caribbean Islands; Steinberg, *The Ethnic Myth*, 180. In 1898 AFL President Samuel Gompers was still pushing a similar proposal; see Lind, *The Next American Nation*, 72. Herbert Hill notes that labor was the chief force behind the Chinese Exclusion Act of 1882; "Race, Ethnicity, and Organized Labor," 40–41. Labor's push for the Davis-Bacon Act in the 1930s had racial underpinnings as well; see Dorothy J. Gaiter, "The Davis-Bacon Act Comes under Attack by an Odd Alliance," *Wall Street Journal*, May 3, 1995, A1. In 1963 the AFL-CIO refused to sponsor King's March on Washington; see Hill, "Race, Ethnicity, and Organized Labor," 33. In South Africa it was the socialists who promoted the "color bar," which later developed into apartheid; Sowell, *Race and Culture*, 99. And in Australia it was the left-wing party that designed discriminatory immigration policies to keep cheap Asian labor out; Hughes, *Culture of Complaint*, 86. Kenneth B. Clark in particular argued that the white working class and white labor have proven unreliable allies (or worse) for the civil rights movement—in part because it is the white working class with whom blacks compete, but also because the white working class is most vulnerable and insecure and relies on its whiteness for status; *Dark Ghetto*, 43.

18. When the issue moved to open housing and school desegregation in the North, the old competition intensified. It was working-class whites, not white-collar suburbanites, who were "asked to share their schools, neighborhoods and places of amusement with blacks," the late journalist Theodore White wrote; *The Making of the President 1968*, 84. For data on white working-class opposition to housing integration, see also Dutton, *Changing Sources of Power*, 118, 142; and Campbell and Shuman, *Supplemental Studies for the National Advisory Commission*, 7. It is "hardly accidental," writes Derrick Bell, "that the most active proponents of fair housing are those liberals living in areas where housing is priced beyond the means of all but a small number of black elites"; quoted in Freeman, "Race and Class," 1888–89. Martin Luther King, Jr., found the most hateful response among working-class whites when he took his civil rights movement north and was confronted by violence in Cicero, Illinois. Liberals invoked

Myrdal's wisdom that the most insecure whites are the most hostile to blacks because, "When the feed-box is empty, the horses will bite each other"; *An American Dilemma*, 70.

In 1971 Frederick Dutton wrote, "The left has long held as a testament of faith that 'the workers' are the main historical agents of social progress, but an important portion of this group is now providing the most tenacious resistance to further broadening the country's social, economic, and political base"; *Changing Sources of Power*, 222. A. H. Raskin wrote that "the typical worker—from construction craftsman to shoe clerk—has probably become the most reactionary political force in the country." Eric F. Goldman called for a new coalition "of the rich, educated, and dedicated with the poor"; both quoted in Rustin, "The Blacks and the Unions," 81. In 1968, David Halberstam noted: "The easy old coalition between labor and Negroes was no longer so easy; it barely existed. The two were among the American forces most in conflict"; *The Unfinished Odyssey*, 41.

19. Moynihan interview (1995).

20. In the 1970s the American public laughed weekly at, not with, Archie Bunker, deservedly ridiculing his racism while undeservedly ridiculing his fears. The idea of rebuilding a coalition between blacks and the likes of Archie Bunker seemed more distant than ever. It was hard to be concerned with Bunker's everyday concerns and struggles because he was the victimizer.

21. The New Left pointed to a series of failed populist coalitions—and the ease with which white working-class people, who seemed at times potential or real allies, could turn on a dime against the interests of blacks. The history of this country is replete with examples to bolster this thesis.

No one better symbolizes the failure of populism than Tom Watson. During the late nineteenth and early twentieth centuries, Watson, a Georgia populist, served in the House and the Senate, ran for vice president with William Jennings Bryan, and ran for president on his own. He began his career, as his biographer C. Vann Woodward explains, with an inspiring and hardheaded call for racial unity; *Tom Watson*, 220. Early in his career, Watson supported antilynching legislation and nominated a black to the state executive committee of the Populist Party, arguing that "the accident of color can make no difference in the interests of farmers, croppers, and laborers" (220–21, 240–41). "Under Watson's tutelage the Southern white masses were beginning to learn to regard the Negro as a political ally bound to them by economic ties and a common destiny, rather than as a slender prop to injured self-esteem in the shape of 'White Supremacy,' " Woodward wrote (221–22); see also Lesher, *George Wallace*, 14–15.

In 1896, when the William Jennings Bryan–Tom Watson ticket was defeated, Watson retired from politics for eight years. When he returned, Woodward notes, he was a different man. By 1904 Watson was calling for officially disenfranchising the Negro (370–72). In 1908 Watson ran for president at the head of the Populist ticket, boasting that he was the only candidate "standing squarely for White Supremacy" (399). In the next two years, he broadened his campaign of hate, warning about "the lusts of the Negro" and railing against Catholics and Jews (405–6, 419, 432, 443, 450). When he died in 1922, the largest funeral tribute was sent by the Ku Klux Klan (486).

Lipset and Raab make the case that Tom Watson was only the first in a long line of right-wing extremists supported disproportionately by lower-middle-income and less educated Americans, from the KKK in the 1920s to Father Coughlin in the 1930s to Joe McCarthy in the 1950s; *The Politics of Unreason*, xvi, 227. In the 1960s the candidate white working America swooned for was none other than the segregationist George Wallace, Mr. Backlash, who had perfected the art of racial demagoguery. In June 1958, after losing the Democratic primary for Alabama, he reportedly vowed that he would never "be out-nigguhed again," and for a time he was not; Leshner, *George Wallace*, 128–29. At his January 1963 inaugural, Wallace pledged, "Segregation now! Segregation tomorrow! Segregation forever!" and six months later he stood at the schoolhouse door, refusing to admit black students to the University of Alabama (234).

In 1964 Wallace ran in the Democratic presidential primaries against the highly popular incumbent Lyndon Johnson and did "astonishingly well," Lipset and Raab note, garnering 33.7 percent of the primary vote in Wisconsin, 29.8 percent in Indiana, and 43 percent in Maryland. In Gary, Indiana, and Baltimore, Maryland, Wallace did especially well in working-class districts; *The Politics of Unreason*, 358. When he ran again in 1968, this time as a third-party candidate in the general election, Wallace drew a larger percentage of the popular vote than any third-party candidate had since 1924. Forty percent of his support came from the North and the West. A 1967 Gallup survey found that Wallace was viewed most favorably by grammar school–educated whites (54–32) and least by university-educated whites (30–65) (360). For further evidence that Wallace did best among the least educated, see *The Politics of Unreason*, 363, 380–82; Converse et al., "Continuity and Change in American Politics," 1102; and Dutton, *Changing Sources of Power*, 118.

22. When Jesse Jackson ran for president in 1984 and 1988, he was unable to appeal significantly to white working-class voters, even while seeming to make all the right populist arguments about the need to move beyond race to class; see West, *Keeping Faith*, 240–41. He voiced all the right words about coalitions, but racist whites, the argument went, refused to vote for him. Instead, the white working class, at least in Louisiana, turned to another figure more horrible than George Wallace himself, an actual former Ku Klux Klan leader, David Duke. My own interpretation of the Jackson vote is different (see notes 71–78).

23. In the 1970s the ethnic revival was in full bloom, with blacks celebrating and rediscovering their African roots and white ethnics getting into the act; Schlesinger, *The Disuniting of America*, 43. Where, a few years earlier, American public policy said yes to private celebration of ethnicity but no to public recognition (with the Civil Rights Act, Voting Rights Act, and Immigration Act), by 1974 the Ethnic Heritage Studies Program Act provided public encouragement for ethnic identification and bilingual education; Glazer, *Ethnic Dilemmas*, 127–36.

Glazer and Moynihan, writing in 1975, noted the genuine failure of both the "liberal expectancy" (that ethnicity would decline in importance as achievement prevailed over ascription) and the "radical expectancy" (that class would become the main dividing line, erasing earlier tribal lines). Instead, "we have been surprised by the persistence and salience of ethnic-based forms of social identification and conflict"; *Ethnicity*, 6–7 (they credit Milton Gordon with the phrase, the "liberal expectancy"); see also Moynihan, *Pandaemonium*, 27.

In explaining this phenomenon, Daniel Bell said that class had proven an ineffective basis of political identity, for two reasons: first, it carried with it, for all but the wealthiest, "a lowered social ranking and esteem and a sense of inferiority"; and second, unlike ethnicity, "'class' no longer seemed to carry any strong affective tie. . . . What had once been an ideology had now become almost largely an interest"; "Ethnicity and Social Change," in Glazer and Moynihan, *Ethnicity*, 157, 167. He contrasted the decline of labor songs with the durability of black civil rights anthems (168). The theme was one Bell had developed many years earlier when he predicted (correctly) that the socialist hope for a union between Jewish and Arab workers in the Middle East was a chimera; see Bell, "Nationalism or Class?—Some Questions on the Potency of Political Symbols," *The Student Zionist* (May 1947), cited in Moynihan, *Pandaemonium*, 7. Bell said the same fate held for the "utopian radical notion" of a "natural" alliance between poor whites and Negroes, for "the greatest store of hate against Negroes . . . lies among the poor whites" (8).

24. Internationally, the story is well-known. Writes Robert Hughes: "Marxism set itself against nationalism, spread by adapting to it, and in the end was laid low by it"; *Culture of Complaint*, 75; see also Moynihan, *Pandaemonium*, 144. Domestically, in the 1980s and 1990s, racial divisions remained high, and ethnic affinities were stronger than ever. Portuguese Americans protested when Portuguese defendants faced gang-rape charges in Fall River, Massachusetts. Black children in Boston rooted for the Los Angeles Lakers against their home-team Celtics, putting race over geography. Hispanics rallied around Lorena Bobbitt and cheered her acquittal on grounds of temporary insanity. And, of course, following the "not guilty" verdict of O. J. Simpson in 1995, the racial chasm widened even further.

25. Moynihan, *Pandaemonium*, 60.

26. See Roper Research poll, cited in Clay Chandler, "It's Getting Awfully Crowded in the Middle," *Washington Post*, December 18, 1994, H1.

27. George F. Will, "Tax Debate Marks Our Class Struggle," *Bergen Record*, August 2, 1984.

28. The first part of the argument says that while class appeals might have worked during the Great Depression, the New Deal worked too well for the Democrats' own good, turning poor Democratic immigrants into middle-class Republicans. Second, even to the extent that there is a working class, its members do not dislike the rich. Says the *New York Times*, "Ordinary people generally do not hate the rich but aspire to be like them. They may be more likely to draw the line between themselves and the people below rather than those above"; Editorial, "Democrats, Democrats, and Plutocrats," *New York Times*, July 22, 1984, sect. 4, p. 20. When George McGovern proposed a stiff inheritance tax on the rich in a speech to rubber workers, the idea fell flat. "To McGovern's surprise he was loudly booed. The workers didn't like the idea. They wanted to leave as much money as possible to their families"; Lance Morrow, "American Liberty," *Time*, July 16, 1986, 19.

29. Moynihan, "The Problem of Crime," *Congressional Record* (May 6, 1992): S6058.

30. Rustin, "The King To Come," 19.

31. See Murray and Herrnstein, *The Bell Curve*; and D'Souza, *The End of Racism*.

32. Mario Cuomo, interview with the author, Albany, N.Y., June 23, 1987.

33. See Rustin, "Conflict of Coalition," 3.

34. Newfield and Greenfield, *A Populist Manifesto*, 9.

35. King, *Why We Can't Wait*, 36.

36. King, *Where Do We Go from Here?*, 17.

37. King, "MLK Defines 'Black Power,'" 101. "The economically deprived condition of the Negro," King told the NAACP Legal Defense Fund, "will remain unless the Negro revolution builds and maintains alliances with the majority white community, alliances with a basic goal: the elimination of the causes of poverty"; quoted in Garrow, *Bearing the Cross*, 326. In 1967 King wrote that white and black workers have a "community of interest that transcends many of the ugly divisive elements of traditional prejudice"; "MLK Defines 'Black Power'," 27, 93. He argued: "Negroes who are almost wholly a working people cannot be casual toward the union movement. This is true even though some unions remain incontestably hostile" (93).

In making the argument that allies were necessary for the second stage of the civil rights movement, King was following the argument of his aide Bayard Rustin. Rustin realized that the second stage, more expensive than the first, required white labor as an ally, making it critical that black demands not be seen as "an attempt to steal [white] jobs . . . there can be no such thing as an exclusively Negro economic program"; "The Lessons of the Long Hot Summer," 45. In 1969, by which time the Nixon administration had imposed the Philadelphia Plan for racial quotas on the construction industry, Rustin saw that racial preferences had become a potent tool to divide working-class blacks and whites. "How," he asked, "can we explain the sudden interest in getting Negroes into the building trades on the part of an Administration which couldn't get a Negro into its Cabinet?"; "Conflict or Coalition," 11. Clearly, Rustin said, Nixon knew no better way to divide black and working-class white. And it was equally clear, Rustin argued, that blacks should not be duped into the role of "stooges"; they should not allow themselves to be "insulted" with reparations and preferential treatment, which, in 1970, 84 percent of black rejected (8); see also Rustin, "The Failure of Black Separatism," 31. If issues are defined by race, Rustin wrote in 1971, "then Nixon will win. But if, on the other hand, they are defined so as to appeal to the progressive economic interests of the lower middle class, then it becomes possible to build an alliance on the basis of common interest between this group and the black community"; "The Blacks and the Unions," 81.

But it is crucial to note that King's new emphasis on class was not merely a reflection of his reliance on Rustin and other aides. One aide recalled that "no one was really enthusiastic about the Poor People's Campaign" except King; Garrow, *Bearing the Cross*, 616. In fact, following the riots, Garrow reports, King was even more eager to take on the class issue than was Bayard Rustin, who for years had tried to move King in the direction of class-based approaches. In a notable reversal of roles, Garrow says, King now felt "that Rustin did not adequately appreciate the movement's responsibility to tackle the basic issues of wealth and class underlying the evils of American society" (455). Rustin initially opposed the Poor People's Campaign, although he believed that "the difficulty with that campaign was rooted not in its perception of the problem, but in its strategy and tactics"; "The King to Come," 20.

38. King, wrote Rustin, "sensed that the passage of civil rights legislation had shifted the focus from purely racial concerns to the broader and less tractable issues of political empowerment and economic justice"—less tractable because, unlike legal racial equality, class issues "will cost the nation something"; ibid.; see also Garrow, *Bearing the Cross*, 537. The fact that the problems were more expensive also increased the need for coalition; King, *Where Do We Go from Here?*, 50, 165. In 1967, King called for a guaranteed income; though it would benefit the two-thirds of the poor who were white, he said, the coalition was necessary "to overcome the fierce opposition we must realistically anticipate"; King, "MLK Defines 'Black Power,'" 102. In contrast to Black Power advocates, King said that "effective political power for Negroes cannot come through separatism"; *Where Do We Go from Here?*, 48.

39. While Lipset, Raab, and Bell have long argued that the white working class is highly conservative, indeed authoritarian, other researchers have questioned that characterization. Hamilton points out that Joseph McCarthy drew his strongest electoral support not from the working class but from upper-middle-class voters in Wisconsin (*Class and Politics in the United States*, 115, 450); and that southern lynching, while often portrayed as the work of poor whites, was in fact often sponsored by the most respected white families (427–28, 482, n51, 431–32).

In addition, while individual labor unions may have dragged their feet on civil rights, they have generally been more progressive than society at large. "Most labor organizations have historically supported equal rights for minority workers," says George Washington Law Professor Charles Craver; *Can Unions Survive?*, 81. And Bayard Rustin notes: "No other mass institution in American society was so fully open to the participation of blacks"; quoted in Wilson, *The Declining Significance of Race*, 126–27. Unions supported the 1964 Civil Rights Act and, indeed, pressed for a fair employment practices section, which President Kennedy and Robert Kennedy had opposed; Rustin, "The Blacks and the Unions," 76. "None of the legislative fights we have had in the field of civil rights could have been won without the trade-union movement," Clarence Mitchell, director of the Washington Bureau of the NAACP, said in the early 1970s (80).

40. Rustin, "The Blacks and the Unions," 81.

41. Those who have looked behind many of the clashes between white labor and black America have often discovered the involvement of wealthy whites; see Wright, *Class Structure*, 202; Wilson, *The Declining Significance of Race*, 57, 72; Bloom, *Race, Class, and the Civil Rights Movement*, 1, 4–5, 36–41; Du Bois, *Black Reconstruction*, 353; Myrdal, *An American Dilemma*, 391; and Kerner et al., *Report of the National Advisory Commission*, 101.

42. Indeed, Daniel Bell himself notes that while ethnicity is often salient, it need not be. "Stagnating" economies "may make economic class issues central again to the political concerns of the society." And to the extent that the question is up for grabs, Bell is by no means for championing ethnicity over class. "If one looks down the dark ravines of history, one sees that men in social groups need some other groups to hate. . . . To replace the politics of ideology with the politics of ethnicity might only be the continuation of war by other means"; "Ethnicity and Social Change," 173–74.

43. Rieder, *Canarsie*, 37; Rieder quotes others as well (82, 99).

44. Lukas, *Common Ground*, 244–45. McGoff was also furious with Ted Kennedy. "As usual, Ted seemed to care more about blacks than he did about his own people," Lukas writes. "The Kennedys had never had it tough in their lives—who were they to sit

down there at Hyannis Port and tell her what to do for the minorities?" (28). She had similar feelings about the media, which painted her and others as unredeemable bigots and condescended to them. "As she watched the images flickering across the screen, and listened to the newsmen summing it all up in their Harvard accents, she thought: . . . They just don't understand" (258).

45. "Louise had tapped a much broader sense of grievance, rooted less in race than in class: the feeling of many working-class whites that they had been abandoned" (ibid., 135).

46. Lukas interview (1995).

47. Eugene Litwak, Nancy Hooyman, and Donald Warren, "Ideological Complexity and Middle American Rationality," *Public Opinion Quarterly* (Fall 1973): 320.

48. Most of the working-class voters in Gary, Milwaukee, and Baltimore who supported Wallace in the 1964 Democratic primary did not in the general election vote for Goldwater; *The Politics of Unreason*, 363. Studies of white working-class Wallace supporters showed there was even greater resentment of white-collar professionals than of blacks; see Thomas F. Pettigrew, Robert T. Riley, and Reeve D. Vanneman, "George Wallace's Constituents, *Psychology Today* (February 1972): 47.

While Wallace was maliciously reactionary on race, his campaign was also economically liberal: his American Independent Party platform called for government job training, a 60 percent increase in Social Security benefits, improvement of Medicare, protection of collective bargaining rights, and guaranteed jobs; Lipset and Raab, *The Politics of Unreason*, 346–47; see also Lesher, *George Wallace*, 448–49 (quoting a 1970 Wallace campaign speech in which he took credit for raising teacher salaries and Medicaid and unemployment compensation increases and proposed lower utility bills). Wallace professed to campaign for "the average cab driver in this country and the beauticians, and steelworker, the rubber worker, the textile worker," who "is sick and tired of all those over-educated ivory-tower folks with pointed heads, looking down their noses at us"; Lipset and Raab, *The Politics of Unreason*, 350. He stressed his own humble origins: "Can a former truck driver who is married to a former dime-store clerk and whose father was a plain dirt farmer be elected President of the United States?"; quoted in Chester, Hodgson, and Page, *An American Melodrama*, 261. Years later Wallace would say he opposed Reagan's economic policy: "He lowered taxes for the rich people and he raised them on the poor. That's wrong"; quoted in Lesher, *George Wallace*, 313.

Moreover, say Lipset and Raab, economic populism was a central component not only of Wallace's rhetoric but of his actual appeal to white working-class voters. A survey of Gary voters showed that Wallace did best among those who had a high degree of class consciousness; Robert T. Riley and Thomas F. Pettigrew, "Relative Deprivation and Wallace's Northern Support" (paper presented at the 1969 meeting of the American Sociological Association, San Francisco), 3. Fifty-seven percent of those who strongly identified with the working class and thought that things were getting worse for the common man supported Wallace, compared with 8 percent of those who strongly identified with the middle class and did not think things were worse.

A nationwide poll by the University of Michigan Survey Research Center confirmed that Wallace supporters not only were more likely to be working-class than Humphrey or Nixon supporters but also had a greater sense of class consciousness; see Scammon and Wattenberg, *The Real Majority*, 195. Sixty-five percent of Wallace voters agreed that "the federal government is run by a few big interests," compared with 39 percent of Nixon voters and 32 percent of Humphrey voters; see Pettigrew, *Racially Separate or Together?*, 236. Wallace knew who his constituents were. In July 1968 he told a news reporter, "You reporters are for McCarthy, aren't you; and your editors are for Humphrey; but your pressmen are for me"; see Halberstam, *The Unfinished Odyssey*, 43.

49. Quoted in Blumenthal, *The Permanent Campaign*, 48. In 1986, I asked the Roper Center to run a cross-tabulation of Gallup poll AIPO761 Voter Ratings of Robert Kennedy and George Wallace, +5 to -5, April 1968. The study confirmed that a majority of white voters who said they liked Wallace also liked Kennedy.

50. See Greenfield and Newfield, *A Populist Manifesto*, 209; Stone and Lowenstein,

Lowenstein, 172; Wills, *The Kennedy Imprisonment*, 221; Adam Walinsky, interview with the author, New York, December 18, 1984; Richard Harwood, interview with the author, Washington, D.C., December 20, 1984.

51. Chester, Hodgson, and Page, *An American Melodrama*, 163. The pollster Louis Harris also argues that if Kennedy had lived and gotten the Democratic nomination, "he probably would have heavily cut the Wallace vote among trade union members"; *The Anguish of Change*, 208.

52. White, *The Making of the President 1968*, 431. See also Archer, *1968: Year of Crisis*, 139.

53. Paul Cowan, "Wallace in Yankeeland," *Village Voice*, July 18, 1968, 19. See also Stein and Plimpton, *American Journey*, 248.

54. Halberstam, *The Unfinished Odyssey*, 173–74, 195.

55. Newfield, *Robert Kennedy*, 300.

56. See Evans and Novak, "Kennedy's Indiana Victory Proves His Appeal Defuses Backlash Voting," *Washington Post*, May 9, 1968. See also Richard D. Kahlenberg, "Electoral Coalition Building and Robert Kennedy's 1968 Campaign," (undergraduate thesis, Harvard University, 1985).

57. Newfield, *Robert Kennedy*, 305.

58. See Don Williamson, "Equity Means No One Can Have It All," *Seattle Times*, October 16, 1990, A8.

59. Jeff Greenfield, interview with the author, New York, January 30, 1995.

60. A survey of businessmen conducted by *Fortune* found Kennedy the most unpopular presidential candidate since Roosevelt. "While President Kennedy was never a great favorite among businessmen," the March 1968 survey found, "the suspicion with which he was regarded is as nothing compared to the anger aroused by his younger brother." Among business leaders, "mention of the name Bobby Kennedy produced an almost unanimous chorus of condemnation ... there is agreement that Kennedy is the one public figure who could produce an almost united front of business opposition"; A. James Reichley, "Bobby Kennedy: Running Himself out of the Race," *Fortune* (March 1968): 113.

61. Newfield, *Kennedy*, 273–74; Peter Edelman, interview with Larry J. Hackman, December 12, 1969, 40, RFK Oral History Program, John F. Kennedy Memorial Library.

62. Bruno and Greenfield, *The Advance Man*, 165.

63. Writes Theodore White, "The very term 'law and order' enraged millions of good, self-styled 'liberals' across the country," whose thoughts ran to vigilantes and A. Palmer Mitchell when they heard the phrase; *The Making of the President*, 236. See also Newfield, *The Education of Jack Newfield*, 93–94.

Nevertheless, law and order was important to the politics of 1968, to Robert Kennedy's campaign, and to his populist appeal to working-class whites and blacks. The law-and-order theme, as Arthur Schlesinger points out, was part of "Kennedy's effort to keep the black and white working class at peace"; *Robert Kennedy and His Times*, 881. In Indiana, Kennedy began referring to himself as "the former chief law enforcement officer of the United States." His commercials showed him talking about law and order to white male factory workers; with the sounds of machines blaring in the background, Kennedy was telling them: "We're going to have to have law and order in the United States. One thing we have to establish is that we won't tolerate lawlessness and violence." The new emphasis on law and order was correctly seen as a shift in emphasis. During the Indiana primary campaign, Warren Weaver argued that Kennedy was beginning to sound like the conservative Republican candidate George Romney on issues of law and order; "Kennedy: Meet the Conservative," *New York Times*, April 28, 1968, sect. 4, p. 1. Kennedy's younger aides complained that he was putting too much emphasis on the issue, and Richard Nixon remarked to Theodore White, "Do you know a lot of these people think Bobby is more a law-and-order man than I am!"; *The Making of the President 1968*, 169.

64. See ch. 1. In fact, Daniel Patrick Moynihan, a Kennedy supporter, gave his speech at the New School in opposition to the growing trend toward racial quotas in

higher education the very day Kennedy was shot; see Peter Kihss, "Moynihan Scores Ethnic Quota Idea," *New York Times*, June 5, 1968, 1.

65. Robert Coles, interview with the author, Cambridge, Mass., February 25, 1985. It is significant to note that, after Kennedy's death, two of his friends and great admirers, Jeff Greenfield and Jack Newfield, wrote a book, dedicated to RFK, whose central theme was the primacy of class. Time and time again, their *Populist Manifesto* argues for a class-based coalition of working-class whites and minorities, united in self-interest. The key to forging a populist majority, they write, is to "unify on the basis of class, rather than divide on the basis of race"; *A Populist Manifesto*, 42. "The real division in this country is not between generations or between races, but between the rich who have power and those blacks and whites who have neither power nor property. Until recently, such an alliance seemed impossible, in part because middle-class liberals have persistently defined public issues primarily in terms of race rather than class. 'White racism,' the Kerner Commission said, was the core of the problem" (20). To focus on race was to marginalize the problem and to mask white liberal hypocrisy. Thus, rallies should protest "overall economic practices of banks," not just their investments in South Africa (60). And liberals should not "sing 'We Shall Overcome' " while at the same time urging acreage and zoning restrictions (54). While Newfield and Greenfield did not explicitly address the issue of racial preferences, their general rule was clear. To unite blacks and white workers, programs must be offered *"all in terms that benefit both groups"* (21, emphasis in original). They emphasize, "Kennedy's program and constituency in 1968 were, in embryo the model for the future we are talking about in this book" (5, 29–30).

66. In addition, the appeal of Democrats to Wallace voters is not completely unique to Kennedy. Patrick Caddell noted that Jimmy Carter appealed to some Wallace voters; cited in Lipset and Raab, *The Politics of Unreason*, 522.

67. Lesher, *George Wallace*, 497–501.

68. Roy Reed, "In Memory of Dr. King: If He Were Alive," *New York Times*, January 20, 1986, A31.

69. Quoted in Lesher, *George Wallace*, 505.

70. Ibid., 505. The key difference between the latter-day Watson and the latter-day Wallace, of course, is that our nation has made progress since Watson's day: where Watson urged the disenfranchisement of blacks, Wallace lived through their reenfranchisement.

71. Quoted in Franklin, *Shadows of Race and Class*, 20.

72. Fuchs, *The American Kaleidoscope*, 198.

73. Campaign newspaper distributed by organizers for Jesse Jackson, cited in Ansley, "Stirring the Ashes," 1033. More recently, during the travails over the white working-class Olympic skater Tonya Harding, Jackson pleaded, "If America cannot find in its heart a sense of plight for Tonya Harding, it says something about our own souls"; quoted in Randall Sullivan, "The Tonya Harding Fall," *Rolling Stone* (July 14–28, 1994), 114.

74. The portion of such voters was probably small. First, we know that whites do seem willing to back another black candidate, Colin Powell. Second, many whites did vote for Jackson. One analyst found: "In many of the 1988 primaries and caucuses, in a field that included a half dozen white candidates, he won more white votes than black." In some states Jackson received "more white votes than major white candidates"; Fuchs, *The American Kaleidoscope*, 198–99.

75. Quoted in White, *American in Search of Itself*, 334.

76. See Mark Hosenball, "Jesse's Business: A Shakedown Racket?," *New Republic* (May 9, 1988): 10ff.

77. Edsall and Edsall, *Chain Reaction*, 205.

78. See "Red Suspenders" [pseudonym], "Minority Interest: Affirmative Action in the Bond Underwriting Business," *New Republic* (November 7, 1988): 23.

79. The Civil Rights Act of 1990 (eventually signed in 1991) was designed to restore civil rights law that had been weakened by the Supreme Court—particularly with respect to disparate impact cases—and to expand to women, religious minorities, and the dis-

abled the right to sue for damages in cases of intentional discrimination, a course of action then already available to African Americans. The portion of the legislation that received the most attention was whether a change in the law regarding disparate impact suits would make it so hard to employ the business necessity test that employers would throw up their hands and resort to quota hiring. But before the bill even came to the Senate floor, a group of moderate senators, including Jack Danforth, Chuck Robb, and others, negotiated a change with the bill's sponsor, Ted Kennedy, to ensure that quota hiring would not result.

The business community was less concerned about quotas than about the second section of the bill—the provision for damages in cases of gender discrimination. It was very difficult, of course, to publicly argue that racial discrimination warrants damages while gender discrimination does not, so the White House shrewdly turned an issue of class (damages, employer versus employee) into one of race (quotas, employee against fellow employee). Sen. Robb, for whom I worked at the time, pointed out the tactic in his speech supporting the Civil Rights Act of 1991; see *Congressional Record*, October 30, 1991, S15, 445–46.

The *Washington Post* reported that big business, including the Business Round Table (BRT), was not concerned about disparate impact and affirmative action. "Most companies have accepted affirmative action," the BRT's attorney Larry Lorber said. "In some respects, they view it as a helpful management tool to keep them from getting sued." What the BRT feared was "huge damage awards"; see Cindy Skrzycki, "Civil Rights and Corporate Qualms: Executives Fear Huge Damage Awards as Result of Hiring Bill," *Washington Post*, June 13, 1991, B11. The media, which had difficulty understanding the complexities of civil rights law, essentially reported the debate as one over quotas; see *Congressional Record*, October 30, 1991, S15, 445–46.

Though the quotas argument was specious in the context of the legislation, the Bush administration had, as Taylor and Liss write, "found political gold"; "Affirmative Action in the 1990s," 35. In the 1990 midterm elections, a number of races arguably turned on the quota issue; the Edsalls say that in *every* 1990 election in which Republicans made quotas "a major factor . . . the Republicans won"; *Chain Reaction*, 257. The most notorious use of the quotas issue came in the North Carolina Senate race: incumbent Jesse Helms ran television ads accusing his black opponent, Harvey Gantt, of supporting racial quotas. Helms's famous (and famously effective) quota ad blamed white unemployment on quotas. "You needed that job," the announcer intoned, as white hands crumpled a rejection notice. Gantt's pollster said the advertisement "swung the election"; Brown, *Minority Party*, 165; see also Edsall and Edsall, *Chain Reaction*, 257; and Brownstein, "Beyond Quotas," 18ff.

80. While Walter Mondale had run with a Democratic Party platform that essentially endorsed quotas (see Edsall and Edsall, *Chain Reaction*, 205) the Clinton-Gore campaign book, *Putting People First*, never uses the phrase "affirmative action" and clearly states the ticket's *opposition* to racial quotas; Bill Clinton and Al Gore, *Putting People First*, 64. The Clinton campaign continually sought to broaden the definition of civil rights; in fact, the campaign book's chapter on "Civil Rights" includes an entirely nonracial section on "Economic Empowerment" (65–66). (Hillary Rodham Clinton also understood the importance of biracial coalition-building around economic issues, having done her thesis at Wellesley on Saul Alinsky; see Elise O'Shaughnessy, "The Moynihan Mystique," *Vanity Fair* [May 1994]: 53.) "New Democrat" Clinton had chaired the Democratic Leadership Council (DLC), which in 1990 declared itself for equal opportunity, not equal results, much to the dismay of Jesse Jackson; Brown, *Minority Party*, 146–47; see also Ronald Brownstein, "Racial Politics," *American Prospect* (Spring 1992): 123.

In a debate during the New York primary, when asked about a local 20 percent racial contracting set-aside, Jerry Brown said, "Sure, I support that," while Clinton gave a highly conflicted answer; see Thomas B. Edsall, "Clinton Admits '60s Marijuana Use," *Washington Post*, March 30, 1992, A1. Edsall describes the confusing answer:

"I think on balance it's worth trying to have an affirmative action goal like that in a city with a large minority population," he said, in an apparent endorsement of the policy. But he then quickly backtracked from the actual practice in many set-aside programs, declaring that he would only support such contracts "if no one gets a contract [who] . . . cannot perform it for the same dollar value than anyone else can. . . . I think price and quality should be determining considerations. I don't think anybody should get business who cannot meet price and quality, but if you look at the whole history of African-American businesses and other businesses in America, what is happening is a lot of our neighborhoods and cities is there are not businesses there." ("The Special Interest Gambit," *Washington Post*, January 3, 1993, C2.)

These comments were overshadowed by Clinton's similarly ambivalent feelings toward marijuana. In the context of voting rights, Clinton expressed some reservations about minority voting districts, telling the story of a friend who said: "Bill, I just don't understand the world I'm living in. We need the federal courts to integrate our schools by race, but we need the federal courts to segregate our legislative districts by race"; quoted in Brown, *Minority Party*, 82.

Mark Shields attributes Bill Clinton's victory to the fact that "he kept his attention and the campaign's focus squarely on the economy and jobs. He was never sidetracked to those issues that have plagued the Democrats through the '70's and '80's, affirmative action for transvestites, taxidermists, and all those sort of bizarre, exotic, boutiquey issues that Democrats increasingly seem to be identified with at the presidential level especially"; Shields appearing on *The MacNeil/Lehrer NewsHour*, November 4, 1992.

Some civil rights leaders were not pleased. Charles V. Hamilton noted that "this was the first presidential election since 1944 where the civil rights of African Americans was not dealt with in some overt form"; "Promoting Priorities: African-American Political Influence in the 1990s," in National Urban League, *The State of Black America 1993*, 59. He scorned the Democratic ticket's emphasis on "those socioeconomic policies that helped *everyone*, not just blacks . . . the 'universal' approach to social policy as opposed to 'race-specific policies'" (60). During the campaign, Rep. Maxine Waters (D-Calif.), who cochaired Clinton's campaign, complained that her candidate never used the term "affirmative action"; see W. John Moore, "On the March Again?," *National Journal* (December 12, 1992): 2825. Black Rep. Charles B. Rangel (D-N.Y.) said, "It appears that at this point we are on the back burner. . . . I feel pretty damn hurt and embarrassed"; see Gwen Ifill, "Clinton Waves at Blacks as He Rushes By," *New York Times*, September 20, 1992, sect. 4, p. 1.

81. William Julius Wilson, "The Right Message," *New York Times*, March 17, 1992, A25. The *Times* said Clinton's impressive showings on Super Tuesday "give healthy evidence, probably for the first time since Robert Kennedy's Indiana primary campaign in 1968, that it is politically possible to bring poor blacks and blue-collar white voters together"; editorial, "Bill Clinton, in Black and White," *New York Times*, March 11, 1992, A22; see also Nicholas Lemann, "Hope Against Hope," *New Republic* (March 13, 1995): 31, 33 (noting that in his first run for Congress in 1974, Clinton carried four counties that had voted for George Wallace in 1968).

82. Moore, "On the March Again?," 2825.

83. Following his election, Clinton became a much stronger advocate of affirmative action, although his campaign instinct—to hedge on the issue—surfaces periodically. One of the first impressions of the new president was his emphasis on diversity in his cabinet. At one point Clinton did lash out at female critics who said he needed to hire more women, calling them "bean counters," but in the next breath he defended himself by proceeding to count beans himself; see "Everybody Happy?," *The Economist* (December 16, 1992–January 8, 1993): 30 (following Clinton's "bean counter" comment, "the news from Little Rock on December 21st was that . . . only women were being considered for attorney-general"); see also John B. Judis, "The Old Democrat,"

New Republic (February 22, 1993): 18. Ben Wattenberg complained, "This administration is turning into a walking billboard for a quota society"; quoted in Ruth Shalit, "Unwhite House," *New Republic* (April 12, 1993): 12. The administration, said Al Kamen of the *Washington Post*, "has elevated the practice [bean counting] to an art form"; "Filling the Robes," *Washington Post*, September 7, 1994, A19. Even after the 1994 election, the Clinton administration was timing its announcement to replace Press Secretary Dee Dee Myers with Michael McCurry until it could announce for another position "the appointment of a woman to offset the departure of Myers"; see Ann Devroy, "President to Name Glickman to Head Agriculture Dept.," *Washington Post*, December 22, 1994, A21.

In mid-February 1993, Secretary of Education Richard W. Riley made good on his confirmation hearing pledge to reverse the Bush position on race-based scholarships; see "Riley Endorses Minority Scholarships," *Higher Education and National Affairs* (January 25, 1993): 1; and Mary Jordan, "Minority Scholarship Rules Relaxed," *Washington Post*, February 18, 1994, A16. Clinton's Justice Department also joined the side of the University of Maryland, whose blacks-only scholarships were challenged by an Hispanic student (in October 1994 the Fourth Circuit Court of Appeals ruled against Maryland and the Clinton administration on the issue; the Supreme Court subsequently let stand the Fourth Circuit decision); see Stephen Labaton, "Educators Scrambling to Assess Ruling That Struck Down a Scholarship Program for Blacks," *New York Times*, October 29, 1994, 1. In 1994, Clinton's Justice Department supported the Piscataway, New Jersey, school board's decision to fire a white teacher in order to preserve diversity—a move that even supporters of affirmative action like Kathleen Sullivan said was unlikely to be sustained in the courts; see Iver Peterson, "Justice Dept. Switches Sides in Racial Case: Backs Board on Layoff of New Jersey Teacher," *New York Times*, August 14, 1994, 37, 46.

While affirmative action did not play an overt role in the 1994 midterm congressional elections, many observers think Clinton's emphasis on diversity registered negatively with many voters; see, e.g., Michael Lind, "What Bill Wrought," *New Republic* (December 5, 1994): 20. The white male vote had been edging away from Democrats for years, but never so dramatically as in 1994. Where white men had split between Republican and Democratic House candidates 51–49 in 1992, the Republican edge over Democrats in House races leaped to 62–38 in 1994, an even more dramatic gap than the 57–43 split in the year of Ronald Reagan's 1984 landslide; see "Portrait of the Electorate: Who Voted for Whom in the House," *New York Times*, November 13, 1994, sect. 1, p. 24. The Democratic pollster Geoffrey Garin said, "The big story of the election is the hostility among blue-collar men who haven't gone to college"; see Dennis Farney, "Have Liberals Ignored 'Have-Less' Whites at Their Own Peril?," *Wall Street Journal*, December 14, 1994, A1.

Republicans were quick to see the link to affirmative action; see ibid. The Senate majority leader, Bob Dole, asked after the election, "Why did 62 percent of white males vote Republican in 1994? I think it's because of things like this, where sometimes the best qualified person does not get the job because he or she may be one color"; R. Jeffrey Smith, "GOP Senators Begin Studying Repeal of Affirmative Action," *Washington Post*, February 6, 1995, A1, A5. While in 1992 Clinton's effort to downplay affirmative action and emphasize nonracial social programs was highly effective, those days appear to be over. Affirmative action is likely to be the centerpiece of the 1996 presidential election— particularly if a California initiative barring racial preferences goes to the voters.

84. This is not to suggest that Phillips ever engaged in the race-baiting of a George Wallace; far from it. But Phillips did shift his emphasis from the social issues (crime, welfare, quotas) to economic populism; see *The Politics of Rich and Poor*, 33 (summarizing his earlier views); and *Boiling Point*, 58 (citing *The Emerging Republican Majority*).

85. See Phillips, *The Emerging Republican Majority*, esp. 83–85, 140.

86. See Edsall, "The Hidden Role of Race [review]," *New Republic* (July 30 and August 6, 1990): 35. Interestingly, the author Tom Wolfe made a parallel shift, from attacking elite liberals in *Radical Chic* in the 1960s to attacking the plutocracy in *Bonfire of the Vanities* in the 1980s. Phillips argued that the class appeal would work, and that

the best Republican strategists knew it; see *The Politics of Rich and Poor*, 30–31.

87. See Al Gore, "The Cynics Are Wrong," commencement address, Harvard University, June 9, 1994, reprinted in *Harvard* (July-August 1994): 30.

88. See, e.g., a 1995 *Washington Post* poll, showing that 76 percent of men and 69 percent of women oppose affirmative action for women; Ladowsky, "That's No White Male . . . ."

89. William Julius Wilson notes that blacks, Hispanics, and the poor represent only about 25 percent of the population; "Race-Neutral Programs," 80. They are an even smaller percentage of the voting population; see Days, "Civil Rights at the Crossroads," 279 ("Strong forces of racism and sexism . . . will make it difficult to forge the type of socioeconomic coalition I am suggesting. But I think that there is no alternative").

90. See Huckfeldt and Kohfeld, *Race and the Decline of Class*, 179–80. Emphasizing class should appeal to poor and working-class blacks, who are much more likely to be concerned about economics than race anyway. Sixty percent of middle-class blacks are more conscious of race than class, compared to 5 percent of poor and working-class blacks; Lind, *The Next American Nation*, 177.

91. See ch. 4.

92. Woodward, *The Agenda*, 24.

93. Michael K. Frisby and Rick Wartzman, "Clinton, Seeking Political Comeback, Uses Speech to Nation to Urge Renewed Faith in Government," *Wall Street Journal*, January 25, 1995, A18.

94. Edsall and Edsall, "Race," 62.

95. Rustin, "The Failure of Black Separatism," 34.

96. Kozol, *Savage Inequalities*, 56.

97. Geoghegan, *Which Side Are You On?*, 30–32. See also Lind, "What Bill Wrought," 22 (on the ineffectiveness of presidents who do not stress class).

98. The left should be wary of its alliances with big business. Although the business community will sometimes prove a powerful ally for good (e.g., when it supported nonviolent desegregation in the South), the alliance usually imposes severe costs on progressives; see Bloom, *Race, Class, and the Civil Rights Movement*, 215. When the Business Round Table negotiated with civil rights groups to help pass the Civil Rights Act of 1991—and the price of support was a cap on damages for gender discrimination, the real concern of business all along—one smelled the faint aroma of the post–Civil War unholy alliance that William Julius Wilson described; *The Declining Significance of Race*, 57.

99. Sleeper, *The Closest of Strangers*, 132, 160.

100. Ronald Steel, "The Bobby Gap," *New Republic* (May 25, 1992): 16.

101. West, *Beyond Eurocentrism*, 1:80.

102. See Peller, "Race Consciousness," 833.

103. Schlesinger interview (1985).

104. Greenfield interview (1985).

105. Rieder, *Canarsie*, 9.

106. Edsall and Edsall, *Chain Reaction*, 186.

107. Mark Shields, ". . . And Blue Collar Wannabes," *Washington Post*, June 7, 1995, A21.

108. Starr, "Civil Reconstruction," 127.

109. As Bayard Rustin wrote: "Any preferential approach postulated along racial, ethnic, religious, or sexual lines will only disrupt a multicultural society, and lead to a backlash. However, special treatment can be provided to those who have been exploited or denied opportunities if solutions are predicated along class lines, precisely because all religious, ethnic, and racial groups have a depressed class who would benefit"; "The King to Come," 21.

110. Thomas and Mary Edsall, in their book about the breakup of the New Deal coalition, write, "Of the four issues—race, rights, reform, and taxes—race has been the most critical, and the most powerful, in effecting political change"; *Chain Reaction*, 5.

111. Edsall, interview (1995).

112. The argument, then, is not that the negative political consequences of pro-

moting a race-conscious effort like affirmative action outweigh the moral arguments in favor of it. While "political" considerations are frequently thought of as competing with "the merits" or the "moral" considerations—especially in the area of civil rights—here, the politics of the situation are inextricably intertwined with the moral considerations, and both point in precisely the same direction. Lyndon Johnson believed that pushing the Civil Rights Act of 1964 "delivered the South to the Republican party" for a generation, but that doing so was a price well worth paying. In switching to class-based affirmative action, however, there is no tension between doing what is politically popular and doing the right thing.

113. Fager, *Uncertain Resurrection*, 14. See also Garrow, *Bearing the Cross*, 358, 439, 536, 540.

114. Garrow, *Bearing the Cross*, 440, 430. King drew on Bayard Rustin's celebrated 1965 article, "From Protest to Politics," in which Rustin argued that the dismantling of Jim Crow was only half the battle. "What," he asked, "is the value of winning access to public accommodations for those who lack money to use them?"; *Commentary* (February 1965): 25. Rustin said that removing legal barriers leaves obstacles "of far greater magnitude," obstacles rooted in "society's failure to meet not only the Negro's needs, but human needs generally" (27).

115. Garrow, *Bearing the Cross*, 536.

116. King, "Showdown for Nonviolence," 24–25.

117. Fager, *Uncertain Resurrection*, 18. King, of course, never saw the Poor People's Campaign, and it is generally acknowledged that it was something of a strategic disaster, run, as it was, by men less able than the slain civil rights leader. The demands were unfocused, the campaigners undisciplined. But poor execution does not undercut the insight that, in proper hands, the coalition is possible, necessary, and desirable.

118. There are worse things in the world than marginalizing. The Civil Rights Act of 1964 was a monumental step forward, even though it addressed only a subset of the larger question of unjust dismissal by employers. (An employer may still fire nonunion employees for no good reason so long as the reason is not related to race, gender, religion, etc.) In 1964 the country was not ready to upset the general rule of "employment at will." Indeed, Hubert Humphrey highlighted the moderate nature of the Civil Rights Act when he noted that it "does not limit the employer's freedom to hire, fire, promote, or demote for any reasons—or for no reasons—so long as his action is not based on race"; Bolick, *Changing Course*, 48. Marginalizing made sense then because it was easier to get people to uphold the principle of color blindness. When the focus shifted to proactive remedies and preferences, the narrow racial focus became a liability.

119. Harrington and Kaufman, "Black Reparations—Two Views," 317, 318.

120. Harrington, *The Next Left*, 144. In 1987, Harrington returned to the theme, arguing that public focus on race, starting with the Kerner Commission, had "diverted attention from the ugly reality dramatized by white male poverty: the class and economic structures that victimize people without regard to race or gender." While blacks and women suffer disproportionately, Harrington wrote, "the issue is not one of race but of class, and the exploitation of the lower classes by the upper"; "The Invisible Poor: White Males," *Washington Post*, February 15, 1987, C1.

121. Cuomo, *Forest Hills Diary*, vii, 117–18. (The first two quotations are from the book's introduction by Jimmy Breslin.)

122. Cuomo interview (1987). During his attempt to resolve the housing dispute, Cuomo played basketball with some middle-class black families in Hollis, Queens, and reported: "They feel that many of the whites who oppose [low-income housing] in Forest Hills are bigots, but then in an interesting contradiction they themselves admit they would oppose it in their own neighborhoods"; *Forest Hills Diary*, 37–38. Years later Cuomo pointed out that when poor black housing was proposed in a middle-class black neighborhood in Baisley Park, the resistance was even "more ferocious" than in Forest Hills, "yet the story never got written"; quoted in Sleeper, *The Closest of Strangers*, 151; see also Freeman, "Race and Class," 1889.

In his famous keynote address at the 1984 Democratic National Convention, Cuomo spoke of "A Tale of Two Cities," drawing on the Dickensian vision of separate cities, divided not by race (as the Kerner Commission saw it) but by class; see "A Tale of Two Cities," in Cuomo, *More Than Words*, 21–31. In his commentary on the speech, James Reston wrote, "So what is developing now is a campaign based on class conflict. . . . The paradox of [Cuomo's] speech was that he was calling for both unity and a campaign stressing class divisions"; "Cuomo's Theme," *New York Times*, July 18, 1984, A23.

Again, in 1987, when Cuomo was confronted with a white attack on an innocent black in Howard Beach, he returned to the theme. "The part of the discussion on Howard Beach that is most important in the long run," Cuomo told the *New York Times*, "is like the one I had at Forest Hills. Underlying all this tension, to some extent, are conditions of deprivation—economic deprivation, basically. In the long run, the best thing you can do to deal with these tensions is to strengthen our education system, strengthen our economy, provide more people with a chance to work"; Jeffrey Schmaltz, "Cuomo and Howard Beach: Recalling Political Roots," *New York Times*, January 19, 1987, B1, B3.

123. Quoted in Mike Barnicle, "Busing Puts Burdens on Working Class, Black and White," *Boston Globe*, October 15, 1974, 23.

124. The interview stirred up "a storm of protest from liberal circles"; Lukas, *Common Ground*, 506. Coles recalls, "There have been two times in my life when I got into a lot of trouble for what I've said. One was that occasion [the *Globe* interview], and the other was when I wrote *The Middle Americans*. And it was the same reaction, namely, one of real criticism and, more than criticism, outrage"; Coles interview (1995).

125. Poor black students were not bused to the wealthy white suburbs—to Wellesley, where Judge W. Arthur Garrity resided, or to Brookline or Lincoln, where the *Boston Globe* editors lived—they were bused to places such as Charlestown, home to the working-class Irish like Alice McGoff. McGoff, Lukas writes, "knew full well which whites would pay the price" for school desegregation. "It wouldn't be those who worked in the big corporate and law offices downtown, the ones who dined in those Back Bay clubs and lived in the comfortable, all-white suburbs. No, as usual it would be the working-class whites who shared the inner city with blacks, competed with them for schools and jobs and housing, and jostled with them on the street corners"; *Common Ground*, 27. McGoff, says Lukas, "had come to understand, it was easy to be liberal about other people's problems. Maybe that was why all the problems were in the city and all the liberals in the suburbs" (269); see also ibid., 27, 135–36, 244–45, 269, 271, 506.

126. Ibid., 22 (paraphrased).

127. Lukas writes of his protagonist, Colin Diver: "As the decade wore on, Colin came to perceive the 'American dilemma' less in purely racial and legal terms, more in class and economic terms. . . . Only by providing jobs and other economic opportunities to the deprived—black and white alike—could the city reduce the deep sense of grievance harbored by both communities, alleviate some of the antisocial behavior grounded in such resentments, and begin to close the terrible gap between the rich and the poor, the suburb and the city, the hopeful and the hopeless"; ibid., 650.

Lukas calls affirmative action "flawed but necessary," saying, "We as a society did such grievous damage to American blacks that compensation is due"; see "Why I Can't 'Bork' Clarence Thomas," A15. But he adds: "On the other hand, I do believe also that we are a society in which class remains an extremely important, if relatively rarely addressed issue and that the people of Charlestown, Southie and Dorchester—the whites of those communities— . . . have suffered because of class. And that it's difficult to argue that they ought not to some degree share in that compensatory justice"; Lukas interview (1995).

128. Beatty, "Race, Class and the City" [review of *Common Ground*], 112.

129. The busing order was a failure in racial desegregation because it accelerated white flight to the suburbs and private education. Beatty notes that whites as a percentage of Boston schools dropped from 60 percent in 1972 to 27 percent in 1985, even though the white population of Boston remained at two-thirds; ibid., 110.

130. In Kentucky, Jefferson County's school superintendent, Stephen Daeschner, had the same idea when he first arrived. As the *Louisville Courier Journal* reports, "Why, he wondered, when everyone was working so hard to implement a voluntary racial integration plan two years ago, didn't the school district also try to balance schools along socioeconomic lines? And why, he wondered, does the school district have so many schools with high concentrations of students from poor families? The questions were met with silence. J. Back, principal of Roosevelt-Perry Elementary School, where 99 percent of the students are poor, recalled later that he felt like leaping from his chair and cheering"; Holly Holland, "Schools Worried by Clusters of Poverty: Superintendent Discusses Spreading Burden More Evenly," *Louisville Courier Journal*, December 11, 1993, A16.

131. Beatty, "Race, Class and the City," 112. If for Beatty many of our problems are not solvable until we reach beyond race to class, so, too, the class emphasis provides strong political dividends for progressives. Writing in 1987 in the wake of the Howard Beach incident, Beatty talked about the importance of emphasizing "the kinds of social programs that might help the races find common ground—national health insurance, quality education for all, more police protection," and derided the Democrats' "suburban agenda," which included, among other things, "affirmative action for middle-class blacks and female graduates of law schools," programs that obviously "have nothing to say to working class whites"; "Howard Beach Portents," A23. Beatty later argued that class-based affirmative action would help provide precisely the political common ground he and other urban populists have sought and would help address the greater inequity, which stems from class unfairness; Beatty interview (1995).

132. DeMott, *The Imperial Middle*, 176.

133. Fallows, "What Did You Do in the Class War, Daddy?," 215, 216. Five years later, when Fallows took a critical look at the SAT, he returned to the same theme. While much had been said of the racial bias of the test, Fallows wrote, "the bias is not racial so much as economic"; "The Tests and the 'Brightest,' " 47.

134. Wilson, *The Declining Significance of Race*, 154. See also Wilson, *The Truly Disadvantaged*, viii. In fact, Wilson considers himself "a social democrat, and probably to the left politically of an overwhelming majority of these critics"; *The Truly Disadvantaged*, viii. In a 1990 article for *American Prospect*, "Race-Neutral Programs and the Democratic Coalition," Wilson again distinguished himself from conservatives who are against both affirmative action and social welfare policies (81). The language employed in *The Declining Significance of Race* is hardly Burkean, with its references to racial oppression and class subordination.

135. Quoted in Clark and Gersham, "The Black Plight," 98. In several articles, Wilson cites his support for Vivian Henderson's call for race-neutral remedies: "Policies, programs, and politics designed in the future to cope with the problems of the poor and victimized will also yield benefits to blacks. In contrast, *any* efforts to treat blacks separately from the rest of the nation are likely to lead to frustration, heightened racial animosities, and a waste of the country's resources and the precious resources of black people [emphasis added]"; see Wilson, "Public Policy Research and the Truly Disadvantaged," in Jencks and Peterson, *The Urban Underclass*, 477; see also "Race-Neutral Programs," 79; and "Another Look at the Truly Disadvantaged," 655–56.

136. While clearly sensitive to matters of race, West praises "race-transcending prophetic leaders" and is himself an honorary chairman of the late Michael Harrington's Democratic Socialists of America; West, *Race Matters*, 40; Jervis Anderson, "The Public Intellectual," *New Yorker* (January 17, 1994): 43. A colleague of West's told *Time*, "He has almost singlehandedly helped us see the importance of economic and class issues within the black community and the larger society"; "Philosopher with a Mission," *Time*, June 7, 1993, 60; see also Steinberg, *Turning Back*, 126.

137. David Mills, "Fire and Race: The Passionate Arguments of Cornel West," *Washington Post Magazine* (August 8, 1993): 25. And as a purely political matter, West says, we must move beyond race and gender and sexual orientation to address class or there will be "many, many more David Dukes by the end of the twentieth century"; *Beyond Eurocentrism*, 2:167.

138. In ch. 5 of *Race Matters*, entitled "Beyond Affirmative Action and Equality and Identity," West criticizes racial preferences, like other preferences, for benefiting "middle class Americans disproportionately," and he says it is "neither a major solution to poverty nor a sufficient means to equality" (63–64). While West believes affirmative action is perhaps "the best possible compromise and concession" and opposes attacks on affirmative action, he prefers, in principle, "a class-based affirmative action," which he sees as a "more wide-reaching" policy (64–65).

139. Friedan now teaches a course, "New Paradigm: Beyond Identity Politics"; see "A Woman's Work: Forget Sexual Politics, Betty Friedan Says. Economic Empowerment Is the Real Issue," *Washington Post*, June 21, 1995, D1, D10.

140. E. J. Dionne, Jr., "Affirmative Action's Limits," *Washington Post*, April 11, 1995, A21.

141. See Taylor, "The Continuing Struggle," 1693–94. See also Ralph Neas, quoted in Moore, "On the March Again?," 2826.

Bibliography

Books

Affirmative Action Review: Report to the President. Washington, D.C., 1995.

Allport, Gordon W. *The Nature of Prejudice.* Cambridge, Mass.: Addison-Wesley, 1954.

American Law Institute/American Bar Association. *The Civil Rights Act of 1991.* Philadelphia: American Law Institute, 1993.

Archer, Jules. *1968: Year of Crisis.* New York: Messner, 1971.

Asian Women United of California. *Making Waves: An Anthology of Writings by and about Asian American Women.* Boston: Beacon Press, 1989.

Bartholet, Elizabeth. *Family Bonds: Adoption and the Politics of Parenting.* Boston: Houghton Mifflin, 1993.

Beatty, Jack. *The Rascal King: The Life and Times of James Michael Curley, 1874–1958.* Reading, Mass.: Addison-Wesley, 1992.

Bell, Daniel. *The Coming of Post Industrial Society: A Venture in Social Forecasting.* New York: Basic Books, 1973.

Bell, Derrick. *Race, Racism, and American Law.* 3rd ed. Boston: Little, Brown, 1992.

————. *Faces at the Bottom of the Well: The Permanence of Racism.* New York: Basic Books, 1992.

————. *And We Are Not Saved: The Elusive Quest for Racial Justice.* New York: Basic Books, 1987.

Bickel, Alexander. *The Morality of Consent.* New Haven, Conn.: Yale University Press, 1975.

Bittker, Boris I. *The Case for Black Reparations.* New York: Vintage/Random House, 1973.

Blackstone, William T., and Robert D. Heslep, eds. *Social Justice and Preferential Treatment: Women and Racial Minorities in Education and Business.* Athens: University of Georgia Press, 1977.

Blanchard, Fletcher A., and Faye J. Crosby, eds. *Affirmative Action in Perspective.* New York: Springer-Verlag, 1989.

Blau, Peter M., ed. *Approaches to the Study of Social Structure.* New York: Free Press, 1975.

Blau, Peter M., and Otis Dudley Duncan. *The American Occupational Structure.* New York: Wiley, 1967.

Bloch, Susan Low, and Thomas G. Krattenmaker. *Supreme Court Politics: The Institution and Its Procedures.* St. Paul, Minn.: West, 1994.

Bloom, Jack M. *Class, Race, and the Civil Rights Movement.* Bloomington: Indiana University Press, 1987.

Blumenthal, Sidney. *The Permanent Campaign.* New York: Simon & Schuster, 1982.

Bolick, Clint. *Changing Course: Civil Rights at the Crossroads.* New Brunswick, N.J.: Transaction Books, 1988.

Brint, Steven, and Jerome Karabel. *The Diverted Dream: Community Colleges and the Promise of Educational Opportunity in America, 1900–1985.* New York: Oxford University Press, 1989.

Brittain, John A. *The Inheritance of Economic Status.* Washington, D.C.: Brookings Institution, 1977.

Brown, Peter. *Minority Party: Why Democrats Face Defeat in 1992 and Beyond.* Washington, D.C.: Regnery Gateway, 1991.

Bruno, Jerry, and Jeff Greenfield. *The Advance Man.* New York: Morrow, 1971.

Califano, Joseph A., Jr. *Governing America: An Insider's Report from the White House and the Cabinet.* New York: Simon & Schuster, 1981.

Campbell, Angus, and Howard Schuman. *Supplemental Studies for the National Advisory Commission on Civil Disorders: Racial Attitudes in Fifteen American Cities.* New York: Praeger, 1968.

Carter, Stephen. *Reflections of an Affirmative Action Baby*. New York: Basic Books, 1991.

Chavez, Linda. *Out of the Barrio: Toward a New Politics of Hispanic Assimilation*. New York: Basic Books, 1991.

Chester, Arthur, Godfrey Hodgson, and Bruce Page. *An American Melodrama: The Presidential Campaign of 1968*. New York: Viking, 1969.

Chester, Ronald. *Inheritance, Wealth, and Society*. Bloomington: Indiana University Press, 1982.

Citizens' Commission on Civil Rights. *One Nation Indivisible: The Civil Rights Challenge for the 1990s*. Edited by Reginald C. Govan and William L. Taylor. 1989.

———. *Affirmative Action to Open the Doors of Opportunity: A Policy of Fairness and Compassion That Has Worked*. Edited by William L. Taylor and Roger S. Kuhn. 1984.

Clark, Kenneth B. *Dark Ghetto: Dilemmas of Social Power*. New York: Harper & Row, 1965.

Clayton, Susan D., and Faye J. Crosby. *Justice, Gender, and Affirmative Action*. Ann Arbor: University of Michigan Press, 1992.

Clinton, Bill, and Al Gore. *Putting People First: How We Can All Change America*. New York: Times Books, 1992.

Cohen, Marshall, Thomas Nagel, and Thomas Scanlon. *Equality and Preferential Treatment*. Princeton, N.J.: Princeton University Press, 1977.

Coleman, James S., et al. *Equality of Educational Opportunity*. Washington, D.C.: U.S. Government Printing Office, 1966.

Coles, Robert. *Privileged Ones*. Volume 5 of *Children of Crisis*. Boston: Little, Brown, 1977.

College Entrance Examination Board. *College Bound Seniors: 1994 Profile of SAT and Achievement Test Takers*. Princeton, N.J.: Educational Testing Service, 1994.

Cose, Ellis. *The Rage of a Privileged Class*. New York: HarperCollins, 1993.

Cottingham, Phoebe H., and David T. Ellwood, eds. *Welfare Policy for the 1990s*. Cambridge, Mass.: Harvard University Press, 1989.

Cox, Archibald. *The Role of the Supreme Court in American Government*. New York: Oxford University Press, 1976.

Craver, Charles B. *Can Unions Survive? The Rejuvenation of the American Labor Movement*. New York: New York University Press, 1993.

Cuomo, Mario Matthew. *More Than Words: The Speeches of Mario Cuomo*. New York: St. Martin's Press, 1993.

———. *Forest Hills Diary: The Crisis of Low-Income Housing*. New York: Vintage, 1983.

Davis, F. James. *Who Is Black? One Nation's Definition*. University Park: Pennsylvania State University Press, 1991.

deLone, Richard H. *Small Futures: Children, Inequality, and the Limits of Liberal Reform*. New York: Harcourt Brace Jovanovich, 1979.

DeMott, Benjamin. *The Imperial Middle: Why Americans Can't Think Straight about Class*. New York: Morrow, 1990.

Dershowitz, Alan M. *Chutzpah*. Boston: Little, Brown, 1991.

Dollard, John. *Caste and Class in a Southern Town*. Madison: University of Wisconsin Press, 1937, 1988.

Douglas, William O. *The Court Years, 1939–1975: The Autobiography of William O. Douglas*. New York: Random House, 1980.

Dreyfuss, Joel, and Charles Lawrence III. *The Bakke Case: The Politics of Inequality*. New York: Harcourt Brace Jovanovich, 1979.

D'Souza, Dinesh. *The End of Racism*. New York: Free Press, 1995.

———. *Illiberal Education: The Politics of Race and Sex on Campus*. New York: Vintage, 1991, 1992.

Du Bois, W. E. B. *Black Reconstruction*. New York: S. A. Russell, 1935.

Duncan, Otis D., David L. Featherman, and Beverly Duncan. *Socioeconomic Background and Achievement*. New York: Seminar Press, 1972.

Dutton, Frederick G. *Changing Sources of Power: American Politics in the 1970s*. New York: McGraw-Hill, 1971.

Dworkin, Ronald. *Taking Rights Seriously*. Cambridge, Mass.: Harvard University Press, 1977.

Eastland, Terry, and William Bennett. *Counting by Race: Equality from the Founding Fathers to* Bakke *and* Weber. New York: Basic Books, 1979.

Edelman, Marian Wright. *Guide My Feet*. Boston: Beacon Press, 1995.

Edsall, Thomas B. *The New Politics of Inequality*. New York: Norton, 1984.

Edsall, Thomas Byrne, and Mary D. Edsall. *Chain Reaction: The Impact of Race, Rights, and Taxes on American Politics*. New York: Norton, 1991.

Ehrenreich, Barbara. *The Worst Years of Our Lives: Irreverent Notes from a Decade of Greed*. New York: Pantheon, 1990.

———. *Fear of Falling: The Inner Life of the Middle Class*. New York: HarperCollins, 1989.

Ehrlichman, John. *Witness to Power: The Nixon Years*. New York: Simon & Schuster, 1982.

Ellwood, David T. *Poor Support: Poverty in the American Family*. New York: Basic Books, 1988.

Ely, John Hart. *Democracy and Distrust: A Theory of Judicial Review*. Cambridge, Mass.: Harvard University Press, 1980.

Epstein, Richard. *Forbidden Grounds: The Case Against Employment Discrimination Laws*. Cambridge, Mass.: Harvard University Press, 1992.

Fager, Charles. *Uncertain Resurrection: The Poor People's Washington Campaign*. Grand Rapids, Mich.: Eerdmans, 1969.

Fallows, James. *More Like Us: Making America Great Again*. Boston: Houghton Mifflin, 1989.

Farber, Daniel A., William N. Eskridge, Jr., and Philip P. Frickey. *Constitutional Law: Themes for the Constitution's Third Century*. St. Paul, Minn.: West, 1993.

Featherman, David L., and Robert Hauser. *Opportunity and Change*. New York: Academic Press, 1978.

Fiscus, Ronald J. *The Constitutional Logic of Affirmative Action*. Durham, N.C.: Duke University Press, 1992.

Fishkin, James. *Justice, Equal Opportunity, and the Family*. New Haven, Conn.: Yale University Press, 1983.

Fleming, John E. *The Lengthening Shadow of Slavery: A Historical Justification for Affirmative Action for Blacks in Higher Education*. Washington, D.C.: Howard University Press, 1976.

Franklin, Raymond S. *Shadows of Race and Class*. Minneapolis: University of Minnesota Press, 1991.

Fried, Charles. *Order and Law: Arguing the Reagan Revolution—A Firsthand Account*. New York: Simon & Schuster, 1991.

Friedman, Milton, and Rose Friedman. *Free to Choose: A Personal Statement*. New York: Harcourt Brace Jovanovich, 1980.

Fuchs, Lawrence H. *The American Kaleidoscope: Race, Ethnicity, and the Civil Culture*. Hanover, N.H.: Wesleyan University Press/University Press of New England, 1990.

Fullinwider, Robert K. *The Reverse Discrimination Controversy: A Moral and Legal Analysis*. Totowa, N.J.: Rowman and Littlefield, 1980.

Funderburg, Lise. *Black, White, Other: Biracial Americans Talk about Race and Identity*. New York: Morrow, 1994.

Fussell, Paul. *Class: A Guide Through the American Status System*. New York: Ballantine, 1983.

Garrow, David. *Bearing the Cross: Martin Luther King, Jr., and the Southern Christian Leadership Conference*. New York: Morrow, 1986.

Geoghegan, Thomas. *Which Side Are You On? Trying to Be for Labor When It's Flat on Its Back*. New York: Farrar, Straus & Giroux, 1991.

Getman, Julius G. *In the Company of Scholars: The Struggle for the Soul of Higher Education*. Austin: University of Texas Press, 1992.

Gilligan, Carol. *In a Different Voice: Psychological Theory and Women's Development*. Cambridge, Mass.: Harvard University Press, 1982.

Glazer, Nathan. *Ethnic Dilemmas, 1964–1982*. Cambridge, Mass.: Harvard University Press, 1983.

————. *Affirmative Discrimination: Ethnic Inequality and Public Policy*. New York: Basic Books, 1975.

Glazer, Nathan, and Daniel P. Moynihan. eds. *Ethnicity: Theory and Experience*. Cambridge, Mass.: Harvard University Press, 1975.

Goldman, Alan H. *Justice and Reverse Discrimination*. Princeton, N.J.: Princeton University Press, 1979.

Goldthorpe, John H. *Social Mobility and Class Structure in Modern Britain*. 2nd edition. Oxford: Clarendon Press, 1987.

Goodwin, Richard N. *Remembering America: A Voice from the Sixties*. Boston: Little, Brown, 1988.

Graham, Hugh Davis. *The Civil Rights Era: Origins and Development of National Policy, 1960–1972*. Oxford: Oxford University Press, 1990.

Greenawalt, Kent. *Discrimination and Reverse Discrimination*. New York: Knopf, 1983.

Greenberg, Jack. *Crusaders in the Courts: How a Dedicated Band of Lawyers Fought for the Civil Rights Revolution*. New York: Basic Books, 1994.

Gross, Barry R. *Discrimination in Reverse: Is Turnabout Fair Play?* New York: New York University Press, 1978.

Guinier, Lani. *The Tyranny of the Majority: Fundamental Fairness in Representative Democracy*. New York: Free Press, 1994.

Hacker, Andrew. *Two Nations: Black and White, Separate, Hostile, Unequal*. New York: Scribner's, 1992.

Halberstam, David. *The Unfinished Odyssey of Robert Kennedy*. New York: Random House, 1968.

Hamilton, Richard F. *Class and Politics in the United States*. New York: Wiley, 1972.

Harrington, Michael. *The Next Left: The History of a Future*. New York: Holt, 1986.

————. *The Other America: Poverty in the United States*. Baltimore: Penguin, 1966.

Hartz, Louis. *The Liberal Tradition in America*. 2nd edition. New York: Harcourt Brace Jovanovich, 1991.

Hastings, Max. *America 1968: The Fire This Time*. London: Gollancz, 1969.

Hayek, Friedrich A. *The Constitution of Liberty*. Chicago: Gateway/Regnery, 1960, 1972.

Herrnstein, Richard and Charles Murray. *The Bell Curve: Intelligence and Class Structure in American Life*. New York: Free Press, 1994.

Hill, Herbert, and James E. Jones, Jr., eds. *Race in America: The Struggle for Equality*. Madison: University of Wisconsin Press, 1993.

Huckfeldt, Robert, and Carol Weitzel Kohfeld. *Race and the Decline of Class in American Politics*. Urbana: University of Illinois Press, 1989.

Hughes, Robert. *Culture of Complaint: The Fraying of America*. New York: Oxford University Press, 1993.

Jeffries, John C., Jr., *Justice Lewis F. Powell, Jr.: A Biography*. New York: Scribner's, 1994.

Jencks, Christopher. *Rethinking Social Policy: Race, Poverty, and the Underclass*. Cambridge, Mass.: Harvard University Press, 1992.

————. *Who Gets Ahead? The Determinants of Economic Success in America*. New York: Basic Books, 1979.

Jencks, Christopher, et al. *Inequality: A Reassessment of the Effect of Family and Schooling in America*. New York: Basic Books, 1972.

Jencks, Christopher, and Paul E. Peterson, eds. *The Urban Underclass*. Washington, D.C.: Brookings Institution, 1991.

Johnson, Haynes. *Divided We Fall: Gambling with History in the Nineties*. New York: Norton, 1994.

Joint Center for Political Studies. *Black Initiative and Governmental Responsibility*.

Washington, D.C.: Joint Center for Political Studies, 1987.

Kahl, Joseph A. *The American Class Structure.* New York: Rinehart, 1957.

Kahl, Joseph A., and Dennis Gilbert. *The American Class Structure: A New Synthesis.* Chicago: Dorsey Press, 1987.

Kahlenberg, Richard D. *Broken Contract: A Memoir of Harvard Law School.* New York: Hill & Wang, 1992.

Karabel, Jerome. *Freshman Admissions at Berkeley: A Policy for the 1990s and Beyond.* Berkeley: University of California Press, 1989.

Karenga, Maulana. *Introduction to Black Studies.* Inglewood, Calif.: Kawaida, 1982.

Kaus, Mickey. *The End of Equality.* New York: Basic Books, 1992.

Kellough, J. Edward. *Federal Equal Employment Opportunity Policy and Numerical Goals and Timetables: An Impact Assessment.* New York: Praeger, 1989.

Kerlow, Eleanor. *Poisoned Ivy: How Egos, Ideology, and Power Politics Almost Ruined Harvard Law School.* New York: St. Martin's Press, 1994.

Kerner, Otto, et al. *Report of the National Advisory Commission on Civil Disorders.* Washington, D.C.: U.S. Government Printing Office, 1968.

King, Martin Luther, Jr. *Where Do We Go From Here?* Boston: Beacon Press, 1968.

———. *Why We Can't Wait.* New York: New American Library, 1964.

Kingston, Paul William, and Lionel S. Lewis, eds. *The High Status Track: Studies of Elite Schools and Stratification.* Albany: State University of New York Press, 1990.

Klitgaard, Robert. *Choosing Elites.* New York: Basic Books, 1985.

Kluger, Richard. *Simple Justice: The History of* Brown v. Board of Education *and Black America's Struggle for Equality.* New York: Knopf, 1975.

Koch, Edward I. *Citizen Koch: An Autobiography.* New York: St. Martin's Press, 1992.

Kotlowitz, Alex. *There Are No Children Here: The Story of Two Boys Growing up in the Other America.* New York: Doubleday, 1991.

Kozol, Jonathan. *Savage Inequalities: Children in America's Schools.* New York: Crown, 1991.

Kuttner, Robert. *The Life of the Party: Democratic Prospects in 1988 and Beyond.* New York: Viking, 1987.

Landes, David S. *The Unbound Prometheus: Technological Change and Industrial Development in Western Europe from 1750 to the Present.* Cambridge: Cambridge University Press, 1969, 1972.

Lapham, Lewis H. *Money and Class in America: Notes and Observations on Our Civil Religion.* New York: Weidenfeld and Nicolson, 1988.

Lebergott, Stanley. *The American Economy: Income, Wealth, and Want.* Princeton, N.J.: Princeton University Press, 1976.

Lemann, Nicholas. *The Promised Land: The Great Black Migration and How It Changed America.* New York: Knopf, 1991.

Lesher, Stephan. *George Wallace: American Populist.* Reading, Mass.: Addison-Wesley, 1994.

Liebling, A. J. *The Earl of Louisiana.* Baton Rouge: Louisiana State University Press, 1961.

Liebow, Elliot. *Tally's Corner: A Study of Negro Streetcorner Men.* Boston: Little, Brown, 1967.

Lind, Michael. *The Next American Nation: The New Nationalism and the Fourth American Revolution.* New York: Free Press, 1995.

Lipset, Seymour Martin, and Reinhard Bendix. *Social Mobility in Industrial Society.* Berkeley: University of California Press, 1959.

Lipset, Seymour Martin, and Earl Raab. *The Politics of Unreason: Right-Wing Extremism in America, 1790–1977.* 2nd edition. Chicago: University of Chicago Press, 1978.

Lukas, J. Anthony. *Common Ground: A Turbulent Decade in the Lives of Three American Families.* New York: Knopf, 1985.

Lynch, Frederick R. *Invisible Victims: White Males and the Crisis of Affirmative Action.* New York: Greenwood Press, 1989.

Marshall, Will. *From Preferences to Empowerment*. Washington, D.C: Progressive Policy Institute, August 3, 1995.

Massey Douglas S., and Nancy A. Denton. *American Apartheid: Segregation and the Making of the Underclass*. Cambridge, Mass.: Harvard University Press, 1993.

Mills, Nicolaus, ed. *Debating Affirmative Action: Race, Gender, Ethnicity, and the Politics of Inclusion*. New York: Delta, 1994.

Mishel, Lawrence, and Jacqueline Simon. *The State of Working America*. Washington, D.C.: Economic Policy Institute, 1988.

Mosteller, Frederick, and Daniel P. Moynihan, eds. *On Equality of Educational Opportunity: Papers Deriving from the Harvard University Faculty Seminar on the Coleman Report*. New York: Random House, 1972.

Moynihan, Daniel P. *Pandaemonium: Ethnicity in International Politics*. Oxford: Oxford University Press, 1993.

———. *Family and Nation*. New York: Harcourt Brace Jovanovich, 1985.

———, ed. *On Understanding Poverty: Perspectives from the Social Sciences*. New York: Basic Books, 1968.

———. *The Negro Family: A Case for National Action*. Washington, D.C.: U.S. Government Printing Office, 1965.

Murray, Charles. *Losing Ground: American Social Policy, 1950–1980*. New York: Basic Books, 1984.

Myrdal, Gunnar. *An American Dilemma: The Negro Problem and Modern Democracy*. New York: Harper & Row, 1944.

Nairn, Allan, and Associates. *The Reign of ETS: The Corporation That Makes Up Minds*. Washington, D.C.: Ralph Nader Report, 1980.

National Research Council. *A Common Destiny: Blacks and American Society*. Edited by Gerald David Jaynes and Robin M. Williams, Jr. Washington, D.C.: National Academy Press, 1989.

———. *Ability Testing: Uses, Consequences, and Controversies*. 2 vols. Edited by Alexandra K. Wigdor and Wendell R. Garner. Washington, D.C.: National Academy Press, 1982.

National Urban League. *The State of Black America 1993*. Edited by Billy J. Tidwell. Washington, D.C.: National Urban League, 1993.

Newfield, Jack. *The Education of Jack Newfield*. New York: St. Martin's Press, 1984.

———. *Robert Kennedy: A Memoir*. New York: Dutton, 1969.

Newfield, Jack, and Jeff Greenfield. *A Populist Manifesto: The Making of a New Majority*. New York: Praeger, 1972.

Newman, Katherine S. *Falling from Grace: The Experience of Downward Mobility in the American Middle Class*. New York: Free Press, 1988.

Nieli, Russell, ed. *Racial Preference and Racial Justice: The New Affirmative Controversy*. Washington, D.C.: Ethics and Public Policy Center, 1991.

Norton, Eleanor Holmes. *A Conversation with Commissioner Eleanor Holmes Norton*. Washington, D.C.: American Enterprise Institute, 1980.

Nozick, Robert. *Anarchy, State, and Utopia*. New York: Basic Books, 1974.

Oakes, Jeannie. *Keeping Track: How Schools Structure Inequality*. New Haven, Conn.: Yale University Press, 1985.

Oates, Stephen B. *Let the Trumpet Sound: The Life of Martin Luther King, Jr*. New York: New American Library, 1982.

Ogbu, John U. *Minority Education and Caste: The American System in Cross-Cultural Perspective*. New York: Academic Press, 1978.

Okun, Arthur M. *Equality and Efficiency: The Big Tradeoff*. Washington, D.C.: Brookings Institution, 1975.

Olson, Mancur. *The Rise and Decline of Nations: Economic Growth, Stagflation, and Social Rigidities*. New Haven, Conn.: Yale University Press, 1982.

Owen, David. *None of the Above: Behind the Myth of Scholastic Aptitude*. Boston: Houghton Mifflin, 1985.

Pessen, Edward. *The Log Cabin Myth: The Social Background of the Presidents*. New Haven, Conn.: Yale University Press, 1984.
————, ed. *Three Centuries of Social Mobility in America*. Lexington, Mass.: Heath, 1974.
Peterson, Merrill D., ed. *The Portable Thomas Jefferson*. New York: Penguin Books, 1975.
Pettigrew, Thomas. *Racially Separate or Together?* New York: McGraw-Hill, 1971.
Phillips, Kevin. *Boiling Point: Democrats, Republicans, and the Decline of Middle-Class Prosperity*. New York: HarperCollins, 1993.
————. *The Politics of Rich and Poor: Wealth and the American Electorate in the Reagan Aftermath*. New York: Random House, 1990.
————. *The Emerging Republican Majority*. Garden City, N.Y.: Doubleday, 1970.
Pinkney, Alphonso. *The Myth of Black Progress*. Cambridge: Cambridge University Press, 1984.
Rainwater, Lee, and William L. Yancey, eds. *The Moynihan Report and the Politics of Controversy*. Cambridge, Mass.: MIT Press, 1967.
Rawls, John. *A Theory of Justice*. Cambridge, Mass.: Belknap Press of Harvard University Press, 1971.
Rieder, Jonathan. *Canarsie: The Jews and Italians of Brooklyn Against Liberalism*. Cambridge, Mass.: Harvard University Press, 1985.
Rodriguez, Richard. *Hunger of Memory: The Education of Richard Rodriguez*. Boston: Godine, 1981.
Rose, Stephen J. *Social Stratification in the United States*. New York: New Press, 1992.
Rosen, Sherwin, ed. *Studies in Labor Markets*. Chicago: University of Chicago Press, 1981.
Ross, Douglas. *Robert F. Kennedy: Apostle of Change*. New York: Trident Press, 1968.
Rossides, Daniel W. *Social Stratification: The American Class System in Comparative Perspective*. Englewood Cliffs, N.J.: Prentice-Hall, 1990.
Rubin, Lillian Breslow. *Worlds of Pain: Life in the Working-Class Family*. New York: Basic Books, 1976.
Rustin, Bayard, ed. *Black Studies: Myths and Realities*. New York: A. Philip Randolph Educational Fund, 1969.
Safire, William. *Before the Fall: An Insider View of the Pre-Watergate White House*. Garden City, N.Y.: Doubleday, 1975.
Sandel, Michael. *Liberalism and the Limits of Justice*. New York: Cambridge University Press, 1982.
Schlesinger, Arthur M., Jr. *The Disuniting of America: Reflections on a Multicultural Society*. New York: Norton, 1992.
————. *Robert Kennedy and His Times*. Boston: Houghton Mifflin, 1978.
Schwartz, Bernard. *Behind Bakke: Affirmative Action and the Supreme Court*. New York: New York University Press, 1988.
Sennett, Richard, and Jonathan Cobb. *The Hidden Injuries of Class*. New York: Knopf, 1973.
Sewell, William H., and Robert M. Hauser. *Education, Occupation and Earnings*. New York: Academic Press, 1975.
Shafer, Byron E. *Quiet Revolution: The Struggle for the Democratic Party and the Shaping of Past Reform Politics*. New York: Russell Sage Foundation, 1983.
Shulman, Steven, and William Darity, Jr., eds. *The Question of Discrimination: Racial Inequality in the U.S. Labor Market*. Middletown, Conn.: Wesleyan University Press, 1989.
Sigelman, Lee, and Susan Welch. *Black Americans' Views of Racial Inequality: The Dream Deferred*. Cambridge: Cambridge University Press, 1991.
Skrentny, John David. *The Ironies of Affirmative Action*. Chicago: University of Chicago Press, forthcoming.
————. "Politics and Possibilities: The Legitimation of Affirmative Action, 1964–1972." Ph.D dissertation, Harvard University, 1994.

Sleeper, Jim. *The Closest of Strangers: Liberalism and the Politics of Race in New York*. New York: Norton, 1990.

Smith, James P., and Finis R. Welch. *Closing the Gap: Forty Years of Economic Progress for Blacks*. Santa Monica, Calif.: Rand, 1986.

Sniderman, Paul M., and Thomas Piazza. *The Scar of Race*. Cambridge, Mass.: Belknap Press of Harvard University Press, 1993.

Sowell, Thomas. *Race and Culture*. New York: Basic Books, 1994.

———. *Preferential Policies: An International Perspective*. New York: Morrow, 1990.

———. *Civil Rights: Rhetoric or Reality?* New York: Morrow, 1984.

———. *Ethnic America: A History*. New York: Basic Books, 1981.

———. *Knowledge and Decisions*. New York: Basic Books, 1980.

———, ed. *Essays and Data on American Ethnic Groups*. Washington, D.C.: Urban Institute, 1978.

———. *Black Education: Myths and Tragedies*. New York: McKay, 1973.

Steele, Shelby. *The Content of Our Character: A New Vision of Race in America*. New York: St. Martin's Press, 1990.

Stein, Jean, and George Plimpton. *American Journey: The Times of Robert Kennedy*. New York: Harcourt Brace Jovanovich, 1970.

Steinberg, Stephen. *Turning Back: The Retreat from Racial Justice in American Thought and Policy*. Boston: Beacon Press, 1995.

———. *The Ethnic Myth: Race, Ethnicity, and Class in America*. New York: Atheneum, 1981.

Stone, Gregory, and Douglas Lowenstein, eds. *Lowenstein: Acts of Courage and Belief*. New York: Harcourt Brace Jovanovich, 1983.

Sullivan, Denis G., Jeffrey L. Pressman, and F. Christopher Arterton. *Explorations in Convention Decision Making: The Democratic Party in the 1970s*. San Francisco: Freeman, 1976.

Takagi, Dana Y. *The Retreat from Race: Asian-American Admissions and Racial Politics*. New Brunswick, N.J.: Rutgers University Press, 1992.

Tawney, R. H. *Equality* [1931]. 4th edition. London: Allen and Unwin, 1952.

Taylor, Bron Raymond. *Affirmative Action at Work: Law, Politics, and Ethics*. Pittsburgh: University of Pittsburgh Press, 1991.

Taylor, Jared. *Paved with Good Intentions: The Failure of Race Relations in Contemporary America*. New York: Carroll & Graf, 1992.

Thernstrom, Abigail M. *Whose Votes Count? Affirmative Action and Minority Voting Rights*. Cambridge, Mass.: Harvard University Press, 1987.

Thernstrom, Stephan. *The Other Bostonians: Poverty and Progress in the American Metropolis, 1880–1970*. Cambridge, Mass.: Harvard University Press, 1973.

Thurow, Lester C. *The Zero Sum Solution: Building a World Class American Economy*. New York: Simon & Schuster, 1985.

———. *The Zero Sum Society: Distribution and the Possibilities for Economic Change*. New York: Basic Books, 1980.

Tocqueville, Alexis de. *Democracy in America*. Edited by J. P. Mayer. Garden City, N.Y.: Anchor, 1969.

Tribe, Laurence H. *American Constitutional Law*. 2nd edition. Mineola, N.Y.: Foundation Press, 1988.

Tucker, Robert C., ed. *The Marx-Engels Reader*. 2nd edition. New York: Norton, 1978.

U.S. Congress, House Committee on Education and Labor. *A Report of the Study Group on Affirmative Action to the U.S. Congress*. 100th cong., 1st sess., 1986.

U.S. Congress, Senate Committee on the Judiciary. *Civil Rights—The President's Program*. 88th cong., 1st sess., 1963.

U.S. Congress, Senate Committee on the Judiciary. *Nomination of Clarence Thomas to Be Associate Justice of the United States Supreme Court*. October 1, 1991, 102nd cong., 1st sess., 1991.

U.S. Congress, Senate Committee on the Judiciary. *Nomination of Ruth Bader Ginsburg*

to Be Associate Justice of the United States Supreme Court. 103rd cong., 1st sess.,
1993.

Urofsky, Melvin. *A Conflict of Rights: The Supreme Court and Affirmative Action.* New
York: Scribner's, 1991.

Van Horne, Winston A., and Thomas V. Tonnesen, eds. *Ethnicity, Law and the Social
Good.* Madison: University of Wisconsin, 1983.

Walzer, Michael. *Spheres of Justice: A Defense of Pluralism and Equality.* New York:
Basic Books, 1983.

Weber, Max. *Essays in Sociology.* Edited by H. H. Gerth and C. Wright Mills. New
York: Oxford University Press, 1958.

Webster, Yehudi O. *The Racialization of America.* New York: St. Martin's Press, 1992.

Weir, Margaret. *Politics and Jobs: The Boundaries of Employment Policy in the United
States.* Princeton, N.J.: Princeton University Press, 1992.

Weiss, Richard. *The American Myth of Success: From Horatio Alger to Norman Vincent
Peale.* New York: Basic Books, 1969.

West, Cornel. *Beyond Eurocentrism and Multiculturalism.* Vol. 1, *Prophetic Thought in
Postmodern Times.* Monroe, Maine: Common Courage Press, 1993.

———. *Beyond Eurocentrism and Multiculturalism.* Vol. 2, *Prophetic Reflections: Notes
on Race and Power in America.* Monroe, Maine: Common Courage Press, 1993.

———. *Keeping Faith: Philosophy and Race in America.* New York: Routledge, 1993.

———. *Race Matters.* Boston: Beacon Press, 1993.

White, Theodore. *America in Search of Itself: The Making of the President, 1956–1980.*
New York: Harper & Row, 1982.

———. *The Making of the President, 1968.* New York: Simon & Schuster, 1969.

Williams, T. Harry. *Huey Long.* New York: Knopf, 1969.

Williams, Walter E. *The State Against Blacks.* New York: New Press, 1982.

Williamson, Jeffrey G., and Peter H. Lindert. *American Inequality: A Macroeconomic
History.* New York: Academic Press, 1980.

Wilson, James Q., and Richard Herrnstein. *Crime and Human Nature.* New York: Simon
& Schuster, 1985.

Wilson, William Julius. *The Truly Disadvantaged: The Inner City, the Underclass, and
Public Policy.* Chicago: University of Chicago Press, 1987.

———. *The Declining Significance of Race: Blacks and Changing American Institutions.*
Chicago: University of Chicago Press, 1978.

Wills, Gary. *The Kennedy Imprisonment: A Meditation on Power.* New York: Simon &
Schuster, 1982.

Woodward, Bob. *The Agenda: Inside the Clinton White House.* New York: Simon &
Schuster, 1994.

Woodward, Bob, and Scott Armstrong. *The Brethren: Inside the Supreme Court.* New
York: Simon & Schuster, 1979.

Woodward, C. Vann. *Tom Watson: Agrarian Rebel.* New York: MacMillan, 1938.

Wright, Erik Olin. *Class Structure and Income Determination.* New York: Academic
Press, 1979.

Yin, Robert K., ed. *Race, Creed, Color or National Origin.* Itaska, Ill.: Peacock, 1973.

Young, Michael. *The Rise of the Meritocracy, 1870–2033.* Baltimore: Penguin, 1961.

Cases

Abbott v. Burke, 575 A2d 359 (N.J. 1990).

Adams v. Richardson, 356 FSupp 92 (1973); *Adams v. Richardson,* 480 F2d 1159
(1973); *Women's Equity Action League v. Cavazos,* 906 F2d 742 (1990).

Adarand Constructors, Inc. v. Pena, 115 SCt 2097 (1995).

Albermarle Paper Company v. Moody, 422 US 405 (1975).

Bakke v. Regents of University of California, 553 P2d 1152 (Calif. 1976).

Board of Education of Oklahoma City v. Dowell, 498 US 237 (1991).

Bob Jones University v. United States, 461 US 574 (1983).

Boston v. Beecher, 679 F2d 965 (1st Cir., 1982).

Brown v. Board of Education of Topeka, 347 US 483 (1954) (*Brown I*).

Brown v. Board of Education of Topeka, 349 US 294 (1955) (*Brown II*).

Califano v. Webster, 430 US 313 (1977).

City of Richmond v. J. A. Croson Company, 488 US 469 (1989).

Contractors Assocation of Eastern Pennsylvania v. Secretary of Labor, 442 F2d 159 (3rd Cir., 1971); cert. denied, 438 US 915 (1978).

DeFunis v. Odegaard, 416 US 312 (1974).

DeRonde v. Regents of University of California, 625 P2d 220 (Calif. 1981).

Diaz v. Pan American World Airways, 442 F2d 385 (5th Cir. 1971).

Drummond v. Fulton County Department of Family and Children Services, 547 F2d 835 (5th Cir. 1977); *Drummond v. Fulton County Department of Family and Children Services*, 563 F2d 1200 (5th Cir. 1977).

Firefighters v. Stotts, 467 US 561 (1984).

Franks v. Bowman Transportation, 424 US 747 (1976).

Fullilove v. Klutznick, 448 US 448 (1980).

Griggs v. Duke Power Company, 401 US 424 (1971).

Hirabayashi v. United States, 320 US 81 (1943).

Hobson v. Hansen, 269 FSupp 401 (1967).

Holder v. Hall, 62 USLW 4728 (1994).

Hopwood v. Texas, 861 FSupp 551 (W. D. Tex. 1994).

International Brotherhood of Teamsters v. United States, 431 US 324 (1977).

Jacobs v. Barr, 959 F2d 313 (DC Cir., 1992).

James v. Valiterra, 402 US 137 (1971).

Jane Doe v. State of Louisiana, 479 So. 2d 369 (1985).

Johnson v. DeGrandy, 62 USLW 4755 (1994).

Johnson v. Transportation Agency, Santa Clara County, 480 US 616 (1987).

Keyes v. School District No. 1, Denver, Colo., 413 US 189 (1973).

Korematsu v. United States, 323 US 214 (1944).

Larry P. v. Riles, 793 F2d 969 (9th Cir., 1984).

Lau v. Nichols, 414 US 563 (1974).

Loving v. Virginia, 388 US 1 (1967).

McAleer v. AT&T, 416 FSupp 435 (DC, 1976).

Metro Broadcasting, Inc. v. FCC, 497 US 547 (1990).

Milliken v. Bradley, 418 US 717 (1974) (*Milliken I*).

Milliken v. Bradley, 433 US 267 (1977) (*Milliken II*).

New York City Transit Authority v. Beazer, 440 US 568 (1979).

O'Donnell v. Washington, D.C., 963 F2d 420 (DC Cir., 1992).

Personnel Administrator of Massachusetts v. Feeney, 442 US 256 (1979).

Plessy v. Ferguson, 163 US 537 (1896).

Plyler v. Doe, 457 US 202 (1982).

Podberesky v. Kirwan, 38 F3d 147 (4th Cir., 1994), cert. denied 115 SCt 2001 (1995).

Regents of University of California v. Bakke, 438 US 265 (1978).

Rosenstock v. Board of Governors of the University of North Carolina, 423 FSupp 1321 (MDNC 1976).

San Antonio Independent School District v. Rodriguez, 411 US 1 (1973).

Shaw v. Reno, 113 SCt 2816 (1993).

Sheet Metal Workers v. EEOC, 478 US 421 (1986).

Sipuel v. Board of Regents of the University of Oklahoma, 332 US 631 (1948).

Spurlock v. United Airlines, 475 F2d 216 (10th Cir., 1972).

Swann v. Charlotte-Mecklenburg Board of Education, 402 US 1 (1971).

Taxman v. Board of Education of Piscataway, 798 FSupp 1093 (NJ, 1992); 832 FSupp 836 (1993).

United Jewish Organizations of Williamsburgh, Inc. v. Carey, 430 US 144 (1977).

United States v. Fordice, 112 SCt 2727 (1992).

United States v. Paradise, 480 US 149 (1987).
United States v. Virginia, 976 F2d 890 (4th Cir., 1992).
United Steelworkers of America, AFL-CIO-CLC v. Weber, 443 US 193 (1979).
Wards Cove Packing Co. v. Atonio, 490 US 642 (1989).
Washington v. Davis, 426 US 239 (1976).
Weber v. Kaiser Aluminum & Chemical Corporation, 415 FSupp 761 (EDLA 1976).
W. R. Grace & Company v. Local Union 759, 461 US 757 (1983).
Wygant v. Jackson Board of Education, 476 US 267 (1986).

Articles
LAW REVIEW ARTICLES
Abram, Morris B. "Commentary: Affirmative Action: Fair Shakers and Social Engineers." *Harvard Law Review* 99: 1312 (1986).
Ansley, Frances Lee. "Stirring the Ashes: Race, Class, and the Future of Civil Rights Scholarship." *Cornell Law Review* 74: 993 (1989).
Ayres, Ian. "Fair Driving: Gender and Race Discrimination in Retail Car Negotiations." *Harvard Law Review* 104: 817 (1991).
Barnes, Robin D. "Race Consciousness: The Thematic Content of Racial Distinctiveness in Critical Race Scholarship." *Harvard Law Review* 103: 1864 (1990).
Bartholet, Elizabeth. "Where Do Black Children Belong? The Politics of Race Matching in Adoption." *University of Pennsylvania Law Review* 139: 1163 (1991).
———. "Applications of Title VII to Jobs in High Places." *Harvard Law Review* 95: 947 (1982).
Becker, Mary E. "Needed in the Nineties: Improved Individual and Structural Remedies for Racial and Sexual Disadvantages in Employment." *Georgetown Law Journal* 79: 1659 (1991).
Bell, Derrick A., Jr. "In Defense of Minority Admissions Programs: A Response to Professor Graglia." *University of Pennsylvania Law Review* 119: 364 (1970).
Belton, Robert. "The Unfinished Agenda of the Civil Rights Act of 1991." *Rutgers Law Review* 45: 921 (1993).
Blumrosen, Alfred W. "Society in Transition I: A Broader Congressional Agenda for Equal Employment—The Peace Dividend, Leapfrogging, and Other Matters." *Yale Law and Policy Review* 8: 257 (1990).
Brest, Paul. "The Supreme Court, 1975 Term—Forward: In Defense of the Antidiscrimination Principle." *Harvard Law Review* 90: 1 (1976).
Byrne, Jeffrey S. "Affirmative Action for Lesbians and Gay Men: A Proposal for True Equality of Opportunity and Workforce Diversity." *Yale Law and Policy Review* 11: 47 (1993).
Cahn, Edmond. "Jurisprudence." *New York University Law Review* 30: 150 (1955).
Cahn, Naomi. "Family Issue(s) [review of Elizabeth Bartholet, *Family Bonds*]." *University of Chicago Law Review* 61: 325 (1994).
"Constitutional Scholars' Statement on Affirmative Action after *City of Richmond v. J. A. Croson Co.*" *Yale Law Journal* 98: 1711 (1989).
Culp, Jerome McCristal, Jr. "Diversity, Multiculturalism, and Affirmative Action: Duke, the NAS, and Apartheid." *De Paul Law Review* 41: 1141 (1992).
Days, Drew S., III. "*Fullilove.*" *Yale Law Journal* 96: 453 (1987).
———. "Turning back the Clock: The Reagan Administration and Civil Rights." *Harvard Civil Rights–Civil Liberties Law Review* 19: 309 (1984).
Delgado, Richard, and Jean Stefancic. "Critical Race Theory: An Annotated Bibliography." *Virginia Law Review* 79: 461 (1993).
Dershowitz, Alan, and Laura Hanft. "College Diversity-Discretion: Paradigm or Pretext?" *Cardozo Law Review* 1: 379 (1979).
Devins, Neal. "Comment: *Metro Broadcasting, Inc. v. FCC*: Requiem for a Heavyweight." *Texas Law Review* 69: 125 (1990).

Ely, John Hart. "The Constitutionality of Reverse Racial Discrimination." *University of Chicago Law Review* 41: 723 (1974).

Espinoza, Leslie G. "Empowerment and Achievement in Minority Law Student Support Programs: Constructing Affirmative Action." *University of Michigan Journal of Law Reform* 22: 281 (1989).

Fallon, Richard H., Jr., and Paul C. Weiler. "*Firefighters v. Stotts*: Conflicting Models of Racial Justice." *Supreme Court Review* 1 (1984).

Foster, Sheila. "Difference and Equality: A Critical Assessment of the Concept of 'Diversity.'" *Wisconsin Law Review* 105 (1993).

Freeman, Alan D. "Racism, Rights, and the Quest for Equality of Opportunity: A Critical Legal Essay." *Harvard Civil Rights–Civil Liberties Law Review* 23: 295 (1988).

———. "Race and Class: The Dilemma of Liberal Reform [review of *Race, Racism, and American Law*, 2nd ed., by Derrick A. Bell, Jr.]." *Yale Law Journal* 90: 1880 (1981).

———. "Legitimizing Racial Discrimination Through Antidiscrimination Law: A Critical Review of Supreme Court Doctrine." *Minnesota Law Review* 62: 1049 (1978).

Fried, Charles. "Comment—*Metro Broadcasting, Inc. v. FCC*: Two Concepts of Equality." *Harvard Law Review* 104: 107 (1990).

———. "Affirmative Action after *City of Richmond v. J. A. Croson Co.*: A Response to the Scholars' Statement." *Yale Law Journal* 99: 155 (1989).

Glazer, Nathan. "Commentary: A Viable Compromise on Minority Admissions." *Washington University Law Quarterly* 93 (1979).

Golick, Toby. "Justice Scalia, Poverty, and the Good Society." *Cardozo Law Review* 12: 1817 (1991).

Gotanda, Neil. "A Critique of 'Our Constitution Is Color Blind.'" *Stanford Law Review* 44: 1 (1991).

Graglia, Lino A. "What's to Be Done about Our Institutions of Higher Learning?" *Policy Counsel* 39 (Fall 1993).

———. "Racially Discriminatory Admission to Public Institutions of Higher Education." *Southwestern University Law Review* 9: 583 (1977).

Harris, Cheryl I. "Whiteness as Property." *Harvard Law Review* 106: 1707 (1993).

Heckman, James J., and J. Hoult Verkerke. "Racial Disparity and Employment Discrimination Law: An Economic Perspective." *Yale Law and Policy Review* 8: 276 (1990).

Higginbotham, A. Leon., Jr. "An Open Letter to Justice Clarence Thomas from a Federal Judicial Colleague." *University of Pennsyvania Law Review* 140: 1005 (1992).

Johnson, Alex M., Jr. "The New Voice of Color." *Yale Law Journal* 100: 2007 (1991).

———. "Racial Critiques of Legal Academia: A Reply in Favor of Context." *Stanford Law Review* 43: 137 (1990).

Jones, James E., Jr. "The Origins of Affirmative Action." *University of California at Davis Law Review* 21: 383 (1988).

———. "The Bugaboo of Employment Quotas." *Wisconsin Law Review* 341 (1970).

Judges, Donald P. "Bayonets for the Wounded: Constitutional Paradigms and Disadvantaged Neighborhoods." *Hastings Constitutional Law Quarterly* 19: 599 (1992).

Kay, Herma Hill. "Commentary: The Need for Self-Imposed Quotas in Academic Employment." *Washington University Law Quarterly* 137 (1979).

Kennedy, Duncan. "A Cultural Pluralist Case for Affirmative Action in Legal Academia." *Duke Law Journal* 705 (1990).

Kennedy, Randall. "The State, Criminal Law, and Racial Discrimination: A Comment." *Harvard Law Review* 107: 1255 (1994).

———. "Persuasion and Distrust: A Comment on the Affirmative Action Debate." *Harvard Law Review* 99: 1327 (1986).

Liacouras, Peter J. "Toward a Fair and Sensible Policy for Professional School Admission." *Cross Reference* 1: 156 (1978).

Mikulak, Brian. "Classism and Equal Opportunity: A Proposal for Affirmation Action in Education Based on Social Class." *Howard Law Journal* 33: 113 (1990).

Morton, Frederick A., Jr. "Note: Class-Based Affirmative Action: Another Illustration of America Denying the Impact of Race." *Rutgers Law Review* 45: 1089 (1993).

Munro, Don. "The Continuing Evolution of Affirmative Action under Title VII: New Directions after the Civil Rights Act of 1991." *Virginia Law Review* 81: 565 (1995).

Neas, Ralph G. "Interview." *Yale Law and Policy Review* 8: 366 (1990).

Nickel, James W. "Preferential Policies in Hiring and Admissions: A Jurisprudential Approach." *Columbia Law Review* 75: 534 (1975).

Norton, Eleanor Holmes. "The End of the *Griggs* Economy: Doctrinal Adjustment for the New American Workplace." *Yale Law and Policy Review* 8: 197 (1990).

"Note: Racial Steering in the Romantic Marketplace." *Harvard Law Review* 107: 877 (1994).

"Note: Rethinking *Weber*: The Business Response to Affirmative Action." *Harvard Law Review* 102: 658 (1989).

"Note: Teaching Inequality: The Problem of Public School Tracking." *Harvard Law Review* 102: 1318 (1989).

Peller, Gary. "Race Consciousness." *Duke Law Journal* 758 (1990).

Posner, Richard A. "The *DeFunis* Case and the Constitutionality of Preferential Treatment of Racial Minorities." *Supreme Court Review* 1 (1974).

"Race, Class, and the Contradictions of Affirmative Action [panel discussion]." *Black Law Journal* 7: 270 (1979).

Ralston, Charles Stephen. "Courts vs. Congress: Judicial Interpretation of the Civil Rights Acts and Congressional Response." *Yale Law and Policy Review* 8: 205 (1990).

Ramirez, Deborah. "Multicultural Empowerment: It's Not Just Black and White Anymore." *Stanford Law Review* 47: 957 (1995).

Rutherglen, George. "After Affirmative Action: Conditions and Consequences of Ending Preferences in Employment." *University of Illinois Law Review* 339 (1992).

Rutherglen, George, and Daniel R. Ortiz. "Affirmative Action under the Constitution and Title VII: From Confusion to Convergence." *UCLA Law Review* 35: 467 (1988).

Sandalow, Terrance. "Racial Preferences in Higher Education: Political Responsibility and the Judicial Role." *University of Chicago Law Review* 42: 653 (1975).

Scalia, Antonin. "Commentary: The Disease as Cure: 'In Order to Get Beyond Racism We Must First Take Account of Race.'" *Washington University Law Quarterly* 147 (1979).

Schnapper, Eric. "Affirmative Action and the Legislative History of the Fourteenth Amendment." *Virginia Law Review* 71: 753 (1985).

Simien, Eulius. "The Law School Admission Test as a Barrier to Almost Twenty Years of Affirmative Action." *Thurgood Marshall Law Journal* 12: 359 (1987).

Solomon, Lewis D., and Judith S. Heeter. "Affirmative Action in Higher Education: Towards a Rationale for Preference." *Notre Dame Lawyer* 52: 41 (1976).

Sullivan, Kathleen M. "The Supreme Court, 1986 Term—Comment: Sins of Discrimination: Last Term's Affirmative Action Cases." *Harvard Law Review* 100: 78 (1986).

Summers, Clyde W. "Individual Protection Against Unjust Dismissal: Time for a Statute." *Virginia Law Review* 62: 481 (1976).

Taylor, Kimberly Paap. "Note: Affirmative Action for the Poor: A Proposal for Affirmative Action in Higher Education Based on Economics, Not Race." *Hastings Constitutional Law Quarterly* 20: 805 (1993).

Taylor, William L. "The Continuing Struggle for Equal Educational Opportunity." *North Carolina Law Review* 71: 1693 (1993).

———. "*Brown*, Equal Protection, and the Isolation of the Poor." *Yale Law Journal* 95: 1700 (1986).

Thomas, Clarence. "Affirmative Action Goals and Timetables: Too Tough? Not Tough Enough!" *Yale Law and Policy Review* 5: 402 (1987).

Van Alstyne, William. "Rites of Passage: Race, the Supreme Court, and the Constitution." *University of Chicago Law Review* 46: 775 (1979).

Verkerke, J. Hoult. "Note: Compensating Victims of Preferential Employment Discrimination Remedies." *Yale Law Journal* 98: 1479 (1989).

White, David M. "Culturally Biased Testing and Predictive Invalidity: Putting Them on the Record." *Harvard Civil Rights–Civil Liberties Law Review* 14: 89 (1979).

Williams, Patricia J. "Comment: *Metro Broadcasting, Inc. v. FCC*: Regrouping in Singular Times." *Harvard Law Review* 104: 525 (1990).

Witten, Samuel M. "Note: 'Compensatory Discrimination' in India: Affirmative Action as a Means of Combatting Class Inequality." *Columbia Journal of Transnational Law* 21: 353 (1983).

OTHER SELECTED ARTICLES

Adelson, Joseph. "Living with Quotas." *Commentary* (May 1978): 23–29.

Alwin, Duane F., and Arland Thornton. "Family Origins and the Schooling Process: Early versus Late Influences of Parental Characteristics." *American Sociological Review* 49 (1984): 784–802.

Beatty, Jack. "Howard Beach Portents." *New York Times*, January 7, 1987, A23.

———. "Race, Class and the City" [book review of *Common Ground*]. *Atlantic* (September 1985): 108ff.

Beer, William R. [Review of *Invisible Victims* by Frederick R. Lynch]. *Social Forces* 69 (1990): 302–3.

Bowles, Samuel, and Valerie Nelson. "The 'Inheritance of IQ' and the Intergenerational Reproduction of Economic Inequality." *Review of Economics and Statistics* 56 (February 1974): 39–51.

Brownstein, Ronald. "Racial Politics." *American Prospect* (Spring 1992): 122–25.

———. "Beyond Quotas: A New Generation of Scholars Is Stressing Class, Not Race, in an Effort to Break the Civil Rights Impasse." *Los Angeles Times Magazine*, July 28, 1991, 18ff.

Bundy, McGeorge. "The Issue Before the Court: Who Gets Ahead in America?" *Atlantic* (November 1977): 41–54.

Bunzel, John H. "In Democracy's Shadow: A Defense of the University's Core Values." *Vital Speeches* (October 1, 1993): 752ff.

Clark, Kenneth B., and Carl Gersham. "The Black Plight: Race or Class?" *New York Times Magazine* (October 5, 1980): 22ff (two articles).

Cohen, David. "Does IQ Matter?" *Commentary* (April 1972): 51–59.

Converse, Paul E., Warren E. Miller, Jerrold G. Rusk, and Arthur C. Wolfe. "Continuity and Change in American Politics: Parties and Issues in the 1968 Election." *American Political Science Review* (December 1969): 1083–1105.

Corcoran, Mary, Roger Gordon, Deborah Laren, and Gary Solon. "The Association Between Men's Economic Status and Their Family and Community Origins." *Journal of Human Resources* (September 22, 1992): 575ff.

Cowan, Paul. "Wallace in Yankeeland." *Village Voice*, July 18, 1968.

Davis, Kingsley, and Wilbert E. Moore. "Some Principles of Stratification." *American Sociological Review* 10 (April 1945): 242–49.

Donahue, John H., III, and James Heckman. "Continuous versus Episodic Change: The Impact of Civil Rights Policy on the Economic Status of Blacks." *Journal of Economic Literature* 29 (1991): 1603–43.

Dworkin, Ronald. "Why Bakke Has No Case." *New York Review of Books* (November 10, 1977): 11–15.

Edsall, Thomas Byrne, and Mary D. Edsall. "Race." *Atlantic* (May 1991): 53–86.

Fallows, James. "The Tests and the 'Brightest': How Fair Are the College Boards?" *Atlantic* (February 1980): 37–48.

———. "What Did You Do in the Class War, Daddy?" *Washington Monthly* (October 1975). Reprinted in *The Vietnam Reader*, edited by Walter Capps, 213–21. New York: Routledge, 1991.

Gates, Henry Louis, Jr. "Heroes, Inc." *New Yorker* (January 16, 1995).

Glazer, Nathan. "Race, Not Class." *The Wall Street Journal*, April 5, 1995, A17.

———. "The Affirmative Action Stalemate." *The Public Interest* (Winter 1988): 99–114.

Hacker, Andrew. "Playing the Racial Card." *New York Review of Books* (October 24, 1991): 14–18.

Harrington, Michael. "The Invisible Poor: White Males." *Washington Post*, February 15, 1987, C1.

Harrington, Michael, and Arnold S. Kaufman. "Black Reparations—Two Views." *Dissent* 16 (1969): 317–20.

Heckman, James. "Affirmative Action and Black Employment." *Social Science* 7 (1986): 125–29.

Heckman, James J., and Brook S. Payner. "Determining the Impact of Federal Antidiscrimination Policy on the Economic Status of Blacks: A Study of South Carolina." *America Economic Review* 79 (1989): 138–77.

Herrnstein, Richard. "IQ." *Atlantic* (September 1971): 43–64.

Hill, Herbert. "Race, Ethnicity and Organized Labor: The Opposition to Affirmative Action." *New Politics* (Winter 1987): 31–82.

Howard, A. E. Dick. "The High Court's Road to the Bakke Case," *Washington Post,* October 9, 1977, C1.

Jencks, Christopher. "Affirmative Action for Blacks." *American Behavioral Scientist* 28 (July-August 1985): 731–61.

Jensen, Arthur. "How Much Can We Boost IQ and Scholastic Achievement?" *Harvard Educational Review* (Winter 1969): 1–123.

Karabel, Jerome. "Berkeley and Beyond." *American Prospect* (Winter 1993): 156–60.

———. "Status Group Struggle, Organizational Interests, and the Limits of Institutional Autonomy." *Theory and Society* (January 1984): 1–40.

Karen, David. "The Politics of Class, Race, and Gender: Access to Higher Education in the United States, 1960–1986." *American Journal of Education* 99 (1991).

Kennedy, Randall. "Orphans of Separatism: The Painful Politics of Transracial Adoption." *American Prospect* (Spring 1994): 38–45.

———. "Race, Liberalism, and Affirmative Action (I): Yes and No." *American Prospect* (Spring 1992).

King, Martin Luther, Jr. "Showdown for Non-Violence." *Look*, April 16, 1968, 23–25.

———. "Martin Luther King, Jr., Defines 'Black Power.'" *New York Times Magazine* (June 11, 1967): 26ff.

Lerner, Barbara. "The War on Testing: David, Goliath, and Gallup." *The Public Interest* (Summer 1980): 119–47.

Loury, Glenn C. "Why Preferential Admission Is Not Enough for Blacks." *Chronicle of Higher Education* (March 25, 1987): 100.

———. "The Moral Quandary of the Black Community." *The Public Interest* 79 (Spring 1985): 9–22.

———. "The Need for Moral Leadership in the Black Community." *New Perspectives* 16 (Summer 1984): 14–19.

Lynch, Frederick R. "Surviving Affirmative Action (More or Less)." *Commentary* (August 1990): 44–47.

Mayer, Susan E., and Christopher Jencks. "Growing up in Poor Neighborhoods: How Much Does It Matter?" *Science* (March 17, 1989): 1441ff.

Moynihan, Daniel Patrick. "Toward a National Urban Policy." *The Public Interest* (Fall 1969): 3–20.

———. "A Family Policy for the Nation." *America* (September 18, 1965): 280–83.

Puddington, Arch. "Clarence Thomas and the Blacks." *Commentary* (February 1992): 28–33.

Rist, Ray C. "Student Social Class and Teacher Expectations: The Self-Fulfilling Prophecy in Ghetto Education." *Harvard Educational Review* 40 (1970): 411–51.

Robinson, Robert V. "Reproducing Class Relations in Industrial Capitalism." *American Sociological Review* 49 (1984): 182–96.

Rustin, Bayard. "The King to Come: The Holiday and the Future Racial Agenda." *New Republic* (March 9, 1987): 19–21.

———. "The Blacks and the Unions." *Harper's* (May 1971): 73–81.

———. "The Failure of Black Separatism." *Harper's* (January 1970): 25–34.

———. "Conflict or Coalition: The Civil Rights Struggle and the Trade Union Movement." Address to AFL-CIO, October 3, 1969.

———. "A Negro Leader Defines a Way out of the Exploding Ghetto." *New York Times Magazine* (August 13, 1967): 16ff.

———. "The Lessons of the Long Hot Summer." *Commentary* (October 1967): 39–45.
———. "From Protest to Politics: The Future of the Civil Rights Movement." *Commentary* (February 1965): 25–31.
Shannon, Patrick. "Reading Instruction and Social Class." *Language Arts* 62 (1985): 604–613.
Skocpol, Theda. "Race, Liberalism, and Affirmative Action (II): The Choice." *American Prospect* (Summer 1992): 86–90.
Slack, Warren V., and Douglas Porter. "The Scholastic Aptitude Test: A Critical Appraisal." *Harvard Educational Review* 50 (1980): 154–75.
Sleeper, Jim. "Race and Affirmative Action: Back to Universals." *American Prospect* (Summer 1992): 91–93.
Smith, James P. "Racial and Ethnic Differences in Wealth in the Health and Retirement Study." *Journal of Human Resources* (Supplement 1995): 158–83.
Smith, James P., and Finis R. Welch. "Black Economic Progress after Myrdal." *Journal of Economic Literature* 27 (1989): 519–64.
Solon, Gary. "Intergenerational Income Mobility in the United States." *American Economic Review* 82 (June 1992): 393–408.
Sowell, Thomas. "The Great IQ Controversy." *Change* (May 1973): 33–37.
Starr, Paul. "Civil Reconstruction: What to Do Without Affirmative Action." *American Prospect* (Winter 1992): 7–14.
Steinberg, Stephen. "How Jewish Quotas Began." *Commentary* (September 1971): 67–76.
Sunstein, Cass R. "Why Markets Don't Stop Discrimination." *Social Philosophy and Policy* 8 (1991): 22–37.
Takagi, Dana Y. "The Retreat from Race." *Socialist Review* 22, no. 4 (1992): 167–89.
———. "From Discrimination to Affirmative Action: Facts in the Asian American Admissions Controversy." *Social Problems* 37, no. 4 (1990): 578–92.
Taylor, William L., and Susan M. Liss. "Affirmative Action in the 1990s: Staying the Course." *Annals* (AAPSS) 523 (September 1992): 30–37.
Thomas, R. Roosevelt, Jr. "From Affirmative Action to Affirming Diversity." *Harvard Business Review* (March-April 1990): 107–17.
Thurow, Lester C. "A Surge in Inequality." *Scientific American* 256, no. 5 (May 1987): 30–37.
Van den Berghe, Pierre. "The Benign Quota: Panacea of Pandora's Box." *American Sociologist* 6 (June 1971): 40–43.
Walzer, Michael. "In Defense of Equality." *Dissent* (Autumn 1973): 399–408.
Wilkins, Roger. "In Ivory Towers." *Mother Jones* (July-August 1990): 10–11.
Wilson, William Julius. "Another Look at *The Truly Disadvantaged.*" *Political Science Quarterly* 106 (Winter 1991–92): 639–56.
———. "Race-Neutral Programs and the Democratic Coalition." *American Prospect* (Spring 1990): 74–81.
Zimmerman, David J. "Regression Toward Mediocrity in Economic Status." *American Economic Review* 82 (June 1992): 409ff.

Interviews

Beatty, Jack. Boston, Mass., January 6, 1995.
Canady, Charles T. Washington, D.C., September 20, 1995.
Cohen, Richard. Washington, D.C., December 13, 1994.
Coles, Robert. Cambridge, Mass., February 25, 1985.
Coles, Robert. February 3, 1995 (telephone).
Corrigan, Jack. February 23, 1995 (telephone).
Cuomo, Mario. Albany, N.Y., June 23, 1987.
D'Souza, Dinesh. Washington, D.C., December 19, 1994.
Edsall, Thomas. January 23, 1995 (telephone).

Faux, Jeff. Washington, D.C., January 20, 1995.
Gans, Marshall. Cambridge, Mass., January 5, 1995.
Garrow, David. January 18, 1995 (telephone).
Geoghegan, Thomas. December 1, 1994 (telephone).
Glazer, Nathan. Cambridge, Mass., January 5, 1995.
Greenfield, Jeff. New York, N.Y., January 30, 1985.
Halberstam, David. December 15, 1994 (telephone).
Harrison, Tubby. Cambridge, Mass., January 5, 1995.
Harwood, Richard. Washington, D.C., December 20, 1984.
Laird, Robert. July 18, 1995 (telephone).
Lukas, J. Anthony. New York, N.Y., January 3, 1995.
Moynihan, Daniel Patrick. Washington, D.C., January 25, 1995.
Ramirez, Deborah. Boston, Mass., January 6, 1995.
Reinstein, Robert. December 14, 1994 (telephone).
Robb, Charles S. Washington, D.C., January 10, 1995.
Schlesinger, Arthur M., Jr. New York, N.Y., January 31, 1985.
Shanker, Albert. Washington, D.C., September 20, 1995.
Slaiman, Donald. Washington D.C., June 14, 1993.
Sleeper, Jim. New York, N.Y., January 3, 1995.
Taylor, William. Washington, D.C., December 15, 1994.
Tucker, Algera. November 4, 1994 (telephone).
Wagner, Carl. Washington, D.C., December 19, 1994.
Walinsky, Adam. New York, N.Y., December 18, 1984.

Index

District of Columbia, 127, 143
Diver, Colin, 191–92
Diversity, xii, 78; and the *Bakke* decision, 26; and compensation for historical wrongs, 75–80; Krauthammer on, 64; and long-run color blindness, 52–64; move from compensation to, xvii, 16, 27–41; occupational, 36–38; reasons for, 38–41
Divorce, 94, 135
Dole, Robert, xvi, 40, 111–12
Douglas, William O., xvi, 25, 139, 149, 174
Dred Scott decision, 4–5
Dreyfuss, Joel, 10
Drinan, Robert, 26
Dropout rates, 66–67
Drug Abuse Education Act, 36
D'Souza, Dinesh, vii, xvi, 44, 77, 133, 173, 185
Dukakis, Michael, 113
Duke, David, 73, 187, 200
Duke Power, 159
Duncan, Beverly, 125
Duncan, Otis, 89, 125, 131
Duncan scores, 88
Dworkin, Ronald, 35, 233n71

Economic Policy Institute, 128
Economist, The, 45
Edelman, Marian Wright, 17, 163–64
Edsall, Mary, vii, 24–25, 199, 201
Edsall, Thomas, 24–25, 199, 201–3
Education, ix, xvii, 200; and the case for class-based affirmative action, 83, 86–92, 94–101; and class reductionism vs. race reductionism, 176–78; and diversity, 34–35, 171; as an equalizer, 95, 96–101; and long-run color blindness, 54–58; and the

mechanics of class-based affirmative action, 121–52; Moynihan on, 4–5; and myths about class-based preferences, 153–58, 162–72, 176–78; of parents, 129; public opposition to racial preferences in, 109–10; and real-life barriers that remain unaddressed, 91–92; and role model theory, 62–64; and social discrimination, 162–64; and the shift from compensation to diversity, 29–31; and social mobility, 86, 87–91. *See also* Admissions policy; Preparatory schools; Public schools
Educational Opportunity Program, 140
Edwards, Alba M., 131
Egalitarianism, 86, 91
Ehrlichman, John, 21, 24
Eisenhower, Dwight D., 57
EITC (Earned Income Tax Credit), 143
Eizenstat, Stuart, 113
Elementary and Secondary Education Act, 96, 208
Ellwood, David, 168–69
Ely, John, 108
Emerging Republican Majority (Phillips), 197
Employment, ix, xvii; and the argument that minority constituencies are better served, 59–60; and the case for class-based affirmative action, 83, 109–10, 115–16; and class reductionism vs. race reductionism, 176–78; and compensation, 19, 78; and disparate impact lawsuits, 31–32, 116, 158–60; full, 10; and increased racial tension, 71–72; and Johnson's view of affirmative action, 9; and liberty rights/rights of association, 30–31; and

long-run color blindness, 52–53, 58–59; and the mechanics of class-based affirmative action, 121–39, 148–57; and myths about class-based preferences, 158–64, 176–78; and occupational diversity, 37–38; and promotions, 44–45, 126, 144; public opposition to racial preferences in, 109–10; and the shift from compensation to diversity, 30–32; and social discrimination, 162–64. *See also* Construction industry; Set-aside programs
Equal Employment Opportunity Commission (EEOC), 26, 79, 158–59
Equality of Educational Opportunity (Coleman Report), 96–97
Equal opportunity, xii, 12, 209; and the case for class-based affirmative action, 83–101; vs. equal result, 171–72; goals of, report card on, 42–52, 80; and income distribution, 92–101; legacy of, 6; and Moynihan on, 14–15; and myths about class-based preferences, 165–66, 171–72; and unequal starting points, 12–13, 86
Ervin, Sam, 11
Espinoza, Leslie, 150
Estrich, Susan, 113
Ethnic groups, differences between the status of, explanations of, 19–20. *See also* specific ethnic groups
ETS (Educational Testing Service), 98, 141. *See also* SAT (Scholastic Assessment Test) scores
Europe, social mobility in, 90, 91
Evans, Rowland, 9
Executive order 11246, 9, 106, 147, 151, 286n141